WITHDRAWN

MUSLIM EURASIA:
Conflicting Legacies

The Cummings Center for Russian and East European Studies
The Cummings Center Series

Muslim Eurasia: Conflicting Legacies

Yaacov Ro'i, Editor

THE CUMMINGS CENTER
FOR RUSSIAN AND EAST EUROPEAN STUDIES
TEL AVIV UNIVERSITY

The Cummings Center is Tel Aviv University's main framework for research, study, documentation and publication relating to the history and current affairs of Russia, the former Soviet republics and Eastern Europe. Its current projects include Fundamentalism and Secularism in the Muslim Republics of the Soviet Union; the Establishment of Political Parties and the Process of Democratization in Russia; Religion and Society in Russia; the Creation of New Historical Narratives in Contemporary Russia; and Soviet Military Theory and History.

In addition, the Center seeks to establish a bridge between the Russian and Western academic communities, promoting a dialogue with Russian academic circles through joint projects, seminars, roundtables and publications.

THE CUMMINGS CENTER SERIES

The titles published in this series are the product of original research by the Center's faculty, research staff and associated fellows. The Cummings Center Series also serves as a forum for publishing declassified Russian archival material of interest to scholars in the fields of history and political science.

Managing Editor – Deena Leventer

MUSLIM EURASIA:
Conflicting Legacies

EDITED BY
YAACOV RO'I

FRANK CASS
LONDON

First published in 1995 in Great Britain by
FRANK CASS & CO. LTD.
Newbury House
890-900 Eastern Avenue, Newbury Park
Ilford, Essex 1G2 7HH, England

and in the United States of America by
FRANK CASS
c/o International Specialized Book Services, Inc.
5602 N.E. Hassalo Street, Portland, Oregon 97213-3644

Copyright © 1995

British Library Cataloguing in Publication Data

Muslim Eurasia: Conflicting
Legacies – (Cummings Center Series)
  I. Ro'i, Yaacov   II. Series
  958.00882971
  ISBN 0-7146-4615-6 (cloth)
  ISBN 0-7146-4142-1 (paper)

Library of Congress Cataloging-in-Publication Data

Muslim Eurasia : conflicting legacies / edited by Yaacov Ro'i.
    p.   cm. — (Cummings Center series)
    Includes index.
  ISBN 0-7146-4615-6 (cloth) — ISBN 0-7146-4142-1 (paper)
    1. Muslims—Asia, Central. 2. Muslims—Caucasus, Northern
(Russia) 3. Asia, Central—Ethnic relations. 4. Caucasus, Northern
(Russia)—Ethnic relations. I. Ro'i, Yaacov. II. Series.
DK855.5.M8B48   1995
305.8'00958—dc20
                                    94-40028
                                    CIP

Typeset by University Publishing Projects, Tel Aviv, Israel
Printed in Great Britain by
Bookcraft (Bath) Ltd, Midsomer Norton

Contents

List of Maps

Preface

Muslim Eurasia: Conflicting Legacies is the first volume of a joint project between the Cummings Center for Russian Studies and the Dayan Center for Middle Eastern and African Studies, both of Tel Aviv University. It focuses on domestic trends and developments in the Muslim regions of the Soviet Union and the Commonwealth of Independent States (CIS). The second volume, *Central Asia Meets the Middle East,* deals with the implications of independence for the new Muslim states in their relations with the Middle East, particularly with Turkey and Iran.

The Cummings Center is indebted to Dalia Ratner and the Chicago Friends of Tel Aviv University for their committment and support of this project.

The editor would like to thank Moshe Gammer and Miri Shefer, and above all, Beryl Belsky for her patience and help in preparing and editing the manuscript.

Note on Orthography

The task of transliterating personal and place names, as well as other words taken from the languages of the ex-Soviet Muslims, is extremely complicated. In this volume, for the sake of uniformity and simplicity, names have been transliterated primarily from Cyrillic. The main exception is the substitution of the letter *j* for the combination of two Cyrillic characters rendered in Latin letters as *dzh*. Thus, one will find in the text *Johar* rather than *Dzhohar*. If, however, such names appear as part of a Russian title or quote, the *dzh* has been retained.

For Arabic names and terms, a simplified transliteration system has been used, dispensing with diacritical and vowel-length marks, but retaining the *q* and ʾ. Hence, *ʾAla* and Qurʾan. For words of Arabic origin in the Soviet Muslim languages, a unified spelling system has been maintained as far as possible, which represents a compromise between Arabic spelling and pronounciation.

All place names have been transliterated from their Cyrillic spelling, with the exception of those that have a generally accepted English spelling which differs from the system used here; hence *Amu-Darya* and not *Amudarʾia*. In the case of places whose names have been changed, the name used corresponds to the period in question. Hence, Kirgiziia and Turkmeniia, as these places were called under Soviet rule, are used up until December 1991, and Kyrgyzstan and Turkmenistan after independence. The people of Kirgiziia/Kyrgyzstan, however, are called Kyrgyz (as they prefer to call themselves) for all periods, and not Kirgiz as the Soviets referred to them.

Introduction

This book focuses on the interaction between the Russian/Soviet heritage in the new independent Muslim states of the CIS and the Muslim areas of Russia, and that of the period prior to their conquest by Russia. Naturally, the residues of the tsarist and Soviet periods are not totally identical; however, on many levels they are similar: colonization, russification, de-islamicization, bureaucratization, centralization. Since each legacy comprises a variety of components, a careful analysis of their manifold aspects is essential in order to examine their mutual relationship and relative weight.

The secularization of society was a prerequisite for and basic postulate of 'socialist construction'. When the Soviet regime decided to reach a *modus operandi* with religion, including Islam, the religious establishment itself underwent a process of secularization as a condition for survival. It was compelled to make concessions in order to be able to function at all. At the same time, cooperation with the regime compromised it in the eyes of the population. Its truncated authority, the constraints under which it worked, and the small number of mosques that were allowed to operate, meant that in the final account, the official registered clergy was incapable of ministering to the spiritual needs of its flock.

Not only were individual lifestyles intricately linked with Islamic tradition in the Muslim regions but the population's collective identity was largely inseparable from it, especially in Uzbekistan, Tajikistan, southern Kirgiziia, the Northern Caucasus and among the Volga (Kazan) Tatars. As this collective identity began to recuperate from the onslaught of the 1920s and 1930s in the relatively relaxed, and more ideologically jumbled years of de-Stalinization, the old legacy began to regain some of the ground it had lost to the new political ethos. With the ultimate collapse and disintegration of the Soviet system, the national intelligentsias, which had received their education under the Soviet aegis (in some cases they owed their *raison d'être* as intelligentsia to Soviet policy) and which had imbibed so much of the Soviet social and political message, found themselves largely unable to adopt the socio-cultural and political implications of a politicized, radical Islam.

The conflict between the two legacies in the realm of religion is, then, extremely complex. Moreover, the commitment to the national culture, such as it is, given that the very nations in many instances derived their existence from the Soviet nationalities policy of the

1

1920s, means that Islamic fundamentalism is hardly a viable option. Nor, of course, does fundamentalism anywhere allow rival ideologies, being by definition an exclusive system. The result seems to be – at least in this initial period of independence – that the role of Islam in the social and political life of the Muslim areas has become a major and very loaded issue among competing political forces. The majority of these forces are extremely wary of laying any undue emphasis upon Islam, let alone making it the fulcrum of their political platforms. At the same time, an Islamic awareness does exist, and the Islamic legacy serves, to an extent, as a divide between the Muslim and non-Muslim states and populations. There is a widespread tendency to revive and re-emphasize Islamic norms and values. It seems, therefore, that Islam may appear in the not-too-distant future as an ascendant, even paramount, feature of at least some of the Muslim states and areas of Russia itself, if growing frustrations and the ever-worsening economic situation are not satisfactorily managed. Four of the chapters in this book (Ro'i, Olcott, Malashenko, Lubin) discuss and analyze the relevance and likelihood of the emergence of some version of politicized Islam, if not full-fledged fundamentalism, in the Muslim areas of the CIS.

The political legacy of the Soviet period is no less intricate. While communism was never a meaningful ideology or lifestyle among any of the Muslim populations (except perhaps for a thin stratum of intelligentsia, who sought in the 1920s to adopt a Muslim national communism), many of the symptoms and components of Soviet rule, especially as applied in the Muslim areas by the local élites, have become a part of their political culture. Indeed, the very frontiers of the new states and other administrative units were determined by the Soviet 'delimitation' (*razmezhevanie*) of the 1920s and 1930s. The RCP(b)/CPSU leadership sought to split the Muslim populations in order to forestall any attempt at unification via movements current at the beginning of the 20th century (pan-Islam, pan-Turkism); today it seems unrealistic to consider any form of unification among the Muslim states and areas. Local animosities and disputes were sometimes created by the Soviet authorities; others had been present before, but these, too, Moscow manipulated in order to give them more relevance and political significance. Thus, for instance, Moscow encouraged the Uzbek leadership to register Uzbekistan's Tajik inhabitants as Uzbeks and the leaders of Azerbaijan to register indigenous Muslim minorities as Azerbaijanis (Wasserman). The system of rule by *nomenklatura* – the group or class that in the USSR comprised the governing élite – has also been maintained, with appropriate changes.

Yet, even under Soviet rule the political leadership in the Muslim areas was characterized by special features that reflected the traditional way of life. Moscow controlled its Muslim populations with the help of local, indigenous clans or the accepted leaderships of certain locales that had long-standing internecine rivalries with neighbouring tribes or regions. In this way it encouraged corruption, nepotism and a mafia-like body politic, which have of necessity been retained in most of the areas under discussion in the post-Soviet era, and have become basic features of their political life. Three of the contributors to this volume (Carlisle, Vaisman, Kosach) address themselves to different aspects of this problem in Uzbekistan and Tajikistan, and two others (Gammer, Wasserman) touch upon its implications for the political development of the northern Caucasus and Azerbaijan. The first three discuss the strength of regionalism, which obstructs the evolution of that sense of loyalty to the nation-state that is a usual concomitant of newly acquired independence, and prevents the creation of a truly national leadership and even the formation of political parties with national programs and differences in the content of their ideologies and platforms. The latter two dwell upon the tense relations and even conflict situations that exist between the various Muslim peoples in the Caucasus. Lubin also discusses the amorphous nature of national identity in Central Asia. Soviet 'nation-building' in Central Asia, Kazakhstan and the Caucasus bore no relation to the sentiments and allegiances of the indigenous population, even of the titular nations of the various union republics, which have changed little since 1917, or even since the Russian conquest (Carlisle, Vaisman, Kosach, Gammer).

Just as the political life of the new Muslim states and the Muslim areas of Russia is characterized by a conflict between the two legacies, so also is their cultural activity. The Soviet period left two major bequests: ubiquitous education and russification, with all that both implied. Yet, inevitably, the acquisition of independence was accompanied by a reassertion and revival of the national language and culture; language laws, enacting the predominance of the eponymous language as sole state language, were passed in all the union republics even before independence as an indication of the 'sovereignty' that they claimed under glasnost. Two chapters demonstrate the paradoxes of the new situation: Kreindler emphasizes the advantages that the Muslim populations continue to enjoy in the realm of education as a result of Soviet policy, despite compulsory russification; Fierman demonstrates the hesitations of the new national leadership in one of the Muslim states (Uzbekistan) as regards implementing the language law because of the lack of a requisite cultural infrastructure. In a third chapter, Tishkov shows that different conditions in the various Muslim states (his findings relate chiefly to Uzbekistan and Kyrgyzstan) have led to different policies and evoked dissimilar problems.

Finally, in the socio-economic sphere, the Soviet legacy seems to be paramount. In some respects, the situation in the Muslim areas of the USSR was typical of the country as a whole; in other respects it was unique. Whereas, since the 1930s the general demographic trend in the Soviet Union was toward a declining birth rate, the Muslim parts, particularly Central Asia, were characterized in the last three decades of Soviet rule by a major demographic boom. This was commonly taken as an indication of the prevalence of their primordial lifestyle. Yet, in the last decade of the USSR's existence, there were clear indications that the modernization that the Soviets had been trying to impose for over half a century was finally having its effect and taking its toll (Tolts).

Certainly, the colonial-type policy pursued by Moscow *vis-à-vis* the Muslim regions subordinated them (except perhaps northern Kazakhstan, the Tatar ASSR and Azerbaijan) to the industrialized European part of the country. This subjugation continues to haunt them and to necessitate a now incongruous dependence on Russia that mars their sense of total independence. This is perhaps the most important conclusion of McAuley's chapter, which also dwells on the distortions created by overcentralized planning and the 'values' peculiar to Marxist state socialism; while Sacks dwells upon the disadvantaged position of the indigenous populations *vis-à-vis* the local Russians in employment and the particularly inferior status of local women in the workforce. Both insist that the Soviet period prevented the establishment of a viable economic infrastructure.

Another aspect of the contention that the Soviet period perpetuated an imperialist Russian superiority in regard to Central Asia is attested to by Tishkov in his discussion of the Soviet, and even tsarist Russian, policy in these areas – namely russification by means of colonization. The considerable Russian populations in the Muslim areas are yet a further constraint upon the realization of nationhood in the new independent nation states, a source of internal tension and even potential conflict, and a bone of contention between them and Russia.

In conclusion, the tale of the conflict between the two legacies does not seem to have ended. On the contrary, in many senses it is in full swing and all the implications may not yet be manifest.

1

The Secularization of Islam and the USSR's Muslim Areas

YAACOV RO'I

As a prelude to discussing the loaded issue of the existence and substance of Islamic fundamentalism in the Soviet Union and its successor states, it is essential to consider the theme of secularism in the USSR's Muslim areas. This is not only because Islamic fundamentalism is by definition a reaction to secularism or secularization, but also because it is impossible to come to grips with the special features of fundamentalism in these regions, indeed with the very question of its existence, without comprehending the *mise-en-scène*, the legacy of the Soviet period.

Islam, like other religions, fell victim to the militant atheism that was an integral component of the materialist ideology of the Bolshevik party. Religion, 'the opium of the masses', was by definition an 'enemy of the people' *par excellence*. As such, the Soviet regime had no alternative but to suppress all its manifestations and institutions that had been formed during the period of capitalism and the exploitation of man by man, the vestiges of which the Bolsheviks were committed to destroying as they set about constructing socialism.

This general objective was made all the more cogent when it came to Islam, because of the fear that the Bolsheviks entertained in the early years regarding pan-Islam, which seemed to threaten the territorial integrity of their new empire in the south and east. Pan-Islam and pan-Turkism,[1] if allowed to prosper,[2] might bring together the otherwise diverse ethnic Muslim groups and enable them to withstand, and even break away from, Russia, whose new rulers' authority had not yet been fully established. Without question, the disintegration of the Ottoman Empire in the wake of World War I and the disappearance of the Caliphate, together with the secularization that was characteristic of several Muslim countries in the first quarter of the

5

20th century, assisted the Bolsheviks in the conduct of their anti-religious campaign in the Muslim areas subject to their rule.

The main thrust of this chapter will be to examine the outcome of Soviet policy regarding religion in the Soviet Muslim areas. The chief hypothesis is that the mobilization of the Muslim 'toiling masses' and the creation of a new Soviet man in the Muslim areas were inconceivable without their secularization. How far, then, was Soviet policy successful? What was the role Islam was to play in the new secular society? And what price was Moscow to pay for the forced secularization of populations that for the most part were not ready for modernization (normally perceived as a precondition for secularization), or for the concomitants of the industrial revolution that had not yet reached them?

At the same time, we must address ourselves to three basic questions that may help us define our terms of reference and delimit the parameters of our discussion: Are the criteria for examining the secularization of Islam the same as those we might use for analyzing the secularization of Christianity or Judaism? Is secularization tantamount to the acceptance of a worldly outlook and of behavioural patterns dictated by non- or a-religious constraints? And does the secularization of Islam mean, or refer to, the religious establishment or also the lifestyle of one or another Muslim society?

Let us first take the second group of questions. When we look at secularization in the context of Christianity, we normally refer to a trend that developed from within the community itself as it imbibed the philosophical values of the Renaissance, rejecting thereby the pervading influence of Christianity upon society, cognition, culture and science.[3] This secularization inevitably affected and reflected both the thought process of the individual as well as his way of life, although it did not necessarily diminish his religious belief, provided that his particular creed or confession accepted this general approach. Indeed, one of the features of the early modern period was the emergence of Christian churches or sects that were prepared to accommodate the emancipation of certain spheres of life from the domination of religion.

The second stage of secularization, or moderniziation, which has swept over Europe in the last 200 years, is a social or sociological, rather than a spiritual, process, and is accompanied by urbanization, industrialization and bureaucratization.[4] Paradoxically, the American fundamentalism of the last century (the term fundamentalism was originally applied in the American Christian context) developed within these parameters.

In Judaism the Haskala, or Enlightenment, movement of the late

18th century led to a secularistic outlook that at first clashed with the religious authority, yet in the course of time what has come to be known as modern orthodox Judaism, adopted something similar to the Protestant model. In both Christianity and Judaism secularization exposed to criticism a tradition or dogma that was by definition comprehensive, self-contained, exclusive and binding, and immune to change whatever the historical or existentialist context. In neither case was secularism forcibly imposed from the outside, even if it was the outcome of external forces and influences. This was especially true with respect to Judaism, which lacks any built-in distinction between ethnos and religion, indeed perceives itself as a chosen people and nation of priests. Thus, the traditional Jewish leadership tends to regard secularization as assimilation, an endeavour, as it were, to fulfil an untenable assignment.[5]

On the level of ideology, Islam perceives all non-Muslims, all infidels, as inferior beings, whose role in society is determined by this definition, and any surrender of the basic tenets of Islam as apostasy. On the practical level, however, Islam, and Sunni Islam in particular, seems on the surface to lend itself a priori to secularization in that it preaches reconciliation, compromise, even cooperation with the powers-that-be. Originally, the intention was to find a *modus vivendi* with an Islamic state, but the contingencies and constraints of history created situations in which the basic hypothesis was projected onto governments that were related to a different brand of Islam, or a different religion altogether, or were totally areligious.[6]

At the same time, Islam makes no distinction between religion and politics. Just as ethics are its personal dimension, so politics constitute the social aspect of Islam. On this level, secularization, which is not a concept inherent to a system that does not recognize the legitimacy of opting out,[7] must be perceived as a political act. However, the punishment for secularism falls within the realm of religion, since it entails a degree of rebellion against God in that it redefines the world as understood by Islam; it leaves no place, for instance, for angels, paradise and other such important components of the Islamic stage-set.

Islam, moreover, like Judaism, remained a way of life in a sense that most Christian denominations did not, and from this point of view changes that might have affected society's or the individual believer's general attitudes and thought processes did not necessarily affect the level of religious practice or Islamic identity or consciousness.[8] This is true in particular when discussing Muslim societies in which the level of education and cognition was generally low.

This was not the case everywhere within the Russian Empire,

among whose Muslims there were major differences, both in the realm of literacy and in the degree of religious practice. The Volga, or Kazan, Tatars, who had initiated and propagated the reformist *jadid* movement in Imperial Russia in the second half of the 19th century,[9] enjoyed a far higher level of education than the other Muslim peoples and were infinitely more russified, or europeanized, having been part of the empire since the 16th century. They fulfiled a special role as the tsars spread their rule into extensive Muslim areas in the mid-19th century, helping in the absorption of these newly conquered populations, among whom they enjoyed something approaching a cultural and commercial monopoly.

The Azerbaijanis, for their part, with the development of the oil industry in the last two decades of the 19th century, had plunged into a new stage of socio-economic development, Baku having become a bustling, capitalist, industrial metropolis. Already, before 1917, the Azerbaijani Turks, often simply known as Turks, were acquiring all the attributes of a nation, whose intelligentsia entertained a strong national consciousness.[10] Both these peoples – the Volga Tatars and the Azerbaijanis – were becoming secular, or, at least, developing significant secular intelligentsias by the turn of the century (although the Azerbaijanis were mostly Shi'ite, the only large Shi'ite population in the Russian Empire).[11]

On the other hand, in the northern and eastern Caucasus and the eastern emirates of Bukhara and Khiva and the Fergana Valley,[12] Islam had become, and remained, part of the political culture and was an essential ingredient in the social consciousness of both élites and 'masses'.[13] In addition, there were the Kazakhs and Kyrgyz, traditional nomads, who had adopted Islam only relatively recently,[14] and perhaps had never been profoundly influenced in their way of life, let alone their world view, by Islam.

The differences in their historical and social backgrounds could not but be reflected in the reaction of these various societies to Bolshevik policy. The Tatar Sultan Galiev, who was Stalin's advisor on the Muslim areas in Narkomnats (the Commissariat for Nationality Affairs), explained in a programmatic article in 1921 that while the country's Muslims could be weaned from Islam, this had to be done in stages and with discretion, the actual dose of anti-religious activity to be prescribed in accordance with the state of health of every specific population as determined by Bolshevik criteria.[15] On the strategic level, the 'national Communists' of the Soviet East headed by Sultan Galiev differentiated in the 1920s between what they considered the fanatical, obscurantist components of Islam, which they condemned, and the *umma*, the community of believers, which they sought to preserve as a potential instrument of social progress. They contended that Islam should not be destroyed but secularized, with total laicization as the ultimate goal.[16]

Bolshevik policy was, in fact, more circumspect in its attitude to Islam than to other religions in the early 1920s. Yet, by the late 1920s it was as generally and totally negative and destructive in its approach to Islam as to all other faiths. Mosques were shut down in vast numbers, the Muslim clergy was persecuted, the property of the *waqf* was sequestrated, Muslim activity in the fields of education and jurisprudence was terminated. With the closing down of schools (the *maktabs* and *madrasas*) and the Shariat courts, certain Muslim practices were declared illegal inasmuch as they fundamentally contradicted the Marxist-Leninist ethos, and atheistic propaganda was conducted with the specific purpose of manifesting the backwardness, harmfulness and irrelevance of Islam to the construction of the new socialist society. The values that were imparted to the youth whom the party and Komsomol sought to mobilize, were consciously intended to replace Islamic norms and teachings. In the 1930s, the *jadid* movement received the brunt of the attack precisely because the contradictions between their teachings and those of the new communist line were by no means clear-cut. The Soviet expert on Islam, Liutsian Klimovich, noted that the jadidists sought to rationalize Islam, to purify it from medieval scholasticism and to bring it into line with the needs of the modern era.[17]

The Islam that remained after the onslaught, or *hujum*, of the late 1920s–early 1930s was, on the whole, subdued.[18] Islam seemed no match for the combination of brutality and sophistication that characterized the regime's anti-religious policy.[19] Religious worship and the fulfilment of religious rites virtually disappeared. Through tradition, however, Sunni Islam developed methods and techniques to help it reconcile itself to unfriendly and even hostile political systems, to enable it to survive in the most adverse conditions.[20] It was, therefore, intrinsically adapted to the kind of political atmosphere in which it found itself under communism. At the same time, we should perhaps make a distinction between institutionalized Islam, the official clergy in the mosques that were allowed to continue functioning, and Islamic custom – folk rites that were deeply embedded in society. While the former operated under a constant threat of punitive measures on the part of the authorities and made every effort to demonstrate the practical and theoretical compatibility of communism and Islam, the latter had endless, often devious, built-in ways and means to evade and obviate the new laws and decrees. The gap between the two became blatant after World War II. On the one hand, the four Muslim 'spiritual directorates' set up in 1943 as a sort of 'transmission belt' between Moscow and the Muslim areas[21] largely filled the role designed for them and showed themselves to be in every sense functionaries of the regime. On the other hand, in many of the Muslim areas, unofficial, illegal communities of believers came into being and gathered strength.

The materials at our disposal have traditionally been severely limited: a good deal of Soviet atheistic propaganda[22] in addition to the texts of some of the decrees that were promulgated by the regime. The frustration of the authorities at the relative failure of its policies was amply evident in much of the former,[23] which indeed reflected the flexibility and deftness of Islam in withstanding external pressures and retaining some, at least, of its basic ingredients and rites. The late Alexandre Bennigsen gave this resilience its due when he described the prosperity of what he called 'parallel' or 'unofficial Islam' in the northern Caucasus and Central Asia.

Today, we are beginning to use official Soviet documentation of religious life in the Soviet period. The picture that permeates this material, in fact, supplements that which we already know. Although from time to time an *imam-khatib* in one of the functioning mosques would try to prevent the erosion of religion in his community in defiance of the authorities,[24] the official, registered clergy was largely subservient. The people who fulfiled functions in, and under the auspices of, the four 'spiritual directorates' that continued to operate until the end of the Soviet period, were on the whole unquestioning lickspittles who accepted without reservation the constraints and limitations imposed by the regime.[25] Thus, for instance, a report on Muslim activity in the year 1948 noted that the spiritual directorates had issued *fetwas* with the intention of averting material damage that might occur to the economy as a result of adherence to Muslim ritual: they forbade absence from work on religious festivals, explained that animal sacrifice was not obligatory, that certain categories of people were exempt from fasting on Ramadan, including people engaged in hard work, and that the payment of the *fitr* (or *zakat*), had lost all significance under conditions of socialism, which had liquidated poverty and need.[26]

To an extent, it could be contended in the defence of the religious establishment that its basic approach to the lay authority was no deviation from the attitude of some, at least, of the Muslim clergy to the secular authority in the pre-Soviet era. The difference would be, however, that at least in those areas which retained a certain autonomy in the Russian Empire, notably in the eastern emirates, the secular powers-that-be were themselves basically Islam-oriented, so that a natural symbiosis was created that did not undermine the authority, the world outlook or the lifestyle of the clergy.[27] Indeed, the principle of accommodating to the regime spelled out or even dictated the inescapable secularization of Sunni Islam and its clergy before the term and its significance penetrated the consciousness even of most political thinkers. In this sense, one cannot claim that the Soviet regime led to the secularization of the Muslim clergy, but rather that this principle was a given, of which the Soviets could and did take advantage to their own ends; it goes without saying that these ends necessarily contradicted those of Islam's religious cadres. Be that as it may, as I have suggested elsewhere,[28] the four spiritual directorates in many ways presided over the secularization process. Seeing this as an inevitable trend and perceiving their own role as that of regime officials, they seemed to have very little alternative. The role that Islam, like other religions, and first and foremost the Russian Orthodox Church, was intended by Gorbachev to fulfil in implementing the social goals of perestroika, and the apparent acceptance of this role by the Muslim establishment, was indicative of the possible coexistence of a secularized Islam with a Marxist-Leninist regime.[29] This had already been borne out by recurrent attempts on the part of the authorities to give a purely secular character to some of the popular and seasonal holidays traditionally observed in the Muslim areas, notably the Nawruz (or Novruz), the Muslim New Year.[30]

The content of Islamic belief, life and practice is a different story. As a way of life that is designed to embody certain beliefs and dogmas, Islam is not by definition, and cannot be, cut off from everyday life. To an extent, it might actually be suggested that Islam, instead of being prone to secularization, sanctifies the believer's every activity, for everything he does is designed to implement the truths laid down in the Qur'an and the *hadith*. By this criterion, as long as a faithful Muslim is true to his credo and makes Islam the focus of his conduct, he is not open to the danger of secularization.

The Islamic practice of Soviet Muslims becomes, then, the crux of our discussion. On this score, however, the evidence at our disposal is problematic. True, the Council for the Affairs of Religious Cults, which, from 1944 through 1965, was responsible for supervising the religious life of all faiths except the Russian Orthodox Church, did register periodically the extent of religious practice performed by the members of the various religions. Yet the evidence on which it based its findings was extremely partial, clearly intended a priori to prove a point, as is true of so much evidence in the Soviet period, not only that which was published and openly propagandistic, but even of documentation provided by junior or medium-level officials for their superiors. A case in point of the former genre was the treatment in literature and the media of many of the customs that characterized the Muslim population and that were generally considered an integral part of religious practice, since they were traditionally performed or consummated by religious or para-religious personnel. Prayer-gatherings at holy places, popular medicine, and so on, were consistently and categorically portrayed as basically shamanistic, non-religious folk habits. I would suggest that the material of the Council for the Affairs of Religious Cults is likewise based on very questionable data. For example, the information concerning the extent of family rites performed by believers is posited on the statements of these believers themselves, and there is every reason to assume that they grossly understated the true situation in order to avoid retribution. I have not yet gathered all the available evidence, or submitted all the material to as careful a scrutiny as is clearly required, but it seems that a number of assertions can safely be made:

1. Some measure of religious practice was maintained in all areas inhabited by a Muslim population throughout most of the post-World War II period.[31] Unfortunately, as already stated, the data available even in the state archives are very incidental and sporadic, and meaningful statistics concerning circumcisions or religious weddings and burials have been difficult to obtain. In fact, there are conflicting testimonies, some insisting that not only all believers, but even some party and Komsomol members, observed all the main life-cycle rituals,[32] others that not even all believers observed them.[33] (Certainly, for example, Muslims who married Russians or other Europeans could hardly be expected to have observed these rites.[34]) When these practices did again become fairly general, probably only in the early 1980s, the intelligentsia, at least, returned to them out of nationalist and not religious motives.

2. Both the extent and the nature of these practices varied considerably from period to period and from place to place. The evidence so far available does not enable one to ascertain if these variations were the result of the policy or attitude of local authorities, whether at the republican or *oblast* level, the result of the initiative or leadership of local imams or mullas, or of the intensity of religiosity among the population.

3. On the whole, it does appear that the mobilized urban intelligentsias of the Muslim populations were generally much less prone to religious practice than the blue-collar urban proletariat[35] or the inhabitants of the countryside.

4. The existence of unregistered, and therefore illegal, religious communities was extremely widespread, at least by the early 1960s, apparently far more than even Bennigsen suspected. Nearly all of them, moreover, had their own imams or mullas. Thus, for instance, while at the beginning of 1963, there were a mere 325 officially registered Muslim prayer houses throughout the Soviet Union, there were more than 2,000 unregistered communities, most of them with their own imam, that came together to practise religious rites, especially on the main Muslim holidays, usually outside in the open air.[36] As against the registered mosques, which often had very large congregations, the unofficial communities were generally small, only rarely exceeding 200, and sometimes numbering only 20 or 30. Nonetheless, their numbers are impressive. If in the Tatar ASSR, there were in all 11 registered communities, no less than 496 unregistered communities were known to the authorities; in Kirgiziia, the numbers were 33 official congregations and 296 unofficial ones. Interestingly, in the Caucasus, very little unofficial activity was reported. In the three Transcaucasian union republics, not one such community was reported; in the Checheno-Ingush ASSR, no communities at all were reported (either official or unofficial), although the Chechen and Ingush were thought to be the most religious of Soviet Muslims,[37] and just twenty years later were said to have no less than 210 unregistered religious communities,[38] whereas Dagestan was said to have only two unofficial communities, as against 27 registered congregations, and the Kabardino-Balkar ASSR nine. The data for the northern and eastern Caucasus are clearly incomplete. Although as yet no systematic research seems to have been done on these areas, there is considerable circumstantial evidence to suggest that such activity was extensive, and one is left to surmise why the CARC was so poorly informed.[39] It should, moreover, be noted that, at least at this stage, it is not clear whether the plethora of illegal, or semi-legal, activity that prevailed in the areas inhabited by Muslim populations was the result of the direct, or even indirect, influence of underground *tariqat,* or brotherhoods of the Sufi type, or simply testimony to the tenacity of religious worship among the population. Some of it, however, undoubtedly was linked with the *tariqat,* above all, but not solely in the northern Caucasus.[40]

In the mid-1980s, the CPSU Central Committee's Institute of Scientific Atheism of the Academy of Social Sciences conducted a major sociological survey in some of the USSR's Muslim areas. Its findings showed a 'comparatively extensive practice of [Islamic] traditions, festivals and rites among all socio-demographic groups of

13

the population, including the young, which indicates not only a relative stabilization of the level of religiosity, but also...a mass basis' for Islam's continued existence in the USSR. The results of the survey refuted the widely held opinion that Islam was becoming 'increasingly ritualistic' (*obriadovyi*) and demonstrated that the 'preservation and reproduction' (*vosproizvidstvo*) of religiosity were 'ensured by the existence of a still fairly significant number of believers characterized by a uniformity of religious consciousness and religious conduct'. The survey also showed the interconnection between 'religious prejudices' on the one hand, and nationalistic and tribal ones, on the other. The 'process of secularization' in the Muslim areas was still proceeding in 'a complex and contradictory fashion'. Islam 'as a system of religious-moral precepts and everyday ritual activity continues to exert its influence over fairly extensive sectors of the population and is closely linked with people's everyday lives and national sentiments'. Even 'many non-believers perceive Islam as a national cultural patrimony, a traditional way of life inherited from their...ancestors'; some of them actually refused to openly admit they were atheists.[41]

The virtually unchanging level of religiosity in the Muslim areas had been made possible by Islam's

> ability to adapt to changing social conditions by transferring the center of gravity to those components of the religious patchwork which are more in harmony with the new conditions and give scope for interpreting the new activities in categories of its confessional teachings (*veroucheniia*).

Thus the Muslim clergy placed primary stress on Islam's moral aspects, particularly in the sphere of family life.[42]

One of the interesting findings was that the degree of religiosity was no longer highest among women, the older generation and the less well educated. Indeed, the high level of religiosity among people with secondary and higher education must be seen as 'a factor in the definite stabilization of Islam's influence, arresting the process of secularization'.[43]

Placing their recommendations before those responsible for atheistic education, the authors insisted that it was no longer tenable to regard Islam as a relic of the past; it must be perceived rather as 'a serious social and spiritual phenomenon with roots...in contemporary society, among others in those negative social and spiritual processes that had become enhanced over recent decades, that were closely linked with national traditions, the relics of the old economic structure, the traditional lifestyle, group, tribal and communal relations, and that were stirred up by hostile propaganda from abroad'. It was similarly necessary to appreciate the interrelationship between the religious and political aspects of contemporary Islam, and the need to operate against the politicization of Islam within the Soviet Union. Finally, it was important to bear in mind the connection and mutual enrichment of Islam and nationalism, the atmosphere of national exclusiveness and narrow-mindedness and ethnic prejudice.[44] The point concerning politicization was certainly well taken, for the new politicization that began to be the focus of attention of students of Islam in the 1980s, stood in sharp contradiction to the Soviet policy of Islam's secularization.[45]

From the evidence, then, it seems fair to say that the Muslim population on the whole, and especially the urban intelligentsia, tended to accept the totally secular norms that the Soviet regime sought to inculcate. In other words, even if at first a departure from religion was imposed upon them by force, in the course of time, this population became basically secularized from conviction, education and/or force of habit. This did not mean that it renounced its Muslim identity, seeing no contradiction in declaring itself at one and the same time Muslim and atheist or non-believing.[46] Some believers, too, adopted a position that was basically secular. Their knowledge of Islam was reduced to a very few practices, and even here it was superficial, and their religious views were far removed, in the words of one scholar, from any genuine Muslim dogma.[47] At the same time, a nucleus persisted in rejecting this trend for whatever reason, and the sole type of religious practice that it could opt for – worship in open places, rather than in any fixed building, with religious leaders who had little or no religious training, and who clearly based their leadership role on folk practices and superstitions – was so blatantly in opposition to the diktat of the regime, that it involved a rejection, *inter alia*, of the secularization that the regime demanded.[48]

These conclusions seemingly have important ramifications for today. In the first place, they indicate significant differences in the basic approach to the question of Islam's place in society. The intelligentsia in most of the successor states and Muslim areas of Russia tend to regard Islam as a national asset, as a political instrument, but not as a spiritual value, let alone a belief system or way of life, which has its own intrinsic significance that should constitute some sort of guiding force in their lives. In other words, a return to religion on the part of these sectors, should it occur, would be instrumental and so, by definition, secularist.[49] The attachment to religion of other strata in the population is less rationalist, and they do indeed see in it an alternative to everything that the Soviet regime represented and stood for, including the secularism that was a basic Soviet value, even if they do not use this terminology. Given their accumulated attitude to the Soviet regime, and their sense of a newly found independence, they may well promote the idea of an Islam that is radical by nature and anti-secular by definition, which might provide a viable alternative to the state authority that they see as a continuation of the previous, Soviet regime and that they seek to reject.

It can be said, then, that the Soviet regime was largely successful in the attempt to deprive Islam of its traditional hold over and influence upon society, even though neither the Bolsheviks, in the first stages, nor the CPSU in later decades, accomplished its total eradication. If in 1917, the religious leadership, except in Tatariia and Azerbaijan, comprised the social and intellectual élite, within less than a generation the mobilized youth of the 1920s and 1930s, which had imbibed Soviet values and norms, constituted a secular intelligentsia from which the new political leadership in these regions was drawn. At the same time, among populations that remained basically rural, indeed whose very retention of their rural composition was in part at least an act of defiance *vis-à-vis* the regime, religious custom and practice remained strong. As the hold of the central authorities weakened following de-Stalinization, and nationalism came to be a main channel of protest, in the Muslim areas – as in Russia itself, in Ukraine and in Lithuania – religion became its handmaiden or sometimes even partner. For the urban intelligentsia this was primarily a secular religion (as I have contended that Sunni Islam often lends itself to being). But for the increasingly large strata of dissatisfied, disenchanted, unemployed and socially dislocated youth, the persistent attempts of the Soviet state to eradicate religion enabled, almost predestined, the attraction of their anti-establishment protest movement to forms of religious practice that contrasted sharply with everything for which the Russian-centred communist regime had stood.

NOTES

1. For these ideologies and their historical context, see Alexandre Bennigsen, 'Panturkism and Panislamism in History and Today', *Central Asian Survey* 3, 3 (1984), pp. 39–49.
2. For the short-lived cooperation between Moscow and the League of Islamic Revolutionary Societies, which sought to organize a worldwide Muslim congress in the immediate postwar period, see Martin Kramer, *Islam Assembled* (New York: Columbia University Press, 1986), Ch. 6.
3. In the words of one attempt to penetrate and analyze the effect of modernity on the consciousness: 'Through most of empirically available human history, religion has played a vital role in providing the overarching canopy of symbols for the meaningful integration of society. The various meanings, values and beliefs operative in a society were ultimately "held together" in a comprehensive interpretation of reality that related human life to the cosmos as a whole....This age-old function of religion is

16

seriously threatened by pluralization' – Peter L. Berger, Brigitte Berger, Hansfried Kellner, *The Homeless Mind* (London: Penguin Books, 1973), p. 75.

4. See Lawrence Stone, *The Past and the Present* (London: Routledge & Kegan Paul, 1981), Ch. 5.

5. Some scholars who have debated the issue of secularism in Judaism in fact contend that it is a contradiction in terms, a superficial or passing phenomenon, which poses one of the central dilemmas of Judaism in modern society – e.g., Jacob Neusner, *Judaism in the Secular Age* (London: Vallentine Mitchell, 1970), Ch. 2. For the meaning of secularization in Judaism, see also Michael Rosenak, 'Jewish Fundamentalism in Israeli Education', in Martin E. Marty and R. Scott Appleby (eds.), *Fundamentalisms and Society: Reclaiming the Sciences, the Family and Education* (Chicago/London: Chicago University Press), 1993.

6. It is perhaps pertinent to note here that Islamic tradition is largely posited on the idea of the model or precedent. For a study of the relationship that developed between Islam and the largely secular states that characterized the Arab world as of the mid-20th century, with the re-emergence of independent Muslim societies, see Olivier Carré, *Le nationalisme arabe* (Paris: Fayard, 1993).

7. It is, rather, an offshoot of rationalism, which in turn was brought in from the outside, first from the Greeks, later from the West.

8. One scholar differentiates between the various groups of secularists within the Muslim world. While all, he says, 'concur on the need to separate religion from politics,...some...are pious believers who maintain the daily observances of Islam'. Others are 'antinomians...who dismiss the whole sacred law as an archaism....For them, the Shariat does more than impede modernization; it also distracts from the message of the Qur'an'; and a third group, the non-believers 'reject religion in its entirety, both faith and laws' – Daniel Pipes, *In the Path of God: Islam and Political Power* (New York: Basic Books, 1983), p. 121.

9. For jadidism, see, for example, Alexandre A. Bennigsen, Chantal Lemercier-Quelquejay, *Islam in the Soviet Union* (London: Praeger, 1967), Ch. 3.

10. For Azerbaijan in the pre-revolutionary period, see Tadeusz Swietochowski, *Russian Azerbaijan, 1905–1920: The Shaping of National Identity in a Muslim Community* (Cambridge: Cambridge University Press, 1985).

11. The third developed and perhaps also truly national group were the Crimean Tatars, but the numbers of those who remained within the Russian Empire were small, and therefore their overall influence was insignificant.

12. The third of the eastern principalities, that of Kokand, ceased to exist in 1876, and became the Fergana Oblast of Turkestan.

13. Even here, cracks were forming in the monolith before the end of the tsarist period. Volga Tatars brought the *jadid* movement to Central Asia and began to help in the creation of a local intelligentsia; while in Dagestan and other areas in the Caucasus foreign influences were beginning to make their mark.

14. This is not true of the area that later became the southern Osh Oblast of Soviet Kirgiziia, that converted to Islam in the 10th century.

15. Bennigsen and Lemercier-Quelquejay, *Islam in the Soviet Union*, pp. 140–4.

16. For this analysis, see Alexandre A. Bennigsen and S. Enders Wimbush, *Muslim National Communism in the Soviet Union* (Chicago: Chicago University Press, 1979), p. 51. They base themselves on Sultan Galiev's article, 'The Methods of Antireligious Propaganda among the Muslims', *Zhizn' natsional'nostei*, 29, 127 and 30, 128 (1921), in ibid., Appendix C, pp. 145–57. Sultan Galiev's comrades, who controlled the government of the Tatar Autonomous Soviet Socialist Republic in 1922, established within the Commissariat of Justice a Shariat commission entrusted with reconciling and coordinating Soviet and Quranic law.

17. L. Klimovich, *Islam v tsarskoi Rossii* (Moscow: OGIZ-GAUZ, 1936). The book devoted an entire chapter to 'Reformist Trends in Islam and Their Political Platform', pp. 171–215.

18. Already in 1923 a first Muslim conference, held under the auspices of the Central Spiritual Directorate of Muslims in Orenburg, resolved to be loyal to the Soviet regime. This position of loyalty was maintained throughout the subsequent period – G. B.

Faizov, 'Rasprostranenie musul'manstva v Povolzh'e i Priural'e', in *Gosudarstvenno-tserkovnye otnosheniia v Rossii* (Moscow: 'Luch' Rossiiskaia Akademiia Upravleniia, 1993), p. 79.

19. In addition to the head-on attack, the authorities employed a series of roundabout tactics to achieve their goal of undermining religion *vis-à-vis* their Muslim population: young men enlisted into the armed forces were necessarily cut off from any religious practice (from many points of view the army served as a melting-pot for the construction of the new society and the creation of the new Soviet man). Sports competitions were invariably fixed for the period of Ramadan, and the audience would mock competitors whose performance was marred by the weakness caused by observing the fast – oral testimony of Michael Zand, who spent several years in Central Asia in the 1950s.

20. For the application of some of these tactics on the part of the jadidists and 'red mullas' in the 1920s, see Gregory J. Massell, *The Surrogate Proletariat* (Princeton: Princeton University Press, 1974), Ch. 1.

21. This was in itself a paradox, given the separation of church and state which was a fundamental principle of the Bolshevik regime from the very beginning, and the clause in the Soviet constitution ensuring freedom of conscience and religious worship (USSR constitution, 1936, article 124).

22. This included some 'scientific' treatises by orientalists on the history of Islam and its existential subservience to the goals and policies of feudalism and imperialism, especially of those of its sects that the Soviet regime believed constituted a political threat. See, e.g., Liutsian Klimovich, *Islam v tsarskoi Rossii*.

23. For recurrent efforts of the party authorities to remedy this situation, see Yaacov Ro'i, 'The Task of Creating the New Soviet Man: "Atheistic Propaganda" in the Soviet Muslim Areas', *Soviet Studies* 36, 1 (Jan. 1984), pp. 26–44.

24. For example, in Andijan in 1948, the 'agitation' of the mosque officials brought large numbers to the mosque, whereas in Bukhara during Ramadan, in the same year, the clergy organized an orchestra that played in the evenings on the mosque roof in order to attract large numbers of believers to evening prayers – N. Tagiev, 'Information on the Month of Ramadan and the Celebration of "Uraz-Bairam" in 1948', no date, GARF, fond (f.) 6991s, opis' (op.) 4, delo (d.) 23, p. 49. In Bukhara in the latter half of the 1960s, a similar situation also prevailed – St. Petersburg Tsentral'nyi gosudarstvennyi arkhiv, f. 2017, op. 1, d. 18, pp. 65–71; even in the one functioning mosque in Leningrad, the imam was constantly reported to be acting in violation of regulations, e.g., f. 2017, op. 1, d. 17, p. 65.

25. One such official, the *imam-khatib* of a mosque in rural Turkmeniia, was reported in early 1980 to have said it was logical that religious observance was declining as society became more advanced. 'No shepherd wants to lose his flock', he said, 'but we consider the peace-loving activities of the Soviet state more important than religion' – *Financial Times*, 6 Feb. 1980. In times of special pressure on the part of the authorities, in particular, the clergy were prone to comply. At the height of Khrushchev's anti-religious campaign, which probably marked an all-time low for the postwar period as far as religiosity and religious practice were concerned, a number of Muslim religious figures in Dagestan were reported to have 'completely voluntarily' renounced the conduct of religious rites in mosques – Report of the CARC representative for the Dagestan ASSR, M. S. Gajiev, at the Council meeting, Jan. 7, 1964; GARF, f. 6991s, op. 4, d, 146, p. 13. Even during perestroika the *imam-qazi* of the Muslims of Turkmeniia, Nasrulla Ibadullaev, noted: 'Islam never says: Let us fight against our own government', a view endorsed by the imam of Ashkhabad, Hezretguly Khanov, when he said: 'A Muslim who does not respect the laws of his own country is no Muslim because such people are going against Allah' – quoted from *Sovet Turkmenistany*, 7 April 1989; JPRS-UPA-89-052, 22 Aug. 1989.

26. GARF, f. 6991, op. 4, d. 23, pp. 12–13. The *fitr* was the contribution made to the poor by every believer who fasted, namely one kilogram of seeds or its market value for every day of the *uraza* – GARF, f. 6991s, op. 4, d. 23, p. 46.

27. There was a certain erosion in the Islamic orientation of the last emirs of Bukhara, who spoke Russian, introduced Russian customs and were subject to Russian influence, but

since this is not the focus of my paper, I am allowing myself some generalizations regarding the pre-Soviet period.

28. See Ro'i, 'The Islamic Influence on Nationalism in Soviet Central Asia', *Problems of Communism* 39, 4 (July–Aug. 1990), pp. 49–64.

29. Ibid., p. 50.

30. The whole issue of substituting its own secular rites – life-cycle, seasonal and historical – for those that had over the centuries been taken over by the local religions, had occupied the Soviet authorities for decades. On the whole, these Soviet rituals had been rejected by the Muslim population, partly because many of them had specifically Russian and/or Christian connotations and associations, partly out of adherence to their own traditional customs. For a study of Soviet ritual, see Christel Lane, *The Rites of Rulers* (Cambridge: Cambridge University Press, 1981). For their attempted application and failure in the Muslim areas, with particular reference to the Nawruz, see Lane, pp. 136, 232–3. For renewed attempts under Gorbachev to impose a new secularized Nawruz, see, for example, *Kommunist Tadzhikistana*, 14, 18, 21 March 1989.

31. These are the years for which I have seen materials, and I would not like to commit myself by making extrapolations regarding, say, the 1930s.

32. E.g., a report in the late 1940s by N. Tagiev, the member of CARC responsible for Islam, GARF, f. 6991, op. 4, d.23, pp. 9–10; the report is undated, but seems apparently to have been made in 1949.

33. E.g., the CARC representative in Karaganda Oblast claimed in 1948 that in the various Muslim communities of the *oblast*, boys were not circumcised and only some were buried according to religious rites – 'Instructional Letter no. 7' circulated to all CARC representatives; appendix no. 3 to the council's meeting of 24–25 Aug. 1948, GARF, f. 6991s, op. 4, d. 22, p. 196.

34. For statistics of mixed marriages among the Muslim peoples, see Viktor Kozlov, *The Peoples of the Soviet Union* (London: Hutchinson, 1988), pp. 188–204. In Kazan itself, where one might expect far more intermarriage than among the rural population, a sociological survey carried out in 1967 showed only 10 per cent mixed marriages – E. K. Vasil'eva, 'An Ethnodemographic Characterization of Family Structure in Kazan in 1967', *Soviet Sociology* 10, 1.

35. Even the blue-collar proletariat, especially among the Tatars and Bashkirs, many of whom lived outside their titular territories, was often totally secularized and had abandoned all religious practice.

36. GARF, f. 6991s, op. 4, d. 429, p. 1, and d. 431 and 435 *passim*. This number includes only those unregistered communities known to the authorities. It is more than possible that some or even many of the Sufi groups operated without the knowledge of the local CARC representative. In early 1950 and 1951, the number of unregistered Muslim communities known to the authorities had been 647 and 830, respectively – Chairman of CARC I. V. Polianskii to Deputy Premier K. E. Voroshilov, 4 Feb. 1950 (RTsKhIDNI, f. 17, op. 132, d. 285, p. 21) and to Central Committee Secretary G. M. Malenkov, 17 March 1951, appendix no. 4 (RTsKhIDNI, f. 17, op. 132, d. 497, p. 31).

37. Alexandre Bennigsen and S. Enders Wimbush in *Muslims of the Soviet Empire* (London: C. Hurst, 1985), p. 183, maintain that according to 'all Soviet sources', the Chechen and Ingush are the 'most religious' of all Soviet Muslims.

38. Michael Rywkin, 'The Communist Party and the Sufi *Tariqat* in the Checheno-Ingush Republic', *Central Asian Survey* 10, 1/2 (1991), p. 134.

39. One possibility is that the people who did the reporting (*kolkhoz* chairmen, for example) were themselves somehow involved in, or at least connected with, unofficial Islamic activity and therefore had an interest in not reporting it. Another might be that the local representatives of CARC were afraid of the consequences of drawing the attention of the central authorities to activity that they knew Moscow could neither ignore nor cope with. In any event, the atheistic propaganda conducted in the area and some central publications did indicate the existence of a very considerable unofficial Islam; see, for instance, my article, 'The Task of Creating the New Soviet Man'. Yet a third possibility, suggested by Rywkin, ibid, p. 136, is that 'the persistence of what the Russians call *krugovaia poruka* (a Sicilian law of silence)', made it difficult

for security agents to penetrate Sufi brotherhoods. (The term *krugovaia poruka* Rywkin apparently found in *Groznenskii rabochii*, 21 Aug. 1986.) Finally, it has been suggested that the *murid* communities are based on the extended family and as such are 'purely family, private matters, having nothing to do with the problems of collective life' – S. Umarov, 'Miuridizm s blizkogo rasstoianiia', *Nauka i religiia* 10 (1979), p. 71, quoted in Fanny E. Bryan, 'Anti-religious Activity in the Chechen-Ingush Republic of the USSR and the Survival of Islam', *Central Asian Survey* 3, 2 (1984), p. 112.

40. A CARC circular of the late 1940s referred specifically to roaming mullas in Kazakhstan and to the presence of fanatic or anti-Soviet *ali-allah*s, dervishes and *murids* – GARF f. 6991s, op. 4, d.22, pp. 204–205. (*Ali-allah* is apparently a distortion of Al-i Ilahi, an extremist, unorthodox, esoteric sect; extraneous to Central Asia, except for Turkmeniia, they had probably penetrated the area with the deported nationalities brought there at the end of World War II from the Caucasus.) For some of the concern of the authorities at the perseverance of Sufi activity, see, e.g., 'Recent Reports on Activities of Living Muslim "Saints" in USSR', RL346/83, 15 Sept. 1983. For such activity, see also Fanny E. Bryan, 'Internationalism, Nationalism and Islam', in Marie Bennigsen-Broxup (ed.), *The North Caucasus Barrier* (London: Hurst & Co.), 1992, pp. 195–218. One of her sources, Kh. Bokov, wrote in *Nauka i religiia* in 1987, that in the Chechen-Ingush ASSR alone 60,000 people actually worked, apparently as full-time employment, within the *murid*, i.e., sufi, groups. Nonetheless, the attribution by Bennigsen of virtually all unofficial activity to the Sufi brotherhoods seems to have been an exaggeration or a misunderstanding of some of the other forces at work.

41. *Sostoianie religioznosti i ateisticheskogo vospitaniia v regionakh traditsionnogo rasprostraneniia islama* (Moscow: Akademiia obshchestvennykh nauk pri TsK KPSS, Institut nauchnogo ateizma; Sovetskaia sotsiologicheskaia assotsiatsiia, 1989), pp. 5–8. The findings of this survey stand in sharp contrast to previous writings on Islam, e.g., Nugman Ashirov, *Islam i natsii* (Moscow: Politizdat, 1975), which has a sub-chapter entitled 'Atheization – the Natural Process of Development of Socialist Nations'.

42. Ibid., p. 26.

43. Ibid., p. 32.

44. Ibid., p. 68.

45. In the words of one commentator, 'Islam in the Soviet Union had been "castrated", for it had been deprived of one of its principal qualities, its politicization or involvement in politics' – Aleksei Malashenko, 'Musul'manstvo i politika', *Nezavisimaia gazeta*, 6 July 1991. See also Malashenko, 'Islam v politike i politika v islame', *Aziia i Afrika segodnia* 8 (1991). The debate on the process of Islam's politicization in the USSR and the implications thereof was opened with the article of one of the doyens of Soviet orientalistica, who enjoyed considerable prestige, among others, in the party establishment – Igor' Beliaev, 'Islam i politika', *Literaturnaia gazeta*, 13 and 20 May 1987.

46. This intelligentsia would probably have had no quarrel with the statement made by the mulla of Tashkent's Shaykh Zaynuddin Mosque in 1973 that 'only he who will publicly declare in front of all believers, in the mosque, that he no longer accepts Allah's commandments will cease to be considered a Muslim' – N. Ashirov, *Musul'manskaia propoved'* (Moscow: Politizdat, 1978), quoted in Azade-Ayse Rorlich, 'Islam and Atheism: Dynamic Tension in Soviet Central Asia', in William Fierman (ed.), *Soviet Central Asia* (Boulder: Westview, 1991), p. 187.

47. V. N. Basilov, 'Everyday [*bytovoi*] Islam in Central Asia and Kazakhstan', in a lecture delivered at the 2nd European Seminar on Central Asian Studies, London, 1987, which, as far as I know, has not been published. Basilov also dwelt on the shamanistic nature of many rites practised by Soviet Muslims.

48. For a short, but careful and apparently objective, resumé of some of the activities and dilemmas of the various groups of Muslim religious sects in different areas of the USSR, see V. G. Sadur, 'Musul'mane v SSSR: istoriia i sovremennost'', in *Na puti k svobodi sovesti* (Moscow: Progress, 1989), pp. 430–43.

49. To date, the intelligentsia has, according to most testimonies, remained basically a-religious.

20

2

Islam and Fundamentalism in Independent Central Asia

MARTHA BRILL OLCOTT

Among the surprises brought by independence in Central Asia was the discovery that Islam proved to have been much more pervasive in Soviet times than was previously imagined. Its persistence was not reflected so much in active participation in dogmatically prescribed rituals (although there was much more of that than we had supposed), as in its role in the identity or self-awareness of most Central Asians, even among those who considered themselves 'non-believers'.

In a way this was merely a continuation of the state of affairs before the revolution, when the people of Central Asia would identify themselves primarily as Muslims, and only secondarily in terms of tribe, clan and language. Although by sharply limiting religious observance and by defining new 'national republics', the Soviet regime was able to elevate what had been essentially tribal or linguistic groups to the level of 'nationalities', it has become obvious since independence that the consciousness of having an Islamic heritage was one of the elements which for the Central Asians continued to define their identities – even if a particular individual knew almost nothing about religion and observed none of its tenets.

Independence has made it plain that during the seven decades of Soviet domination most of the people of Central Asia continued to observe important Islamic holidays and rites of passage, even if they called these 'national' rather than religious customs, and observed them mostly in the privacy of their homes. These rituals included male circumcision (which remained almost universal in Central Asia throughout the Soviet period) and its celebration, marriage and mourning. During festivals like Qurban-Bairam, Central Asia's official mosques were described as filled to overflowing;[1] and there is no reason to suppose that the many unofficial mosques of which we are now aware were any less crowded. Even Ramadan seems to have been widely observed, at least outside the major, Europeanized cities.[2]

It is no doubt for this reason that all the new constitutions of Central Asia, save that of Kazakhstan, specify that Islam has a special place in the heritage of the titular people, even as they also specify that these new states will be non-denominational and secular.

However, in a process which began before independence but which has accelerated significantly since, large segments of Central Asian society have increasingly come to understand – or to remember – that these defining 'national' rituals are specifically Islamic. All strata of the native populations of Central Asia now generally accept that they are Muslim, owing to Islam at least the honour of acknowledging their apostasy, even if they are unable to meet such minimal injunctions as not drinking alcohol or eating pork.

As a consequence, Islam has become a feature of all of the élites of Central Asia, except in those parts of Tajikistan which are controlled by the Rahmonov government. This 'return to Islam' is most pronounced in Turkmenistan and Uzbekistan, where Sapurmurad Niiazov and Islam Karimov, the respective presidents, have both made *hajj*. Ironically, both are Communist Party *apparatchik*s who were originally put in power by Moscow, with one of their responsibilities being to contain and curtail Islam. Of the two, Niiazov's is the more public 'conversion', with the president (whose atheist past the republic's formidable propaganda machine has diplomatically forgotten) sponsoring numerous mosques and *madrasa*s, many of which bear his name. He has even erected a large statue of himself making pilgrimage, on the site where Ashgebat's main Lenin monument once stood.

Karimov's transformation has been less pronounced, in part because the threat of religious opposition is more serious in his republic, but he too has made such symbolic gestures as swearing his presidential oath of office on a Qur'an. Even Kazakhstan's Nursultan Nazarbaev, who continues to make his own atheism plain, has praised the historical contributions which Islam has made to society, and he has participated in public ceremonies which have a religious dimension, such as the burial of his predecessor, Dinmuhammed Kunaev.

This new regard for Islam by the élite is a reflection of a process which began among the Central Asians a decade or more ago, for much the same reason and at much the same time that Russia itself began to see an upswing of Russian nationalism, including a growth in the public presence of the Russian Orthodox Church. As innumerable sources now confirm, Soviet life had, by about the mid-1970s, proven itself to be spiritually and morally bankrupt; as a result, many people began to look around for alternate ideologies. Increasingly, the authorities in Moscow promoted this rebirth of Russian and Slavic nationalism, as part of a tactic to reinvolve and reinvigorate a citizenry which was rapidly sinking into drunken, degenerate indifference. If Russians were encouraged to 'seek their roots', then Central Asians could not easily be denied the same privilege, even if the 'roots' were very different. Consequently, the Islamic dimensions of Central Asian life became increasingly evident once again, as an integral constituent of national self-identity. Once Gorbachev began to demand that the leaders of the republics validate their positions by parliamentary and popular vote, it became inevitable that the republics' élites would have to mirror, at least to some degree, the growing religiosity of their constituents.

This necessity to accommodate Islam has, however, placed the leaders in a quandary. They are all sovietized, secular intellectuals who, because of their orientation toward European models and values, agree with Western tendencies to define Muslim believers as unyielding, fanatical, and ultimately dangerous. This has made the new quasi-religiosity of the Central Asian leaders something in the nature of a rear-guard action, which is designed to provide them with sufficient Islamic 'credentials' to allow them to set limits on the further spread of Islam.

Curbing this trend would probably have a real chance for success if the 'official' clerics, whom the current leaders support and empower, had managed to retain control of religious life in their respective countries. Certainly such control had been the Soviet intention, when the Central Asian Spiritual Directorate of Muslims (SADUM) was established during World War II. This body, fulfilling instructions from Moscow, sharply limited access to religious education, training and worship, and also painstakingly worked out a limited practice of Islam which was compatible with Soviet citizenship.

Yet, although they had created SADUM, the Soviet authorities remained suspicious of its leaders, because they understood that the teachings of Islam were at odds with those of the state. The Muslims who served in SADUM underwent elaborate scrutiny, but no security system is flawless. This is especially true in the case of religious believers, whose behaviour is difficult to predict, since religious belief dictates that people obey their conscience, which is an extremely fungible organ. This became particularly evident as the processes of Islamic revivalism intensified in Central Asia, where even the Muslim clerics of SADUM were doing no more than attempting to demonstrate that the social and moral teachings of Soviet law did not conflict with Islamic teachings; none seem to have explained that Soviet law took precedence over Islamic law.

One of the things which independence has revealed is that during the Soviet period SADUM and its clerics actually played a far smaller role in Central Asian Islam than did the enormous network of unrecognized and frequently untrained 'volunteer' clerics, who established Qur'an schools, preserved shrines, presided at burials, weddings and other rituals and, in the urban Muslim settings at least, monitored the observation of 'traditions' – most of which were Islamic. In Uzbekistan this last function was served through neighbourhood *mahallas*,[3] while in Turkmenistan the watchdogs of traditional Islamic practice were *elats*, or kinship groups of twenty to forty families.

It is impossible to know with any certainty how many unsanctioned mosques and *madrasas* there were in Soviet times, although all indications are that Soviet scholar Sergei Poliakov is not exaggerating in his assertion that there was some form of mosque or prayer house, sometimes called a 'study group' for purposes of obfuscation, in every Central Asian community.[4] Certainly this is consistent with findings by Uzbek ethnographer Nadira Azimova, who claims that in 1985 there were 194 unofficial clerics, each with his own congregation, in Namangan Oblast alone.[5] The long list of 'unofficial' mosques which Alexandre Bennigsen and Enders Wimbush provide in their book[6] seems to omit at least as many as it contains.

In Soviet times only a dozen or so Muslims annually were granted the right to formal Islamic education, through admission either to the Mir-i Arab Madrasa in Bukhara, which in the late Soviet period had a total enrolment of about fifty, or to the Imam al-Bukhari Institute in Tashkent, which had about thirty. It was only graduates of these two institutions who could legally conduct religious services, and even they could not actively proselytize, and had to submit their sermons for official approval. The numbers of clergy required to service the network of unsanctioned mosques, shrines and *madrasas* make it obvious that the overwhelming majority received their training 'illegally', at home or in informally organized *madrasas*.

A considerable portion of this 'underground' clergy came from the traditional Central Asian élites, and especially from the traditional religious élites. Soviet sources generally concealed the information that several religious 'dynasties' flourished in Central Asia, among both the officially-recognized clergy and the unofficial clergy. Two of the last three SADUM muftis, Muhammed Sadyq Mama Yusupov and his predecessor, Shamsuddin Babakhanov, were from clerical families. Other unofficial clergy were from families known as *seyyids* (descendants of Muhammad), *khojas* (those whose ancestors had made pilgrimage), and, in Turkmenistan, *awlads* (alleged descendants of Abu Bakr, Uthman and Ali). Conveyance of élite authority by right of birth, either to family or to clan, is one of the most difficult factors for outsiders to understand about élite politics in Central Asia, even as it is one of the most crucial elements – indeed, perhaps the single most crucial element – which decides an individual's potential for authority. Even the few glimpses we have of the roles played by clan and family in Central Asian politics suggest the power of these 'invisible' factors: the antipathy between Nazarbaev and Kunaev is said to have been caused largely by the fact that they were descended from two different *zhus* (hordes)[7] or, according to those who claim that Kunaev and Nazarbaev both originate from the Great Horde, from different (and often) rival clans. The majority of Kyrgyzstan President Askar Akaev's most sensitive (and lucrative) appointments have gone to members of his wife's clan; while Niiazov is said to be able to balance rivalries among the five major clans of Turkmenistan (whose seals are represented by the medallions of the state flag) only because he is an orphan, who was raised in a Soviet *internat* (boarding school), and 'clan-neutral'.[8]

It is crucial to understand that clan politics convey privilege, but also confer responsibility; members of particular clans are not only expected to look out for one another's interests, but are also encouraged, by group and family pressure, to continue the traditional activities in which the group has invested its self respect. It may be presumed that a large part of the pressure to maintain Islamic belief and practice in the years when the Soviet authorities struggled so actively to extirpate them came from this internal definition: one of the central characteristics of the élite clans was that they were part of the Muslim hierarchy, and so individuals strove, sometimes at substantial risk to position and career, to maintain family tradition.

Of course, a great distinction should to be made between élites which incorporate Islam as part of their claim to station, and élites which exist within Islam. Very different roles will be played in the future of Central Asia by élites who are now adopting an Islamic dimension as part of a general claim on power, and by the élites of the religious hierarchies themselves, official and unofficial.

In part, the difference between these two élites is a reflection of the fact that there are essentially two religious revivals occurring in Central Asia simultaneously. One is a broad-based popular return to a lost national and Islamic heritage, the other a much more narrowly-based attempt, on the part of a comparatively small number of believers, if not actually to introduce an Islamic state, then at least to reduce the gap between public behaviour and the tenets of Islam. Before 1990, contact between the two revivals was limited; now, however, the two movements are increasingly overlapping, especially as official uncertainty about how to contain the first revival increasingly enhances the authority of clerics in the second.

THE GENERAL RETURN TO ISLAM

The wide-scale return by most Central Asians to some form of Islamic worship might best be called a general return to Islam, as large numbers of people attempt to incorporate Islamic practices into lives which remain essentially secular. Most of this return to Islam is being led by the official clerics of the old SADUM hierarchy, which has now split into individual simulacra by republic. These clerics no longer see their role as the containment of Islam, but rather as its revitalization. Although Uzbekistan did not pass a law on freedom of conscience until July 1991, SADUM policies began to change dramatically in 1989, after the appointment of a new mufti, Muhammed Sadyq Mama Yusupov. Mama Yusupov was born in Andijan in 1953, the son of the mulla of Bulagbesh mosque. He received his formal education in the seminaries of Bukhara, Tashkent and Libya, but he is also said to have been a student of Rahmatulla Alloma, the major fundamentalist figure of Andijan (see below). Before he became mufti, Mama Yusupov served as deputy rector and then rector of the Imam al-Bukhari Institute in Tashkent.

The way in which Mama Yusupov came to power tells a great deal about the changing relationships between believers and the official clergy in the late Soviet era, for the circumstance necessitating a new mufti amounted to a rebellion by believers. The long-time Soviet-era mufti, Shamsuddin Babakhanov (grandson of SADUM's founding mufti, Ishan Ziyauddin Babakhanov), was forced to resign on 6 February 1989, following several days of demonstrations in Tashkent's main mosque, during which protesters accused Babakhanov of drunkenness and licentiousness.[9]

Appointed in February, Mama Yusupov was confirmed as mufti at a full congress of SADUM representatives and foreign guests in March 1989. At that convocation he delivered a major speech in praise of recent actions by Moscow, such as the return of the Caliph Uthman Qur'an to Tashkent (which Russian Imperial troops had taken after the conquest of Turkestan), and the restoration of the Abu Isa al-Termezi Mausoleum, the Bahauddin Mausoleum and Mosque, the Kalyan Mosque in Bukhara, and the Jami Mosque in Kokand, all of which were signs of new policies. However, the new mufti went on, these were not enough. Islam could not be returned to its former vitality without more mosques and better trained clerics; at the same time he thanked the Uzbek government for the support it had given, by building new dormitories and academic buildings at the *madrasa* in Bukhara and the institute in Tashkent.[10]

Mama Yusupov was no supporter of secular nationalism, as his speech before the second session of Uzbekistan's Supreme Soviet (in June 1990) made clear; he insisted that the Uzbeks, Kazakhs, Kyrgyz and Tajiks were historically one Muslim people, and that efforts to drive them apart should be viewed with suspicion.[11] Even so, his views were far more cautious than those of Central Asia's leading fundamentalists, who saw the creation of an Islamic state as their eventual and undisguised goal. In the years before Uzbekistan's independence the mufti was a public supporter of Mikhail Gorbachev, glasnost and perestroika, and gave enthusiastic public support to Moscow's anti-alcohol, anti-bribery and anti-corruption campaigns. This devotion was rewarded by the mufti's election to the USSR Congress of People's Deputies, from the podium of which he spoke out in favour of the USSR's foreign policies in the Middle East and Gorbachev's domestic initiatives.[12]

As the influence of SADUM grew under Mama Yusupov, Central Asia's secular leaders began to see the role that religion was going to play in the national revival of their various republics, prompting each to try to guarantee that this return to Islam was at least partly under his control. In Kazakhstan, even though the Islamic revival there was proceeding more slowly than was the case in Uzbekistan or Tajikistan, Islam had become a significant enough social force in the republic by late 1989 to make the country's new leader decide he could no longer afford to have it outside his control. Accordingly, Nazarbaev formally removed Kazakhstan from the jurisdiction of SADUM in November 1989, creating a separate muftiate for Kazakhstan; the fact that Nazarbaev made this move even though it was far from clear that he had the authority to do so under Soviet law, is some measure of how pressing this problem was.

Qazi Ratbek Nysanbai, who had been the senior SADUM official in Kazakhstan, was named Mufti of Kazakhstan, a decision formalized in January 1990, at the first *kurultai* of the Muslims of Kazakhstan.[13] Like Mama Yusupov, Nysanbai also became a deputy, in his case of the Kazakhstan Supreme Soviet (representing Chimkent).

Nysanbai's authority derives entirely from Nazarbaev, and it is not clear how much support the mufti enjoys among Kazakhstan's believers. A significant portion of Kazakhs consider Mufti Ratbek to be politically co-opted by his years in SADUM. In December 1991 a delegation from Alash, the closest thing Kazakhstan has to an Islamic party (although the party program actually calls only for recognition of Islam as a state religion), tried physically to remove Nysanbai from office; this ended with the mufti having his leg broken, and the jailing of Alash leaders.[14]

Religious revival has also proceeded by fits and starts in Kyrgyzstan, in part because the republic's leadership has retained control of the formal governing bodies. SADUM-appointed Qazi Sadyqjan Kamalov, speaking for reform elements within Kyrgyzstan's Islamic community, also became a champion of Kyrgyzstan's fledgling democratic movement, the DDK (Demokraticheskoe dvizhenie Kyrgystana), but the ties between believers and secular activists became much looser after Akaev came to power, and the DDK transformed itself from anti-regime activism into pro-government opposition.

During the political unrest of 1990 (following the Osh disturbances in June), the administration of Absamal Masaliev kept Sadyqjan Kamalov under close official supervision. After Akaev came to power, in October 1990, Sadyqjan's position improved quickly. He and his followers were allowed to create an Islamic centre in an office building on the capital's showy main square.[15] When independence brought the effective end of SADUM, Kamalov was named Mufti of Kyrgyzstan.

However, in September 1993, at the first *kurultai* of Kyrgyz Muslims, a new mufti was chosen. A possible explanation for this was Kamalov's association with Islamic fundamentalists on the Uzbek side of the Fergana Valley, which was demonstrated publicly in 1991, when Uzbek followers of Abdulwali Qari (see below), to whom SADUM denied '*hajj* passes', travelled to Mecca with the Kyrgyz delegation. Another reason why Akaev may have turned against Kamalov was because of differences occasioned by the forceful overthrow of the Iskandarov coalition in Tajikistan, and the installation of the Rahmonov government, which has been vigorously anti-Islamic.

It is in Uzbekistan that the potential conflicts between official Islam and the secular government have become most obvious. The change in state policy towards religion has made the post of head of SADUM a very powerful one, with the mufti responsible for collecting – and dispensing – enormous sums of money. The revenues collected by SADUM have increased dramatically as the number of mosques and schools under its jurisdiction has grown. Power, though, still depends a great deal on the secular authorities, who have retained control of SADUM, just as its republican analogues after independence, and their muftis, although ratified by an assembly of Islamic believers, have served at the behest of the respective republics' presidents.

In April 1993 Uzbekistan's President Islam Karimov turned against Mama Yusupov, alleging that the mufti had misappropriated funds. In fact, however, Karimov had targeted Mama Yusupov for dismissal some six months before, when the Uzbek cleric began defending the actions of Qazi Akbar Turajonzade in Tajikistan (see below); it was, *inter alia*, alleged that the qazi was advocating formation of an Uzbek branch of the Islamic Renaissance Party (IRP). The Islamic Renaissance Party was created in Astrakhan in June 1990, by Ahmedqazi Akhtaev, who is an Avar from Dagestan, and Valiahmed Sadur, a Tatar living in Moscow.[16]

Uzbek activists made repeated efforts through late 1990 and early 1991 to hold an organizational meeting, as part of the process necessary to register the IRP in Uzbekistan. It was not until 26 February 1991 that 300 people were able to gather in Tashkent, in defiance of the Tashkent *gorispolkom*, which had decided to ban the meeting after lengthy consultation with communist party and security officials. The organizers of that meeting included Abdulla Uta, who was to become chairman of the IRP in Uzbekistan, and Abdurrahim Pulatov, the co-chairman of Birlik (the secular nationalist movement). The meeting was broken up and the organizers were fined.[17]

The Islamic Renaissance Party never succeeded in gaining legal registration in Uzbekistan, but it has established chapters in Tashkent and in the principal cities of the Fergana Valley; although the fundamentalist leaders, like Abdulwali in Andijan, and Aqilbeq Ishanbaev and Abdulahad in Namangan, all claim to be independent of the IRP, there would be no reason for them to publicly claim membership in an illegal organization.

The relationship between Birlik and the IRP is a complex one. Although Pulatov was present at the IRP organizing meeting, Birlik leaders have said they do not endorse the IRP agenda; they do, however, support the right of this group to exist. Birlik members imply in interviews[18] that one of the reasons for the decision to outlaw their movement in 1992 was that it was presumed to be a potential partner for coalition with the IRP, as the democrats had been in Tajikistan.

Although Mama Yusupov was alleged to be sympathetic to fundamentalism in general and the IRP in particular, the mufti's public position toward the formation of the IRP was consistently negative; in both 1990 and 1991 he spoke out openly on many occasions against the formation of the party, claiming that the IRP was fracturing the community of believers.[19]

In fact, the mufti's position on the IRP exacerbated the splintering of the clerics of Uzbekistan, into pro-mufti, pro-fundamentalist and pro-Babakhanov factions. In July 1991 the combined opposition was powerful enough to attempt to unseat Mama Yusupov, who was forced to appeal to President Karimov for support. The mufti's leadership was reaffirmed, but he was weakened by his victory, because in order to convince believers of his independence, Mama Yusupov needed to distance himself from the Karimov government. This made Karimov a new and powerful enemy, not only of Mama Yusupov, but of an independent Muslim establishment more generally.[20] Because the mufti's support was considered a political asset during Uzbekistan's presidential election campaign (when Karimov ran against the slight but nevertheless real opposition of Erk party founder Muhammed Salih), Karimov maintained very good public relations with the SADUM leader until after the December 1991 elections. After that point, however, relations soured rapidly, culminating in Mama Yusupov's dismissal, and the bringing of criminal charges (for malfeasance) against him; he is reported to have fled Uzbekistan for Saudi Arabia, rather than face court proceedings.

Saudi Arabia has also been at least a temporary current address of another Islamic cleric,[21] who got caught in the politicization of the religious revival; this is Qazi-Kolon Hojiakbar Turajonzade, who was named Qazi of Tajikistan in August 1988. Like Mama Yusupov, who was both his counterpart in Uzbekistan and his contemporary in the Soviet seminary system, Turajonzade received training outside the USSR, in his case at the law faculty of Jordan State University.

Turajonzade, born in 1954, seems typical of his generation of official clerics, at least in his attempts to reconcile state and unofficial Islam. Like Mama Yusupov, Turajonzade was a vocal supporter of Gorbachev in the final years of the USSR, arguing that perestroika had returned to believers the possibility to pursue their faith; in turn, although Turajonzade never stated this trade-off explicitly, he acknowledged the right of the state to restrict the participation of Islam in politics. Under Turajonzade the official clerics were made to sign guarantees that they would obey the laws only of the Shariat and the Tajik SSR,[22] and that they would not join any political parties.

The object was to forestall formation of a Tajik branch of the IRP. After the establishment in May 1992 of the coalition government of National Reconciliation comprising Nabiev and his supporters, as well as democrats and the IRP, who together had one-third of the seats, Turajonzade explained his reasoning for being opposed to an IRP: namely, that all of Islam should be considered a single party, or unit of interest. Turajonzade has also stated consistently that he sees no possibility of establishing an Islamic government anywhere in Central Asia, because the seven decades of Soviet rule have so destroyed faith and knowledge among believers that, as he put it, less than three per cent of them can read a *namaz* (daily prayer) properly.[23]

What appears to have pushed Turajonzade from clerical activities into politics was the attempt by President Rahmon Nabiev in early

1992 to assert control over the muftiate, of which Turajonzade had become head with the de facto collapse of SADUM's authority outside Uzbekistan. Rather than accept the sort of presidentially-appointed muftiate which Karimov and Nazarbaev had maintained in their republics, Turajonzade preferred to let Tajikistan's believers assert their independence, which they did in a series of demonstrations. Nabiev also moved against the IRP at this time, which further destabilized the situation.

By May 1992 Nabiev had been forced from office, and an attempt was made to install a coalition government, led by Parliamentary Speaker Akbarshoh Iskandarov, with active participation of the democratic party, led by Shodmon Yusuf. The appointment of IRP head Dawlat Usman as deputy premier, however, seems to have convinced both Russia and Uzbekistan that Tajikistan was in eminent peril of 'going Muslim'; it was the active intervention of these two states, and especially of Russia, which greatly escalated the intensity of the country's civil war.

In interviews since the collapse of the Iskandarov coalition and the imposition of the Rahmonov government, Turajonzade has portrayed the civil war as a battle of communists, backed by Russia, against a coalition of democrats, IRP supporters, and representatives of his own qaziate. He has stressed that he has no wish to impose Islam as a state religion, and indeed points out that he was removed from the Presidium at the time that Iskandarov became its chairman;[24] however Turajonzade was identified by the Rahmonov faction as one of its main enemies, and in December 1992 was forced to flee. Although he expressed a willingness to work with the Rahmonov government at that time, Turajonzade has been made the subject of criminal investigations by that government,[25] and so prudently took refuge, first in Saudi Arabia, and subsequently, it seems, in Afghanistan.[26]

THE FUSING OF FORMAL AND INFORMAL ISLAM

The careers of Sadyq Kamalov, Mama Yusupov and Qazi Turajonzade illustrate how the general 'legalization' of Islamic revivalism disturbed the relations between the civil and religious authorities, in large part because the revitalization of SADUM also led to a partial fusing of formal and informal Islam. SADUM began actively to court Central Asia's unofficial clerics, which brought hundreds, perhaps thousands, of once 'illegal' mosques under the supervision of the Spiritual Directorate. What the self-appointed imams and muftis of these mosques received in return was support for local building drives, as community after community replaced small, illicit worship and assembly houses with large public buildings, some of them full-scale 'cathedral' mosques. SADUM also provided believers with the clout necessary to facilitate the spontaneous repossession of pre-revolutionary mosques, *madrasa*s and holy sites which the Soviet authorities had nationalized or otherwise converted to secular use. A prominent example was the Jami (cathedral) Mosque in Andijan, where Abdulwali's supporters managed to take control both of the mosque and of the adjoining warehouse, which blocked access to it. Another was in Osh (Kyrgyzstan), where believers forced the municipality to relinquish a 'museum' on the grounds of the *madrasa*-made-storehouse which stood at the foot of Suleiman mountain. Some of the properties seized in this way became affiliated with SADUM; some, like the Jami Mosque in Andijan, did not.

There were other incentives to ally with SADUM. Mullas who did so gained access to 'pilgrimage passes' for themselves and their followers. Annual '*hajj*' charter flights began in 1990, funded by Saudi Arabia – as was much of the abovementioned construction of mosques – but administered at SADUM discretion. More importantly, the leadership of SADUM began to make overtures towards unofficial Islam on a theological level. SADUM clerics were now encouraged to preach the faith openly, and to try to attract as many new believers as possible. SADUM also endorsed some of the social programs of the funda-mentalists, urging the population to live lives shaped by Shariat law. Finally, it strongly advocated increased Arabic language education, as well as plans to return written Uzbek to its original, Arabic, script, in order to enable the return of Uzbeks to their pre-revolutionary religious heritage.

ISLAMIC FUNDAMENTALISM

It should not be surprising then that formal, official Islam has played so large a part in the second process which was unfolding simul-taneously in Central Asia, parallel to that of revivalism, but largely independent of it. This second movement, involving far fewer people than does the revivalist movement, resembles much more what outside observers would consider Islamic fundamentalism, in which adherents reorder their lives to comply fully with Islam's teachings, and speak of the desire to return society to 'the true path of Islam'. Of course, this fundamentalist movement ran contrary to Soviet law, because it was posited on the belief that the law of Allah must be placed above that of the state. Thus SADUM officials were forced to condemn the fundamentalists in public. In reality, though, many within the official clerical establishment not only tolerated the revival, but actively helped to facilitate it. Even today, the dimensions of this fundamentalist revival are still difficult to estimate, in large part because the presidents of the new republics are no more in favour of fundamentalist Islam now than they were when they were Moscow-appointed first secretaries of Soviet union republics.

The Soviet authorities began to recognize the existence of the fundamentalists by the early 1980s; in the conclusion to the second edition of his book *Islam and Society* (*Islam i obshchestvo*), Kazakh orientalist T. S. Saidbaev mentions two such communities of revivalists, the *ahl-i qur'an* (people of the Qur'an) from outside Tashkent and a group near Osh; he calls them 'isolated dangerous fanatics trying to live their lives within the confines and dictates established by Islam',[27] further arguing that these small communities posed a political threat because their decision to educate their children at home was an explicit rejection of the authority of the secular Soviet regime.

Yet Saidbaev does not seem to have been aware of the full dimensions of the fundamentalist movement which was developing in the Fergana Valley; but the Egyptian journalist (and reputed Muslim Brother) Fahmi Hawadi has described the activities of another fundamentalist group around Namangan which was active at about the time that Saidbaev was doing his research.[28]

Today the Fergana Valley is the 'educational centre' for Central Asia's fundamentalists. Most of Central Asia's religious figures are still in the 'proselytizing phase', more interested in training new clerics and increasing the level of religious learning among the population than in getting the laws of society to conform to those of Islam. Obviously they see that effort as a necessary next stage, but as Qazi Akbar Turajonzade who, though an official cleric, maintained strong ties with Tajikistan's fundamentalist movement, said on numerous occasions, this next stage could be as much as a generation away.[29]

Certainly before 1989 or 1990, when new laws on religion and regulations, permitting the formation of political movements and organizations, came into force, Central Asia's Islamic fundamentalists concentrated entirely on educational activities, and on the construction or restoration of mosques, schools and *madrasas*. While Soviet propagandists excoriated 'foreign forces' for trying to use Islam to destabilize Central Asia, in reality the spread of fundamentalism within the Fergana Valley was largely generated and sustained from within.

Neither the Islamic revolution in Iran, nor the Soviet-Afghanistan war seems to have had much responsibility for the development of Fergana fundamentalism. Certainly, Turkmen religiosity was sustained and stimulated by Islamic broadcasts on Iranian Radio Gorgan, which began transmitting to its neighbour well before the advent of Khomeini;[30] however, Turkmenistan has played a peripheral role in

Central Asia's religious revival, and there is only secondary evidence to suggest that these broadcasts have had a broader impact.[31]

As for Afghanistan, while there is no question that Islamic fighters from Tajikistan were definitely receiving direct support from groups within Afghanistan's Islamic government in 1992 and 1993, there is little evidence to suggest that there was any contact during the Soviet occupation. Some Central Asian soldiers serving in the Soviet Army in Afghanistan did go over to the *mujahedin*, but they seem to have numbered no more than a few hundred; only a handful of these have returned home with the intention of establishing Islamic states there.

The Afghan war seems, however, to have illustrated to the leaders of Islamic revivalism in Soviet Central Asia the depth of conviction of religious forces in Afghanistan, whose battle they understood as a manifestation of revivalism. As teachers of the faith, the fundamentalists of Central Asia saw it as their responsibility to seek out the sources of the Afghan revival, which they found in the works of Muslim brethren like the brothers Sayyid and Muhammed Qutb, or Sayyid Abu 'Ala Mawdudi, whose books were already entering the Soviet Union through contacts in the Middle East, even before they were attainable through Afghanistan.

Although Soviet Muslims welcomed foreign missionaries when they came, relatively few such missionaries seem to have been able to penetrate the Soviet security system,[32] and those 'caught in the act', as was Fahmi Hawadi when he travelled the region as a journalist in the late 1970s, were quickly deported. However, Qur'ans and books of religious commentary and current Islamic political thought did find their way to the region, where they were duplicated on rudimentary copy machines, or clandestinely reprinted at state printing plants, bound with covers taken from Communist Party publications. Such books were quite rare, as were surviving copies of major pre-revolutionary religious primers, such as jadidist reformer Munawwar Qari's *Adib-i awwal* (*First Teacher*, ca. 1901) and *Adib-i thani* (*Second Teacher*, 1903), or Uzbek language primers (written in Arabic script) that provided an introduction to the Qur'an and to Islamic studies.[33]

During his 1980 visit to an 'underground *madrasa*' in Namangan, Hawadi found the students reading copies of Sayyid Qutb's *Ma'alim fi al-tariq* (*Landmarks along the Way*) and Muhammed Qutb's *Shubhatun hawla al-islam* (*Ambiguities Surrounding Islam*) which had been borrowed from the SADUM library in Tashkent.[34]

Officials in SADUM also appear to have been instrumental in training Sufis of the Naqshbandi order, and probably of other Sufi groups as well. The Naqshbandi movement developed around Bukhara in the 13th century, but spread throughout Central Asia, the

North Caucasus, into Iran, down to Turkey, and then south to Egypt and Yemen and east into India.

Throughout the Soviet period the Naqshbandi order was formally banned, as were other secret religious societies. However, the key role played by Naqshbandi *ishans* in the Basmachi movement in Central Asia and in resistance to Soviet rule in the North Caucasus guaranteed that known Naqshbandi *ishans* became a particular target of Stalin's police.

Despite that, the Naqshbandi did survive. Ziyauddin Babakhanov, a popularly revered Naqshbandi *ishan*, was selected by Stalin to be the first head of SADUM in 1943 at the age of 84. His grandson, Shamsuddin Babakhanov, also became head of SADUM; though he was often criticized by local believers for what they saw as his lax personal observance of Islamic teachings, Babakhanov told visiting Egyptian journalist Hawadi that he too was an 'adherent of the way'.[35]

SADUM Mufti Muhammed Sadyq Mama Yusupov was never linked to Sufi groups, but his successor, Muftarkhan Abdullaev, rector of Bukhara Madrasa and head of the (SADUM) Mavarannahr Mosque in Bukhara until his appointment as mufti in April 1993, is a Naqshbandi, who claims to have trained over a thousand Sufi adepts (or followers) in study groups held outside of the *madrasa* while serving as a SADUM official.[36]

Much has been written about the 'fighting' nature of Central Asia's Naqshbandis, particularly by Alexandre Bennigsen. The Naqshbandi Sufism described by Abdullaev was far more spiritual in orientation than it was political. His aims, as he described them, were to restore Islam to Central Asia through Sufism, so that each believer could come to be at peace with himself – or herself, since he mentioned having trained dozens of women as well.

Not all of the fundamentalist strains of thought are as contemplative as that which Abdullaev appeared to profess. Some Central Asian fundamentalist groups are already active politically, and as the events in Tajikistan show, these groups can feel pushed to respond to deteriorating political conditions, with or without the approval of their leadership.

The main impetus for the development of the politicized strains of contemporary Central Asian fundamentalism comes from the *madrasas* of the Fergana Valley, particularly from the students of Hakim Qari, a spiritual leader (b. ca. 1897) in Margilan.[37] The analysis of Hakim Qari's importance by Uzbek scholar of fundamentalism, Abdujabbar Abduvakhitov, has been borne out by other sources. In the last decades of Soviet rule, Margilan (the older eastern city on the outskirts of Fergana) functioned as a state within a state, and served as a centre for Uzbekistan's 'second' or 'black-market' economy. Margilan's clans are key to the regulation of trade throughout Central Asia; during the Soviet period local authorities simply ignored Margilan's economic activities, probably in part because they profited from them handsomely as well. The city appeared to be a Central Asian backwater, a first impression which visitors from Moscow and other authority centres were encouraged to accept as reality.

The fact that the city was a well-preserved economic secret also made Margilan an ideal centre for a religious revival, since Hakim Qari's students were essentially free to come and go as they wished. In such an environment, Hakim Qari was able to become a figure of great local standing, a Central Asian 'holy man' on the model of his pre-revolutionary predecessors. Nor did it hurt that Margilan had long been a centre of Sufism in the Fergana Valley; the 1898 anti-Russian revolt, led by the Naqshbandi Shaykh Muhammed Ali (known also as Madali) had its roots in Margilan.

It is unclear whether Hakim Qari is himself a Sufi, but the fact that his course of study featured the works of Uzbek *jadid* reformers such as Munawwar Qari (1880–1933), Mahmud Hoja Behbudi (1874–1919) and Abdulrauf Fitrat (1886–1938) suggests that he may not be, since these men saw Sufism as a force of obscurantism. However, lines of intellectual inheritance were not always rational in the Soviet Union, so that Hakim Qari's relationship to Sufism should still be seen as an unresolved question. Indeed, in many ways the question of whether or not the Islamic fundamentalists of Fergana are Sufis is irrelevant. Although the two groups could some day come together, the origins of the fundamentalists in Fergana are distinct from those of the Naqshbandis of Bukhara, and the fundamentalists' religious education and political programs are distinct from those of mainstream Sufism.

Still reported to be alive in 1993, Hakim Qari has lived quietly in Margilan, teaching and proselytizing. His work has now been largely passed on to a group of students whom he trained in the late 1970s. The student who is said to have most closely approached his teacher in charisma and depth of intellect was a cleric named Rahmatulla.

According to Abduvakhitov, Rahmatulla and another promising student, Abdulwali, lived with Hakim Qari for six months in 1978. Shortly afterwards, in 1979, Rahmatulla broke with his mentor, calling Hakim Qari a 'collaborator' at a public meeting, and accusing him of having been subservient to the Soviet authorities. Abdulwali and Rahmatulla left Margilan for Andijan, where they embarked on a kind of personal crusade to revitalize Islam through a net-work of clandestine schools in the cities, towns and villages of the Fergana Valley, which taught from religious materials produced by underground printing presses. The schools were financially self-sufficient, supported through various commercial enterprises which Rahmatulla and his followers established solely for that purpose.

These small schools (five to ten students each) introduced their pupils to the study of the Qur'an and the founding teachings of Islam, as well as to the writings of contemporary Islamic thinkers such as Hasan al-Banna (1906–49), the philosopher of the Muslim brethren, and the more modern works of Mawdudi and the Qutb brothers.

Rahmatulla died in an automobile accident in 1981, at the age of 31. Some adherents have claimed that the cleric was killed, but if the purpose of such an assassination was to curtail Rahmatulla's influence, the killing – if it was such – was in vain.

Some activist disciples were arrested for their activities, but Rahmatulla's underground schools flourished throughout the 1980s. His companion Abdulwali has become a major spiritual leader in the Fergana Valley, the shaykh of a large mosque and *madrasa* in Andijan, which believers seized from the state and restored in the late 1980s.

Abdulwali himself is not actively – or at least publicly – engaged in politics, but his colleagues and students run the fundamentalist mosques and *madrasa*s of Uzbekistan, Kyrgyzstan and Tajikistan, and are prominent in the leadership of the Islamic Renaissance Party in both Tajikistan and Uzbekistan.

CONCLUSION

The official response to Islam in Central Asia seems almost designed to transform the general return to Muslim observance, which characterizes society's attempt to reclaim its lost identity into the sort of political Islam that the present leaders fear the fundamentalist revival will become. Turajonzade and Mama Yusupov represent relatively moderate clerical positions, with the emphasis upon the moral and intellectual regeneration of a society artificially cut off from an important part of its identity. There is nothing in that search which should be threatening; as Turajonzade pointed out in an interview published on 15 August 1993:

> Islam is a religion of the patient. It can not threaten anyone...We want people in Tajikistan to be able to profess any religion and to express any opinion without having to pay for this with their lives or freedom, as is the case right now.[38]

However, if the other leaders of Central Asia choose to follow the lead of Uzbekistan's Karimov, and of Russian Foreign Minister Andrei Kozyrev, in seeing Islam as an inherently destabilizing force which can be extirpated by force, then it seems as if the further politicization of Islam in Central Asia is inevitable.

NOTES

1. *Islam v SSSR* (Moscow, 1973), p. 68.
2. Nadira Khaitbaevna Azimova, *Sistema traditsionnogo vospitaniia detei v uzbekskikh sel'skikh sem'iakh* (Moscow: Moscow State University, Department of History, 1987), pp. 84–103.
3. For a detailed description of the workings of the *mahalla*, see Sergei P. Poliakov (ed.), *Everyday Islam: Religion and Tradition in Rural Central Asia*, Introduction by Martha Brill Olcott (Armonk, NY: M.E. Sharpe, 1992), pp. 53–95.
4. Ibid.
5. Azimova, *Sistema traditsionnogo vospitaniia detei*, p. 101.
6. Alexandre Bennigsen and S. Enders Wimbush, *Muslims of the Soviet Empire* (Bloomington: Indiana University Press, 1986), Ch. 7.
7. *Moskovskie novosti*, 19 Jan. 1992, p. 1.
8. For the importance of clan or tribal politics, see Donald Carlisle, 'Geopolitics and Ethnic Problems of Uzbekistan and Its Neighbours'; Grigorii G. Kosach, 'Tajikistan: Political Parties in an Inchoate National Space'; Demian Vaisman, 'Regionalism and Clan Loyalty in the Political Life of Uzbekistan', in this volume.
9. *Pravda vostoka*, 16 Feb. 1993.
10. TASS 14 March 1989, as quoted by *FBIS Daily Report Soviet Union* (FBIS), FBIS-SOV-89-049, 15 March 1989.
11. Muhammedsadyq Muhammed Yusuf, *Esli-by my vse byli nabozhnymi* (Tashkent: Chulpan, 1992), p. 10.
12. *Al-Anba* (Kuwait), 11 May 1989, as translated in FBIS-SOV-89-096, 19 May 1989, p. 8.
13. *Izvestiia*, 27 Jan. 1990.
14. *Kazakhstanskaia pravda*, 11 Dec. 1991.
15. *Izvestiia*, 29 March 1991.
16. For details, see Alexei Malashenko, 'Does Islamic Fundamentalism Exist in Russia?', in this volume.
17. *Pravda vostoka*, 1 March 1991.
18. Conducted by the author in May and Aug. 1992, and in March 1993.
19. *Komsomol'skaia pravda*, 8 Dec. 1990, and 3 April 1991.
20. *FBIS Daily Report Central Eurasia*, FBIS-SOV-91-136, 16 July 1991 p. 103.
21. *Rossiiskaia gazeta*, 27 Aug. 1993, p. 7.
22. *Komsomol'skaia pravda*, 21 Sept. 1990, p. 1.
23. *Rossiiskaia gazeta*, 27 Aug. 1993, p. 7.
24. *Nezavisimaia gazeta*, 25 Aug. 1993, p. 1.
25. *Al-sharq al-awsat*, 11 Jan 1993, p. 7, as translated in FBIS-SOV-93-018, 29 Jan. 1993, p. 60.
26. *Keyhan*, 24 July 1993, p. 14, as translated in FBIS-SOV-93-163, 25 Aug. 1993, p. 44.
27. T. S. Saidbaev, *Islam i obshchestvo* (Moscow: Nauka, 1984), 2nd ed., p. 282. See also Yaacov Ro'i, 'The Impact of the Islamic Fundamentalist Revival of the Late 1970s on the Soviet View of Islam', in Y. Ro'i (ed.) *The Soviet Union and the Muslim World* (London: George Allen & Unwin, 1979), pp. 167–72.
28. *Al-arabi* (Kuwait), No. 254, 1980; JPRS-UPA–80–1058, 21 Aug. 1980, pp. 82–105, and information received in dicussions between the author and Hawadi in 1992.
29. See, for example, the interview of Qazi Turajonzade with Interfax, FBIS-SOV-92-156, 12 Aug. 1992, p. 56.
30. There were complaints that Iranian and other radio sources were broadcasting Islamic materials as early as 1965. See Muriel Atkin, *The Subtlest Battle: Islam in Soviet Tajikistan* (Philadelphia: Foreign Policy Research Institute, 1989), p. 58.
31. For such evidence, see Ro'i, 'The Islamic Influence on Nationalism in Soviet Central Asia', *Problems of Communism*, 39 (July–Aug. 1990), pp. 62–3.
32. Abdujabar Abduvakhitov, 'Islamic Revivalism in Uzbekistan', in Dale F. Eickelman (ed.), *Russia's Muslim Frontiers* (Bloomington: Indiana University Press, 1993), p. 84.
33. For Qari, see Edward Allworth, *The Modern Uzbeks From the Fourteenth Century to the Present* (Stanford: Hoover Institution Press, 1990), p. 133. For a description of the

sort of educational materials available to Islamic activists, see Abduvakhitov, 'Islamic Revivalism in Uzbekistan', pp. 81–2.

34. *Al-arabi* (Kuwait), No. 254, 1980; *JPRS Report, USSR Political and Social Affairs* 1058, 21 Aug. 1980, pp. 82–105. Information also received in dicussions between the author and Hawadi in 1992.

35. Ibid., p. 89

36. Interview conducted by author, May 1992.

37. For greater detail on Hakim Qari, see Abduvakhitov, 'Islamic Revivalism in Uzbekistan', pp. 82–4.

38. *Moskovskie novosti*, No. 33, 15 Aug. 1993, p. 8.

3

Does Islamic Fundamentalism Exist in Russia?

ALEXEI MALASHENKO

At first glance the existence of Islamic fundamentalism in Russia may be considered a very secondary problem that is hardly discernible in the country's political and religious life. Russian political *apparatchiks* associate fundamentalism with the situation in Central Asia (notably Tajikistan), but refuse in effect to recognize its influence in Russia itself. In the opinion of the majority of Russia's top level officials, even the political developments in the 'semi-independent' republics of the Northern Caucasus have nothing to do with fundamentalism. An exception was a statement made by former Vice-President Aleksandr Rutskoi to President Johar Dudaev of Chechnia in 1991: 'All of you here are bandits and Muslim fundamentalists.'[1] As for Russian society, its attitude to Muslim fundamentalism is generally critical or negative, and to Islam, indifferent.

One question must be answered by everyone who tries to analyze the position of the Muslim nations[2] and the place of Islam as a confession and culture within the Russian Federation. This question may be formulated as follows: Is there a 'common Islamic space' in the Russian Federation, and even more important – inside the frontiers of the Commonwealth of Independent States? (Since the disintegration of the Soviet Union some politicians, ·including Mikhail Gorbachev, who seek to emphasize the unity of the USSR, often use the terms 'common economic, cultural, military and even spiritual space'.)

The existence of such an 'Islamic space' may be proved, first by the similarity of the social and cultural processes which are developing within different Muslim ethnic groups in Russia and throughout the CIS, specifically, the so-called 'Islamic renaissance' and the wide politicization of Islam; second, by the tacit or sometimes open confrontation between Muslim and non-Muslim ethnic groups; and third, by their aspiration to elaborate their own way of development based on some of the social, political and cultural values of Islam: an Islamic totality, comprehension of Islam as a mode of life, the cohesion of Islam and politics, and the idea of an Islamic economy.

Moreover, Russia's Muslims are beginning to feel themselves to be a confessional community of ethnic minorities (the number of Muslims is estimated variously between 11 and 20 million people[3]). This feeling is strengthened by numerous political contacts between political leaders of the Muslim republics – Tatarstan and Chechnia, Tatarstan and Dagestan and, of course, between the different republics in the Northern Caucasus. (These contacts do not rule out contradictions and even disputes or confrontation between neighbouring Muslim nations, for instance, between Tatarstan and Bashkortostan.[4])

The Muslim nations of Russia are seeking their national identity, which cannot be separated from their religious rebirth. Their national consciousness is tied to their religious feeling. Of course, every Muslim nation has its own degree of religiosity, which is defined by its level of secularization, stage of urban and rural culture, degree of westernization, etc. An analysis by Tatar Professor Roza Musina in 1990 tells us that two-thirds of the Tatar urban population (in Tatarstan) consider themselves Muslims and in the rural areas the percentage is higher.[5] We have no analogous statistics for the Northern Caucasus, but there is no doubt that the level of religiosity there is higher than in Tatarstan or Bashkortostan.

In any event, according to information given out by the Board of Social Assemblies and Confessions of the Ministry of Justice of the Russian Federation, the number of Muslim associations (including religious communities) increased during 1991–92 from 870 to 4000 (most of them in the Northern Caucasus).[6]

Such is the background to the appearance of the 'shadow' of Muslim fundamentalism on the political map of Russia at the beginning of the 1990s. Muslim fundamentalism appeared because it could not fail to arise as a social and political phenomenon: the Islamic rebirth (after the long years of a totalitarian, atheistic regime) means a restoration of the typical features of this religion: among them, its involvement in politics and its profound influence on state and society.

Fundamentalism has not become a strong and powerful movement in Russia. It looks like a mere shadow of the fundamentalism prevalent in the Middle East, North Africa or Tajikistan. The reason for its weakness does not require a complex interpretation: the Muslim community in Russia is not large and it is dispersed; moreover, it is unready to accept the main ideas of fundamentalism, above all the creation of an Islamic state. This is so, first, because of the low level of knowledge of Islamic dogma and the absence of a coherent religious and political literature and second, because of the lack of experience in religious and political activity. At the same time the majority of the Muslim population in the cities as well as in the rural areas is influenced by the mass media, whose attitude toward fundamentalism is negative. Even those politicians who try to use fundamentalist slogans recognize that in practice they have no chance of achieving their main strategic goals.

Nevertheless, fundamentalism exists and its ideas and slogans are popular among a certain section of Russia's Muslims; under favourable conditions, one might suggest that it could acquire great significance. These conditions include a quick deterioration of the living standards of the Muslim nations, growing contradictions between the Muslim republics and the central power and an outbreak of nationalism, as has already occurred in Chechnia and Tatarstan.

Groups of Muslims sympathizing with the ideas of fundamentalism exist virtually in every region populated by Muslims. The number of such groups is not very large. But sometimes they are active enough to influence the situation inside the local Muslim community.

The emergence of political Islam in Russia (or rather in the Soviet Union) dates back to June 1990, when the Islamic Renaissance Party (IRP) was created at a constituent conference held in Astrakhan. The IRP became the embryo of an organized Islamic political movement across the former USSR which culminated in 1992–93 in Tajikistan, whose own IRP was transformed into the most powerful opposition force.[7]

The organizational committee of the IRP was registered in Moscow. But its activity and its very existence were prohibited in the republics of Central Asia. It operated legally only in Tajikistan, from November 1991 till March 1993.

From the beginning, the leadership of the IRP tried to avoid the word 'fundamentalism'. They preferred to talk about an Islamic rebirth in the fields of culture, spiritual life or religious education. At the same time, they affirmed that direct ties existed between Islam and politics.

The IRP, which claimed to be an 'all-union party', was active in most of the Muslim areas of the Soviet Union. (The IRP actually supported the idea of the Soviet Union as a united state and strongly criticized its disintegration.) IRP sections have been organized in Makhachkala (in the Republic of Dagestan), in the Republic of Karachai, in some *oblasts* of the Volga-Ural region and in Moscow, which since 1991 has become a centre of Muslim political activity. The majority of the IRP's members are Volga Tatars and Avars (the largest ethnic group in Dagestan).

The IRP considered itself 'a religious and political organization uniting Muslims who disseminate Islam'.[8] It declared the necessity of regulating the economy 'on the basis of the Shariat' and rejected 'the artificial schemes of social development which have brought humanity to a full crisis in all fields of life'.[9]

There is no mention of 'fundamentalism' in the IRP program or in its official documents. Its amir (or leader) Ahmedqazi Akhtaev denied any connection with Islamic fundamentalism. However, a lot of party members shared the ideas of fundamentalism laid out in the IRP newspaper *al-Vahdat* (only three issues of *al-Vahdat* were published), where it was said that fundamentalism would soon occupy 'one of the leading roles in the Muslim world'.[10] Some of the paper's contributors tried to prove that the Muslim nations and Muslim civilization in general must elaborate its own model of development based on Islamic norms and principles in the realm of individual and social behaviour. They also developed the idea of an inevitable and growing confrontation between Islam and Christianity and held that Islam has a special mission in the world.

There were two main wings of the IRP – the radical one, headed by Heidar Jemal from the Independent Centre of Information 'Tawhid', and Sergei Dunaev, the 'coordinator of spiritual contacts' (*koordinator po dukhovnym kontaktam*), who both openly acclaimed fundamentalism and sometimes spoke of an Islamic state; and the moderate wing represented by the party press secretary, Valiahmed Sadur.

In April 1992 the IRP underwent an undeclared split. The moderate group organized a regional conference (of the European part of Russia and Siberia) in Saratov, which was ignored by the radicals. The radical fundamentalist trend was now represented by Heidar Jemal (its leading personality) and a small group of his followers. Jemal took over the IRP newspaper which then changed its name to *Edinenie* (the Russian translation of *al-Vahdat*), with the subtitle 'Islamic political newspaper'. Up till the time of writing (the end of 1993), Heidar managed to edit only one issue of the newspaper (in December 1992). In spring 1993 Russian Federation Supreme Soviet deputy, Murad Zargishiev, who lives in the steppes of the Nogai nation north of the Caucasian mountains and who was a supporter of Supreme Soviet chairman Ruslan Khasbulatov, said that Heidar Jemal might well become 'the leader of Russian Islam'.[11]

In summer 1993, Sadur's group made efforts to reconstruct the party on a new base. He insists that the IRP is not a fundamentalist party, completely rejects any idea of radicalism and affirms that the party will continue to act within the framework of the Constitution of the Russian Federation.

At the same time, the appeal for an Islamic rebirth was tied by

Sadur to the idea of the resurrection of the Tatar nation, an issue that came to the fore at the above-mentioned IRP conference in Saratov. There the appeal for Tatarstan's independence was vigorously supported by the IRP leadership, though they never stopped insisting on the necessity of ensuring strong relations between Russia and Tatarstan.

Despite its growing 'Tatar accent', the IRP still claims – and some-times not without success – to be a 'trans-national' party and considers the Islamic parties in the newly-born independent states – Uzbekistan, Tajikistan and Kazakhstan – as its filials. It maintains ties with its brothers-in-faith and colleagues in Tajikistan, Uzbekistan and the other newly-born Muslim states. The IRP tries to give assistance to those members of the Islamic Renaissance Party of Tajikistan who emigrate to Moscow or to other cities in Russia, helping them to get jobs or find lodging. The IRP also provides the mass media with information about the situation in Central Asia, in particular, concerning the persecution of the opposition, and organizes joint press conferences with Islamic activists from Kazakhstan, Tajikistan and the other Muslim states.

The regional conference of the IRP in Saratov was attended by several delegations from outside Russia – Kazakhstan, Uzbekistan and even Belarus – who took an active part in it.

All this proves that the IRP is acting in a so-called 'common Islamic space', which continues to exist despite the disintegration of the Soviet Union. Of course, we should not exaggerate the political significance of this space. But it is necessary to emphasize that this CIS 'Islamic space' is a part of Muslim civilization and the situation in the Muslim world at large influences the Muslim regions of the CIS.

The IRP is not the only Islamic political organization in Russia. The appeal to Islam is characteristic of several political groups in the Northern Caucasus as well as in Tatarstan. Among them are several small detachments of armed young men in Chechnia who call themselves 'Muslim Brothers', local religious groups like the 'Jama'ati Muslimi' in Dagestan, or the Islamic Democratic Party (also in Dagestan). There is evidence that the most radical national party of Tatarstan, Ittifaq (Alliance), includes a wing whose young members also identify with the Muslim Brotherhood.[12]

Of course, the 'Muslim Brothers' of the Russian Federation cannot be compared with their famous namesake in the Middle East. There is no chain of Muslim Brotherhood in Russia. With very few exceptions the young Muslims – males and females – who say that they adopt the main ideas of the Brotherhood are not consolidated in special groups. Nor do they have a powerful or charismatic leader able to organize a wide religious and political movement.

At the same time, according to information from Tbilisi, armed groups of volunteers calling themselves 'Muslim Brothers' came from the Northern Caucasus to aid the Abkhazian troops in the war against Georgia.

Could all these be called 'fundamentalists'? It is hard to answer this question. But their leaders favour the cohesion of religion and politics as well as the application of some norms of Islamic law, first and foremost, the criminal code. Their activities are at this point confined to relatively narrow areas, but their influence may grow among certain social strata of both the urban and rural population. (In August 1993 a news correspondent from Russian television asked a Chechen peasant what he thought about a Muslim holy war, a *gazavat*, or *jihad*. 'Islam is linked with blood', was the answer.)

Muslim political opposition organizations in Russia have no permanent connections with Muslim radicals abroad. Certainly, the ruling regimes in the Middle East prefer to deal with official structures in Russia rather than with the opposition. 'They do not notice us', an IRP representative said to this author. Saudi Arabia, Kuwait, the other Arab countries, Turkey and even Iran avoid establishing relations with Islamic organizations and refuse to subsidize them.

However, there is evidence that several Islamic groups from the mountainous regions of the Northern Caucasus have ties with Muslim Brothers in the Middle Eastern countries, in particular Jordan. These contacts are explained not by a common Islamic ideology or common aims, but by family ties. (Some Chechen Muslim Brothers even assert that they are getting arms directly from the Muslim Brotherhood in the Middle East. But in practice they buy them from officers of the Russian army or from the Chechen 'National Guard'.)

In the Muslim regions of Russia the appeal to Islam is characteristic not only of the political opposition. Islam as a political instrument is widely used by the secular authorities who in crises or difficult situations are able to exploit certain ideas akin to those of fundamentalism. This is manifest, for example, from the political behaviour of Chechnia's President, Johar Dudaev.

In 1991–92 Dudaev rejected the idea of using Islam in politics. 'Where any religion prevails over a secular constitutional organization of state, either the Spanish inquisition or Islamic fundamentalism will emerge', he said in an interview with the Moscow *Literaturnaia gazeta*.[13] But at the beginning of 1993 Dudaev, frightened by the activity of his political adversaries, formed a bloc with religious forces and in particular with 'Mehk Khel' (the Council of Elders) that called for the 'formation of organs of state power in the republic based on the historical traditions of the Chechen nation, the principles of Islam, the

Shariat and the priority of human values'. In February 1993 Dudaev published a draft of a new constitution that proclaimed Islam the state religion.[14]

In April 1993 the local National Guard demanded the creation of 'an Islamic republic' in Chechnia, and Dudaev's followers suggested that he declare himself 'Imam of Chechnia'. Dudaev did not accept this rank officially. But he sought to convince the local population that *in extremis* he might play the role not only of the national and political (that is, secular) leader but also of a spiritual guide.

Dudaev, then, does not insist on the creation of an Islamic republic or on the transformation of the secular president into an imam. Moreover, the idea of the islamicization of the Chechen republic met resistance among urban Chechens. Nor was it supported by the local Muslim spiritual directorate, which did not want to give up its monopoly of control over religious life.[15] But the conflict over the islamicization of social and political life is very significant and proves that the politicization of Islam is an important trend in Chechnia.

We have already mentioned the position of the Council of Elders, which is mostly composed of tribal chieftains and Muslim clergymen. The Muslim clergy plays an important role in the development of the fundamentalist trend and the politicization of Islam. The younger generation is disappointed with the policy pursued by the top officials of the religious establishment. And they accuse the older clergy of servility and collaboration with the secular administration both in the past – under the communist regime – and currently (in the first years of post-communism).

In 1992 the Spiritual Directorate of the Muslims of the Northern Caucasus was suspended and in its place several small Muslim directorates were organized, each based on a single autonomous republic. In practice this meant that each ethnos in the Northern Caucasus got its own spiritual administration. The Muslims of the republic of Karachai proclaimed IRP member Muhammed Biji-Ulu (Bijiev) their mufti and spiritual leader. The IRP also maintained a certain influence on the Muslim directorate of Dagestan.

Meanwhile, a part of the Muslim clergy of Tatarstan and Bash-kortostan, supported by local nationalists and proclaiming the idea of the sovereignty of both republics, organized in summer 1992 national Muslim directorates independent of the Spiritual Directorate of the Muslims of the European Part of Russia and Siberia (*Dukhovnoe upravlenie musul'man evropeiskoi chasti Rossii i Sibiri* – DUMES).[16] The head of DUMES, Talgat Tajuddin, refused to recognize the new spiritual administrations and declared that the disintegration of the existing official 'spiritual' structure might transform any national conflict into a confessional one. 'And this', he said, 'is the most dangerous path for the Muslims of Russia.'[17]

In October 1992 a group of young clergymen organized in Kazan, the capital of Tatarstan, a Supreme Coordinating Centre of the Muslim spiritual directorates. The new 'independent' muftis of Tatarstan and Bashkortostan, Gabdulla Galliulin and Muhammet Nigmatullin joined this centre, which became a structure parallel to DUMES. Among its organizers we should mention the *imam-muhtasib* of the mosque in Saratov, Muqaddas Bibarsov, who collaborates with the IRP. Since 1990 Bibarsov has been editor of the newspaper *Musulmanskii vestnik* (*The Muslim Messenger*), in which he personally has endeavoured to prove the legitimacy of the link between Islam and politics.[18] *Musulmanskii vestnik* published several articles about Islamic fundamentalism defining it as 'the new birth of Islam' (*novoe rozhdenie islama*).[19]

Even the *imam-khatib* of the Moscow cathedral mosque, Ravil Gainutdin, whose influence inside the Muslim community throughout Russia has recently increased considerably and who is known for his cautious attitude, sometimes speaks about 'true fundamentalism' reviving the Islamic traditions of the epoch of the Prophet. 'Fundamentalism is a silence, a reflection; it has no aggressiveness', he said.[20] The participation of Muslim clergymen in politics is one of the characteristic features of the fundamentalist trend. Yet, so far, although many Muslim clerics are young, not many of them are involved in politics.

The Islamic parties and organizations and the 'new' Muslim clergy are thus seeking their place in Russian political life. They wish to become the nucleus of the political life of the Muslim minorities. But in 1993 they still seem a long way from reaching their goal.

The radical wing of the Muslim political movement has realized the necessity of some form of cooperation with other political groups. It may seem a paradox, but certain Islamists have collaborated with the Russian opposition forces – the so-called 'patriots' or 'people of red-brown colour'. For instance, Jemal Heidar published a series of articles under the general title of 'Reflections', in the nationalist-cum-communist newspaper *Den'*.[21]

* * *

The Russian national-communists were partly ready to accept the idea of Islamic fundamentalism. Like Muslim fundamentalists, Russian 'patriots' repudiate the idea of democracy and maintain the 'consonance' of religion and politics. According to one of the ideologists of the

Russian 'patriotic' movement, General Viktor Filatov, Islamic fundamentalism and Orthodox fundamentalism, which is founded on Russian patriotism, are the two main forces obstructing the cultural and spiritual intervention of the West in the Muslim and Russian lands and help to maintain a high moral and spiritual level among the population.[22]

Den' (closed by President Eltsin on 5 October 1993) published a series of articles about Islam under a special rubric entitled 'Slavo-Islamic Academy'. From time to time it reproduced for its readers abstracts from Ayatolla Khomeini's speeches.

If we compare the ideology of both fundamentalist trends – the Islamic and the Russian Orthodox – we discover some interesting parallels, emanating from analogies between Islam and Orthodoxy. Among them are the priority of the spirit of community over individuality; the claim to be more than a religion – that is, a way of life or 'totality'; the ties between religion and politics. All these create favourable conditions for fundamentalism, whether of Russian Orthodox or Islamic style.

Both fundamentalisms must be considered as a kind of compensation for the failure of the Muslim nations and the Russians in the economic and political fields, where they lost out in competition with the West. The resultant inferiority complex pushed the disciples of fundamentalism toward a search for a specific Islamic or Russian path of development – based on religious tradition. They subsequently made it absolute, repudiating the 'Western model'.

The fundamentalists speculate on the slogan of 'social justice', which derives from Islamic or Orthodox traditions and their norms of social and individual behaviour. They also propagate the idea of an ideal society which needs a 'strong ruler', who personifies simultaneously both secular and spiritual power. For the Muslims such absolute power is incarnated in the prophet or messiah. For the Russian Orthodox – in a monarch or tsar whose power is 'blessed' by Almighty God.

However, Islamic and Orthodox fundamentalists are similar only up to a point. Russian Orthodox fundamentalism is not an autonomous political movement, but rather an ideological trend within a conglomerate of dissimilar political forces, including communists, who are antagonistic to the transformation of Russian society. It is inseparable from Russian nationalism and in effect subordinate to it. The ideas of Russian Orthodox fundamentalism are often used by communists. Its ideologists, among them representatives of the clergy – Metropolitan Ioann of St. Petersburg and Ladoga, Metropolitan Anthony of Krasnoiarsk and Enisei, the famous preacher Dmitrii

Dudko and others – openly support the idea of the restoration of Soviet power.

The attitude to Islam of the Russian national, as well as the clerical Russian Orthodox, opposition is ambiguous. They criticize the fundamentalists of Central Asia, in particular of Tajikistan, and propagate the idea of a permanent Islamic threat to Russia. But the tendency towards a mutual understanding of the two fundamentalisms was becoming more and more evident in 1993 on the eve of the October coup.

As far as Muslim fundamentalists are concerned, they do not accept any form of communist regime. Islamists, moreover, consider nationalism an obstacle to the consolidation of the Muslim *umma*. In general, Islamic fundamentalism, despite its political weakness within Russia, is more 'logical' and self-sufficient than its Orthodox counterpart.

Interestingly, Muslim secular politicians and intellectuals deny that Islamic fundamentalism can take root in Russia, with the exception of some small areas in the Northern Caucasus. In addition, many Muslim clergymen who collaborate with the administration, consider that fundamentalism is a threat to political stability and contend that it is unnatural to the Muslims of Russia. However, both groups agree that Russia's Muslims comprise an integral part of Islamic civilization and therefore should become familiar with the cultural and religious processes of the Muslim world. Such a position is a tacit recognition of the possibility of the cohesion of Islam and politics inside Russia.

Political Islam remains a reality of Russian public life. The patterns of its presence are visible in the different Muslim territories of Russia. Its activity may increase or diminish. But it exists and will preserve its influence on Russia's Muslim community. Nor it is a deviation from 'normal Islam', as many scholars and statesmen would like to think.

Political Islam in Russia will never be on the same scale as that in Tajikistan and some other Muslim territories of the former USSR. But it would be a mistake to ignore its presence within the Russian Federation.

NOTES

1. This statement, never published in the press, became well-known in Chechnia and beyond its borders.
2. The term 'Muslim nation' is used to denote a member of an ethnic group whose cultural tradition is, or was until the Soviet period, Islamic.
3. Murad Zargishiev estimates that there are 20 million Muslims in Russia – *Segodnia*, 10 March 1994; Ravil Gainuddin that there are 19 million – *Moskovskii komsomolets*, 22 Sept. 1992, and *Nezavisimaia gazeta*, 3 March 1994; Talgat Tajuddin told the author he believes the number to range somewhere between 14 and 15 million, while the author

reckoned the number at approximately 11 million, *Druzhba narodov* 10 (1990). In fact, the 1989 population census gave the figure of 12,233,124 (including just over 400,000 Ossets, of whom approximately two-thirds were Christians) Goskomstat RSFSR, *Natsional'nyi sostav naseleniia RSFSR: po dannym vsesoiuznoi perepisi naseleniia 1989 g.* (Moscow: Respublikanskii informatsionno-isdatel'skii tsentr, 1990), pp. 8–10. (We are grateful to Mark Tolts for this information.) This number must clearly have grown fairly considerably since then, although some Kazakhs, for example, have returned to Kazakhstan.

4. For conflict situations between Muslim nations in the Caucasus, see Moshe Gammer, 'Unity, Diversity and Conflict in the Northern Caucasus,' in this volume.

5. See 'The Muslim-Christian Frontier' (*Musulmansko-khristianskoe pogranichie*), international seminar held in Kazan, 26–29 October 1993.

6. *Put'*, newspaper of the Russian Christian Democratic Movement (Moscow), 3–4 June 1993.

7. The Tajik section of the all-union IRP was created in Dec. 1990 at a conference held not far from Dushanbe. In Nov. 1991 this section broke away from the all-union IRP and registered in December as the Islamic Renaissance Party of Tajikistan. The IRP of Tajikistan was the backbone of the Tajik opposition to the regime. From April 1992 it participated in a government coalition. Since the break-up of the coalition and the beginning of the civil war, the IRP of Tajikistan has been actively fighting against the ruling regime headed by Imomali Rahmonov. For the Tajikistan IRP, see G. Kosach, 'Political Parties in an Inchoate National Space,' in this volume.

8. 'Programma i ustav Islamskoi Partii Vozrozhdeniia' (The Program and Charter of the IRP), p. 6.

9. Ibid., p. 8.

10. *Al-vahdat* (Moscow), 9 Jan. 1991.

11. *Segodnia* (Moscow), 18 May 1991. Zargishiev's other candidates for the role were Shaykh ul-Islam Talgut Tajuddin and the imam of the Moscow mosque, Ravil Gainutdin.

12. There are, in addition, some phantom Islamic organizations like, for instance, the 'Party of the Islamic Path' in Chechnia mentioned by several journalists and experts, but which in practice never existed.

13. *Literaturnaia gazeta*, 12 Aug. 1993.

14. *Golos Chechenskoi respubliki* (Groznyi), 28 April 1993.

15. According to information provided by Aleksei Kudriavtsev of the Moscow Institute of Oriental Studies who visited Chechnia, and by Chechen observers.

16. Actually DUMES changed its name and is officially called the Spiritual Directorate of the Muslims of the European Part of the CIS and Siberia, but its former name is much better known and is used still (in 1993) in the Russian mass media.

17. *Nezavisimaia gazeta*, 22 Sept. 1992.

18. *Musul'manskii vestnik* (Saratov), March 1991.

19. Ibid., Nov. 1990.

20. *Moskovskii komsomolets*, 20 July 1993. In January 1994, Gainutdin became mufti of the Muslim Spiritual Directorate of Russia's Central European Region.

21. 'An Islamic Republic – Not Tomorrow, but Today!' *Den'*, 25 Oct.–8 Nov. 1991; 'From Europe to Vladivostok or from Asia to Dublin?', *Den'*, 18–25 Sept. 1992; and 'In Memory of the Five Million,' *Den'*, 21–27 March 1993.

22. *Den'*, 30 May–5 June 1993.

4

Islam and Ethnic Identity in Central Asia: A View from Below

NANCY LUBIN

The role of Islam and ethnic identity in Central Asia has dominated academic and policy research on this region for some time. Answers to questions regarding the adherence to Islam in the region; the extent to which a growth in Islam may represent a political threat to the current leadership in Central Asia and to Western interests there; the way individuals define themselves relative to others, and where ethnic animosities may lie; and the extent to which Islamic or ethnic identity may affect the foreign policies of these new Central Asian states, not only help shape our understanding of the region but underlie much of Western policy there.

Traditionally, these kinds of questions in Central Asia have been examined from the top down or from the outside looking in. The purpose of this chapter is to examine some of these questions from the bottom up. In the eyes of Uzbekistan's population, how strong is Islam, and does it in fact represent a significant political challenge to current authority? What are the most important individual identities, and where do strong antagonisms lie? Should these new Central Asian countries seek foreign assistance from other countries, and if so, do these kinds of identities strongly affect their choice of most desirable partners?

As a small step towards understanding some of these popular views, this author, under the auspices of the US Institute of Peace* and

* The author gratefully acknowledges the support and assistance of the US Institute of Peace in carrying out the research and survey for this chapter; much of this chapter is adapted from a USIP Quickprint, 1994. The author also greatly appreciates the support of the National Council for Soviet and East European Research for much of the background research; the assistance of John Loncle in working with the large quantities of data and analysis; and the invaluable help and advice of Steven Grant, Richard Dobson and Michael Swafford.

in conjunction with the 'Expert' Centre in Central Asia, conducted a public opinion survey in June and July, 1993, among 2000 respondents in Uzbekistan and Kazakhstan – countries that together comprise almost three-quarters of Central Asia's population and about 80 per cent of its land mass. The survey results could be broken down by most major indicators – age, sex, nationality, urban/rural, place of habitation (*oblast*), level of education and profession – and closely follow the 1989 census data in most of these indicators. The survey was conducted in face-to-face interviews in one of four languages: Uzbek, Kazakh, Russian, and Karakalpak. The margin of error was roughly six–seven per cent (Table 4.1).

TABLE 4.1 COMPARISON OF OVERALL POPULATION DISTRIBUTION AND THE SURVEY SAMPLE IN KAZAKHSTAN AND UZBEKISTAN

| | | Kazakhstan | | | Uzbekistan | |
| | | Census data | | | Census data | |
	Year	(1989)	Survey	Year	(1989)	Survey
Total	1990	16,464,464	801	1991	20,613,123	1266
Male	1990	48.43%	47.80%	1991	49.44%	52.70%
Female	1990	51.57%	52.20%	1991	50.56%	47.30%
Urban	1990	57.11%	52.30%	1991	40.14%	66.70%
Rural	1990	42.89%	47.70%	1991	59.86%	33.30%
Age 18 - 29	1991	33.50%	27.00%	1991	21.58%	28.00%
Age 30 - 39	1991	24.00%	26.50%	1991	12.90%	29.90%
Age 40 - 49	1991	14.00%	19.60%	1991	5.96%	18.20%
Age 50 - 59	1991	13.70%	14.20%	1991	5.98%	11.90%
Age 60 +	1991	14.60%	11.40%	1991	6.45%	11.90%
Higher Ed.	1991	13.00%	20.10%	1991	9.17%	21.30%
Secondary Ed.	1991	64.00%	59.90%	1991	57.70%	62.80%
Unfinished Secondary	1991	23.00%	18.10%	1991	33.13%	14.60%
Titular Nationality	1991	41.00%	42.90%	1991	71.39%	70.40%
Russian	1991	36.00%	31.70%	1991	8.35%	10.50%
Other	1991	23.00%	25.40%	1991	20.26%	19.10%

By themselves, the responses in our survey by no means paint a definitive picture of the views of the citizens of Uzbekistan or Kazakhstan. Responses were undoubtedly influenced, for example, by the prevailing 'party' line, by fear, or by a desire among many respondents to give a 'right' answer – that is, an answer that the respondent believed the interviewer would like to hear rather than his or her personal opinion. This may have been particularly true in Uzbekistan, where the regime of President Islam Karimov has tended, sometimes brutally, to suppress views contrary to those of the government. As with other types of research, the survey was also undoubtedly influenced by outside events and local media coverage at the time it was conducted. For example, relations then between Uzbekistan and the US were depicted in Uzbekistan as somewhat more strained than they had been just a few months earlier; also shortly before the survey, several opposition figures had been arrested or had fled. And survey research generally, as any other type of research, is plagued by a host of other uncertainties and inexactitudes.

The effect of these problems on our survey, however, may have been less than anticipated. First, for a good number of questions, it was unclear what the proper answer or 'party line' was at the time the survey was taken. Official government pronouncements at this time were quite contradictory on the question of Islam, simultaneously supporting and condemning the renewed interest in Islam throughout Central Asia. The survey questionnaire was designed to minimize these problems further by including, for example, a good deal of overlap where the same type of question was asked several times in different contexts and in different ways. Personal observation on the part of this author (in rural and urban areas of the Fergana Valley and Tashkent Oblast) and the survey takers (throughout Uzbekistan and Kazakhstan) suggest that respondents were far more forthcoming and honest about their answers, including in Uzbekistan, than one might have expected.

Thus, despite the limitations, the results are intended, albeit superficially, to provide a broad sense of some of the attitudes among the people of Uzbekistan and Kazakhstan, in order to gain some additional appreciation of the challenges in this region that may lie ahead, both for the Central Asians themselves and for the West. Our survey results challenged some commonly held assumptions, and raised new questions. The purpose of this chapter is to present some of the survey results regarding attitudes towards Islam, ethnic identity and foreign policy orientations. The survey responses suggest that many of our judgments and stereotypes may require more investigation if we are to better understand where Uzbekistan and Kazakhstan may be headed and what role the West could most productively play there.

ISLAM

In the past, Islam has often been viewed as one of the strongest sources of identity and belonging in this region, likely to grow rapidly and present important political challenges for both Central Asia and the rest of the world. Certainly this prospect has been played up by some of the regional leaders. As Central Asian leaders consolidate their power in the wake of the disintegration of the USSR, they often present the spectre of growing Islamic political movements as the biggest challenge to their own power and authority, and to stability within their new countries. President Karimov of Uzbekistan has used the threat of an allegedly growing Islamic opposition in Central Asia to justify a crackdown on his own population.

While interest in Islam is growing rapidly throughout Central Asia, however, our survey highlights more ambiguous conclusions, and suggests that at least currently, these fears may be overemphasized. Certainly Islam is deeply ingrained in Central Asian ethnicity and culture. But largely because of a long history where religious teaching and practice were either forbidden or co-opted by successive political regimes, personal understanding of Islamic doctrine in Central Asia remains limited or distorted. Although this could certainly change, our survey suggests that Islam tends to be viewed much more in traditional and cultural terms than in religious ones. In terms of political power, our survey suggests that Islamic leaders are seen as relatively weak, and few respondents hope for an Islamic state. Although Islam may be important in the long term, then, our survey results tend to weaken the claims of some Central Asian leaders that an already widespread Islamic fundamentalism poses a threat to their very survival.

In terms of Islamic awareness, for example, respondents were asked to select several of a number of groups to which they felt it was most important to them to belong. 'Each person simultaneously belongs to different groups or communities of people', respondents were told. They were then asked to look at a list of choices, and select the groups to which they felt they most belonged. Respondents identified much more readily with community – with family, neighbours, neighbourhood (*mahalla*), relatives, region and country – than with Islamic communities as such. For example, two-thirds of our Uzbekistani sample selected their family, followed by their neighbours (40 per cent), neighbourhood (*mahalla*, 36 per cent); and then their relatives (35 per cent). Only about one-tenth of all respondents in Uzbekistan selected 'people of my belief', consisting of about one-eighth of the Uzbeks and only four per cent of the Russians. Many of those who selected this option were from Fergana Oblast, but they still represented a small proportion of people from this *oblast*. In

Kazakhstan, an insignificant proportion of respondents included 'people of my belief' in the list of groups to which they felt it was most important for them to belong. Of course, it is likely that most members of one's family and neighbourhood may already be of the same Islamic background.

Likewise, while Islamic awareness may be growing in Central Asia, the way this awareness expresses itself may be more complex and contradictory. In terms of personal belief, fewer than half (46 per cent) of all respondents in Uzbekistan, and about one quarter of all respondents in Kazakhstan, said they were 'believers' and practised Islam. (Actually, more than half – 52 per cent – of respondents in Uzbekistan said they were 'believers', while 46.4 per cent of the entire sample, said they practised Islam. It should be borne in mind that not all respondents were Muslims) (Table 4.2).

Among these Muslim 'believers', however, knowledge or practice of the main pillars of Islam appeared weak. Almost one-third of Uzbekistan's 'Muslims', and two-thirds of Kazakhstan's 'Muslims' could not translate 'There is no God other than Allah and Mohammad is his prophet' from the Arabic, or they gave an incorrect translation. (Indeed, close to 20 per cent of the small number of Kazakhstani respondents who said they were believing Muslims also said that they disagreed with this statement, which is a fundamental tenet of Islam!) In terms of rituals, over three-quarters of those Kazakhstanis who said they were Muslim believers do not pray at all, and three-quarters say they never fast. In Uzbekistan, responses suggest slightly greater adherence to rituals, although the level is still low: 44 per cent of those who said they were religious Muslims do not pray at all, and 23 per cent do so only occasionally; roughly one-third do not fast at all, while another third do so 'only sometimes'.

Age and regional differences were striking, especially in Uzbekistan, where expressed adherence to Islam was higher. Despite a reported spread of Islam among Uzbekistan's younger population, it would appear that Islamic belief is still weakest among the younger generation. Roughly 39 per cent of the 18–29-year olds in our survey consider themselves to be Muslim believers, compared to 47 per cent of the 50–59-year olds and two-thirds of respondents over 60.

Regionally, adherence to Islam was stronger in the Fergana Valley than elsewhere in Uzbekistan, especially in Andijan Oblast, where about three-quarters of respondents see themselves as practising Muslims – versus 25 per cent of respondents from Tashkent, or between 13 and 20 per cent in the western regions of the country. At the same time, the majority of even these respondents said their primary allegiances are to neighbourhood, *mahalla* and family, with

TABLE 4.2 RELIGIOUS BELIEF BY AGE AND REGION

Do you consider yourself a believer? If so, which belief do you profess?

	Islamic Believers		Other Believers *		Non-Believers		Don't Know / Difficult to Say / No Answer	
KAZAKHSTAN								
Total	196	24.5%	147	18.4%	397	49.6%	61	7.6%
UZBEKISTAN								
Total	587	46.4%	72	5.8%	564	44.5%	43	3.3%
Oblasts								
Tashkent City	52	35.4%	32	21.8%	56	38.1%	7	4.7%
Tashkent	93	68.4%	0	0.0%	43	31.6%	0	0.0%
Bukhara	18	36.0%	1	2.0%	31	62.0%	0	0.0%
Karakalpakistan	37	50.0%	3	4.1%	31	41.9%	3	4.1%
Navoi	19	25.3%	8	10.7%	45	60.0%	4	5.3%
Khorezm	22	24.4%	0	0.0%	68	75.6%	0	0.0%
Samarkand	59	43.1%	5	3.6%	66	48.2%	6	4.3%
Syr-Darya	28	50.9%	7	12.7%	18	32.7%	2	3.6%
Kashka-Darya	57	40.4%	1	0.7%	79	56.0%	4	2.8%
Andijan **	53	74.6%	7	9.9%	9	12.7%	2	2.8%
Namangan **	48	52.2%	3	3.3%	33	35.9%	8	8.7%
Fergana **	101	51.0%	5	2.5%	85	42.9%	8	4.0%
Age								
18 - 29 years	138	38.9%	16	4.6%	186	52.4%	16	4.5%
30 - 39 years	184	48.7%	18	4.8%	160	42.3%	16	4.3%
40 - 49 years	94	40.7%	16	6.8%	112	48.5%	9	3.9%
50 - 59 years	71	47.0%	14	9.3%	64	42.4%	2	1.4%
60 and more years	100	66.2%	9	6.0%	43	28.5%	0	0.0%

* Category includes Russian Orthodox, Catholic, Protestant, Buddhist, Jewish, Baptist and Adventist
** Located in the Fergana Valley

only a tiny proportion naming 'people of my belief'. The proportion of Muslim believers was also lower in the other two *oblasts* included in our survey from the Fergana Valley: 47 per cent of respondents in Namangan consider themselves to be practising Muslims, and 41 per cent in Fergana Oblast – roughly the same proportion as in Syr-Darya Oblast and only slightly higher than in the *oblasts* of Samarkand and Bukhara.

As far as the threat of political Islam is concerned, our survey also suggests that, so far, Uzbekistanis and Kazakhstanis tend to view the political role of Islam as weak. It indicated that Islamic leaders are generally viewed as exerting little power and influence; moreover, few respondents support the establishment of an Islamic state in Uzbekistan. For example, when asked in Uzbekistan to rank on a scale of one to nine how much real power different individuals and institutions wield in Uzbekistan (with one signifying no power, and nine signifying unlimited power), 96 per cent of all respondents put President Karimov between seven and nine on the scale, that is, as wielding significant power; 86 per cent of all respondents actually gave President Karimov a nine, that is, suggesting he is perceived as wielding unlimited power. Almost 70 per cent of respondents put *oblast* leaders (*hokimiaty*) on the scale between seven and nine; 60 per cent put *raion* and city leaders there; and 43 per cent put local soviets, or councils, there.

Only 27 per cent of respondents, on the other hand, put the Muslim clergy in this category – a level which was only slightly lower than the number of people who put the mafia in this category! Twenty-eight per cent of all respondents put the Muslim clergy between one and three on the scale, that is, as exerting little if any power – again, about the same level of responses as for the mafia. Interestingly, Russians tended proportionately to ascribe more power to Muslim leaders than Central Asians did (Table 4.3).

When asked what kind of state would best resolve the problems of Uzbekistan or Kazakhstan, the majority of respondents, or slightly over half of all respondents (50.4 per cent), selected the answer of 'any system, as long as there is order'. The proportion of Central Asians and Slavs, males and females, and different age groups did not diverge greatly on this answer. In Uzbekistan, less than one-eighth (or 127 people, consisting of about 11 per cent of all Central Asians, but only 2 per cent of all Slavs) selected an Islamic state – slightly less than the one-eighth of respondents (about ten per cent of all Central Asians and 25 per cent of all Slavs), who selected a Western-style democracy; in Kazakhstan, only 18 people, or less than two per cent of all respondents, chose an Islamic state.

TABLE 4.3 POWER/INFLUENCE OF MUSLIM CLERGY

Nationality:	Total		Has no power 1		2 - 3		4 - 6		7 - 8		Has unlimited power, 9		Don't know		No answer	
Total	1242	100%	210	16.9%	136	11.0%	315	25.4%	212	17.1%	119	9.6%	233	18.8%	17	1.4%
Uzbek	878	70.7%	177	14.3%	93	7.5%	232	18.7%	120	9.7%	82	6.6%	160	12.9%	14	1.1%
Other CA	114	9.2%	7	0.6%	19	1.5%	30	2.4%	31	2.5%	11	0.9%	16	1.3%	0	0.0%
Russian / Other Slav	141	11.4%	7	0.6%	10	0.8%	32	2.6%	39	3.1%	15	1.2%	36	2.9%	2	0.2%
Other	110	8.9%	19	1.5%	14	1.1%	21	1.7%	23	1.9%	11	0.9%	21	1.7%	1	0.1%
Don't know	1	0.1%	0	0.0%	1	0.1%	0	0.0%	0	0.0%	0	0.0%	0	0.0%	0	0.0%
No answer	1	0.1%	0	0.0%	0	0.0%	1	0.1%	0	0.0%	0	0.0%	0	0.0%	0	0.0%

Of those who selected an Islamic state, moreover, it was unclear if their notion of such a state was the same as that which is normally envisaged in other countries, and answers were contradictory. For example, when asked what traits were considered most important in a politician, only 17 per cent of those who supported the creation of an Islamic state in Uzbekistan believed it was important for the politician to be a Muslim. Instead, the most important traits were honesty and decency (68 per cent), and experience (49 per cent). Also more important than religious affiliation were defence of the poor (24 per cent); a good understanding of people (23 per cent); and maintenance of law and order (19 per cent). For the survey as a whole, religious affiliation was viewed as one of the least important traits for a prospective leader of Uzbekistan.

Likewise, when asked which leaders they most respected as a government leader, 90 people, or over 70 per cent of those who selected an Islamic state, named President Karimov. This represented both a higher number and a higher percentage of people who chose Karimov than was found among those who selected any other desired system of government – and this despite the fact that Karimov has been quite vocal in his opposition to the establishment of an Islamic state. Next in line were 11 people (or nine per cent) who named Sharaf Rashidov and eight who named Lenin. Only one person said he or she most respected the Ayatolla Khomeini.

Finally, when respondents were asked about their party affiliations, 12 per cent said they belonged to the People's Democratic Party and over half (52 per cent) that they belonged to the trade unions. Only two respondents who supported the creation of an Islamic state said that they belonged to the Islamic Renaissance Party, although this data is difficult to interpret as the party is outlawed in Uzbekistan.

Certainly, responses about personal belief may be underestimated in our survey, as respondents probably sought to provide the politically correct answers to our questions. At the time the survey was taken, however, it was unclear what the 'correct' answers to these questions were, since most Central Asian leaders presented a dual approach to ethnic identity and Islam. They tended to support the growth of traditional values and Islam as a faith, while steadfastly denouncing the growth of any potential fundamentalist or political Islam that could challenge their political power. Thus, while this could possibly account for the low proportion of those who support an Islamic state, it would not explain the low level of personal belief in Islam. On the contrary, it would conceivably have seemed more embarrassing to assert that one is a practising Muslim but to then display little knowledge of, or interest in, the content of Islam.

If this is true, then our survey responses suggest that, with the possible exception of parts of the Fergana Valley, adherence to Islam may be seen today more in cultural or traditional terms than purely religious ones. Notions of an Islamic state may also be more idealized in Uzbekistan. In the minds of our respondents, Islamic governments tend to be associated with fairness, goodness and other traditional or cultural values related to Islam, but not with the clergy or religion as such. Most important to our Uzbekistan respondents was the question of maintaining order and stability in the wake of the chaos of political and economic disruption throughout the former Soviet Union. While Islam may be gaining ground in Uzbekistan, public opinion would suggest that the threat of the growth of a politicized Islam as an alternative power source to Presidents Karimov or Nazarbaev is at least, so far, a relatively weak one.

This is not, however, to minimize the importance of Islam in Central Asian society or politics. Certainly, the practice of Islam is growing throughout Central Asia, and these fears may become reality in the future. As we have seen elsewhere in the world, Islam can be a powerful political tool in fomenting conflict and unrest. What our data do suggest, however, is that adherence to Islam in personal terms might mean something quite different from that which it signifies just across the border to the south or in the Middle East. They also suggest that were an 'Islamic' conflict to explode in the very near future, it is unlikely that Islam itself would be the root cause of the conflict, as much as it would be an umbrella, or vehicle, for expressing other grievances that in Central Asia are far more immediate causes of dissension and despair.

ETHNIC AND NATIONAL IDENTITY

It is difficult in any analysis to separate ethnic, religious, cultural and other identities from each other, and our survey again presented mixed results with regard to ethnic and national identity. As described above, when respondents were asked, for example, to which groups it was most important for them to belong, most selected family and community over religious or specifically national identity. Only 13 per cent of respondents in Uzbekistan, and only four per cent in Kazakhstan, selected 'people of my nationality'. This probably reflects the fact that the groups they selected – family, relatives and community – are often of the same nationality to begin with. But it also suggests the importance of other identities – family, relatives, community, region, etc. – in individuals' thoughts and actions.

Most respondents tended to feel a greater sense of belonging to their family, neighbourhood and community, although there were interesting differences among nationalities. Whereas over 40 per cent of the Uzbeks selected their neighbourhood community (*mahalla*), for example, among Russians, 27 per cent selected 'Soviet people' (even though they, as such, no longer exist), and 23 per cent selected 'people of my profession'.

Responses to other questions, on the other hand, suggested schisms as much within Central Asian and Muslim communities as between them and others. Indeed, aside from the most pronounced dislike they seemed to display towards Jews and Armenians, Central Asians showed almost as much wariness of each other as they did of Russians.

For example, when respondents were asked whom they would like to see as a son/daughter-in-law, a neighbour and a colleague at work, most respondents – and especially ethnically Central Asian respondents – tended to have strong preferences and biases. Over 90 per cent of our Uzbek and Kazakh respondents said they would like their son or daughter to marry someone of their own nationality; only four–five per cent said it did not matter what nationality the individual was. But the second highest remaining percentage of people, roughly 10 per cent of both groups, also said they would like their son or daughter to marry a Russian. Between half and two-thirds of all Russian respondents (with a higher percentage in Uzbekistan) said they would like to see a Russian as a son- or daughter-in-law; about 13 per cent said an Uzbek, and ten per cent, a Kazakh; while about a quarter of the Russians in both countries said it did not matter what nationality the individual was.

When asked whom they would *not* want to see as a son- or daughter-in-law, Central Asians likewise had strong feelings. The least favoured in both countries were Jews and Armenians. But about the same proportion of Kazakhs who named a Russian as an undesirable son- or daughter-in-law (37 per cent) also named Uighurs (36 per cent) and Uzbeks (35 per cent); and about the same proportion of Uzbeks who named a Russian (23 per cent) as undesirable also named a Kyrgyz (21 per cent) and a Kazakh (20 per cent). Only four per cent of the Kazakhs in our Kazakhstani survey, and six per cent of the Uzbeks in the Uzbekistani survey, said that they did not have strong feelings about whom their children might marry.

Respondents naturally became more tolerant the greater the distance from their immediate personal lives; but prejudice and intolerance remained high. Again, Jews and Armenians were at the top of the list regarding the undesired nationality of their neighbours, with almost one-third of all Uzbek respondents, for example, stating that they would not want to have a Jew as a neighbour, and 26 per cent that they would not like to have an Armenian neighbour. But here again, more Uzbek respondents named Tatars (19.4 per cent), Koreans (15 per cent), Kazakhs (12 per cent), Kyrygz (11 per cent) and Tajiks (8 per cent), than named Russians (7 per cent); and more Kazakh respondents named Uzbeks (14 per cent), Tatars (20 per cent), Koreans (19 per cent) and Uighurs (17 per cent), than named Russians (10 per cent). Only nine per cent of the Uzbek respondents, and about 20 per cent of Kazakh respondents, said it made no difference who their neighbour was.

Finally, a good proportion of respondents preferred not to have Jews and Armenians even as colleagues at work: almost one-quarter of all Uzbek respondents said they would prefer not to have a Jewish colleague at work, and one-fifth said they would prefer not to have an Armenian one. But again, more people said they would prefer not to have as work colleagues other Central Asian and non-Russian nationalities generally than Russians. More Kazakhs would prefer not to have an Uzbek (11 per cent), Tatar (13 per cent), Korean (11 per cent) or Uighur (11 per cent) colleague at work than would prefer not to have a Russian (6 per cent) one; and more Uzbeks would prefer not to have a Kyrgyz, Tajik, Tatar, Kazakh or Korean co-worker than a Russian one. Only ten per cent of the Uzbeks, versus 26 per cent of the Russians, said that it made no difference.

These patterns, moreover, prevailed among the younger generations and more highly educated portions of our sample, who proved to be no more tolerant than their older or less educated counterparts. Indeed, generally they were less tolerant.

Nonetheless, with the increased emphasis on 'indigenization' after such a long period of colonial rule, and with increasing economic hardship, Russians and Central Asians, not surprisingly, displayed a different sense of attachment to these countries. When asked whether, given the opportunity, they would like to leave Uzbekistan or Kazakhstan and live somewhere else, well over 90 per cent of the Uzbeks and Kazakhs replied no; by contrast, about 43 per cent of the Russians in Kazakhstan, and over one-third of the Russians in Uzbekistan, replied in the affirmative, despite the fact that many probably had roots in Central Asia going back two or three generations and had established their own communities there. Most of these Russians wanted to go to Russia, Ukraine, or Belarus, or else to Europe, the US or Canada. Most wished to leave because they feared for the future of their children, or else were seeking better economic conditions. They tended to be concentrated in the lower age groups and were among the more highly educated.

The survey results suggest that while divisions among nationality groups in Central Asia run deep, they may be as acute among Central Asians as between them and Russians. Divisions between Central Asians and Russians, or Muslims and non-Muslims, are not as clear-cut as is often assumed. Our survey suggests that discord may be expressed in terms of ethnic group, family, neighbourhood and region as much as along religious lines. It also suggests that the younger generation – of all nationalities and educational levels – may be just as intolerant of other national groups as the older respondents. These divisions will probably have an enormous influence on Uzbekistan's and Kazakhstan's paths to reform; but the splits and schisms will not always be well-defined.

FOREIGN POLICY

Facing a litany of political, economic and social challenges at home, Central Asian citizens are often expected to be in favour of turning to other countries for aid and assistance. With a strong sense of separate ethnic and cultural identity that permeates Central Asian societies, questions of religious and ethnic identity are often viewed as playing an important role in their determinations of partners abroad. For example, many Western observers have tended to view the granting of foreign assistance in Central Asia as largely a contest between Turkey and Iran, given their proximity to Central Asia and their shared cultural if not religious values. But the contradictory contextual nature of identity in Uzbekistan and Kazakhstan seems to be reflected in foreign policy orientations as well.

First, despite the economic hardship at home, our survey suggests that attitudes towards foreign investment or assistance to their countries may be ambiguous. When asked to rate the importance of a number of possible measures to address Uzbekistan's problems, only about one-third of respondents in both Kazakhstan and Uzbekistan said that the widespread attraction of foreign capital is important, with more Russians in Uzbekistan arguing against this than Uzbeks.

Likewise, when asked if their country should turn to other countries to help solve its economic and environmental problems, respondents in both countries were split: almost half of all respondents in Uzbekistan said no, while 40 per cent said yes; in Kazakhstan, these proportions were reversed. About one-tenth did not know or found it difficult to answer.

Interestingly, these responses were somewhat contradictory according to nationality. In Uzbekistan, for example, more Russians argued against the widespread attraction of foreign capital than did

Uzbeks (19 per cent of Russian respondents said that this was totally unimportant, and 17 per cent said it was even undesirable; this was more than twice the number of Uzbek respondents who were not in favour). When asked whether Uzbekistan should turn for help to other countries to solve its problems, however, about half the Russians answered yes, while only about 38 per cent of the Uzbeks said yes; more than half of the Uzbeks said no.

The overwhelming reasons for this wariness to turn to other countries for assistance were the sense that the Central Asian new states can 'do it themselves'. In Uzbekistan, for example, 68 per cent of the 620 people who said no to outside assistance stated the reason as 'we have our own capabilities and possibilities'; Central Asians comprised 81 per cent of them. In Kazakhstan, 61 per cent of the 231 people who rejected outside assistance gave this reason, with Central Asians comprising 44 per cent of them. Other reasons included the perceived humiliation that would come with receiving outside assistance, and the fear of becoming dependent on Western countries.

Among those who do welcome foreign investment, however, most are seeking this not from Turkey or Iran, but overwhelmingly from the West or Japan. Of the 519 in Uzbekistan and 423 people in Kazakhstan who said that their countries should turn to other countries for assistance, most did not name Turkey or other Islamic countries as the most desirable source. Instead, the largest proportions of respondents named European countries (one third of Uzbekistani respondents, and over half of Kazakhstani respondents), and Japan (34 per cent of Uzbekistani respondents and 29 per cent of Kazakhstani ones). One third of respondents in Uzbekistan also named the United States; but the US was named by only 15 per cent of Kazakhstani respondents – about the same proportion who advocated turning to Russia (Fig. 4.1).

The most striking answers to this question in Uzbekistan were in the younger age groups of the survey (17–29 years of age). The first three choices were: the US (44 per cent of all 17–29 year olds selected the US, versus 22 per cent of those over sixty); Japan (40 per cent of all 17–29 year olds); the European states (37 per cent); and Muslim states (31 per cent). Only 20 per cent of this age group selected Russia, compared to almost half of those over sixty.

By contrast, only about a quarter (26 per cent) of Uzbekistani respondents, and about six per cent of Kazakhstani respondents, said that they should turn to Turkey. For Uzbekistan, this was slightly less than the 29 per cent who said Uzbekistan should turn to Russia for assistance, and about the same proportion (25 per cent) who said it should turn to other governments of the CIS, and also to other Muslim countries. Only nine of the Uzbekistani respondents, or less than two per cent of those who responded to this question – and only about a half of one per cent of respondents in Kazakhstan – believed their countries should turn to Iran.

Central Asians predominated both among those selecting Muslim countries, and among those seeking aid and assistance from the West. Nor were these answers divided strictly along nationality lines (see Table 4.4). While 88 per cent of the 135 people in Uzbekistan who selected Muslim countries, and 85 per cent of the 137 people who selected Turkey, were of Central Asian nationalities, 70 per cent of the 150 people who selected Russia and the 159 people who chose European countries were also Central Asians. Moreover, eighty-one per cent of the 153 people who selected the US were Central Asian. In Kazakhstan, over 40 per cent of those who chose European countries, and more than half of those who selected the US, were ethnic Kazakhs.

When asked from which countries Uzbekistan and Kazakhstan should keep the greatest distance, those most frequently named were Afghanistan (over one-third of respondents in both countries), followed by Israel, Iran and Pakistan. One-third of Kazakhstani respondents also named China. When asked from which countries Uzbekistan should keep the greatest distance, Uzbekistani respondents most frequently named Afghanistan (36 per cent of respondents), Israel (21 per cent), Iran (16 per cent) and Pakistan (16 per cent). Kazakhstani respondents named Afghanistan (35 per cent), China (33 per cent), Israel (14 per cent), Iran (13 per cent) and Pakistan (12 per cent); 30 per cent of Kazakhstani respondents did not know or could not answer.

Uzbeks in Uzbekistan were wary of Afghanistan (34 per cent), Israel (23 per cent) and Iran (15 per cent). Russians were most wary of Afghanistan (50 per cent of Russians in Uzbekistan, and 41 per cent in Kazakhstan), Pakistan (33 per cent in Uzbekistan, versus 14 per cent for Uzbeks, and 18 per cent of the Russians in Kazakhstan); and Iran (29 per cent of Russians in Uzbekistan, and 16 per cent of Russians in Kazakhstan). A quarter of the Russians in Kazakhstan were also most wary of China. Kazakhs in Kazakhstan wanted to keep the greatest distance from China (45 per cent), Afghanistan (30 per cent) and Israel (17 per cent); 31 per cent of the Kazakhs did not know or could not answer.

President Karimov has long argued that with Uzbekistan's great wealth, the country does not need outside assistance or investment, but that it needs partners to work with on an equal basis. He has consistently argued that Uzbekistan is not looking to Turkey, Iran, or to any one country for assistance or for a model of development, but is

TABLE 4.4 COUNTRIES PREFERRED AS DONORS TO UZBEKISTAN OF ECONOMIC AND ENVIRONMENTAL AID BY AGE AND NATIONALITY

Age	European states		Muslim states		Russia		Iran		CIS states		Turkey		USA		Arab states	
17 - 29 yrs	55	10.6%	46	8.9%	30	5.8%	3	0.6%	29	5.6%	39	7.5%	65	12.5%	13	2.5%
30 - 39 yrs	61	11.8%	42	8.1%	42	8.1%	2	0.4%	52	10.0%	45	8.7%	50	9.7%	17	3.3%
40 - 49 yrs	25	4.8%	22	4.2%	31	6.0%	3	0.6%	25	4.8%	27	5.2%	25	4.8%	7	1.4%
50 - 59 yrs	24	4.6%	16	3.1%	26	5.0%	1	0.2%	16	3.1%	14	2.7%	22	4.2%	4	0.8%
60 yrs and up	11	2.1%	9	1.7%	22	4.2%	0	0.0%	10	1.9%	12	2.3%	10	1.9%	3	0.6%
Total	176	34.0%	135	26.1%	151	29.2%	9	1.7%	132	25.5%	137	26.4%	172	33.2%	44	8.5%
Nationality																
Uzbek	111	21.5%	104	20.1%	97	18.8%	8	1.5%	81	15.7%	110	21.3%	105	20.3%	29	5.6%
Other Central Asian	17	3.3%	16	3.1%	8	1.5%	0	0.0%	8	1.5%	7	1.4%	21	4.1%	10	1.9%
Russian / Other Slav.	27	5.2%	6	1.2%	29	5.6%	0	0.0%	28	5.4%	8	1.5%	28	5.4%	1	0.2%
Other	20	3.9%	9	1.7%	17	3.3%	1	0.2%	14	2.7%	12	2.3%	18	3.5%	3	0.6%
Don't know	1	0.2%	0	0.0%	0	0.0%	0	0.0%	0	0.0%	0	0.0%	1	0.2%	1	0.2%
Total	176	34.0%	135	26.1%	150	29.0%	9	1.7%	131	25.3%	137	26.5%	172	33.3%	44	8.5%

Age	Japan		CA states		Israel		Asian states		China		Germany		All states		Don't know	
17 - 29 yrs	59	11.4%	31	6.0%	3	0.6%	11	2.1%	6	1.2%	1	0.2%	0	0.0%	2	0.4%
30 - 39 yrs	62	12.0%	49	9.5%	3	0.6%	18	3.5%	7	1.4%	0	0.0%	2	0.4%	1	0.2%
40 - 49 yrs	29	5.6%	20	3.9%	1	0.2%	7	1.4%	1	0.2%	0	0.0%	1	0.2%	1	0.2%
50 - 59 yrs	19	3.7%	14	2.7%	2	0.4%	4	0.8%	2	0.4%	0	0.0%	0	0.0%	2	0.4%
60 yrs and up	8	1.5%	16	3.1%	1	0.2%	3	0.6%	2	0.4%	0	0.0%	1	0.2%	0	0.0%
Total	177	34.2%	130	25.1%	10	1.9%	43	8.3%	18	3.5%	1	0.2%	4	0.8%	6	1.2%
Nationality																
Uzbek	122	23.6%	89	17.2%	3	0.6%	28	5.4%	12	2.3%	1	0.2%	2	0.4%	1	0.2%
Other Central Asian	20	3.9%	19	3.7%	2	0.4%	5	1.0%	0	0.0%	0	0.0%	0	0.0%	1	0.2%
Russian / Other Slav.	19	3.7%	12	2.3%	3	0.6%	6	1.2%	1	0.2%	0	0.0%	0	0.0%	3	0.6%
Other	16	3.1%	9	1.7%	2	0.4%	4	0.8%	5	1.0%	0	0.0%	2	0.4%	1	0.2%
Don't know	0	0.0%	0	0.0%	0	0.0%	0	0.0%	0	0.0%	0	0.0%	0	0.0%	0	0.0%
Total	177	34.2%	129	25.0%	10	1.9%	43	8.3%	18	3.5%	1	0.2%	4	0.8%	6	1.2%

FIGURE 4.1 COUNTRIES TO WHICH REPUBLIC SHOULD TURN FOR
ASSISTANCE WITH ECONOMIC AND ENVIRONMENTAL
PROBLEMS

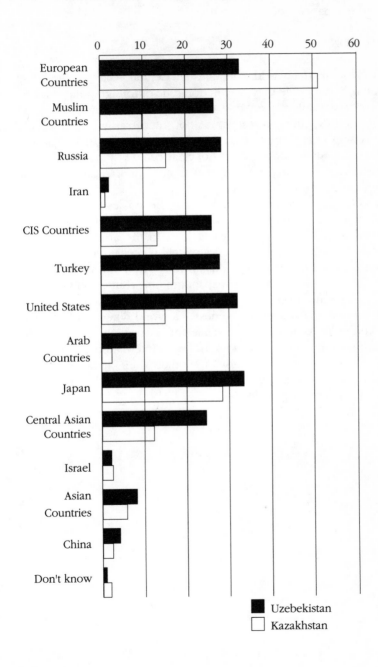

probing contacts with a wide range of countries, and is seeking its own path to development. Regardless of the success he may attain in these endeavours, our survey suggests that his words may have found profound resonance with his citizenry.

CONCLUSION

As anywhere in the world, identities in Central Asia are fluid and contextual, and the role they play in domestic or foreign policy may be ambiguous. Islam plays a key role, especially in Uzbekistan, in the way people identify themselves, but not necessarily in the all-encompassing or strictly religious way often ascribed to it. National differences are also strong, but are not clear cut: divisions and tensions may be as deep among, and even within, Central Asian groups as between Central Asians and Slavs.

The role of Islam and nationality may be no less ambiguous in foreign policy. Although the responses above give a cursory and superficial view, they suggest that at least in the area of economic assistance, foreign involvement is not widely perceived to be a contest between Turkey and Iran, or the Muslim versus non-Muslim worlds.

Certainly, our survey is but a snapshot in time. But overall, it seems to portray a picture of populations seeking to build a stable world out of their current chaos and divisiveness – a world where their Islamic, ethnic and cultural heritages are perceived as playing a central role, without precluding integration with the wider international community or a reduction in ethnic tension at home. Their answers paint a confused and contradictory picture of how successful they ultimately may be in reaching these goals.

5

Geopolitics and Ethnic Problems of Uzbekistan and Its Neighbours

DONALD S. CARLISLE

Since the independence of the former Soviet Central Asian republics was proclaimed in September 1991, observers have speculated over the future course they will choose. The key questions are: what system will they adopt and in which direction will they orient themselves?

Three factors must be considered in answering these questions. First, in the domestic sphere, what political and socio-economic system will replace the communist one-party regimes? Or, will there be little or no change, the former Soviet regimes continuing into the post-Soviet period largely unreconstructed? Second, in regard to foreign policy, the Soviet Union's Central Asian successor states are being tugged in opposite directions. Which direction will they choose? On the one hand, as sovereign states they are drawn to exercise their new-found freedom in the international arena; this urge to turn outwards is reinforced by their Turkic/Muslim heritage – so long repressed under Soviet rule – which suggests establishing close ties with the Middle East and Asia along with exploring relations with the non-Islamic West. Pulling in a contrary direction is a northern magnetic attraction, towards Russia, the region's lodestar for well over one hundred years. There is yet a third alternative to consider: the possibility of giving priority to problems and relationships within the Central Asian region itself. Will the new states perhaps opt for some sort of confederation? A regional orientation is not in conflict with whatever choice might be made regarding the north/south axis, which, in turn, need not interfere with turning inward so as to create regional harmony. However, an inward-oriented focus might set a different agenda and require tough decisions that could complicate relations with the outside world.

This study focuses on the domestic dimensions of the political context emergent in Central Asia; it highlights new realities while drawing attention to the persistence of old patterns and the possible resurrection of still older configurations in novel guises. An important aim is to appraise the prospects for unity and diversity within this region which is presently – but probably not permanently – divided into independent units based on national/ethnic principles. The analytical prism adopted here is a geopolitical one which stresses the centrality of local and sub-regional realities as opposed to reliance solely on national/ethnic categories.[1]

Attention will be given in this study to foreign policy, but only when it relates to internal political evolution and domestic stability; naturally the external policies of these states as they affect one another will be addressed. Of course, the role of Russia and Russians in the politics of the region will not be ignored.

THE PAST IN PERSPECTIVE

The approach adopted in this chapter is largely geopolitical in its orientation and national/ethnic in its focus. This is not to say that these two rather different vantage points are always synchronized and congruent. Quite the contrary. It is the major premise undergirding this study that 'geopolitics' provides the most useful framework and that it is through this grid that national/ethnic issues can best be understood. For our purpose geopolitics is understood as political context and configuration viewed through the prism of location or locale. It emphasizes geography – both physical and human – in its interface with personal identity and political allegiances.

One must avoid geographic determinism or geopolitical fatalism in assessing the present and future. It must be stressed that the approach adopted does not emphasize the former Soviet Central Asian republics' relations with neighbouring states on the far side of the USSR's old borders. Rather, the focus is on interaction within Central Asia itself; emphasis is on relations between regions and groups within individual states. The argument is that each state's domestic political geography and internal regional politics provide the best framework for understanding how national and ethnic relations unfold.

The geopolitical approach demonstrates its power when applied, for instance, to the origins of Uzbekistan and Tajikistan – the two main foci of this study.[2] The 1924–25 'national delimitation' from which Uzbekistan and the other Central Asian republics emerged, pre-supposed the existence of distinct Uzbek, Turkmen, Tajik, Kazakh and Kyrgyz nations and supposedly responded to their demand for statehood. It was actually quite a different endeavour; what it did was to carve out state formations (Soviet republics) for historically well-known groups that were not yet consolidated as distinct peoples let alone modern nations. National delimitation lumped together diverse, sometimes divergent, and certainly different communities under a single ethnic principle. Certain groups were identified as the Uzbek nation and territorially delimited within the boundaries of an entity called 'Uzbekistan' which had never existed previously.[3] Other groups who made up anything but consolidated nations were also delimited by territory and frontiers and assigned a new juridical status similarly based on unreal or not-yet real nations.

Essentially what transpired was not national delimitation, which presupposed nations-in-being, but the creation of states for ideal nations, not yet existing. Political engineering and boundary delineation, not national delimitation, took place in 1924–25. One might say it was an example of nation-building 'from above'. In 1925 Uzbek national consciousness did not, so to speak, exist 'below' and national consolidation had barely begun. The argument of this study is that even at present these objectives remain unachieved and these processes are incomplete.

Another insight follows from this argument. The history of Soviet Uzbekistan should be read as the attempt to create modern nations (Uzbeks, Tajiks etc.) where previously there were ethnic groups (Uzbeks, Tajiks etc.). The nature of this enterprise calls to mind the 19th century Italian politician's quip: 'We have made Italy. Now we must make Italians.' The major corollary to this nation-in-the-making approach is the contention that pre-1924 realities lived on during the Soviet period and proved as salient as the artificially-contrived nationality; subnational and pre-national allegiances complemented and sometimes superseded 'Uzbek' and 'Uzbekistan' as primary realities. In various guises, pre-revolutionary Kokand, Khiva, Bukhara, and Turkestan persisted. It is postulated here that even today they provide, as they did in the past, a useful compass alongside the notion of nation and nationalism for getting one's bearings regarding the present and future in Uzbekistan and Tajikistan.

National politics in Central Asia today have a peculiar shape and acquire distorted and sometimes disturbing contours. This is because of the persistence of traditional societies with their pre-national patriotisms and the presence, under the umbrella of the nation-state, of lively subnational and regional realities. Consequently, one must be very cautious in applying categories like 'nation', 'nationalism' and 'nationalists' to former Soviet Central Asia. There, the real referents for these abstract concepts remain elusive and the context is extremely complicated; these peoples are only in the early or intermediate stages of modern political development, if that, with a confused and chaotic present and an uncertain future.

THE ORIGINS OF UZBEKISTAN

It must be underlined that local and regional politics provide a key to the national delimitation in Central Asia and the character of the republics that emerged in its aftermath. The cooperation of native politicians with Moscow was essential for success. Answering the questions why national delimitation took place, and who was advantaged or disadvantaged by the dismemberment of Turkestan and the elimination of Bukhara and Khiva, requires attention to regional and local politics.

Exploring the differences between Central Asian communist leaders and introducing their personal ambitions are the best guides here. The momentous events of the 1920s have too often been explained largely in ethnic terms but are better understood in other ways. The local leaders' allegiances were by no means national in nature; the identities in conflict were essentially political and produced patriotisms that were locale-based not primarily 'national' (whatever that could mean where the notion of the nation was quite new and identity based in clan and family was very old).

The geopolitical approach contends that the principal instigators and main local beneficiaries of the 1924–25 national delimitation were the *jadid* reformers of Bukhara, in particular Faizulla Khojaev and his followers.[4] The essential point to make is that 'Uzbekistan' – which initially appeared in 1925 on the map with its capital at Samarkand – was the Bukhara *jadids*' pet project and its creation reflected their influence. In fact, what emerged as Uzbekistan could be viewed as a Greater Bukhara or Bukhara 'writ large'.

The 1924–25 national delimitation restructured local boundaries and introduced a new principle of political administration and identity. It eliminated Turkestan and erased the ancient states of Bukhara and Khiva. At first glance it appeared to dissolve the Bukharan Soviet People's Republic, the successor state to the Bukharan Emirate, into new national units. Bukhara did actually disappear from the map as a discernible political entity. In the post-1925 republics, most of old Bukhara was to be found in new Uzbekistan, although some western territory was ceded to Turkmenistan. Its most isolated and mountainous terrain, East Bukhara, and the Pamir region were re-packaged as 'Tajikistan' to form an entity named for the Persian-speaking peoples, the Tajiks. Until 1929 this section of defunct Bukhara remained intact – as did virtually all of the former emirate – within Uzbekistan, although assigned a special status (see Maps 5.1 and 5.2).

However, if we shift the analytical prism somewhat and re-focus attention, it becomes obvious that Bukhara's fate was not as disastrous as a cursory glance at pre- and post-1925 maps might suggest. On the post-1925 Soviet map Bukhara officially disappeared as an independent unit, its territory supposedly incorporated in the new republics. But if we look again, we see that what actually reappeared as Uzbekistan could be viewed as a Greater Bukhara: new Uzbekistan was old Bukhara writ large. The contention is that, aside from some western territory transferred to Turkmenistan, historic Bukhara re-emerged intact from the national delimitation. It reappeared as a larger and stronger unit, augmented by land, resources and peoples co-opted from defunct Turkestan and what had been the Khiva Khanate – and, since 1920, the Khorezm Soviet People's Republic. And it was to be ruled by the Bukharan political élite!

Faizulla Khojaev, leader of Soviet Bukhara (1920–24) and Chairman of Uzbekistan's Sovnarkom from 1925 to June 1937, was the main figure on the Central Asian scene seeking Turkestan's (and Khiva's) dismemberment. He was opposed by other native politicians, especially Turkestan's leaders, who recognized that the projected Uzbekistan would dominate the region. Geopolitically the creation of Uzbekistan in place of Turkestan meant the rise to prominence of Bukhara and the Bukharans in Soviet Central Asia.

Let us consider what transpired in territorial terms. As Turkestan and Khiva were liquidated, the Samarkand region of Soviet Turkestan, as well as the Tashkent area and the major part of the rich Fergana Valley, were merged with virtually all of the Bukharan Soviet People's Republic – and much of ancient Khiva/Khorezm – to constitute a new entity. What surfaced in 1925 under Faizulla Khojaev and the Bukhara *jadids'* auspices with its capital at Samarkand was old Bukhara enlarged and disguised as new Uzbekistan. Faizulla Khojaev had in effect achieved the objectives which for centuries had eluded the Bukharan emirs: with the backing of the Russians, he orchestrated the absorption by Bukhara of much of what had belonged to the Khiva and Kokand khans.

THE ORIGINS OF TAJIKISTAN

The centuries-old antagonism between Uzbeks and Tajiks had, by the late 19th century, been partially mitigated through gradual 'turkicization' of the Tajiks. The emergence of a hybrid native, the so-called 'Sart', especially in urban areas, reflected this merger of peoples. There appeared a native type that transcended the Turco-Iranian division. In Bukhara, for instance (as in the Samarkand region), Uzbek and Tajik not only intermeshed but numerous other peoples were able to coexist as well.

Certainly, perfect harmony did not exist, and there were periodic religious outbursts and ethnic/cultural difficulties; nonetheless, a *modus vivendi* seemed to have been worked out and various 'nationalities' and related groups adjusted to one another. Mutual accommodation had not required the radical solution of sharpening ethnic differences by creating national units – which was the Soviet approach to the region.

These Soviet measures undercut the assimilation processes and singled out the Tajiks as one of the primary ethnic formations to be preserved; this probably saved them from sublimation in other formations and absorption through 'turkicization'. It is very likely that the Tajik-oriented wing of the Bukharan *jadid* movement lobbied for this outcome. Faizulla Khojaev's main opponents in Bukharan politics, Abdulla Muhiddinov and his family, were probably the key figures here. In 1924 Tajiks were given a special role and acquired a distinct, but not independent, territory. In fact the Uzbek lobby among the Bukhara *jadids* initially intended to give them only a minor role as a mere *oblast* within Uzbekistan; however, it was upgraded to autonomous republic status, but was still contained within Uzbekistan and subordinate to its authorities.[5]

Tajik spokesmen presented ethnic, cultural and historic reasons for including the renowned city of Samarkand (and Bukhara) within Tajikistan. Their petition was rejected and Samarkand was named as Uzbekistan's capital. Another Tajik/Uzbek bone of contention was Khujand and the surrounding region abutting the Fergana Valley. It apparently was the prime candidate to become the Tajik capital, but in 1924 this area was allocated to Uzbekistan. Then in 1929 the whole region was transferred to the jurisdiction of Stalinabad (formerly Dushanbe).

Whether it was because of Faizulla Khojaev's skills, the weight of the Bukhara Uzbek lobby, the influence in Moscow of Khojaev's patrons such as V. V. Kuibyshev, or simply the correlation of his project with Stalin's objectives, Uzbekistan finally emerged from the delimitation as the strongest Central Asian republic.[6] This was the case in terms of population, resources and territory; it also incorporated most of the prize area at stake – the fertile Fergana region. The ancient historical and cultural centres, Bukhara and Samarkand, as well as Khiva, fell within Uzbekistan's borders. The major strategic centre and Russian stronghold, Tashkent, was also allocated to the Uzbeks, not to the Kazakhs as the latter had demanded. That this was to prove more of a bane than a boon was obvious from the political tale that unfolded.

Moscow's recognition of Uzbekistan's special position within Central Asia was made clear. In February 1925 Mikhail Kalinin remarked in Bukhara when he addressed the First Congress of the republic's Communist Party:

> Naturally, Uzbekistan must play a large role in Central Asia, a role, one might even say, of hegemony. This role must not be lost sight of, Comrades, leaders of the Central Committee of Uzbekistan. I consider this proper. Certainly, Uzbekistan has at its disposal sufficiently large cultural forces...great material possibilities, a large population, it has the most wealthy cities. I consider it a fully valid and natural desire to play first violin in Central Asia. But, if comrades want to play first violin, then it is reasonable that this will be achieved in our Soviet Union only by increased work, great generosity, huge effort, and sacrifices for the neighbouring republics, which will come in contact with you. For when you are strong and mighty, then great tact will be demanded from you toward these republics. In a word, you must relate to them as Moscow relates to you.[7]

One could argue that a second phase of national delimitation was to be launched in 1929; this time it undermined rather than reinforced the 1925 grand design of the Bukharan politicians. Indeed, as mentioned, there was evidence that considerable territory held by the Uzbek SSR was about to be transferred to Stalinabad's jurisdiction, but this feature of what would have proved to be a more extensive second national delimitation was abandoned.

Evidence points to Moscow's intervention in Uzbek politics in 1929 to undermine Faizulla and the Bukhara lobby; the detaching of Tajikistan should be seen as something of a political punishment dealt out to him. The September 1930 movement of Uzbekistan's capital from Samarkand to Tashkent was part of the same attempt to discipline him and to shift the centre of political gravity from a Bukhara/ Samarkand axis to a Tashkent/Fergana orientation and in the process, to draw it closer to Moscow.

Stalin used other Uzbek politicians (initially, Akmal Ikramov and his Tashkent/Fergana cadres) against the Bukhara/Samarkand *jadids*.[8] Moscow's manipulation of local cleavages and differences provides a major key to the divisive game it played during the 1920s and 1930s; the First Secretary of Uzbekistan's Party organization, Ikramov, was Stalin's main agent in exploiting the various native feuds and ambitions. Later, he too would be jettisoned by Stalin and replaced by Usman Yusupov and a more authentic Stalinist clique – also based in the Tashkent/Fergana area – which served Moscow's interests.[9]

The momentous turning point of 1929, the year of the launching of the revolution from above, also marked a second phase in national delimitation. The Tajik 'autonomous' republic was detached from the Uzbek SSR with the unexpected addition of the Khujand region, and was proclaimed a separate union republic. It appears that additional dismemberment of Uzbekistan was planned when it was announced that the whole Surkhan-Darya region was to be transferred to Tajik jurisdiction. However, this step was not taken.

These territorial changes can hardly be linked to the application of ethnic criteria. They were a punishment dealt to Faizulla Khojaev and the Bukhara Uzbeks who in 1925 had successfully lobbied for inclusion of all Tajik terrain in the Uzbek state. Ultimately, Faizulla and his followers – as well as all the Uzbek politicians who benefited from his predicament – were killed in Stalin's Central Asian version of the Great Purge. The Tajik communists of various ilk who had prospered in the twenties and thirties – whatever their origin – suffered the same fate.

SOVIET UZBEKISTAN AND RASHIDOV

The regional paradigm discussed at the beginning of this chapter as a supplement to, and sometimes as a substitute for, ethnic analysis casts light on the origins of Uzbekistan (and Tajikistan). It is also a window on leadership patterns and élite politics throughout the history of Soviet Uzbekistan. During the years of so-called mature Stalinism, the Tashkent/Fergana area was the principal source of the native personnel that ruled the republic. The core contingent that dominated the Party's Bureau and Secretariat was usually recruited from the Tashkent and Fergana districts. Samarkand, Bukhara and other outlying areas were largely ignored, relegated to secondary importance. Unexpectedly in 1959 the lock of the Tashkent/Fergana cohort on top leadership positions was broken when Sharaf Rashidov, who was born and raised in Samarkand, became the Party's First Secretary.

Born in 1917, Rashidov served as Uzbekistan's First Secretary from March 1959 until his death in October 1983. The Rashidov era largely coincided with the Brezhnev era in the USSR as a whole.[10] Once known as the period of 'developed socialism', Brezhnev's time in office came to be regarded as the period of 'stagnation'. Whatever the label, certain important features stand out. An emphasis on stability and a reluctance to risk change by reform were obvious traits.

The Rashidov regime in Uzbekistan mirrored the centre's conservative personality, its oligarchic politics and its status quo policies. During this time the USSR functioned as a looser, less integrated, imperial edifice in which the claims of unity were diluted and the pull of the centre on the periphery was somewhat relaxed. The republics enjoyed increased autonomy when compared to the totalitarian integration of the Stalin era.

Moscow's approach to ruling the empire's periphery gave substantial leeway to the republic's *nomenklatura*, allowing first secretaries like Rashidov to function with a great deal of autonomy in local affairs. In Uzbekistan, a variant of communist feudalism surfaced. In an Uzbek version of 'oriental despotism' Rashidov appeared to rule as the republic's khan or emir; the party Bureau functioned something like a Council of Vizirs. A great deal of autonomy was also delegated to the party secretaries of the various regions, who administered their provinces as *beks* had ruled their dominions in pre-revolutionary Bukhara, Khiva or Kokand.

But after Brezhnev's death in 1982, Moscow under Andropov launched an assault on the Uzbek status quo established during Rashidov's reign.[11] The so-called Uzbek Affair which followed saw an attack on local corruption, and Rashidov was blamed for its pervasiveness. Under the guise of 'de-Rashidovization', a process of 'de-uzbekization' and 're-muscovization' was carried out. The scale of this purge was astonishing. In 1988 the First Party Secretary in Uzbekistan, Rafiq Nishanov, sent from Moscow to preside over the house-cleaning, claimed that during a four-year period 58,000 senior officials in Uzbekistan had been replaced.[12]

POST-SOVIET UZBEKISTAN AND KARIMOV

The choice in June 1989 of Islam Karimov as Uzbekistan's Party leader was unexpected. The explanation for his appointment sheds light on why he remained politically insecure during the next five years. In fact, his consolidation of power after August 1991 has not been as smooth and uncomplicated as it might at first appear. Indeed, even Karimov's present, seemingly unchallenged, position in Uzbek politics is deceptive and his future may be problematic. This insecure domestic position needs to be addressed as well as his increasing dominant position on the Central Asian scene as a result of the war in Tajikistan.

The emergence of Islam Karimov as the dominant leader in Uzbekistan was unprecedented; the story includes puzzling twists as well as some mysterious turns. Without examining Soviet political culture and Moscow's attempt between 1983 and 1988 to 'purge' Uzbekistan, it is impossible to understand how Karimov got where he is today. One needs to appreciate his almost miraculous emergence out of the political limbo to which he had been consigned in 1988 by Nishanov, then the Party's First Secretary who preceded him, and who implemented Moscow's directives to discipline Uzbekistan.

Karimov's unexpected elevation to Nishanov's post after riots in the Fergana Valley in June 1989 initially set limits on his independence. At the outset he was dependent on local politicians who engineered his promotion and who perhaps thought of him as their puppet. This prolonged and complicated his consolidation of power, which really did not take off until January 1992.

Karimov's career passed through several phases. Nothing in his early life – he was born in Samarkand in 1938 – or in mid-career suggested he was likely to emerge at the top of the political pyramid. Karimov was simply an economic technocrat; he was never a politically driven figure. He served for many years as a Gosplan bureaucrat and eventually, in 1986, became Minister of Finance. It is important to note that he was not a typical party apparatchik and was never a member of the *nomenklatura's* inner circle.

Before 1986 he had not held a party post and was never a member of a party bureau at any level, let alone of the central republican Politburo; he never served in the Party Secretariat. He did not even qualify for Central Committee membership and had never attended a Party Congress until 1986. Consequently, his appointment as First Secretary of the Communist Party in June 1989 was, to say the least, startling.

As of December 1986 everything pointed to Karimov's continued prominence as a technocrat in a high level government post with little likelihood of further advancement. His real rise to power begins with his demotion in that month: he lost his government post in Tashkent and was exiled in disgrace to the distant terrain of the Kashka-Darya Oblast. True, there he was to be the dominant figure, for he was appointed *obkom* first secretary. But there was no reason to see this demotion as anything but a political dead-end; certainly the transfer to this backwater region was not meant to serve as the launching pad for a career that included promotion to the post of First Secretary of the republic's party and subsequently President of Uzbekistan.

Regarding his years as First Secretary, it appears he travelled a rocky road after the mysterious June 1989 appointment which took him from Karshi back to Tashkent (and subsequently to the position of President in March 1990). The contention here is that the period 1989 through August 1991 should be viewed as a time of official pre-eminence but continued dependence on those who had orchestrated his appointment, especially the Tashkent Establishment. In fact during this time he informally shared power with Shukurulla Mirsaidov, the leading Tashkent politician, a former colleague, and temporary ally; I believe it was Mirsaidov and his friends who were instrumental in bringing Karimov to power. A fierce power struggle between the two men and their entourages immediately got underway.

Only after the failed August 1991 coup did Karimov defeat Mirsaidov and begin consolidating power in his own hands. Consequently, it could be contended that the period after January 1992 was the first time that Karimov was really in charge politically. It was only after his election as President in December 1991, and his installation as President in January 1992 that he was reasonably secure and, after dispensing with Mirsaidov, was able to unveil his own policies.

Unfortunately for Karimov and his more reform-minded allies, two developments in 1992 complicated matters mightily. The initial event was the January student demonstrations in Tashkent which had lethal consequences and fuelled an anti-Karimov opposition movement; it was met by a regime crack-down and rigorous repression of dissent which continued throughout 1992 and well into 1993.

The other turning point was likewise ominous and proved a watershed. The upheaval in neighbouring Tajikistan during 1992, resulting in May in a government shake-up and in September the forced resignation of the Tajik President, the vicious civil war and that state's virtual disintegration, reinforced authoritarian attitudes in Uzbekistan. Although it occurred beyond the borders of Uzbekistan, it had major domestic implications as well as regional ramifications. Karimov and his supporters contended that the Tajik conflict could spill over into Uzbekistan, triggering similar processes there; he closed the borders with Tajikistan and continued the campaign to crush dissent.

The danger of domestic instability and the exaggerated fear of Islamic fundamentalism – although the situation in Fergana gave reason for apprehension – provided justification for continued repression within Uzbekistan; the Islamic threat was cited *ad nauseum*. Karimov's economic reforms and domestic initiatives were decisively influenced by the Tajik events; the escalating Tajik catastrophe reinforced the repressive mood of his regime at home and accelerated its intrinsic authoritarian tendencies.[13]

THE KARIMOV/MIRSAIDOV STRUGGLE

As part of the June 1989 deal that must have been struck, something like a power diarchy ensued. At first Mirsaidov served as Prime Minister, occupying the key governmental post. When in March 1990 Karimov took on the post of President (like Gorbachev in Moscow), Mirsaidov became the Vice-President in the revamped political system.

The impasse that followed over the next year was described to me by a reliable Uzbek source in the summer of 1991 as a 'struggle between two bears that could not continue unresolved much longer'. It appears that the August coup attempt in Moscow helped break that deadlock in Uzbekistan. Its failure benefited Karimov and undermined Mirsaidov who had aligned himself with the anti-Gorbachev putsch. It is widely believed that the Uzbek authorities (Karimov was usually mentioned) immediately declared martial law and identified with the coup-makers. Careful consideration of the events, however, reveals a more complicated situation. Karimov had been on a visit to India just before the Moscow crisis broke. Although he immediately returned home, there is every reason to believe that the emergency measures imposed in Tashkent were initiated by Mirsaidov and his allies who hoped to profit from them. Nor is it far-fetched to argue that they intended to replace Karimov at the first opportunity. The failure of the coup thus politically weakened the so-called 'Tashkent mafia', not Karimov.

The subsequent rise in Karimov's fortunes, and the decline in Mirsaidov's, during the autumn and winter substantiates this interpretation. Then, in December, Karimov was elected President in a contested election which gave him enhanced legitimacy; it provided the opportunity to break free from his previous 'handlers' and the Tashkent Establishment and allowed him to move decisively against Mirsaidov. In January 1992 he took two essential steps to consolidate power. First, he diminished the role of the vice-presidency – and eventually abolished the post – in an attempt to isolate Mirsaidov. The provocation worked. The latter soon resigned.

Demonstrations in Tashkent followed, ostensibly over economic conditions and price increases, but possibly also related to Mirsaidov's fall from power. There were several deaths; these events triggered Karimov's crack-down on dissent which figured so highly in Uzbekistan's growing reputation for repression. But if this interpretation is correct, the actual explanation had little to do with economic protests and was intimately tied to a raging succession struggle within the Uzbek political élite. This explanation seems to have been missed by foreign observers, although it was clearly understood in Tashkent by everyone to whom I spoke.[14]

RASHIDOV'S REHABILITATION

Perhaps the most surprising expression of Karimov's domestic strategy has been his commitment to the rehabilitation of Sharaf Rashidov. In the summer of 1992, a concerted campaign was launched to return Rashidov to good graces. During the autumn this effort gathered momentum. By the end of 1992 his birthday was being celebrated in lieu of the usual November anniversary of the Revolution. The spot in Tashkent where he had been buried after his October 1983 death – and from which his body was disinterred later – now has a large statue of Rashidov, dedicated in November 1992.[15] The nearby main thoroughfare, once called Lenin Prospekt, is now named after

Rashidov. Numerous articles in the press as well as pamphlets have appeared seeking to restore his reputation, tarnished by Moscow's assault from 1983 through 1988 on what it called 'Rashidovism' and the corruption it was said to have spawned.

Karimov's lack of a personal political machine helps explain his reliance on the old Communist Establishment. His recent rehabilitation of Sharaf Rashidov should be viewed as a concession to it and a means for enhancing his own legitimacy; this unexpected turnabout must be read as a Karimov tactic in a continuing struggle to win the support of Uzbek regional élites which are still rooted in the old order.

Almost as surprising as Rashidov's rehabilitation has been Mirsaidov's re-emergence. After his demotion and resignation in 1992 he repeatedly spoke out against Karimov. He spent much time in Moscow but returned to Tashkent in the summer of 1993. There he was arrested, tried and found guilty; but in a surprising dénouement, he was amnestied and has remained free. Given his potent connections in Tashkent this is a puzzling act on Karimov's part; it suggests he may need Mirsaidov and is seeking reconciliation with him and the forces he represents in the Tashkent Establishment. A split in the Tashkent power élite produced by the Karimov/Mirsaidov struggle continued to plague the President. Perhaps he needed to repair the rupture in relations by reaching out to his former friend and recent enemy.

THE CATASTROPHE IN TAJIKISTAN

The unreality of relying on ethnic categories alone and the need to supplement them is illustrated by Professor Barnett Rubin's observations about identity in Tajikistan:

> Among the Muslim, settled (as opposed to nomadic) population of Central Asia, region of residence rather than language or descent has long been a principal axis of identity. Such 'regionalism' (*mahalgasrai* in Tajik) cut across linguistic or ethnic lines. In many areas of Central Asia, the original Persian-speaking populations have long undergone a process of acculturation to the dominant Turkic invaders and settlers. Regions in Tajikistan differ significantly in the degree to which this process of 'Turkicization' has advanced. In some areas the lines separating Tajiks from Uzbeks are far more fluid than the mutually exclusive juridical categories of nationality would suggest.[16]

Tajikistan has a very complicated internal structure; suffice it to say that its most striking feature is that mountains constitute over 90 per cent of its territory and that it has an extensive border with Afghanistan. Eastern Tajikistan, or the Pamir region, makes up about one half of the country and is truly a distinct area. Professor Rubin emphasized how deceptive national identity is. 'The official ethnic categories...correspond only partially to people's actual identities', he observed:

> Some groups of 'Tajiks' have distinctive cultural features. The autono-mous region *(oblast)* of Gorno-Badakhshan is home to a sub-nationality, the mountain Tajiks or Pamiris (after the Pamir mountains which are their home). The Pamiris speak languages related to Persian but distinct from Tajik. Unlike other Tajiks, who are Sunni Muslims, they follow the Ismaili sect of Islam...As Ismailis are generally minorities among other Muslims, they have tended to support secular politics, as the Pamiris have in Tajikistan. In addition, many of those classified as Tajiks in the southern province of Quarghan Teppa (Kurgan Tiube) consider themselves to be Arabs by descent, though members of this traditionally nomadic group speak Tajik.[17]

The western half of Tajikistan can be divided on a horizontal axis with another high range of mountains separating the north from the central and southern regions. The terrain to the south borders on Afghanistan, where there are extensive Tajik (and Uzbek) minorities. South Tajikistan should also be divided into at least two distinct parts: the Kulab and Kurgan-Tiube regions.

To the far north beyond the mountains and distant from the capital, Dushanbe, is a distinct area with Leninabad/Khujand and Kanibadam as its major urban centres. When Uzbekistan was created in 1925, this region was not included in the Tajik autonomous republic. As explained earlier, in 1929 the Khujand region was transferred from Uzbek to Tajik jurisdiction.

What becomes clear is that Soviet Tajikistan was never an in-tegrated modern state built on a single united nationality; it was a fragile composite of regions, cobbled together because of local political ambitions and controversy in 1925 and in 1929. It was not a reflection of the will of its peoples who were never consulted about their preferences. Its ruling élite mirrored the regional cleavages that existed below the surface of the superficial national veneer. Tajikistan's northern region, Khujand/Leninabad, the most highly developed and closely linked with Uzbekistan, dominated the republic's politics and provided its top politicians. Even before the Great Purge this was the case. Then after 1938, there was a short hiatus in which 'outsiders' were in the saddle.

By 1946 the Leninabad/Khujand cadres were in command again; they dominated Tajik politics until September 1992 when President Rahmon Nabiev was forcibly removed and again newcomers – this time from the south and the Pamirs – took over. The northerners were considered particularly beholden to Moscow and Tashkent. In fact those trying to discredit Nabiev among his compatriots argued that he was an Uzbek in disguise.[18]

To understand the civil war that ripped Tajikistan apart, it is necessary to frame it against a larger backdrop. Serious attention should be paid to two distinct but related sets of events. The first began to unfold with the 1979 Soviet invasion of Afghanistan and culminated in the collapse of the Kabul regime in April 1992. The second is connected to Gorbachev's domestic and foreign innovations and their impact on Tajikistan. They triggered the political upheaval which had been underway since 1992 and the power realignment in the region.

The traumatic events that followed forced the Central Asian states – with Uzbekistan in the lead – to focus on security issues and to reaffirm their interests in common with Russia. The war accelerated the emergence of Uzbekistan as the major state in the region (and the decline of Kazakhstan as a regional player) and brought Russia's return as a Central Asian power.

It was in May 1992 that the ongoing political struggle in Tajikistan erupted, just after the fall of Kabul. By September the conflict had escalated into a full-scale civil war. *Moscow News* observed in early November 1992:

> Central Asia has not only broken the monopoly of the Transcaucasus on lengthy armed conflicts but also shown that the tragic 'records' of Caucasian wars may be beaten...In battles lasting from 20-28 October more people were killed in Kurgan-Tiube region alone than in all the armed conflicts on USSR territory from 1987 to 1991.[19]

It is possible that 40,000 to 50,000 were killed within the span of a few months. The refugees numbered well over 100,000 with many thousands, ironically, fleeing across the border to Afghanistan for safety. Another commentator observed:

> No conflict around the edges of the former Soviet empire can compare with the Tajik tragedy. The exact number of its victims will never be known. The losses run into the hundreds of thousands, and if 200,000 refugees rushing to the southern borders of Tajikistan are taken into account, the situation takes on catastrophic proportions.[20]

In some ways, the war was a rebellion of south Tajikistan against the north. Uneven economic development and widely divergent living standards between the north and the south were a root cause. According to this view, 'a split occurred between the residents of the comparatively well-off northern city of Leninabad, bordering on Uzbekistan, and the Pamir and Garm highlands where the living standard is much lower'.[21] This notion of a revolt against the domination of the Leninabad élite and its Uzbek supporters in the south, is an accurate although a somewhat schematic statement. It does, however, draw attention to the regional bases for the conflict and helps transcend the usual juxtaposition of democrats/Islamicists (the so-called Opposition) to communists in a more sophisticated analysis.

The Gorbachev reforms stimulated political activity in Tajikistan, which led to perhaps the first multiparty system in the USSR. Regions produced their own political organizations:

> The sleepy life of this remote Central Asian province was disrupted by Moscow's 'perestroika'. People from regions inhabited almost exclusively by Tajiks (Pamir, Gharm, Karategin), mainly from representatives of the intelligentsia, made up the core of the Democratic Party...founded in 1991. In the same year, the Islamic Party of Revival was instituted which embraced mostly Kurgan-Tiube peasants led by their mullas – as a rule uneducated people. Societies uniting Tajiks on the basis of their origin emerged in Dushanbe. Lali Badakhshan represented those from the Pamir Region; Zarafshan, those from Penjikent in the south of the Leninabad Region; Rastokhez, the intelligentsia from Leninabad; Vatan, former residents of Gharm; Yagnob, those who came from the centres of the Zarafshan Valley.[22]

By autumn 1992 'the opposition' had won: the former Communist Establishment based in Leninabad that had dominated for so long was overthrown. This triggered a reaction of people from Kulab and from Uzbek communities in Tajikistan against the new rulers, and a vicious civil war ensued. The intervention of Russia and Uzbekistan in the winter of 1992 decisively tilted the scales, bringing about the restoration of the political status quo ante and ensuring the opposition's defeat.

Today, however, a conflict among the victors is a danger, threatening political stability. The Kulabis now dominate Dushanbe politics and have refused to defer to the Leninabad/Khujand politicians. The dispute is personified in a struggle between the Kulabi representative, Imamali Rahmonov, who is in effect Head of State, and Abdumalik Abdulojanov, the Prime Minister, his bitter foe who is spokesman for the Khujand region. As the controversy heated up, there were rumours that North Tajikistan had petitioned to be absorbed by Uzbekistan, thus turning the clock back to 1929; we are told that Karimov rejected the demand.[23]

Uzbekistan's primary interest in solidifying its own present territorial/ethnic arrangements counselled against what may have been a logical but untimely solution. Of course, Tashkent may simply prefer to achieve this objective indirectly without running the risks that a formal territorial realignment would generate.[24]

THE ROLE OF RUSSIA AND RUSSIANS

What of Russia's future in the region? The still unresolved Tajik crisis and confrontation with Afghanistan, and Russia's intervention in alliance with Uzbekistan, have set in motion new processes that run counter to the contraction of Russian power that followed its failure in Afghanistan and the collapse of the USSR. The Tajik catastrophe reversed these trends and ended the Russian retreat from the region. True, Central Asia's relation to Moscow will never again approximate its subordinate role in the old imperial order; but the Tajik situation is a watershed, producing a reorientation in Moscow's direction.

The relationship will certainly be much closer than during the period immediately after the USSR disappeared. This is certain to prove the case so long as the present communist élite or its secular successors remain in power; it will remain true so long as Moscow and Tashkent believe there is a serious threat to the former Soviet and present CIS borders from Islam, whether based at home or abroad.

Russia reappears here in the role of guarantor of the new states' territorial integrity and perhaps also of their internal stability. In the latter context it seeks to provide assurance to the local Russians about their future prospects. Concomitantly, Russia has adopted as its allies authoritarian rulers such as Sapurmurad Niiazov in Turkmenistan and Karimov in Uzbekistan. Karimov and his regime appear to be the main beneficiary of Russia's new posture in Central Asia.

The Central Asians after a period of euphoric hopes that Turkey, the US the UN or other external sources would provide short-run solutions to long-term problems through foreign aid and investment, have been forced to retrench. They have shed idyllic illusions about foreign solutions to domestic problems. The crush of local and regional crises has introduced a healthy dose of realism, underlining the need for *realpolitik*. It has turned the leaderships in the direction of Moscow and reliance on the security shield only it can provide.

THE PRESENT IN PERSPECTIVE

At least two realities caution against adopting the nation-state model as the wave of the future for Central Asians. Within each state the unity and integration expected of a viable nation-state are lacking. Units like Uzbekistan or Tajikistan were artificial entities, concocted in 1925 and subsequently stifled in their operation during the Soviet years as subordinate provinces of the union. The sub-republic realms, where real loyalties were rooted, persisted and promised to reassert themselves. That promise is being fulfilled today; pre-national identities have lived on. They have spawned allegiances that sometimes complement, and at other times undercut, an identity such as Uzbek and Tajik – or Kyrgyz, Turkmen and Kazakh for that matter.

In Uzbekistan there are internally at least five major 'regions' that have had a life of their own and that are the fundamental building blocs of the country. Tajikistan's regional complexity yields at least a three-fold axis: northern Tajikistan which is more closely linked on virtually every score with Uzbekistan than with its southern and eastern areas; the south, whose Tajiks have more in common with their ethnic compatriots across the border in Afghanistan than with Tajiks north of Dushanbe; and finally the Pamirs which divide the country on a west/east axis, and which are inhabited by 'Mountain Tajiks' who have little in common – including language and religion – with their ethnic kin in the valleys.

In addition to divisions among Tajiks themselves, there exists the very real rift between the Uzbek and Tajik communities. It is important to remember that Uzbeks make up 23 per cent of the country's population, while Tajiks in Uzbekistan also constitute a sizable minority, much larger than census data would suggest.

In Kazakhstan, of course, everyone recognizes the basic but unofficial horizontal division between northern 'Russian Kazakhstan' and southern Kazakhstan. This is a paramount fact of life, making Kazakhstan much more a Eurasian than a Central Asian state. And within the Kazakh community itself there are also differences, recognized relations of superior and inferior based on lineage and alleged descent from the various Hordes. Kyrgyzstan too has a fundamental line of division between its northern and southern regions; in addition, there are tribal/clan differences on which political affiliations are based.

Leaving aside geopolitical/regional divisions within an individual state, one must also consider more purely ethnic dimensions; they exist between the major nationalities within particular states and between the states. There is the persistent problem of large ethnic enclaves consisting of major minorities: for example the Tajiks in Uzbekistan and the Uzbeks in Tajikistan and Kyrgyzstan. And of course, there is the issue of the Russians as a minority, present everywhere, but exiting the southern tier states at a rapid pace over the last few years.

The initial exodus of Russians from Uzbekistan, however, seems to have stopped. Some attribute this turnabout to the positive effect of Karimov's policies; the local Russians seem reasonably confident that his commitment to a secular state and his authoritarian posture are in their interest. In Tajikistan, however, the exodus continued and even accelerated after independence. In Dushanbe in September 1993, a UN delegation found few Slavs or Europeans – except for diplomats and soldiers – visible in the city. Non-Muslims have streamed out of the region, some stopping temporarily in the Leninabad/Khujand region but most leaving permanently, probably never to return.

As history repeatedly shows, one of the most important forces stimulating national integration is the threat of foreign enemies, real or imagined, at home or abroad. Consolidation of national identity and political unity is often enhanced by inflaming national hatreds across borders and within the boundaries of established but fragile states. National integrity is threatened by such border/territorial disputes and majority/minority divisions between regions and states. Moreover, the problem is not always between but rather within states – although in perverse ways this also strengthens national consciousness. Paradoxically, the disintegration of Tajikistan may not only signal the victory of regionalism in the near term, but enhance the prospects for a Tajik national identity over the long run – that is, if new Tajik leaders decide to play the ethnic card so as to mobilize local support against Afghanistan, or to counter Russian and Uzbek influence. Not for the first nor the last time, could defensive nationalism, mobilized against aliens, serve the cause of national integration.

The internal issues confronting the Central Asian states are multiple, complex and dangerous. One observer ventured to appraise the individual states' viability and their likelihood of surviving.[25] Turkmenistan – largely because of abundant economic resources – and Uzbekistan fare best; Kyrgyzstan was judged to have a dismal future ahead. The problems are daunting and the prospects are problematic. There are many ethnic and economic flashpoints providing fertile ground for intra-national as well as inter-national strife in Central Asia. A mapping of disputed areas recently identified four areas as the most likely near-term candidates where conflict may surface: they include Tajik claims on Bukhara and Samarkand and disputes among Kyrgyz, Uzbeks and Tajiks in the Fergana region.[26] But these are only a small sample of the many possible territorial/ethnic claims in the region.

THE FUTURE IN PERSPECTIVE

In competition with the nation-state framework inherited from the Soviet era and subnational patriotisms, one finds evidence of a more inclusive community surfacing. There is a potential pan-Turkic identity that could be mobilized to draw the different peoples (excluding the Tajiks) of Central Asia together. And there lurks in the background – but much less potent – the spectre of pan-Islamic or fundamentalist forces attempting to unite the region on religious grounds.

Regional differences and economic difficulties encountered in the post-Soviet period conceal an ongoing search for what the peoples of the region share in common. Numerous efforts have been made since

1991 by the Presidents and the governing élites to promote joint solutions to common problems. But so far little has been accomplished in translating high rhetoric into real endeavours. The idea of 'Turkestan' or 'Central Asia' as an entity remains an ideal, closer to dream than to reality, yet potent as propaganda nonetheless. But ideas and ideals should not be underestimated, and perhaps what the region will eventually embrace is some variant of that dream. Nothing in their history or culture suggests that the nation-state and nationalism, pitting one people against another, will suffice to satisfy in the long run their longing for unity.

Given the dialectics of intra-CIS politics, one would think that the Central Asian states would have an objective interest in advancing regional unity so as to confront the Slavic states with a common front. Surely the lesson learned from the Stalinist period – when the strategy was to keep Central Asia divided – has to be absorbed for use in the post-Soviet period. Separation into quasi-nation states served Moscow's interests in the Soviet years and threatens to do the same in the post-Soviet period.

But there are major obstacles in the way of promoting a common front against Russia and creating a compact Muslim/Turkic cohort within the CIS; such increased unity threatens some Central Asian states more than others. In the southern tier (Turkmenistan, Uzbekistan and Tajikistan), there is a general fear that Uzbekistan would acquire leverage over the rest. The Tajiks, as a non-Turkic people, hold back on principle. Turkmenistan fears Uzbek dynamism and the dominance of its massive population. The Kazakh/Uzbek competition is centuries old and their leaders, Nursultan Nazarbaev and Karimov, have been intensely jealous of each other.

Developments over the course of 1992–93 sorted out some of the uncertainties and moved things in a direction that has brought greater involvement of Russia in the region and increased the power and prestige of Uzbekistan and its leader Karimov. In January 1993, the leaders of the five states proclaimed a common commitment to 'Central Asia' as an entity with a promising future, and some steps were taken to promote relations on a regional basis. Russia's military involvement in Tajikistan, which all of Central Asia's incumbent politicians agreed was necessary, may persuade them to transcend differences.

Assuming that steps taken to seal the Afghan border are successful, and that within Tajikistan some sort of reconciliation takes place, normality may return to the region.[27] But what is normal in Central Asian conditions and what does the political stabilization of the present regimes imply for the future? In the southern-tier states authoritarian political regimes are likely to be around for some time to come. The promise of pluralism will have to be implemented in the economic realm before prospects for political democratization become real.

The near-term difficulties that the Karimov regime (and others) are likely to face in the Fergana region should not be underestimated. The conventional wisdom that Tashkent has exaggerated the Islamic fundamentalist threat has some merit; but this should not lead to the facile conclusion that Karimov's fears are based on a mirage; Fergana is in fact a boiling cauldron of economic and ethnic tensions ready to overflow at almost any time with terrible consequences for Uzbekistan, Tajikistan, and especially Kyrgyzstan.

Nor should the focus on Uzbekistan's nationalist and hegemonic tendencies lead to minimizing the reality of regional differences arising within Uzbekistan; centrifugal tendencies there are real, not imaginary. It would not come as a surprise to see Bukhara emerge as an autonomous if not an independent area in the not-too-distant future. A movement for political unification of the Fergana Valley, which would threaten more than Uzbekistan, is something that should be anticipated. In addition, it is in the Namangan region of Fergana that religious fundamentalism has surfaced. Thus, regional fragmentation of some sort – if not disintegration on the Tajik model (one hopes without bloodshed) – while not likely, should not be excluded.

Any evaluation of Karimov's internal politics should take into account this threat from his own regional élites. In recent informal remarks during his visit to the UN, he hinted as much when he observed that regional disintegration posed the greatest danger for Eltsin.[28] It is inexplicable that all commentators on Uzbekistan focus only on national or religious facets of problems or stress economic dilemmas. Indeed, these are there, but they should be factored through a geopolitical framework, if we are to anticipate the future.

The increased role of Uzbekistan in Central Asia generally is an ongoing trend and, assuming Uzbekistan contains its internal problems, its increased role in Central Asia is likely to continue for some time to come; this should produce a reaction from its neighbours. For this reason, pan-Turkic unity or a Turkestan/Central Asia confederation is a very distant prospect; other leaders hesitate to risk taking any steps toward regional unity because of the fear that Uzbek hegemony will follow. However, Russia's increased presence on the Central Asian stage may stimulate movement in that direction. It all depends on whether Central Asian élites fear Uzbekistan or Russia more and how they interpret and react to the Tajik catastrophe.

NOTES

1. For a detailed explanation of the 'geopolitical approach' and its application to leadership politics in Uzbekistan, see Donald S. Carlisle, 'The Uzbek Power Elite: Politburo and Secretariat (1938–83)', *Central Asian Survey*, 5, 3/4 (1986), pp. 91–132.
2. This argument is presented and documented in Donald S. Carlisle, 'Soviet Uzbekistan: State and Nation in Historical Perspective', in Beatrice F. Manz (ed.), *Soviet Central Asia in Historical Perspective* (Boulder: Westview Press, 1994).
3. The original settlers who created the region's civilization were groups whose descendants were known as Tajiks and who were Persian in culture. In the wake of the Arab conquest, the culture was islamicized. Subsequently, the hordes of Genghis Khan conquered the area. Thereafter, the high-point of Central Asian civilization was the Chagatay period when Tamerlane established his capital at Samarkand in the 14th century.
   In the 15th century, Turkic nomads from the north, the Uzbeks, conquered the region. Eventually the Uzbeks adapted to the urban civilization and adopted Islam; they moved their capital from Samarkand to Bukhara. By the late nineteenth century, antagonism between Uzbeks and Tajiks had been partially sublimated and a hybrid entity known as the 'Sart' was emerging, especially in urban centres.
4. Early in the twentieth century, *jadids* emerged throughout Central Asia to challenge the grip of Islamic obscurantism; initially they sought to westernize the educational system and to make room for the study of secular subjects. Later, in the wake of the 1905 Russian revolution and the 'Young Turk' takeover in the Ottoman Empire, they moved in a political direction. In fact, the radical jadidists in Bukhara called themselves the 'Young Bukharans'.
5. As a reward – or more likely as punishment – Muhiddinov was sent to Dushanbe to serve as the first chairman of Tajikistan's Sovnarkom, a post he held until 1929. He was replaced in that year but remained active in the government for a while. In 1933 he was arrested and then disappeared.
6. In late 1919 V. V. Kuibyshev had been sent to Tashkent by Lenin as a member of the so-called 'Turkestan Commission'. In Sept. 1920 he went to Soviet Bukhara as emissary for Moscow and the Comintern. During this time, he became an especially close friend of Faizulla Khojaev. It is the contention here that Kuibyshev (and Sergo Ordzhonikidze who travelled to Bukhara) were the main lobbyists in Moscow for Bukhara's interests.
7. M. Kalinin, *Izbrannye proizvedeniia, Tom I (1917–1925)* (Moscow, 1960), p. 630.
8. From 1925 until 1937 there was a political tug-of-war between Faizulla Khojaev, who headed the government, and Akmal Ikramov, the Communist Party chief. Ikramov, who initially benefited from Khojaev's arrest in June 1937, was himself arrested in September. Both were tried and sentenced to death at the infamous Moscow Show Trial in March 1938.
9. See Carlisle, 'Power and Politics in Soviet Uzbekistan: From Stalin to Gorbachev', especially pp. 99–103, in William Fierman, *Soviet Central Asia. The Failed Transformation* (Boulder: Westview Press, 1991).
10. For an extended treatment of the Rashidov era set in the context of Soviet Uzbekistan's history, see Carlisle, 'Uzbekistan and the Uzbeks', *Problems of Communism* (Sept.–Oct. 1991), pp. 23–44.
11. In fact, Tel'man Gdlian and Nikolai Ivanov of the All-Union General Prosecutor's Office were appointed to look into corruption in Uzbekistan in Sept. 1982; see also note 36 in Demian Vaisman, 'Regionalism and Clan Loyalty in the Political Life of Uzbekistan', in this volume.
12. The story is told in detail in James Critchlow, *Nationalism in Uzbekistan* (Boulder: Westview Press, 1991); the figure is given in FBIS-SOV-88-183, 21 Sept. 1988 (cf. Vaisman, 'Regionalism and Clan Loyalty').
13. For details on individual cases of repression, and there were many, see Helsinki Watch, *Human Rights in Uzbekistan* (May 1993).
14. During two trips to Uzbekistan (Oct. 1992 and Jan. 1993), I raised this question with everyone I met, both inside and outside the government; there was a consensus that the timing of the demonstration was suspicious and should be related to Mirsaidov's

fall from power. Tashkent's power élite – both formal and informal – was unreconciled to Karimov's rule. His main intra-élite problem has, in fact, been to bring Tashkent under his control. I believe that as of early 1994, this has not been achieved.

15. See *Pravda vostoka*, 8-9 Nov. 1992.
16. Barnett R. Rubin, *The Fragmentation of Tajikistan*, (unpub. manuscript), p. 6. The best study of Tajikistan's political history is Teresa Rakowska-Harmstone, *Russia and Nationalism in Central Asia* (Baltimore: Johns Hopkins Press, 1971). An analysis which deals with more recent developments is Muriel Atkin, 'Tajikistan: Ancient Heritage; New Politics', in I. Bremmer and R. Taras (eds.), *Nations & Politics in the Soviet Successor States* (Cambridge: Cambridge University Press, 1993), pp. 361–83.
17. Rubin, *The Fragmentation of Tajikistan*, pp. 5–6.
18. The same tactic was used in Uzbek politics. Rashidov's enemies, in order to discredit him, said that he was a Tajik. Recently the same charge has been made about Karimov; there is something in this contention since Karimov's mother was Tajik.
19. *Moscow News*, No. 45 (8–15 Nov. 1992), p. 1.
20. Arkady Dubnov, 'The Tajikistan Catastrophe', *New Times* 4 (Jan. 1993), p. 10.
21. Ibid., p. 11.
22. Ibid. For a more detailed analysis of Tajikistan's political scene, see Grigorii Kosach, 'Political Parties in an Inchoate National Space', in this volume.
23. Bess Brown, 'Central Asian States Seek Russian Help', *RFE/RL Research Report* 2, 25 (18 June 1993).
24. By Feb. 1994 Abdulojanov had been removed. He was replaced by a 44-year old technocrat named Abdujalil Samadov. This may mark a victory of the south over the north and a decline in the fortunes of Khujand (and Tashkent) in Tajikistan. Since this key personnel change is unlikely to have been taken without Moscow's approval, does this also signify a turn in Russian-Uzbek relations and a new phase in the struggle for hegemony in Tajik affairs?
25. See Igor Rotar, 'Will Central Asia Explode?', *Nezavisimaia gazeta*, 21 Jan. 1993, trans. in *Current Digest of the Post-Soviet Press* XLV, 3 (1993), pp. 9–12.
26. Igor Rotar, 'A Mine Laid By the Kremlin Mapmakers', *Nezavisimaia gazeta*, 22 Dec. 1992, trans. in *Current Digest of the Post-Soviet Press* XLV, 1 (1993).
27. See Kevin Martin, 'Tajikistan: Civil War without End?', *RFL/RL Research Report* 2, 33 (20 Aug. 1993).
28. On 28 Sept. 1993 Karimov spoke at a private dinner in New York City. It was arranged by the Neumount Mining Company of Colorado. This is my interpretation of his remarks, which I relate to the geopolitical framework presented in this chapter. The contention is that Uzbekistan is a fragile entity made up of major regions (Bukhara, Fergana, Tashkent etc.), that have a life of their own and which have the potential for undermining the integrity of the state in a crisis. I submit that the problem of regions is central to Karimov's intra-élite politics and his domestic manoeuvring.

DONALD S. CARLISLE

MAP 5.1 CENTRAL ASIAN REPUBLICS BEFORE NATIONAL DELIMITATION

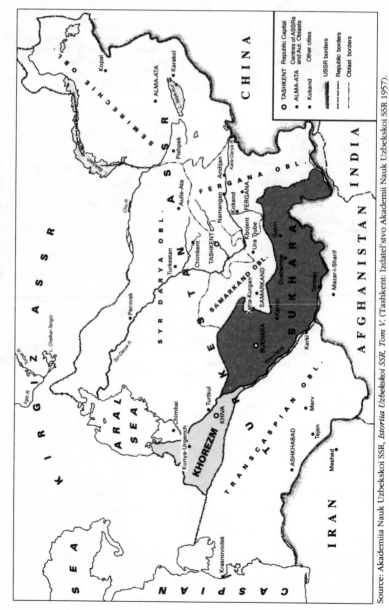

Source: Akademiia Nauk Uzbekskoi SSR, *Istoriia Uzbekskoi SSR, Tom V.* (Tashkent: Izdatel'stvo Akademii Nauk Uzbekskoi SSR 1957).

MAP 5.2 CENTRAL ASIAN REPUBLICS AFTER NATIONAL DELIMITATION

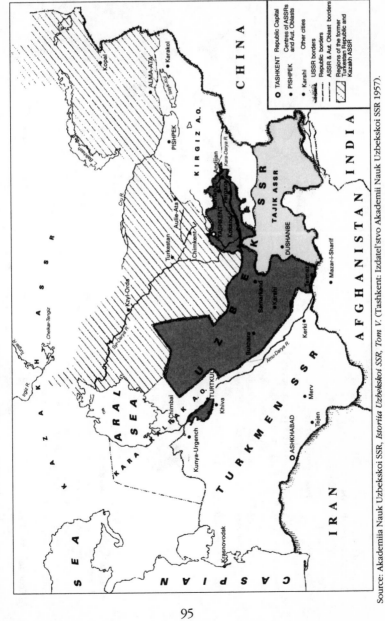

Source: Akademiia Nauk Uzbekskoi SSR, *Istoriia Uzbekskoi SSR, Tom V.* (Tashkent: Izdatel'stvo Akademii Nauk Uzbekskoi SSR 1957).

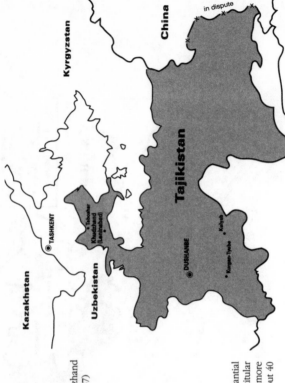

MAP 5.3 TAJIKISTAN

Declared independence 9 September 1991

Basic Demographic Data

Total population: 5,248,000 (1990)

Growth rate: 3.0% (1979–89)

Urban: 33%   Rural: 67% (1989)

Net migration rate: 2.4 migrants/1,000 population (1979–88);
                        7.7 migrants/1,000 population (1989–90)

Birth rate: 38.7 births/1,000 population (1989)

Age composition: 0–14, 43%; 15–24, 19%; 25–64, 34%; 65+, 4% (1989)

Largest cities (population in thousands): Dushanbe, 602 (1989); Khudzhand (formerly Leninabad), 163 (1989); Kulyab, 77 (1987); Kurgan-Tiube, 59 (1987)

Ethnic Composition (per cent)

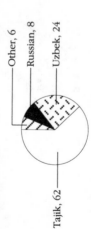

Other, 6
Russian, 8
Uzbek, 24
Tajik, 62

Trends in Ethnic Composition

Tajikistan was the fastest growing republic during the 1980s, despite substantial outmigration. This is because Tajiks have the highest birth rate of all 15 titular nationalities. The Tajik proportion of the republic's population grew by more than 3 percentage points between 1979 and 1989. Tajiks make up only about 40 per cent of the population of Dushanbe, the republic capital.

Economic Significance

A primarily agricultural republic, Tajikistan produces cotton, fruit and vegetable oil. The republic also boasts significant hydroelectric potential.

96

MAP 5.4 'DISPUTED AREAS'

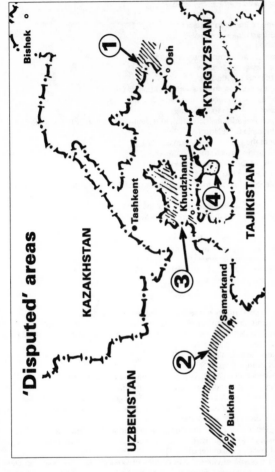

KEY

1. Fergana Valley, Kyrgyzstan.
2. Parts of Samarkand and Bukhara Provinces (Zeravshan Valley).
3. Tajikistan territory that was part of Uzbekistan, 1924-1929.
4. Isfara-Batken conflict (enclave immediately to right of number is part of Tajikstan; the two enclaves to its right are parts of Uzbekistan).

Map drawn by Vladimir Streletsky, Institute of Geography, Russian Academy of Sciences.

DONALD S. CARLISLE

APPENDIX 5.1 MAP OF UNREST IN THE USSR

WHO CLAIMS WHAT?
Main territorial-ethnic claims and conflicts in the USSR
WEST

1. Part of Murmansk Region of Russia to Karelia (A)
2. Part of Pskov and Leningrad regions of Russia (A)
3. Part of Latvia to Estonia (F)
4. Establishment of Russian-speaking autonomy in Estonia (B)
5. Part of Pskov Region of Russia to Latvia (A)
6. North-western part of Belarus to Lithuania (C)
7. Establishment of a Policy autonomy in the south of Lithuania (B)
8. Klaipeda with surrounding area to secede from Lithuania (C)
9. Part of Kaliningrad Region of Russia to Lithuania (C)
10. Creation of a German political-administrative unit in Kaliningrad Region of Russia (C)
11. Southern disttricts of Lithuania to Belarus (A)
12. Part of Zhitomir Region of the Ukraine to Byelorussia (A)
13. Part of Gomel Region of Byelorussia to the Ukraine (A)
14. Part of Chernovtsy Region of the Ukraine to Moldova (C)
15. Northern part of Moldova to the Ukraine (A)
16. Creation of the Dniester SSR Moldova in the south-east of Moldova and the north-west of Odessa Region of the Ukraine (C)
17. Creation of the Gagauz autonomy in the south of Moldova (B)
18. Creation of Bulgarian autonomy on the borderlands of Moldova and Odessa Region of the Ukraine (B)
19. Part of Odessa Region of the Ukraine to Moldova (A)
20. Creation of the Crimean Tatar Republic in the Crimea (B)
21. Secession of the Crimea from the Ukraine (D)
22. South-eastern Region of the Ukraine to Russia (B)
23. Part of Rostov Region of Russia to the Ukraine (A)

CAUCASUS

24. Seaside districts of Krasnodar Territory to the Adygei Autonomous Region (B)
25. Creation of the Karachai and Circassian Republics (C)
26. Creation of the Kabardin and Balkar Republics as part of the federative Kabardino-Balkaria (C)
27. Creation of the Karachai-Balkar Republics (E)
28. Creation of the Kabardino-Circassian Republic (E)
29. Restoration of autonomy of Ingushetia (D)
30. Eastern part of North Ossetia to the Chechen-Ingush Autonomous Republic (C)
31. Part of North Ossetia with city of Mozdok to Kabardino-Balkaria (C)
32. Part of Chechen-Ingush Autonomous Republic with city of Malgobek to Kabardino-Balkaria (C)
33. Creation of a united Circassian Republic within the boundaries of Circassia, Kabardin and Adygei Republics and the seaside districts of Krasnodar Territory (C)
34. Western districts of Daghestan to the Chechen-Ingush Autonomous Republic (B)
35. Restoration of the Gorskaya Republic within the boundaries of the Chechen-Ingush Republics North Ossetia, Kabardin and Circassian Republics (D)
36. Creation (restoration) of ethnic and cultural autonomies of Cossacks in Krasnodar and Stavropol territories; of Greeks on the seacoast of Krasnodar Territory; of Turkmens in Stavropol Territory; of Noghays in Stavropol Territory and the north of Daghestan; of Germans in Krasnodar Territory (B)
37. Territory of Greater Sochi to Georgia (A)
38. Secession of Abhasia from Georgia (G)
39. Secession of South Ossetia from Georgia (G)
40. Creation of the South Ossetian Autonomous Republic as part of Georgia (G)
41. Abolition of the South Ossetian autonomy (G)
42. Unification of South and North Ossetia (E)
43. Nagorny Karabakh to Armenia (E)
44. South-western part of Georgia (Dzhavakheti) to Armenia (B)
45. South-eastern part of Georgia to Azerbaijan (B)
46. North-western part of Azerbaijan to Georgia (B)
47. Southern part of Armenia to Azerbaijan (B)
48. Abolition of Adzhar Autonomous Republic (G)
49. Restoration of Shaumyanovsky District in Azerbaijan (B)
50. Return of Meskhetian Turks to their historical homeland (B)

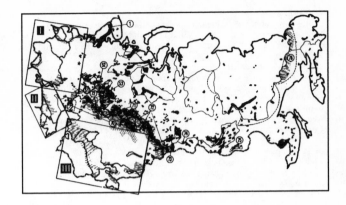

MAIN FACTORS OF CONFLICT

A. change of borders
B. settlement of corresponding ethnic groups in the past and today
C. A+B
D. past changes in the status of autonomy or its territorial-state status
E. historical, ethnic and/or economic unity
F. B+E
G. revival or suppression of national consciousness

SYMBOLS

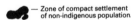 — Zone of compact settlement of non-indigenous population.

— Same in boxes.

—Zone of conflict.

— Territories that changed their adminstrative status.

— Open clashes resulting in casualties.

WHERE THE CLAIMS COME FROM

① — The press.

② — The programmes of influential socio-political movements

③ — Declarations at the state level

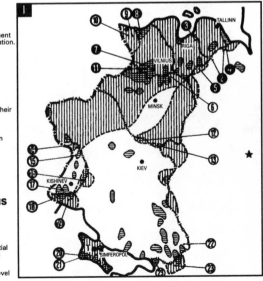

DONALD S. CARLISLE

THE VOLGA REGION
51. Creaton (restoration) of the Republic of Germans in the Volga Region (D)
52. Partition of Tataria into districts of Kazan Tatars and Mesharis (B)
53. Creation of a united Bashtatarstan; mutual territorial claims of Bashkiria and Tataria (F)

CENTRAL ASIA AND KAZAKHSTAN
54. Secession of Kara-Kalpak Autonomous Republic from Uzbekistan (G)
55. Annexation of Kara-Kalpakia to Kazakhstan (D)
56. Part of Mangistausky Region of Kazakhstan to Turkmenia (B)
57. Amu-Darya part of Tashauz Region of Turkmenia to Uzbekistan (F)
58. North-western part of Bukhara Region of Uzbekistan to Kara-Kalpakia (A)
59. South-eastern part of Kara-Kalpakia to Khorezm Region of Uzbekistan (F)
60. Amu-Darya part of Chardzhou Region of Turkmenia to Uzbekistan (F)
61. Amu-Darya part of Bukhara Region of Uzbekistan to Turkmenia (F)
62. Southern part of Chemkent Region of Kazakhstan to Uzbekistan (F)
63. Parts of Samarkand and Bukhara regions of Uzbekistan (Zeravshan River Valley) to Tajikistan (F)
64. Surkhan-Darya Region of Uzbekistan to Tajikistan (F)
65. Southern mountainous regions of Osh Region of Kirghizia to Tajikistan (F)
66. Part of the Gorno-Badskhshan Autonomous Region of Tajikistan (northern Pamir-Alai) to Kirghizia (F)
67. Part of Osh Region of Kirghizia (in Ferghana Valley) to Uzbekistan
68. Southern districts of Alma-Ata and Taldy-Kurgan regions of Kazakhstan to Kirghizia (F)
69. Northern districts of Issyk-Kul Region of Kirghizia to Kazakhstan (F)
70. Part of Russia's regions bordering on Kazakhstan (Astrakhan, Volgograd, Orenburg, Omsk, Kurgan, Altai Territory and others) to Kazakhstan (C)
71. Creation of German political-administrative units in North Kazakhstan and neighbouring districts of Russia (B)
72. North Kazakhstan, Kokchetav, Tselinograd, Kustanai, East Kazakhstan, the Irtysh part of Pavlodar and Semipalatinsk, northern parts of the Urals and Aktyubinsk regions of Kazakhstan to Russia (B)

SIBERIA AND FAR EAST
73. Eastern part of Gorno-Altai Autonomous Region to Tuva (B)
74. Part of Krasnoyarsk Territory to Tuva (B)
75. Annexation of Achinskoye Buryat Autonomous Region to the Buryat Republic (D)
76. Part of Magadan Region to Yakutia (A)

Letters on the map indicate the districts of the present-day settlements of deported Germans (G), Koreans (K), Crimean Tatars (T) striving to return to their historical homeland and/or ethnic-territorial autonomy.

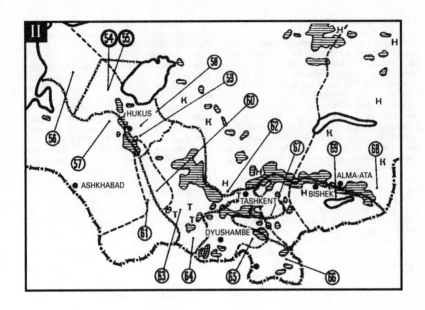

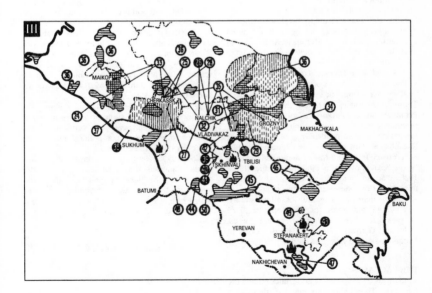

DONALD S. CARLISLE

CENTRAL ASIA AND KAZAKHSTAN

Inhabited from antiquity by peoples of Iranian and Turkic (or Turkic-Mongolian) origin, Soviet Central Asia and Kazakhstan have accepted over the past and current centuries millions of newcomers from other parts of the country.

In the past few years, the area has seen the horrors of the Ferghana and Osh carnages, bloody dramas in Alma-Ata and Dushanbe, and armed conflicts on the pastures of the Pamir-Alai mountains and the Novy Uzen oil fields. The reasons for escalating ethnic clashes lie in the economic, social and political instability that is characteristic of the entire Soviet Union, having deep historic roots.

There are several factors which contribute to the worsening situation in the Asian Republics. First, there is the varied ethnic composition of the population in the Ferghana Valley, the areas adjoining Lake Issyk-Kul, Semirechye (a historical territory located in the south-east of Kazakhstan and north of Kirghizia, named for the seven rivers which flow through its territory), and several other regions.

Second, the current national-administrative division into Republics has a short history dating back only to the early years of Soviet power. The new boundaries cut through formerly mono-lithnic states. The Bukhara Emirate was divided between Uzbekistan, Turkmenistan and Tajikistan, the Khiva Khanate – between Uzbekistan, Kara-Kalpakstan, Turkmenistan and Kazakhstan, and the Kokand Khanate – between Uzbekistan, Tajikistan, Kyrghyzstan and Kazakhstan.

Thirdly, several Asian peoples living for centuries on the same territory consider themselves rightful heirs to the cultural traditions of their ancestors. For example, both present-day Uzbeks and Tajiks claim to be descendants of Timur and Ulugh Beg and heirs to the great cultural tradition from Al-Biruni to Avicenna and Jami. In 1924–1926, when new boundaries were set, some of the Uzbeks were registered as 'Tajiks', and some Tajiks as 'Uzbeks'.

Fourth, the memories of one's historical native land are still strong. For example, large groups of Turkmenians once inhabited the Mangyshlak Peninsula in Kazakhstan; a group of Kirghiz populated the Karategin country in Tajikistan; many Uzbeks lived near the city of Chemkent in Kazakhstan. Many of them, like Karategin Kirghiz, were ousted from their historical motherland long before Soviet power was established there. In the 1920s, Soviet authorities organized massive migrations from one Asian Republic to another.

Lastly, there are demands for administrative and cultural autonomy for, and repatriation of peoples that suffered during the Stalinist purges, including Germans, Koreans, Kurds, Crimean Tartars, Assyrian-Aysors and Meskhetian Turks.

THE CAUCASUS

As many as 60 indigenous nationalities inhabit the Caucasus. Thoroughly inter-mingled, they often belong to different language groups and even to different language families, the mountainous landscape contributing to the secluded way of life of many of them. Two world religions – Christianity and Islam – meet here.

The Caucasus is home to four Union Republics, seven Autonomous Republics and four Autonomous Regions. Only in this area (specifically in the Northern Caucasus) can one find autonomies embracing two nationalities: Karachais and Circassians, Kabardinians and Balkars, Chechens and Ingush (in Daghestan alone there are more than 30 nationalities). Only in the Caucasus do people of one nationality have their autonomies separated by the boundaries of Union Republics: Ossetian autonomies exist both in the Russian Federation and Georgia, while Armenians have an Autonomous Region in Azerbaijan known as Nagorny Karabakh.

Nowhere have the boundaries of politico-administrative units changed so often as in the Northern Caucasus, particularly in the 1920s, 30s and 50s. Just more than half of its terriotory has retained its administrative division.

Deportation is a special feature of the history of the Caucasian peoples. All in all, more than 600,000 people, among them Meskhetian Turks, Kurds, Karachais, Balkars, Ingush and Chechens were forced to leave their homeland. These areas were promptly settled by other peoples who now lay claims to the territory they occupy.

Most of the demands being voiced today in the Caucasus have to do with the restoration of former administrative-territorial units or the upgrade in the status of already existing ones. There are demands to set up separate autonomies for Karachais and Circassians, to create a federation for Kabardinians and Balkars and to restore autonomy for the Ingush people. Abkhasians and South Ossetians want to secede from Georgia.

A specific feature of all these national-territorial claims is that the move to reunite with fellow-nationals is seen as a means of survival. The most vivid example here are appeals to restore the Mountain Autonomous Republic which existed until the early 1920 and was known as the Gorskaya ASSR.

Quite often territorial claims against one neighbouring national come up against territorial claims from another neighbour. Territorial claims are put forward by major political movements and even at government level.

Contradictions arising from territorial disputes in the Caucasus now total around thirty. But talking to the local population gives the impression that there are no territories in the area which cannot be called into question. All this is taking place in a region rich in land and resources.

Source: *Moscow News* weekly, No. 11, 1991.

APPENDIX 5.2 PROSPECTS OF CONFLICT

	KYRGYZSTAN	UZBEKISTAN	TURKMENISTAN
Likelihood of national-territorial conflicts	Significant	Insignificant	Significant
Likelihood of regional conflicts	Significant	Insignificant	Significant
Likelihood of islamization	None	Significant	None
Likelihood of getting out of the crisis on its own	Miniscule	Significant	Significant
Political style of republic leadership	Democracy	Authoritarianism	Authoritarianism
Irrigated land per capita (hectares)	0.29	0.20	0.33

6

Regionalism and Clan Loyalty in the Political Life of Uzbekistan

DEMIAN VAISMAN

A significant role is played in the political life of the Central Asian republics by what can be described as 'traditionalism'. There are few studies on this theme, though publications on it have recently become more frequent.[1] The term 'traditionalism' is understood as the way of life based on customs, traditions and rules of conduct accepted in a pre-industrial society. One manifestation of traditionalism are the political forces in a regional clan-based society such as Uzbekistan, which are the result of the ethnic history of its people . The aim of this chapter is to analyze the impact of some aspects of traditionalism on the political life of Uzbekistan, the most populous state in Central Asia.

The creation of the modern Uzbek people was a complex development. Until the 19th century the territory of Central Asia was divided between the khanates of Bukhara, Kokand and Khiva which were ruled by Uzbek dynasties. These states were not ethnically homogeneous; their inhabitants included, among others, Turkmen, Tajiks, Arabs, Bukharan Jews, along with the Uzbeks. Even by the beginning of the 20th century, the Uzbek ethnos was still in the making. One illustration of this was the fact that the inhabitants of cities and their vicinities continued to call themselves 'Tashkentis', 'Bukharans' or 'Samarkandis', instead of using the ethnic self-appellation 'Uzbeks'.[2] Moreover, the Uzbeks considered themselves not only Uzbeks but also members of regional, local and tribal communities.

In the course of the events that followed the 1917 October Revolution, the Turkestan Governorate, the Bukharan Emirate and the Khiva Khanate vanished from the political map. In the middle of the 1920s the Bolsheviks created new states on the territory of Central Asia: Uzbekistan, Turkmeniia, Tajikistan and Kirgiziia, thus dividing the different nationalities from each other. This process was accompanied by attacks on the traditional power structures, which forced them to find ways to adapt to the new realities. While doing so, the traditional power structures tried to preserve their main elements in order to achieve a synthesis. Were they successful? It appears that they were indeed, especially in view of the events in Central Asia following the disintegration of the USSR at the end of 1991.

The forming of traditional power structures begins at the *mahalla* level. This term is derived from the Arab word meaning 'a city neighbourhood'. The *mahalla* system of territorial rule dates back many centuries. Each *mahalla* incorporated several dozens of families held together by either kinship or profession, and grouped around the neighbourhood mosque. In the Uzbek regions of the Khiva Khanate at the end of the 19th century, *mahalla*s were called *mechet'-qaums* (mosque communities). They were headed by *aksakals* (or elders, literally 'whitebeards'), who were men of means. An *aksakal* maintained order and carried out the instructions of the authorities. He was not paid and the *mechet'-qaum* provided him with a livelihood.[3]

It is characteristic that at the beginning of the 1920s, after the khanate was abolished, the *mechet'-qaum* was preserved as the basic form of social organization. According to the Constitution of the Khorezm People's Soviet Republic (KPSR), the executive power in the *mechet'-qaums* belonged to the *aksakals*, as before. But, to distinguish them from the khan's *aksakals*, they were called 'red *aksakals*' (*kyzyl-aksakal*). In 1923, there were 430 such *aksakals* in the 14 *shuras* (regional councils) of the KPSR.[4]

Today in Uzbekistan the *mahalla* is still an efficiently working system of regional government.[5] As before, it is headed by an *aksakal* chosen by a general meeting of the inhabitants. Preference is given to persons occupying eminent positions in society. Everybody, irrespective of his position in society, must obey the *aksakal* in matters of internal order. Nobody is better informed than the *aksakal* concerning the social position of each family. The *mahalla* system of self-government has, however, changed somewhat. Now, an elected *mahalla* committee helps the *aksakal*. The committee coordinates the activities of the internal organizations of the *mahalla*: the women's council, the veterans' council, the funeral commission, etc. The mahalla committee controls a fund which is collected by the inhabitants and from which it helps the needy and finances expensive rites such as marriage ceremonies, funerals or memorials that are held on the seventh, twentieth and fortieth day after the death of a relative, as well as after a year. When someone dies, the family of the deceased does not prepare food for three days; it is fed by the *mahalla*. There is also a custom in the *mahalla* called *khashar*, voluntary work for the benefit of all the *mahalla*'s members. People help each other in building and repairing houses, in cleaning irrigation canals, etc.[6]

Several *mahallas* compose a *raion* union. These *raions* form a traditional hierarchical structure that serves as a power basis for regional political élite groupings. As a rule, they are headed by a man from a locally well-known family group. This system of power is indeed a replica of the pre-Bolshevik power structure. The principle of 'democratic centralism', the theoretical basis of Bolshevik rule, was integrated completely into the feudal system of power, contributing to its preservation and consolidation. Only the names of the offices held by local politicians were changed. Rashidov (First Secretary of Uzbekistan's Communist Party in the years 1959–83) would previously have been the republic's khan or emir; the party Bureau, his vizirs; and the central party bureaucrats, court figures along the Bukharan, Kokand or Khivan patterns. It could also be argued that the secretaries of Uzbekistan *oblast* party committees ruled their provinces as *beks* had governed their bekdoms in pre-revolutionary Bukhara.[7] Under the Bolsheviks, regional political élite groupings too were formed, as in the past, on the basis of large historical regions that could comprise an economic zone and incorporate several administrative divisions.

THE REGIONS

The term 'region' usually means a territory larger than an *oblast*. The term describes larger subdivisions of Uzbekistan, that were formed in the course of history and were united by the similarities in the way of life and by the language of the local inhabitants.

The Fergana Valley includes three *oblasts*: Andijan, Namangan and Fergana. In the 18th–19th centuries the region was part of the Kokand Khanate which was destroyed after the conquest of Central Asia by Russia. The climate of the valley is most favourable to agriculture; consequently, the majority of the local population traditionally works on the land. The Fergana Valley, which is a very important cotton-growing centre, is the most densely populated area of Uzbekistan. While in 1989 the average number of inhabitants per square kilometre in the whole of Uzbekistan was 45.4, in Andijan Oblast it was 419.3, in Namangan Oblast 191.7, and in Fergana Oblast 308.2.[8]

Khorezm region includes the Khorezm Oblast and the Karakalpak Autonomous Republic. Khorezm is an ancient land which was known as early as the 5th–4th centuries BCE. The centre of the *oblast*, the city of Urgench, was from the 11th–13th centuries the capital of a mighty empire and a large cultural and trade centre. From the 16th to the beginning of the 20th centuries the region of Khorezm was a part of the Khiva Khanate, and in 1920–24 – part of the KPSR. At present, it too is a major cotton-growing region and here also the majority of the population works in agriculture.[9]

The Samarkand-Bukhara region includes two *oblasts*: those of Samarkand and Bukhara which centre on two most important nuclei of ancient oriental civilization. For many centuries, these cities were centres of the caravan trade between Europe and Asia (the 'silk route'). From the end of the 16th century up to the Russian conquest of Central Asia, the territory of these *oblasts* was part of the Bukharan Emirate. One of the regional centres, Samarkand, was in 1924–30 the capital of Uzbekistan. Samarkand is the second most important city after Tashkent from the point of view of both its population and its industrial development. The city of Bukhara is also a cultural and industrial centre, but agriculture is the main occupation of the *oblasts'* population.[10]

The Tashkent region consists of the city of Tashkent and Tashkent Oblast. Tashkent is a large centre of industry, transportation and culture. Historical sources first mention its existence as early as the 4th–5th centuries. It began to grow rapidly in the second half of the 19th century due to developing trade with Russia. In 1865 Tashkent was annexed to the Russian Empire, and in 1867 it became the administrative centre of the Turkestan General-Governorate. By the turn of the 20th century the Trans-Caspian railway reached Tashkent and later the Orenburg-Tashkent line was constructed. The railroads transformed the city into a main railway junction, and the trade and transport centre of Central Asia. This status has been preserved up to the present. From 1930, Tashkent became the capital of Uzbekistan. Tashkent Oblast, with Tashkent as its capital, is the most industrially developed part of the republic.[11]

The Kashka-Darya—Surkhan-Darya region consists of the two southern *oblasts* of Kashka-Darya and Surkhan-Darya. Until 1920 the territory was a part of the Bukharan Emirate. At present the region is a cotton-growing centre and its industrial development is at a low level. The largest cities are Karshi, Termez and Shakhrisabz. The latter two were administrative and trade centres already in ancient times. In the 18th–19th centuries, Shakhrisabz was the capital of an independent Shakhrisabz state ruled by a *bek*.[12]

CLANS AND POLITICS: THE CASE OF SHARAF RASHIDOV

Since its creation, power in the republic of Uzbekistan has been held by three regional élite groupings: those of Fergana, Samarkand and Tashkent. Periodically replacing each other at the top party and state positions, their representatives controlled the main power structures (see Appendix 6.1).[13] A regional élite consists of clans that are connected by blood relationships and/or a common place of birth. The inner relationships within a clan are based on principles of paternalism, hierarchy and coercion, thus forming an institution of government characteristic of a traditional rural community. The main bearers of the traditional mentality are the villagers. In 1990, Uzbekistan's rural population still comprised 59 per cent of the total population.[14] The villagers are accustomed to the idea of a society built on the extended family model, in which family elders have indisputable authority. In accordance with the traditional mentality, the role played by a political leader is comparable to that of a family/clan head. A bitter competitive struggle is constantly waged, in which the strongest clans become predominant. It is their leaders that later occupy key positions in a regional élite. This further enables them to contend for positions in the republican power bodies. Whilst occupying these positions, they are able in turn to exercise control over society and, more importantly, to influence the distribution process of material goods.

A characteristic example of the functioning of a leading political clan is provided by that of Sharaf Rashidov which belonged to the Samarkand-Bukhara regional élite. There is no evidence that this clan existed in any form before the establishment of Bolshevik power. One may assume it was just a result of the social consolidation that accompanied this process. The clan representatives connected to the pre-revolutionary establishment were removed from their leadership roles as early as the first half of the 1920s. The coalition of clans led by Akmal Ikramov and Faizulla Khojaev supported by smaller clans that eventually replaced them, represented the Tashkent and Bukhara *oblasts*. The clans of Ikramov and Khojaev were politically defeated and, in the main, physically destroyed during the purges of the 1930s. The purges continued up to Stalin's death. The total number of those arrested in Uzbekistan from 1939–53 was 61,799, of whom 7,100 were executed. Among them were a large number of party, state, economic and military functionaries, as well as intelligentsia.[15] Taking into account the system of the formation of leading cadres that were, for the most part, recruited from the ranks of the ruling regional élite groupings, one may conclude that they comprised the main mass of those persecuted. The repressions created opportunities for the advancement of new leaders from among the regional élites. Sharaf Rashidov was one such leader.

SHARAF RASHIDOV: THE WAY TO THE TOP

The most important condition for the successful functioning of a clan is the personal calibre of its leader. He should possess charisma and indisputable authority. He must be a subtle psychologist. In the eyes of his clan he should be the patriarch, the wise and experienced tribal chief who understands the power mechanisms in a society that, in the main, lives according to the deeply ingrained laws of a rural community. Sharaf Rashidov undoubtedly conformed to these requirements. He was born in November 1917 into a peasant family in Jizak, Samarkand Oblast. Rashidov imbibed with his mother's milk all that was characteristic of a rural community, its hierarchy and system of values. His strong and complex personality was formed against the backdrop of the Bolshevik attempts to destroy the basis of a society that had been formed over the centuries. Adapting to the new conditions, Uzbek society produced new people from its ranks who, while renouncing the less important features, would preserve its main foundations intact. Therefore, histrionic abilities became a main requirement for the new leaders. Indeed, they became the quintessence of Sharaf Rashidov, endowing him with a self-styled wisdom and a kind of self-defence. Rashidov was an exacting and shrewd person and a good organizer. This was noted even by non-sympathizers. One of them, Kamil Ikramov, wrote four years after his death:

> As a journalist, I met him several times, had lengthy conversations with him and I can definitely affirm that he was a very able man, had an excellent memory, and was able to win the favour of any person who saw him for the first time. Rashidov's path to crime was a real personal tragedy. Had Rashidov's sophisticated tactical mind been directed towards chess he would, in due time, have become a chess master, if not a champion.[16]

Rashidov graduated from the pedagogical seminary in Jizak and Samarkand University. In 1935–36 he became a schoolteacher and in 1939 joined the party. From 1937-40 he was the executive secretary and deputy editor of the Samarkand Oblast newspaper *Lenin Yuli* and from 1941 was its chief editor. In August 1941 he was drafted into the army, but in 1942, after being severely wounded at the Volkhov front, was discharged. He was decorated for his active participation in the fighting. Having returned to Samarkand, he again began to work as editor of *Lenin Yuli*.

Rashidov's party career began in 1944, when he was 'elected' secretary of the Samarkand *obkom*.[17] According to Donald S. Carlisle, Rashidov owed his promotion to a Stalin favourite, Usman Yusupov who headed the party organization in the republic from 1937 to

1950.[18] From 1947 Rashidov was editor of the republic's newspaper *Kyzyl Uzbekiston*, and then became chairman of the Writers' Union of Uzbekistan. From 1950 to 1959 Sharaf Rashidov was already one of the three leading figures of the republic – as Chairman of the Presidium of the Uzbek SSR Supreme Soviet.[19] Although this was a purely representative office, it provided him with an opportunity to be seen, to establish contacts in the highest echelons in Moscow. A person who held this office became automatically one of the vice-chairmen of the USSR Supreme Soviet.

The second half of the 1950s was the period when the USSR began to expand its contacts with the developing countries and high-ranking governmental delegations visited the Third World. One of the first such delegations headed by Khrushchev himself visited India at the end of 1955. Rashidov was a member of the delegation, fulfilling the role of a leader representing Soviet Central Asia that flourished under communist rule. Personal acquaintance with Khrushchev soon played a decisive part in Rashidov's career. In spring 1959, after Sabir Kamalov was removed from power, a struggle began for the position of First Secretary of the Central Committee of the Uzbekistan Communist Party. Rashidov was one of the strongest candidates. There was a split vote on his candidature. Eventually all was decided by a vote cast from Moscow, that of Khrushchev. Rasul Gulamov, then a member of the Central Committee Bureau, recalls:

> The date of the Central Committee plenary session was already announced, but the bureau members continued to argue. Then the representatives of the Central Committee of the CPSU who had came to Tashkent for the occasion phoned N. S. Khrushchev: 'The Uzbek comrades still cannot agree.' 'Who is on the candidates' list?' asked the leader of the Union. They read him the list. 'Of them all, I know only Rashidov', Khrushchev said, and this sentence decided the vote in Rashidov's favour.[20]

From March 1959 he became First Secretary of the Communist Party.

RASHIDOV'S CLAN: CONSOLIDATION OF POSITION

In order to consolidate their power, the new clans need first to undermine the influence of the old groupings. Therefore, the first years of dominance of a new clan are a period of purges and cadre shifting. A manifestation of this phenomenon was the replacement, in 1959–65, of five Central Committee secretaries for agriculture, four for industry and two for ideology in Uzbekistan. In each *obkom* three to four secretaries were replaced. Cadre changes at lower levels of the leadership were even more considerable.[21] After this, the situation stabilized.

FAMILY CONNECTIONS

The core clan consists of blood relatives of the family of the clan head, who occupy important positions. The core is extended by marriage connections: Rashidov had one son and four daughters. The son was married to a daughter of the first secretary of the Karakalpak *obkom*, Kalibek Kamalov, who occupied this important position for 21 years. He was a member of the Central Committee Bureau of the Uzbekistan Communist Party and was dismissed only in 1984, one year after the death of his influential relative. The family connection with Kamalov enabled Rashidov to control the Karakalpak Autonomous Republic that occupied a third of Uzbekistan's territory. Clans usually strengthen their position through family connections among regional élite groupings. This cements the clan's power and helps to extend it.

Establishing a family connection between the Rashidov and Muminov families consolidated internal ties within the Samarkand-Bukhara regional élite. The best known of the Muminovs was Ibrahim Muminov (1908–74), born in Samarkand Oblast. His career began in Samarkand, where he lectured in history and philosophy in various institutes. In all probability, it was then that he became acquainted with Rashidov, who was a student at Samarkand State University. Later this acquaintance was strengthened by a marriage union. One of Rashidov's daughters married Muminov's son, who almost immediately became first vice-president of the prestigious Institute of Nuclear Physics of the Uzbek SSR Academy of Sciences.[22] Another daughter became the wife of Muminov's nephew. Ibrahim Muminov himself specialized in Marxist-Leninist philosophy. As vice-president of the Uzbek SSR Academy of Sciences for almost 20 years, responsible for humanities, he played an important role in ideology, directing it into the requisite channels. At three congresses, the 15th, 16th and 17th, of the Uzbekistan Communist Party, Muminov was elected a member of its Central Committee, and for many years he was also a deputy of the republic's Supreme Soviet. The list of positions he held simultaneously occupied a solid portion of his obituary in summer 1974. First among the signatures was, of course, Rashidov's.[23]

As a rule, the clan entrusted close relatives with the most pres-tigious positions. In the 1960s, for instance, Sahib Rashidov, Sharaf's brother, was head of the People's Inspectorate (*narodnyi kontrol'*). Sarvar Azimov and Normakhamadi Khudaiberdyev, both relatives of Rashidov, were Vice-Chairman of the Uzbekistan Council of Ministers and Secretary of the Central Committee of the Uzbekistan Communist Party, respectively. The most important positions were indeed the Central Committee *nomenklatura*, where no serious appointment was made without Rashidov's consent.[24]

In order to strengthen the clan's position, a new Jizak Oblast was formed at the end of 1973. It was made up of nine districts from the Syr-Darya and Samarkand *oblasts*. Jizak, the home city of Rashidov was made its capital.[25] The first secretary there was a relative of Rashidov – U. Turakulov. Rashidov's wife, Khursanda, also played an important role in the life of the clan. In the Qur'an one can find many statements denigrating women, holding their mental capacity in low esteem. For instance, the Qur'an says: 'What! Make they a being to be the offspring of God who is brought up among trinkets, and is ever contentious without reason?'.[26] A wife is totally dependent on her husband, who earns the means to support the family. 'Men are superior to women on account of the qualities with which God hath gifted the one above the other, and on account of the outlay they make from their substance for them.'[27]

The postulates of the Qur'an logically imply the submission of the woman to the man within a family. The home of a Muslim should be divided into two parts: the public and the private one. In the women's half, called *ichkari* by Uzbeks, all the women in the family live and no stranger is admitted. A woman may enter the men's area, called *dyshgari*, only to serve food. According to recollections of people who visited Rashidov's home and had the opportunity to observe his attitude towards his wife, the rules and customs pertaining to a Muslim's home as, for example, the division of the living quarters into separate areas for men and women, were not observed. One reason was that party functionaries of such high rank were obliged to conduct a secular lifestyle, to make their families, at least on the surface, an example of the equality of men and women.

But one should also take into account other aspects. Rashidov who, undoubtedly, was aware of the traditional way of life,[28] spent most of his life in constant intrigues and power struggles, and he regarded his wife Khursanda as his closest and most loyal associate. This fact determined her pivotal position within the clan. Her functions were not limited to creating a pleasant atmosphere within the family. She not only maintained friendly relations with the wives of the Moscow leaders, trying to raise Sharaf Rashidov's prestige in the eyes of the central leadership, but had greater influence than a wife usually has. She actively influenced the positioning of forces within the clan by taking part in its leader's key cadre decisions. An eyewitness remembers:

> The wife, an ambitious and clever woman, interfered in all his [Rashidov's] affairs. He always took her opinion into account. No important decision was made by him without previously consulting her.[29]

Her relatives were an important reserve for Rashidov as he sought to strengthen the clan's position, and were a part of its main core. Khursanda's nephew, Academician Uktam Aripov, for instance, occupied important positions in the republic's health service, and was rector of the Tashkent Medical Institute, which was the largest in Central Asia.

Rashidov's family connections were not advertised. Apparently nobody, except himself, could tell how many of them were integrated into the party apparatus or economic and state structures. 'I never thought that so many leaders were his relatives!', exclaimed one person who had worked with him for many years, at Rashidov's funeral.[30]

After his direct relatives, came Rashidov's companions from his regional élite. Thus, for instance, the key post of Minister of Internal Affairs was occupied for many years by M. Iakhaev who was born in the Samarkand region and who had worked in the apparatus of that same ministry for a long period. R. Gaipov, the very influential secretary of the Kashka-Darya *obkom*, was also a native of Samarkand. The interests of the Fergana élite were also accounted for. M. M. Musakhanov from Fergana region came to be first secretary of the Tashkent *obkom*. All these leaders kept their posts up to Rashidov's death.

Rashidov's attitude to the representatives of the Tashkent regional élite was less benevolent. The reason for this, according to people who worked with him, was his conviction that the natives of Tashkent had lost their awareness of patriarchal values. Tashkent natives were included in the system of power, but, as a rule, were given secondary posts. It is characteristic that during the quarter of a century of Rashidov's regime none of them became Chairman either of the Council of Ministers or of the Supreme Soviet Presidium. Representatives of regional élite groupings who were not part of the ruling triangle also occupied lower rungs on the ladder of power. Anyone who showed the slightest opposition to figures promoted by the clan at any level was punished.[31]

STYLE OF LEADERSHIP

Rashidov was aware that his personal authority within the clan depended on how efficient he was in stemming attempts to undermine his leadership. Therefore, he waged an uncompromising campaign against anything that threatened the clan, or that might destroy its influence in society. According to the Uzbek writer Timur Pulatov, 'any attack against a member of his clan was considered by Rashidov as an attack against himself'.[32] A certain pattern existed in the attitudes of leaders towards their subordinates. Its essence was to prevent the formation of alliances that could become a threat to the clan and its leaders. A member of the Central Committee staff noted in his memoirs:

> 'Divide and rule' was the basis of the relationship between Rashidov and his staff. He was often called a Genghis Khan for his slyness and cruelty. He encouraged informers, and could make best friends quarrel. His tactics were as follows: one of the friends would be invited to his office. As if in passing, he was told that another friend had said something unpleasant about him. After that, the other friend was summoned and told the same. Usually this sufficed for the closest friends to become not only enemies, but informers against each other, to Rashidov.[33]

The clan acted efficiently under Rashidov's leadership. However, from time to time, it did face acute problems, mainly in its relations with the leaders of other regional élite groupings which had attained power by virtue of agreements on the division of spheres of influence. In such cases,. each clan leader would appeal to the supreme arbiter in Moscow, trying to tar his allies' rivals by quoting cases of corruption and power abuse. These court intrigues were an integral part of the power struggle in which there was nothing extraordinary. In an alliance formed on the basis of ambition and private profit, rather than on kinship, personal relations are inevitably weaker.

CRISIS AND STRUGGLE FOR LEADERSHIP

In all probability, there occurred many such crises in the course of Rashidov's rule that were solved by agreements and mutual concessions. However, with the clan-geographic division of power, crises crop up which may threaten the very existence of a coalition of regional élite groupings. The relations between the latter can break down when some members conclude that the leader of an élite clan has risen too high and not taken into due account their own interests; this causes a breach in the rules of conduct accepted in a traditional society. The most serious crisis of Rashidov's leadership was apparently connected to such an occurrence. In 1969, Chairman of the Supreme Soviet Yadgar Nasdriddinova and Secretary of the Central Committee Rafiq Nishanov, representing, respectively, the Tashkent and Fergana regional élite groupings, concluded an alliance with Rahmankul Kurbanov, Chairman of the Council of Ministers, who was of Bukharan extraction and, therefore, close to the core of the Samarkand-Bukhara regional élite. All three were members of the Central Committee Bureau, thus belonging to the inner circle of the political leadership. The conspirators aimed to remove Rashidov from power. Nasreddinova, explaining her reasons for coming out against Rashidov, later recalled:

> His activity as the highest party leader began to manifest autocratic features all too clearly. Over the years, he began to perceive any objections and remarks that I made to him as too acute and painful.[34]

The anti-Russian demonstration at a football match at the Pakhtakor stadium in 1969 seemed to the conspirators a convenient pretext for discrediting Rashidov in the eyes of the Kremlin leaders.[35] In undertaking this action, the leaders of the rival regional élite groupings naturally sought to secure support from Moscow. However, Rashidov's ties there turned out to be stronger. Apparently, Brezhnev himself stood behind him. The well-informed investigators of the USSR Procurator's office, Tal'man Gdlian and Nikolai Ivanov, who were sent to Uzbekistan in 1983 to look into corruption there, have described the relations of these two men as follows: 'The former party leader, Brezhnev, was Rashidov's chief patron. Due to their "special" relationship, Uzbekistan was out of bounds to any critics.'[36]

After the attempt to depose Rashidov had failed, Yadgar Nasdriddinovaa was able, through her connections, to find a position in Moscow as Chairman of the Council of Nationalities of the USSR Supreme Soviet. Nishanov became Ambassador in Ceylon. The fate of the third conspirator, Rahmankul Kurbanov, was less fortunate. He had betrayed his clan and had thus to be punished most severely. Kurbanov was arrested and convicted, and served a long prison term. As a result of the attempted coup, the Fergana regional élite lost its place in the republican leadership. The traditional alliance temporarily disintegrated. The place of Chairman of the Council of Ministers was taken by Normakhamadi Khudaiberdyev, a native of Rashidov's home province, while the post of Chairman of the republic's Supreme Soviet was given to Nazar Matchanov, a representative of the Khorezm regional élite, which, for the first time in the existence of the Republic of Uzbekistan, occupied one of the three highest posts. However, Rashidov was unable to ignore the Fergana regional élite for long. Five years later, Matchanov was dismissed from his post and replaced by Inamjon Usmankhojaev, a native of Fergana.[37] The alliance had been restored. The Tashkent regional élite continued to be represented. In 1971, Nishanov was replaced by Akil Salimov, also from Tashkent. However, his influence on the decision making processes was incomparably less than Nishanov's had been. Salimov did not show himself to be a serious political figure during all his twelve years in office as Central Committee Secretary for Ideology.

DEATH OF THE CHIEF AND SUBSEQUENT TURMOIL

This state of affairs was preserved until Rashidov's death in October 1983.[38] That event was catastrophic for the clan. The process of searching for a new leader often brings about collisions among the clan's most influential leaders. This, in turn, weakens its standing. Taking advantage of this, other regional élite groupings may push the rival from the leading roles. This is what happened in Uzbekistan. The Fergana regional élite took advantage of Rashidov's death to place its own candidate, Inamjon Usmankhojaev in the post of First Secretary of the Central Committee. Tashkent's representation was apparently intact. Tashkent-born Akil Salimov became Chairman of the Supreme Soviet Presidium. The new leadership, undoubtedly, had plans to replace a number of the leading cadres. However, under pressure from Moscow, where it was decided to make an example of Uzbekistan in the struggle against corruption, it lost control of this process. Brigades of investigators were sent to Uzbekistan. Their leaders, Gdlian and Ivanov, were beyond the control of the republican leadership, for they were directly responsible to the centre. This fact predetermined the scale of the purge. In just three years, from 1984 to 1987, 90.4 per cent of the *nomenklatura* of the CPSU Central Committee in Uzbekistan and 76.6 per cent of Uzbekistan's party *nomenklatura* were replaced. About 300 high officials were sent from the Soviet Union's central regions to replace the dismissed 'national cadres',[39] thus upsetting the positioning of forces that had been formed over the decades.

In 1984, the Bukharan regional élite lost its place at the top of the ruling hierarchy, for the first time for many years. Khudaiberdyev was replaced by a Tashkenti, Gairat Qadyrov, as Chairman of the Council of Ministers. Thus, the Tashkent group held two of the three most important posts. However, the position of the new leaders was weak, especially that of the top person. Having grown up in the shadow of Sharaf Rashidov, Usmankhojaev could not be compared to him in any respect. His authority was minimal. There was discontent over his appointment in the republic, since he was unable to withstand Moscow's pressures. In Moscow, also, the Kremlin leadership was disappointed with him, because he was not sufficiently active in the fight against corruption, in which he himself was entangled. The reappearance in Uzbekistan of Rafiq Nishanov, who had spent many years outside the republic, was an expression of Moscow's discontent. First, he became Minister of Foreign Affairs, and in December 1986, he replaced Salimov as Chairman of the Supreme Soviet Presidium.[40] It was clear that a replacement of the leadership was being prepared. However, the position of the Tashkent people was not shattered. Nishanov himself was one of them. In January 1988 he replaced Usmanhojaev who was arrested on charges of corruption.[41]

In his address to the 19th All-Union Party Conference in July 1988, the new leader, in a flourishing, oriental style, described the representatives of the dead rival's clan:

> There are also forces that try to resist. They are insignificant, but one cannot underestimate them. Avicenna once said: 'Beware of a fly sitting on a dead serpent.' The people of the republic, communists, will not calm down till they have swept off the road all those who have bitten off a tasty morsel and are now trying to hold onto it.[42]

Soon after the conference, in the course of 'democratic elections', many leaders lost power. At plenary sessions of the *oblast* party committees held in October 1988, secretary of the Fergana *obkom* Hamdan Umarov was made to retire, while the secretaries of the Bukhara and Samarkand *obkoms*, Ismail Jabbarov and Nazir Rajabov, were dismissed from their posts for having compromised themselves.[43]

In the course of the election campaign, about 40,000 party functionaries of all ranks were elected to various party posts.[44] In this way, apparently, Nishanov tried to replace those who survived the 1984–87 purge. During the year after Nishanov came to power fifteen ministries and government bodies were liquidated in Uzbekistan and the Syr-Darya and Jizak Oblasts created under Rashidov were annulled. Sixty other structural administrative sections were reorganized. About 30,000 officials lost their posts.[45] This caused significant cadre shifts. Members of Rashidov's clan, or people connected to it, were thrown out of the power structures at all levels under various pretexts. At the same time, an attempt was made to split the Samarkand-Bukhara élite.

Upon Nishanov's transfer to the post of First Secretary of the Central Committee, the vacancy of Chairman of the Supreme Soviet Presidium was filled by the Samarkandi, Pulat Habibullaev. During the last period of Rashidov's life, he had been head of the Central Committee Department for Science, and later president of the Uzbekistan Academy of Sciences, and had been a member of the Supreme Soviet. However, he did not justify the hopes placed in him. Habibullaev took the post but refused to denounce Rashidov. As a result, after just a year, in January 1989, he was dismissed following the speech of a 'rank-and-file communist' obviously inspired by Nishanov. Characteristically, patronizing members of Rashidov's clan was among the many sins blamed on Habibullaev.[46] He was replaced by M. Ibrahimov, which meant that the Fergana élite had restored its position. Rafiq Nishanov ended his career as First Secretary of the Central Committee in summer 1989.

In 1990 in Uzbekistan the process of Rashidov's rehabilitation began.[47] When the independent Uzbek state was formed, it needed this, above all to preserve continuity in time. Despite his equivocal character, he was undoubtedly one of those who laid the foundations for modern Uzbekistan. However, the point is not only the struggle for the preservation of historical memory. Islam Karimov, who became President in 1991, needed to consolidate all his forces, and, first and foremost, his Samarkand-Bukhara regional élite. An important role in his efforts to achieve this were to be played by the former head of the élite, Sharaf Rashidov. This is the reason why streets and towns are again being renamed after him, why the republican government took a special decision to celebrate officially Rashidov's 75th birthday[48] and why monuments to him are being erected.[49]

Nishanov's resignation was preceded by the tragic events in the Fergana region – a conflict between Uzbeks and Meskhetian Turks, during which more than 100 people lost their lives. The fact that the timing of these disturbances coincided with the anti-Rashidov campaign led some to assume that it was caused by some reason other than inter-ethnic frictions. Judging by its efficient organization, it was an action that had been planned in advance. The clans that were being persecuted in connection with the anti-Rashidov campaign made an attempt to defy their persecutors. Having aggravated the situation under conditions of a weakened central authority, they tried to bring about changes in the republican leadership by discrediting it. They succeeded. In July 1989 Nishanov was replaced by Islam Karimov, a native of Samarkand.[50] This implied, among others, the dismissal of Qadyrov, a Tashkent native.

A POSSIBLE SCENARIO FOR THE FUTURE

With the collapse of the USSR and the removal of the centre that had supported the leading regional élites as of the mid-1920s, the importance of the clan-geographical factor can be expected to increase. The socio-economic crisis now being experienced by Uzbekistan is accompanied by a sharp decline in the living standards of its population. This situation is likely to strengthen the willingness of people to return to tested, traditional forms in defence of their interests. Emerging groups having transformed into clans will then try to challenge the traditional élite clans on the regional levels and to replace them. Eventually, this may result in a struggle of regional élites for the redistribution of power and subsequent socio-political upheavals. There may well be a long period of political instability, continuing until a new leading group or coalition of regional élites is formed. In any event, the clan-geographical factor will influence the formation of power structures in the most important republic in former Soviet Central Asia for many years to come.

NOTES

1. See, for example, William Fierman (ed.), *Soviet Central Asia. The Failed Transformation* (Boulder: Westview Press, 1991).
2. O. A. Sukhareva, *Bukhara v XIX-nachale XX veka* (Moscow, 1966), pp. 263-4.
3. Girshfeld, *Voenno-statisticheskie dannye po Khorezmskomu Oazisu*, Part 2 (Tashkent, 1902), p. 23.
4. N. Kalandarov, *Obrazovanie i deiatel'nost' Khorezmskoi kommunisticheskoi partii* (Tashkent, 1975), p. 95.
5. In accordance with the law promulgated in September 1993 – see 'Zakon Respubliki Uzbekistana. Ob organakh samoupravleniia grazhdan'. *Pravda vostoka*, 21 Sept. 1993.
6. R. Siddikov, 'Obshchestvennoe territorial'noe samoupravlenie', *Chelovek i politika* 8 (Tashkent, 1991), p. 42.
7. Donald S. Carlisle, 'Uzbekistan and the Uzbeks', *Problems of Communism* (Sept.–Oct. 1991), p. 29. See also Carlisle, 'Geopolitics and Ethnic Problems of Uzbekistan and Its Neighbours', in this volume.
8. *Bol'shaia sovetskaia entsiklopediia (BSE)*, 3d ed., Vol. 27 (Moscow, 1977), cols. 870–3; *Narodnoe khoziaistvo SSSR v 1989:* 'Statisticheskii ezhegodnik' (Moscow: Sovetskaia entsiklopediia, 1990), p. 23.
9. *BSE*, 3rd ed., Vol. 28, cols. 1092–5.
10. *BSE*, 3rd ed., Vol. 4 (1971), cols. 485–90; 3rd ed., Vol. 22 (1975), cols. 1574–6.
11. *BSE*, 3d ed., Vol. 25 (1976), cols. 914–21.
12. *BSE*, 3d ed., Vol. 11 (1973), cols. 1656–7. *BSE*, 3d ed., Vol. 29 (1978), cols. 904–5.
13. The appendix was compiled using the following sources: *BSE*, 2nd ed., Vol. 1 (1949–58), p. 14; Vol. 3, p. 570: Vol. 30, col. 44; *BSE*, 3d ed., Vol. 10 (1970–78), col. 360; Vol. 15, col. 1529; Vol. 17, cols. 913–14; Vol. 21, cols. 1532–3; Vol. 28, cols. 960, 1222–3; Vol. 30, col. 1252; *Malaia sovetskaia entsiklopediia*, 3rd ed., Vol. 6 (Moscow, 1959), pp. 321–2; *Revoliutsiei prizvannye. Biograficheskie ocherki* (Tashkent, 1987), p. 222; *Pravda vostoka*, 28 Dec. 1978, 1 Nov. 1983; 4 Nov. 1983; 2 Oct. 1990; 14 Jan. 1992; *Who's Who in the USSR, 1965–1966* (Montreal: Intercontinental Book and Publishing Co., 1966), p. 1115; Donald S. Carlisle, 'The Uzbek Power Elite: Politburo and Secretariat (1938–1983)', *Central Asian Survey* 5, 3/4 (1986), p. 103; FBIS-SOV-84-226, 21 Nov. 1984, p. R/1; FBIS-SOV-83-250, 28 Dec. 1983, p. R/10.
14. *Narodnoe khoziaistvo SSSR v 1989. Statisticheskii ezhegodnik* (Moscow, Sovetskaia entsiklopediia, 1990), p. 23.
15. 'Ob obshchestvenno-politicheskoi obstanovke i zadachakh partiinykh organizatsii respubliki. Doklad pervogo sekretaria Ts.K. kompartii Uzbekistana. I. A. Karimova na chrezvychainom XXIII s'ezg Kommunisticheskoi partii Uzbekistana, 14 Sept. 1991,' *Chelovek i politika* 11 (1991), p. 16.
16. K. Ikramov. 'I probil chas', in *Rashidov i rashidovshchina, Sbornik statei* (Perm, 1992), p. 19.
17. 'Sharaf Rashidovich Rashidov. An Obituary'. *Pravda*, 1 Nov. 1983.
18. Donald S. Carlisle, 'Uzbekistan and the Uzbeks', p. 29.
19. *Pravda*, 1 Nov. 1983.
20. T. Pulatov,'Pod sen'iu ottsa natsii, in *Rashidov i rashidovshchina*, p. 41.
21. 'Soprotivlenie', in *Rashidov i rashidovshchina*, p. 28.
22. V. Artemenko. 'Sluchainyi prezident', *Pravda*, 18 Mar. 1989.
23. 'Ibrahim Muminov. Obituary'. *Voprosy filosofii* 9 (1974), p. 186; *Pravda vostoka* 23 June 1974.
24. S. Rizaev, *Sharaf Rashidov. Shtrikhi k portretu* (Tashkent: Tzuvkhi-Nur, 1992), pp. 50, 59–60.
25. *Pravda vostoka*, 1 Jan. 1974.
26. *The Qur'an*, tr. Rev. J. H. Rodwell, Everyman's Library (London: J. M. Dent & Sons, 1939), XLIII, 18.
27. *The Qur'an*, IV, 34.
28. Memoirs of a colleague of Rashidov in the author's possession.
29. Ibid.
30. Ibid.

31. For instance, the composer M. Burhanov, author of the text of the Uzbek SSR anthem, was ostracized for a long time, after he spoke out against the candidate for the post of chairman of the Union of Composers proposed by Rashidov.
32. T. Pulatov, 'Pod sen'iu ottsa natsii', p. 42.
33. Manuscript of memoir in the author's possession.
34. Ia. Nasreddinova. 'Do i posle korruptsii', *Rashidov i rashidovshchina*, p. 24.
35. The incident at the stadium was understood somewhat differently by Carlisle, in his extremely interesting article 'The Uzbek Power Elite', p. 116. Carlisle maintains that Rashidov made use of the events in order to remove the clans of Nasreddinova and Kurbanov. I think that both sides tried to make use of the tragic events. In addition, an exceptionally active role was played by Nishanov about which Carlisle did not write. According to sources in my possession, Nishanov was meant to replace Rashidov as First Secretary of the Uzbekistan Central Committee.
36. T. Gdlian and N. Ivanov, 'Protivostoianie', *Rashidov i rashidovshchina*, p. 8.
37. *Pravda vostoka*, 4 Nov. 1983.
38. The death of Rashidov from heart failure was officially announced at the beginning of November 1983. However, one cannot exclude the possibility that there was another reason for his death. Andrei Aleksandrov-Agentov, an Andropov aide, wrote ten years later: 'Andropov himself summoned Rashidov and during the talk informed him of all the facts gathered at the time by the Central Committee and KGB about corruption within the Uzbek leadership, in which Rashidov, too, was involved. I do not know how Andropov ended that talk, but I myself witnessed how Rashidov looked when leaving the office, white in the face. Soon after he commited suicide in Tashkent.' *24*, 20 April 1993 (published under the aegis of ITAR-TASS, the official Russian news agency).
39. I. Usmankhojaev, 'Prodolzhaia delo Oktiabria', *Kommunist Uzbekistana* 11 (1987), p. 4.
40. FBIS-SOV-88-007, 12 Jan. 1988, p. 49.
41. FBIS-SOV-86-238, 11 Dec. 1986, p. 29.
42. *Izvestiia*, 1 July 1988..
43. FBIS-SOV-88-205, 24 Oct. 1988, p. 54 and FBIS-SOV-88-206A, 25 Oct. 1988, p. 78.
44. FBIS-SOV-88-183, 21 Sept. 1988, p. 68.
45. FBIS-SOV-89-061, 31 March 1989, p. 61.
46. V. Artemenko. 'Sluchainyi prezident'.
47. FBIS-SOV-89-160, 21 Aug. 1989, p. 87.
48. A. Orlov, 'Snova Rashidov?' *Izvestiia*, 27 Nov. 1990; *Pravda vostoka*, 1 Oct. 1992.
49. *Pravda vostoka*, 11 June 1992.
50. *Golos Uzbekistana*, No. 36, 1992. For the Fergana Valley disturbances of May–June 1989, see also Yaacov Ro'i, 'Central Asian Riots and Disturbances, 1989–1990: Causes and Context', *Central Asian Survey* 10, 3 (1991), pp. 23–33.

APPENDIX 6.1 UZBEK LEADERS

FIRST CC SECRETARIES	PLACE OF BIRTH	CHAIRMAN, PRESIDIUM OF SUPREME SOVIET	PLACE OF BIRTH	CHAIRMAN, COUNCIL OF MINISTERS	PLACE OF BIRTH
A. Ikramov 1925 - 1937	Tashkent	Iu. Ahunbabaev 1925 - 1943	Fergana 1925 - 1937	F. Khojaev	Bukhara
U. Iusupov 1937 - 1950	Fergana Oblast	A. Muminov 1943 - 1947	no data	S. Segizbaev 1937 - 1938	Tashkent
		A. Niiazov 1947 - 1950	Fergana	A. Abrurahmanov 1938 - 1950	Tashkent
A. Niiazov 1950 - 1955	Fergana	Sh. Rashidov 1950 - 1959	Jizak, Samarkand Oblast	A. Mavlianov 1950 - 1951	Kazakhstan
				N. Mukhitdinov 1951 - 1953	Tashkent
				U. Iusupov 1953 - 1954	Fergana Oblast
N. Mukhitdinov 1955 - 1956	Tashkent			S. Kamalov 1955 - 1957	Tashkent
S. Kamalov 1957 - 1959	Tashkent			M. Mirzaahmedov 1957 - 1959	no data
Sh. Rashidov 1959 - 1983	Jizak, Samarkand Oblast	Ia. Nasreddinova 1959 - 1970	Fergana	A. Alimov 1959 - 1961	no data
				R. Kurbanov 1961 - 1971	Bukhara
		N. Matchanov 1970 - 1978	Khorezm	N. Khudaiberdyev 1971 - 1984	Jizak, Samarkand Oblast
		I. Usmankhojaev 1978 - 1983	Fergana		
I. Usmankhojaev 1983 - 1988	Fergana	A. Salimov 1983 - 1986	Tashkent	G. Kadurov 1984 - 1989	Tashkent
		P. Khabibulaev 1986 - 1989	Samarkand		
R. Nishanov 1988 - 1989	Tashkent	M. Ibragimov 1989 - 1991	no data		
I. Karimov 1989 - 1991	Samarkand	Sh. Iuldashev 1991	Fergana	M. Mirkasymov 1989	Tashkent
				Sh. Mirsaidov 1990. office annuled	Leninabad, Tajikistan

7

Tajikistan: Political Parties
in an Inchoate National Space

GRIGORII G. KOSACH

The territorial disintegration of the former Soviet empire and the emergence on its ruins of new state entities were the natural outcome of profound, latently maturing processes which surfaced in the period of glasnost and perestroika. Today the root causes of these processes seem clear enough: economic degradation, an unprecedented out-pouring of social tension and the breakdown of inter-ethnic relations which had been based on a model that comprised two mutually exclusive elements – 'the flourishing of the socialist nationalities' and the desire to mould the 'Soviet people as a new historical community'. The attempts to solve the problems inherent in the implementation of these contradictory goals by traditional political and administrative methods and the tried and tested ideological clichés which the Soviet leadership was so reluctant to abandon proved utterly ineffective and abortive.

The Soviet ruling élite's political opponents in the union republics put forward their own perception of how to overcome the country's social and economic difficulties. Moreover, when choosing priorities in their practical programs of action, they resolutely discarded the quintessence of the ideological legitimization of the all-union com-munist system, namely, the proposition concerning its internationalist character. This basically set them apart from their adversaries. The parties and movements that stepped into the political arena in the republics in the latter half of the 1980s appealed to their national histories and values. In these they saw a prerequisite for the reform of the prevalent socio-economic structures. These parties and movements were established by the local 'educated class', which strove to achieve a nationally-oriented political space which, they presumed, would be an earnest of the rebirth and prosperity of the peoples inhabiting it. Only the resolute and complete eradication of the ideas and practices of communism from society's spiritual, social and political life could ensure progress towards this goal.

In the early 1990s, developments in Tajikistan were taking the course common to all the national regions in the Soviet periphery in the last years of the USSR's existence. In Tajikistan the process culminated when, at an extraordinary session on 9 September 1991, the republican Supreme Soviet adopted a Declaration of State Independence, which proclaimed the establishment of a 'new independent entity of international law' that was coming into being in accordance with the aspiration of its people to self-determination.[1]

By the time Tajikistan gained sovereignty a secular and religious opposition to the ruling regime already existed and had assumed clear-cut organizational and ideological forms. The Rastokhez (Renaissance) Movement of the People of Tajikistan and the Democratic Party of Tajikistan (DPT)[2] formed the secular wing of the opposition, and its religious wing was represented by the Islamic Renaissance Party (IRP) which had grown out of the Tajik branch of the all-union party of the same name.[3]

Formally, the republican organization of the Communist Party was diametrically opposed. But in September 1991, processes which had been at work in the party for some time and which were the local replica of the attempts to renovate the All-Union Communist Party, took a distinct turn towards greater radicalism. The party's extra-ordinary 22nd Congress decided to rename it the Socialist Party of Tajikistan,[4] and 'change its programmatic aims, tasks and functions'; the decision was never actually implemented. The communists 'resolutely' rejected all 'claims to absolute truth and a vanguard role in society', and became 'a political action party of a parliamentary type'. They declared that the proclamation of independence by Tajikistan had radically altered their position, the Tajik Communist Party with-drew from the Communist Party of the Soviet Union, and declared that it was an association of like-minded people acting in accordance with the laws of the republic as a national force, as a movement integrating into the political system of the new sovereign state entity.[5]

Subsequent developments led to a meaningful change in the position of the party. On 30 September 1991, the Supreme Soviet of Tajikistan banned the activities of the Communist Party and its successor, the Socialist Party, and nationalized its property.[6] The ruling élite decisively abandoned both the ideology which fettered it, and the party which professed and implemented this ideology. The com-munists were not in a position to resume their legal activities until December 1991, when the ban on them was lifted.[7] But by now this was a party that had been divorced from Tajikistan's power structures and had lost not a few adherents, although still retaining a significant number of its supporters.[8]

The political map of Tajikistan took final shape in the autumn of 1991. The two opposing camps in the political alignment of forces were the secular and the religious opposition on the one hand, and the communists on the other. It seemed that the struggle between these polar forces, which was seen as a confrontation between totalitarianism and democracy with national overtones, would ultimately determine the republic's future regime.[9] However, viewing developments in this light distorted the picture. Such an approach ignored the struggle of the regional élites, who were out to change the distribution of power in the republic, that had previously been determined in Moscow. The absence of the centre's tutelage and the communists' loss of direct control over the entire ruling élite turned the confrontation between the two political camps into an open bid for power by the opposition, in which the differences in ideology and principle became ancillary to other considerations. This set the scene for the emergence of various coalitions of parties that seemed to have utterly incompatible platforms and ideals.

PARTIES IN TAJIKISTAN: POLITICAL PLATFORMS

There are at least two proximate central elements in the conceptual formation of the political parties and movements in Tajikistan and the formulation of their platforms: first, the idea of national renaissance and, second, the attendant social determinants. Both elements can be traced back to the enlightenment tradition disrupted under the Soviet regime and to jadidism, which had been an active force in the period of the Emirate of Bukhara.[10] They correspond to trends that formed the basis of national revival in other Asian countries during the period of European colonial expansion.

Reformulating concepts and images in order to justify the central elements of their programs and make them acceptable in con-temporary circumstances, the parties and movements of independent Tajikistan turned to the political parlance of the last years of the Soviet era. 'General human values' occupied the most prominent place in this jargon. 'Today', according to the IRP, 'these values have assumed significance';[11] whereas Rastokhez talked of their primary importance as 'the ideals of the overwhelming majority of those who championed the ideals of freedom, equality, and fraternity as preconditions for the... advance towards progress';[12] and the DPT spoke of 'democracy and the establishment of a state governed by law and order.[13] These positions fully reiterated the declarations of the communists, who aspired 'to uphold...the humanitarian ideals of justice, freedom, equality, and the principles of democracy and humanism of our people'.[14] The rival camps referred to these terms in order to raise the issue of how to overcome the country's backwardness and under-development that had resulted from it having been a part of the Soviet Union. All the parties referred to the Soviet period as in many ways a colonial epoch.

The communists put the blame for 'preserving' the republic's 'distorted economic structure' and 'perpetuating its status as a raw material appendage to the militarized economy of the metropolitan state' on the 'administrative-command centre and the bureaucratic party-state leadership'. They agreed that the standard of living in the republic was lower than in any other former Soviet region; moreover, the central leadership's policy of the 'merging of the nations...and the population's atheization ...had narrowed down the sphere of application of the Tajik language, and generated a nihilistic sentiment towards the Tajik people's historical heritage and contempt for Islamic moral values'.[15]

The secular opposition emphasized the same points. In the opinion of the DPT, 'the republic remains today essentially a raw materials appendage to the former Soviet Union, with undeveloped industry and backward extracting and processing sectors'.[16] 'As a result of Tajikistan's integration into the so-called "single Soviet economic complex", Rastokhez insisted,

> not one integrated economic organism was formed in the republic. Its economy is deficient and irrational...The state policy of the bureaucratic administrative command system wrought havoc with the habitat of the Tajik people. It distorted its history...caused the degradation of the moral and ethical foundations of its existence...violated the citizen's basic rights and freedoms, and made any profound social transformations in the republic impossible.[17]

Formally, the IRP did not raise issues that would have been appropriate and natural for secular parties. Its ideologues were pre-occupied with purifying Islam of 'pagan' prejudices and the distortions of later epochs. However, the way they raised these outwardly, purely religious, issues implied that the present sorry state of Islam was just another manifestation of the general decline of Tajikistan caused by its having been included in the Soviet state. Of course, the IRP said, the denigration of Islamic values began from the time they spread into Central Asia, but the official atheism of the Soviet period and the general policy of imposing 'false Western wisdom' on the republic made the process almost irreversible. The disruption of cultural tradition distanced believers – and the Islamists regard the entire indigenous population of Tajikistan as believers – from the Qur'an and the *tafsir* (the commentary of the Qur'an) and made them hostages to a mystique that was utterly incompatible with the true faith.[18]

In this context the programmatic precepts of the IRP that emphasized the party's aspirations to 'expand Islam's sphere of influence' in society, to 'bring to the people the values of the Qur'an and the Sunna', and 'to eradicate state atheistic propaganda' acquired a special nuance. This applied in equal measure to the declaration that 'the IRP's activities are based on acknowledgement of a single Creator, humanism and respect for human rights' and to the accentuated attention given to establishing 'an integral economic system...to be subsequently transformed into an Islamic-type economy'.[19] This implied opposition to the existing state administrative mechanism with its indifference towards the individual, and the substitution of an Islamic way of life based on the tradition of true Islamic civilization, with models that did not correspond to the genuine interests of those to whom the party was appealing.

All the parties viewed statehood as the principal precondition of Tajikistan's rebirth. Naturally, this new reality alone could not guarantee solutions to all the problems besetting the republic. To achieve this, the spokesmen of the two opposing camps offered an almost identical set of measures in the various spheres of economic, social and political life, as well as in culture, education and science. These were laid down in more detail in the programs of Rastokhez, the DPT and the communists and less so in that of the IRP. In the IRP's case, these were matters of the implicit ideological postulates of religious political movements concerning the centrality of books of divine revelation for the process of transformation within a society that had deviated from the predestined road.

Irrespective of the degree of detail, the measures suggested by the various parties looked like a tool kit which could be put to successful use provided national unity was achieved within the already existing framework of the newly acquired statehood. The Tajik population of the republic was viewed as the core of this unity. The emphasis on this aspect of the problem was natural for Rastokhez, which had emerged and was acting as a national movement. 'Inasmuch as Tajikistan is the historical homeland of the Tajik people, the development of the Tajik nation, language and culture takes priority in Rastokhez activities.' Of course, the movement's ideologues were not oblivious to the problems facing the other nationalities living in the country. This was in keeping with 'the principles of democracy and inter-ethnic equality', 'justice', 'the impermissibility of inter-ethnic conflict' and 'free expression of the will and self-determination of peoples'.[20] The DPT, for whom the implementation of the measures designed to bring about the Tajik national rebirth by no means ran counter to 'recognition of the equality of all the republic's citizens irrespective of their nationality or religious affiliation',[21] set itself the same task.

On the whole, the communists formulated the issue in the same way as did the opposition. Inasmuch as the previous, Soviet period in Tajikistan's development had 'created a threat to the nation's *genofond*' (that is, its very genotype and existence as a nation) and to 'its habitat', the primary task of the present day was the 'consolidation of the Tajik people...the development of the national culture and the state language'.[22]

The political parlance used by the two sides could differ in some of its stock phrases, betraying their adherence to varying theoretical concepts. Whereas the communists pressed for the 'formation of a Tajik national working class and for rectifying the errors committed...at previous stages of development',[23] Rastokhez pointed to the import-ance of 'creating a natural social structure of the Tajik nation'.[24] But these dissimilarities did not alter the essence of the issues raised by both blocs.[25]

It would seem that the IRP could not pose the problem as the secular parties did. The Islamic movement's evident distancing from national issues and accentuated interest in supranational religious values seemed to corroborate this impression. Party membership was permissible only to people who sought to base their activity on the Qur'an and the Sunna,[26] in other words, to Muslims and not to people belonging to other national communities. However, some nuances in the Islamists' program allowed another interpretation of their ideological postulates.

'The IRP is guided by constitutional principles', and 'condemns the basis and practice of terrorism and reaction'. It thus conducts its activities within the confines of the state space it recognizes and whose integrity it pledges to respect. However, this space is populated by an ethnic majority and national minorities, believers and non-believers. 'The IRP is in favour of equality between believers and non-believers based on mutual understanding.'[27] The natural orientation for a party of this kind, towards the support of Muslim believers whom its activists address in the language of the ethnic majority, indicates that its seemingly simplistic treatment of the nationalities problem, which it appears to dismiss perfunctorily, is more profound and multifaceted than meets the eye. This party is very young and has been in the political arena only for a very short period of time, hence its rigorous attitude to its doctrine and the methods of its implementation. But that is not the essence of the problem.

The IRP exists and operates in a society whose state structure throughout the Soviet period was based on the national principle, with all its distortions, to the detriment of the denominational principle. Today the IRP has revived the factor of religious affiliation and strives to make it the cornerstone of Tajikistan's statehood, which does not mean simply a rigorous adherence to Islamic sources. This is also a return to the tradition of confessionalist statehood of the Bukharan Emirate or Afghanistan before 1978, which in the former case did not rule out the primacy of the Tajik language and culture, and in the latter, the domination of the Pushtuns.

Social determinants as an instrument of achieving national rebirth within the framework of the newly acquired statehood were the second element common to the ideological and political platforms of the parties and movements in what looked like opposing camps. The programmatic documents of all these parties viewed ensuring 'social justice' as one of the main objectives of their political practice.

For all the plethora of measures, primarily of an economic character, that were proposed for the national rebirth, this could not be achieved without appealing to the values inherent in the very structure of Tajik society. A direct orientation towards economic instruments – the market and its attendant infrastructure, contacts with countries boasting high labour productivity – could prove just a technocratic semblance of a solution, as had been the case in the Soviet period, and would not of themsleves lead to national prosperity. Rastokhez was the first political association to advance and consistently uphold these concepts. The DPT held identical views.

Rastokhez considered 'man and his all-round development to be the prime value of history and social life. On this basis alone would it be possible to achieve universal happiness and prosperity', and eradicate social differences and antagonisms?[28] The country's stark reality was such that 'half the population was destitute', the people were deprived of the basic values of their existence – language and culture – social links had been severed and society was 'rent by contradictions'.[29] DPT leader Shodmon Yusuf maintained that indeed society was devoid of all 'national characteristics and tradition', and without these, democracy, the most important achievement of world civilization, was out of reach.[30]

The transition to democracy would be possible only after the restoration of national identity and consolidation. To achieve these, programmatic measures that would alleviate social tension and contribute to social stabilization would be necessary. The state had to carry out these steps to demonstrate that it was an effective instrument of 'government by the people' (*narodnovlastie*) in that it could tackle the problems of poverty, health care for workers in both city and countryside, restoration of the ecological balance, mother and child welfare, and the ensurance of an appropriate place for women in society.[31]

The formulation by the communists of the problem of national distinctiveness and their list of measures associated with 'social justice' which the state must implement, were virtually identical with those offered by Rastokhez and the DPT.[32]

The IRP viewed the basic principles of social justice, which it understood as 'Islamic-type justice', and the measures required to achieve it in much the same light as the secular parties. Needless to say, it justified its attitude in the context of the necessity to restore the role of Islam and raise the status of believers rather than of the nation's rebirth.[33]

SOCIAL BASE OF THE PARTIES AND MOVEMENTS IN TAJIKISTAN

All the parties and movements in Tajikistan appeal in their programmatic documents to the 'people' (*mardum*) as their natural social base. Naturally, in some cases this broad and vague notion may, implicitly or explicitly, indicate specific social parameters that would make it possible to single out the social strata which could potentially provide the electoral base for the relevant political association. Yet, the attempts to do this are generally formal; moreover, their formal character can considerably distort the real picture of the political confrontation between the parties.

As a Muslim party (*hizb musulmonani*), the IRP, by virtue of its goal-oriented self-identification, must necessarily dissociate itself from Tajikistan's Russian-speaking population, although theoretically it could win a measure of support even from some sections of this group, such as Tatars or Russian-speaking and culturally assimilated Tajiks living in the major urban centres. Moreover, inasmuch as it proclaims 'mutual understanding with non-believers' in the context of the 'compulsory termination of state-conducted atheistic propaganda', theoretically again the European minorities are not excluded from the IRP's circle of activity denoted in the concept of 'the people'. 'The truth of Islam should be brought to them',[34] albeit in proselytic form. On the other hand, the political vocabulary that the IRP resorts to is oversaturated with Arabisms. Suffice it in this context to recall the Arab word *nahzat* (renaissance) in the party's name (its official name in Tajik is Hizbi Nehzati Islomi), designed apparently to place it in contrast with Rastokhez, which also means 'renaissance', Rastokhez consciously referring to itself with a word of Persian origin.

Lastly, the communists, in specifying their notion of 'the people', refer to the 'working people', meaning 'the workers, *dekhkans* (peasants), intelligentsia, young people and other strata'.[35] In their appeals to this 'people' and their attempts 'to give expression to the people's innermost aspirations', their position in many respects coincides with that of Rastokhez and the DPT. The programmatic documents of Rastokhez and the DPT, which directly or indirectly specify their objectives in the spheres of economics, ecology, social relations and national culture and regard their realization as a guarantee of the national rebirth, link the two notions of 'people' and 'labour'. It is relevant to note here that the notion of an 'Islamic economy' (*iktisodi islomi*) in the IRP political vocabulary, that is common to Islamic political movements, is regarded as an integral part of a broader system of 'Islamic social justice' in which property is the fruit of righteous labour to be placed at the disposal of society as a whole, the actual owner just managing it on the people's behalf. Again, the question touches upon what the secular parties mean by 'the working people'.[36]

Sociological surveys, statistical data and some conclusions drawn by Tajik scholars give a more concrete, although far from fully accurate, picture. (The conclusions of Tajik scholars are often based on personal contacts with the activists of the political movements, which makes them no less interesting than the sociological surveys or the statistics.)

In the opinion of two well-known Tajik scholars, S. Olimova and M. Olimov, the Rastokhez movement that 'represents almost exclusively free-thinking intellectuals...has in effect no ties with other social strata and to all intents and purposes does not seem to make any attempts to broaden its social base'. Essentially, 'its isolation from the people' accounts for the fact that Rastokhez does not have a broad base of social support and, moreover, cannot alter this situation. In the opinion of the Olimovs, 'fundamentalism is mainly represented by people in the younger and middle-age brackets...who are wholly disenchanted both with socialist ideals and the wisdom of their elders'. Fundamentalism has gained 'wide currency' in Tajikistan inasmuch as the communist ideology buttressed by 'all the might of the Soviet state' failed to gain the upper hand in its struggle with Islam. Islam 'as it were, went underground but did not surrender its positions. The bulk of the population rejected the very possibility that a Tajik could be a sincere atheist.' Besides being inherently hostile to communism, the Islamic political movement, in the opinion of these two authors, is also a protagonist of the secular opposition parties, which 'preach a program of national rebirth based on the idea of progress and the Western development model'.[37]

Russian researchers studying today's problems in Central Asia have arrived at the same conclusions. In particular, they ascribe the weakness of the secular opposition and the fact that democratic norms have not taken root in the Central Asian states to precisely the same reasons. They visualize the local democrats as a force that – even though their programs are allegedly different from that of the Islamists – has to ally itself with the Islamic political movements in the common confrontation with 'the successors of the post-communist system' because the prospects of restoring links between the people and the intelligentsia lie in this course of action.[38]

Though this is undoubtedly an interesting point of view, its adherents, both Russian and Tajik, suffer from an aberration of vision caused by their own democratic ideals. While explaining the failures of the secular opposition and its virtual absorption by its Islamist allies during the Dushanbe events of May 1992 and subsequent developments in Tajikistan, they reject out of hand the idea that the platforms of Rastokhez, the IRP and other parties are virtually parallel. They believe that Islam as a system of religious norms, and the Islamist political movements which strive to revive these norms so that they regulate the life of society, are fully identical. They tend to forget that the Soviet system – of which Tajikistan was a part – sought to legitimize itself ideologically, among other things, by absorbing the national-religious heritage and making it a component of the mythology that it had created. They ignore the fact that nationalist parties in other Islamic countries legitimized their existence and the regimes they set up for the same reasons and in the same ways as did the former Soviet state. In Tajikistan, as distinct from these countries, the establishment of Rastokhez and the DPT was a first attempt at implementing a 'nationalist revival program' and, therefore, political Islam could not be a response to the program's shortcomings; apart from which both branches of the opposition, the religious and the secular, emerged at virtually the same time. Finally, the very thesis that certain ideological tenets of the 'educated class' derive from their isolation from 'the people', is somewhat surprising. In other words, such conclusions concerning the social base of political parties and movements require substantial additions or even correction.

Sociological studies conducted in the latter half of the 1980s in various regions of Tajikistan produced the impression that the younger generation had a growing interest in religion. Thus, in 1987, 49.6 per cent of the students of five institutions of higher learning, 65.4 per cent of nursing school students and 68 per cent of students from four secondary vocational schools in Dushanbe celebrated the feast denoting the end of Ramadan (Qurban-Bairam). Some graduates of the

Oriental languages faculty of the Tajik State University in the republican capital actually became 'ministers of religion'.[39]

These facts seem to corroborate the conclusion that young people make up one of the groups, which in the past constituted the social base of the 'Wahhabis'[40] and which now support the IRP. However, the author of the monograph containing this information overlooks many points that are important for processing sociological research data, including the respondents' social origin and the region of their birth. On the basis of customary Soviet practice, it can be presumed that these students were born in the countryside surrounding Dushanbe and had come to the capital to study at secondary vocational schools, including the nursing school, and the medical, pedagogical and agricultural institutes established in every *oblast* centre to train the requisite cadres for the rural settlements and small towns within the *oblast*. In equal measure this applied to students of the Oriental languages faculty who took courses, among others, in order to qualify as teachers of the native language and literature and who more often than not came from the countryside, rather than from the capital and big cities, where the Tajik language was not considered prestigious.

There is another important point. Religiosity among the population in general and young people in particular does not necessarily lead to the political affiliation that would seem to be associated with it. This was the case in the history of the jadidist tradition in the Bukhara Emirate and the Muslim regions of Tsarist Russia and the subsequent groups into which its adherents broke up, some of them actually choosing a socialist orientation, as well as in other Muslim countries where people who joined the communist fold could be profoundly religious. Though such a situation was hardly probable in the Soviet Union, the Soviet experience showed quite clearly that youthful dissidence more often than not gave way to career considerations and adaptation to ideological and political realities. Muslim beliefs that assumed the form of popular Islam were, of course, widespread in Tajikistan. According to a survey conducted in Leninabad Oblast in 1985, over half the respondents had immediate family members or close relatives who were religious and 55 per cent actually took part in religious festivities.[41] However, this in no measure reflected the real geography of the spheres of political influence in Tajikistan in subsequent years.

In October–November 1991 and in June 1992, the Moscow-based Russian Academy of Management conducted sociological surveys in Tajikistan. They covered the north of the republic (Leninabad Oblast), Kurgan-Tiube and Kulab Oblasts in the south, the capital, Dushanbe, and several of its neighbouring towns and *raions*, such as Tursunzade and Gissar. Despite all the errors, which are unavoidable in this type of work, these surveys obtained information on the social base of the political parties which can be considered generally accurate.[42]

A considerable section of the respondents – 39 per cent – said in the 1992 survey that they did not trust a single political party, and all respondents rejected the idea of conducting elections to the Supreme Soviet on the basis of party lists. The political associations were much less popular than public figures of republican or regional calibre who had formerly belonged to the CPSU élite and were not currently affiliated with any party.

Nonetheless, when asked which political parties and movements they trusted, the overwhelming majority of respondents thought it necessary to support secular associations. On the republican scale, communists topped the list – 36 per cent in 1991 and 40 per cent in 1992, the DPT was second – 21 per cent in 1991 and ten per cent in 1992, and Rastokhez gained the support of six per cent and three per cent of the respondents, respectively. Both in 1991 and 1992, the IRP was trusted by six per cent of those polled. On the whole, these figures coincided with the respondents' reaction to the idea of the islamicization of Tajikistan. In 1991 it was supported by five per cent of those polled, in 1992, by six per cent. In 1991, 74 per cent and in 1992, 77 per cent of those polled considered it necessary to preserve the republic as a secular state. Those not sure constituted 21 per cent and 17 per cent, respectively.

Attitudes of respondents to the emigration of the non-Tajik population and to the state's regionalization are also worthy of note. On the republican level, 84 per cent said they saw no reason why people who hailed from different regions of Tajikistan should not live where they chose in Tajikistan. Some 83 per cent of the respondents did not approve of Uzbek and Kyrgyz emigration, 81 per cent of Russian and Ukrainian emigration, and 75 per cent felt the same about Germans, Jews and other ethnic groups.

In 1992, three of Tajikistan's leading political forces – the Communists, the DPT and the IRP – enjoyed varying measures of support among different strata. Whereas the communists enjoyed the sympathy of 57.7 per cent of *dekhkans* (peasants), 48.7 per cent of agricultural experts (agronomists, livestock specialists, veterinarians, etc.), 28.4 per cent of industrial workers and 37.2 per cent of students, other social strata expressed less confidence in them – 21.7 per cent of professionals (teachers, doctors, research institute workers, university lecturers), 21.5 per cent of state officials, and only 9.2 per cent of industrial engineers and technicians. The latter group clearly preferred the DPT and the IRP (27.7 per cent and 16.8 per cent, respectively).

Each of these two parties enjoyed the sympathies of 10.9 per cent of professionals, while 10.8 per cent of government officials preferred the DPT. The support shown the DPT by students was quite considerable – 23.3 per cent. However, it dropped sharply among the *dekhkans* (5.9 per cent), agricultural experts (3.9 per cent) and industrial workers (7.8 per cent). The IRP received the support of only 5.9 per cent of *dekhkans*, 5.3 per cent of agricultural experts, 3.9 per cent of industrial workers, 1.1 per cent of government officials and 4.7 per cent of students.

But these overall republican data did not reflect many of the important aspects of the situation in Tajikistan. They did not include any data for the Gorno-Badakhshan Autonomous Oblast (GBAO), whose territory comprises 44.5 per cent of that of the entire republic, although its total population in 1989 numbered just 164,000 out of a population of over five million. Nor did they furnish direct information about the national breakdown of the adherents of each of the three political parties, although such information could be inferred: the countryside was the main sphere of employment of the indigenous population,[43] and at big factories Russian-speakers constituted the overwhelming majority. The Tajiks among the respondents belonging to the categories of industrial workers, professionals, government officials and students clearly supported the IRP. With certain reservations, the same may be said for the DPT, for it must be borne in mind that the survey was conducted in June 1992, that is, right after the Dushanbe events of May 1992, during which the DPT and the IRP collaborated. This collaboration alienated the Russian-speaking population from the DPT, was an impetus to its emigration from the republic, and to all intents and purposes transformed the DPT into a mono-ethnic party.

Nor was that the only problem. All the groups of respondents could be defined as what the platforms of the leading parties referred to as 'the people'. This 'people' constituted the aggregate social base of all the political parties in the republic. Its horizontal stratification, which it inherited from the Soviet period, provided no basis for defining the actual social groups that could comprise a real social core for this or that political party. It was precisely this circumstance that accounted for the similarities in their programmatic documents.

Finally, the overall republican indices of the 1992 opinion poll differed substantially for individual cities and regions.[44] In this case the traditional Soviet social model proved to be ineffectual. For instance, 18.6 per cent of those polled in Kurgan-Tiube Oblast and 14.7 per cent in Dushanbe (naturally, representing different categories of respondents) supported the idea of establishing an Islamic republic in

Tajikistan. However, this idea was almost fully rejected in Leninabad and Kulab Oblasts, as well as in Gissar and Tursunzade. Sixteen per cent of respondents in the technological professions, 10.9 per cent of professionals, and 9.3 per cent of the students favoured islamicization. This was resolutely opposed by industrial workers and the government apparatus.

As many as 25.8 per cent of those polled in Leninabad Oblast were in favour of the autonomization of their region, while for Kurgan-Tiube the figure was 13.9 per cent, and for the republic as a whole, only 10 per cent. Of all the Tajik respondents, 9.4 per cent welcomed the emigration of Russians and Ukrainians from Tajikistan – the figure had increased by a third since the survey conducted in 1991. The proportion among IRP supporters was considerably higher (39 per cent), with 20 per cent of them favouring the departure of Uzbeks, and 24 per cent that of Germans, Jews and others. At the same time, some 24 per cent of the IRP's supporters thought that people from the various regions of Tajikistan should live in the places where they were born.

Many of these data coincided with the geographical distribution of the supporters of the various political associations. The IRP got the support of 18.4 per cent of those polled in Dushanbe and of 17.5 per cent of the respondents in Kurgan-Tiube Oblast. The DPT received its highest level of support in Dushanbe – 25.7 per cent. The communists held the leading positions in Leninabad and Kulab Oblasts and in Gissar. Their position was weakest in Dushanbe, a mere three per cent. The published materials of the survey did not give data on the influence of Rastokhez in the various regions.

The survey results showed that not only horizontal social relations in Tajikistan were inapposite, but that vertical social ties of a national character were also non-existent. Society was split first and foremost along regional lines. The formal existence of the union republic of Tajikistan, that had been regarded as a sovereign entity within the Soviet state, by no means changed the orientation of its regions towards external economic centres or towards Dushanbe. On the whole, these lines of gravitation corresponded to the boundaries of the Central Asian states which had existed in the region on the eve of, or after, the Russian conquest. Tajikistan's Leninabad Oblast gravitated economically towards the territory of the Kokand Khanate, abolished in 1876 by the Russian Imperial administration and made into a single administrative formation, the Fergana Oblast of the Turkestan General-Governorship that included present-day Khujand (Leninabad). The oblasts of Kulab and Kurgan-Tiube in southern Tajikistan, for their part, were oriented towards contemporary Uzbekistan, repeating the bends and curves of the political and economic map of the Bukharan Emirate.

Finally, there was the GBAO, formed within Tajikistan in January 1925. The inclusion in Russia in 1885 of the part of historical Badakhshan which lay north of the River Panj broke up an integral region, the southern part of which was incorporated in Afghanistan. No substantive ties, however, were formed between northern Badakhshan and the Bukharan Emirate, to which it was formally transferred by the Russian administration. This was due to the maintenance of effective control over Badakhshan by the Russian army's Pamir military detachment that was quartered on its territory and whose commander was directly subordinate to the governor-general of Fergana. The GBAO had only weak economic links with the rest of Tajikistan throughout the Soviet period, remaining a permanently subsidized region. The predominance among its population of ethnic groups who speak East Iranian languages also distinguished this region from the rest of the republic (Tajik is a West Iranian language), as did their affiliation to the Ismaili sect of Islam. Political currents and processes in Dushanbe, too, had little impact in the GBAO, which was hardly even affected by the civil war that flared up in Tajikistan in 1992, although people from this region who lived in Dushanbe were active in the ranks of the opposition and formed the political group Lali Badakhshon (Badakhshanskii Lal) on the basis of local ties.

The development, or preservation, of the backwardness of certain regions within the republic was determined by the all-union strategy of economic development rather than by Tajikistan's internal requirements. The affluent Kurgan-Tiube Oblast, which specialized in the cultivation of long-fibre cotton (in the Vakhsh Valley) and was practically the only producer of this crop throughout the Soviet Union, was contiguous to another southern *oblast*, Kulab, that was probably the poorest and most backward region in the republic. Industrialized Khujand in Leninabad Oblast with its high share of military-industrial enterprises was in effect the economic, westernized capital, while Dushanbe was the political capital. This latter city with its major concentration of educational establishments and research centres had grown since the 1920s out of several *kishlaks* in a region where Tajik was the native language for only 18.7 per cent of the population;[45] Bukhara and Samarkand, the spiritual centres of Tajik culture, were not included in the republic's territory.

Tajikistan's population was ethnically heterogeneous, and naturally its various ethnic communities adhered to different value systems. Moreover, the Tajiks themselves, who constituted throughout most of the Soviet period slightly over half of the population[46] were, as we have seen, not a single national formation. The social structure of the Tajik people did not possess the obligatory parameters of a 'socialist nation', of which the most important was the existence of a national working class. Both in urban and rural society important elements of earlier pre-Soviet social relations were retained.[47] The various regional groups that together constituted the Tajik nation held different views regarding the state's integrity, the presence of other ethnic minorities and the possibility for those professing non-Sunni Islam,[48] and even for Tajiks born in neighbouring regions, to live outside their place of origin. Regional links proved significantly stronger than national ones, and this applied in equal measure to industrialized and agrarian regions. Sometimes these links provided a basis for creating local associations with pronounced political leanings.[49]

The same held true for ostensibly republican political associations. Notwithstanding the tasks and aims they proclaimed, they were essentially regional rather than national parties.

POLITICAL PARTIES OF TAJIKISTAN: FOUNDATION AND POLITICAL PRACTICE

Tajikistan's political parties were set up by representatives of the republic's 'educated class' with its inherently contradictory internal structure. Its motley groups and strata (in Soviet parlance they were defined as 'the scientific-technical, humanities and creative intelligentsia') had at times diametrically opposed leanings and interests.

S. Olimova and M. Olimov have put forward some interesting ideas about the internal structure of Tajikistan's intelligentsia and the orientations of its composite groups. These two authors point out that, first of all, there is a marginal social stratum represented by Russian-speakers of mixed origin or those of the upper élite. They have only a scant knowledge of the national culture, but are dynamic and well- educated in the European sense of the word. Some of them are cosmopolitan, while others want to move out of their marginal status and acquire their own national identity. Second, there is the numerous rural intelligentsia (teachers, doctors, agricultural experts), together with low-ranking government officials, and the engineers and technicians of the urban industrial plants. People in this group originate mainly from rural areas, and preserve close economic and spiritual links with the population of their native parts. In their new places of residence these people form associations which reproduce the political sentiments of the corresponding regions. Finally, there is a group comprising people from humanities research institutes and republican and local-level administrators, that is led by writers and poets. This group is oriented towards the ideals of national revival on the basis of the values of the pre-Islamic Iranian-speaking zone – Zoroastrianism, the grandeur of Iran under the Sassanid dynasty – and of Iran under the last Shah as the embodiment of a truly democratic renovation and of progress. Some 'marginals' from the first group who strive to regain their national roots, including members of the republican political élite, and some of the 'rural intelligentsia' also gravitate towards this group.[50]

The conclusions of the Olimovs indeed coincide in part with the data of the surveys conducted in Tajikistan by the Russian Academy of Management regarding the political leanings of certain strata of the 'educated class'.

However, both the conclusions arrived at by the Olimovs and those based on the social surveys reveal the inapplicability of the simplistic Soviet scheme of the stratification of the 'educated class' to the realities of Tajikistan. The picture of the internal divisions in the ranks of those who founded Tajikistan's political movements and parties is much more complex than it seems at first glance. Thus, despite the temptation to see the second group of the 'educated class' as the founders of the IRP, this is not borne out by the survey results concerning the level of support given to communists by the so-called 'agricultural intelligentsia'. Moreover, it is apparent that representatives of the first and third groups were the founders of Rastokhez and the DPT and initiated the reform from within the Communist Party. In other words, Tajikistan's political parties and movements were united not only by the identity of their political platforms and their common social base but also by a similar formative background – an aggregate of groups and strata of the 'educated class' that penetrated and influenced each other.

All three factors made these parties not just rivals but rivals-cum-allies; hence the seemingly inconceivable 'democratic-Islamic' alliance. In the future, too, new political blocs and coalitions are possible, if this or that party sees prospects of snatching part of the following of a present ally or associate. These new supporters would be drawn by pragmatic considerations, which could always be justified by a similarity of ideology.

Acting, as they were, in a transitional society, these parties emulated the ploys and methods of political struggle customary in this society. And if, as Shodmon Yusuf, says 'the tribal consciousness' of the Tajiks recognizes 'the right of survival only of the representatives of a given tribe', and if 'the so-called Tajik people have not a single song that is acceptable to all regions',[51] clearly the only way for any political association to achieve success was to put its faith in a popular personality, or group of the political élite, or specific region.

Thus regional élite groups have become a real political force in post-Soviet Tajikistan. Their emergence, which began in the last years of the Soviet era, was determined by the specific traits of the mechanism of power that operated in the republic, which was outwardly unified and centralized, yet each of its components was to a large degree autonomous within the framework of its own functions and prerogatives. The union centre supported the situation in which the ruling élite originated in Leninabad Oblast and shared some of its power with people from Kulab and served as guarantor of the status quo; Dushanbe, for its part played the same role as Moscow vis-à-vis those regional élites that were subordinate to the republican authorities. The weakening and subsequent disappearance of the union centre caused the progressive erosion of Leninabad Oblast's dominant position in Tajikistan's administration and destroyed the unwritten accord between the regional élite groups concerning the principles underlying the republican pyramid of power. Those who had previously been far removed from the top believed that a power vacuum was forming and were out to fill it.

It was only natural and easily understandable that the communists should rely on the backing of Leninabad and Kulab Oblasts. The opposition parties, on the other hand, could not turn for support to people from the north and their satellites from Kulab, who in the years of their long rule had discredited themselves in their eyes. So these parties had perforce to choose from among prominent figures who had belonged to the same communist *nomenklatura* but had not been admitted to the summit of power and were therefore believed to be consistent advocates of democratic change. This circumstance alone could make the parties in Tajikistan look alike. But there were also the common features of their political platforms, social base and background, as well as methods of political action. These methods, in their turn, were determined by the absence of any national space and by links of regional and local loyalties. Each party believed that using these links was its sole road to power.

All this made these parties not just tools to be manipulated by the regional élite groups. Since the parties' attachment to specific regions was utterly fortuitous, they became entities that could be used by present-day or future élite groups. This meant that these parties became completely distanced from their proclaimed goal – the preservation of the integrity of the national territory and attaining the rebirth of the people who inhabit it.

NOTES

1. Text of the Declaration of State Independence of the Republic of Tajikistan – *Narodnaia gazeta* (Dushanbe), 11 Sept. 1991.
2. Rastokhez was formed in September 1989 and the DPT in August 1990. By the time Tajikistan's independence was proclaimed, both were officially registered associations. The DPT was formed by former Rastokhez members.
3. The activists of the Tajikistan branch of the all-union IRP were known locally as Wahhabis. The Wahhabis were a puritan Sunni sect founded in the 18th century in the Arabian peninsula, which called for a return to the simplicity of early Islam and which rejected later developments, including Sufism, as a corruption of the true faith. The designation in Tajikistan probably originated from a desire by the official religious establishment in the mid-1980s, when the term began to appear in the press, to denigrate political opponents of the Soviet regime and of its own status and activity. Tajikistan's so-called Wahhabis seem to have had no connection in fact with the Wahhabi movement in Saudi Arabia.
   The Tajikistan branch of the IRP was officially registered, as a separate republican party, on 11 Dec. 1991 – see *Narodnaia gazeta*, 12 Dec. 1991.
4. Appeal of the delegates of the extraordinary 22nd Congress of the Communist Party of Tajikistan to the communists and all the toiling people of the republic – *Narodnaia gazeta*, 27 Sept. 1991.
5. Programmatic statement of the Socialist Party of Tajikistan – *Narodnaia gazeta*, 28 Sept. 1991.
6. *Narodnaia gazeta*, 1 Oct. 1991.
7. *Narodnaia gazeta*, 28 Dec. 1991.
8. In Jan. 1993, there were still officially 126,000 members in the Communist Party – *Narodnaia gazeta*, 6 Feb. 1993. After the registration in the spring of that year, only 70,000 members remained – *Golos Tadzhikistana*, 28 April–5 May 1993.
9. This view was held by, among others, some Russian democrats. In particular, Anatolii Sobchak, who visited Dushanbe in Sept. 1991 as one of a group of President Gorbachev's personal envoys, spoke in this vein.
10. S. Olimova and M. Olimov, 'Obrazovannyi klass Tadzhikistana v peripetiiah XX veka', *Vostok. Afro-aziiatskie obshchestva: istoriia i sovremennost'* 5 (Moscow, 1991), pp. 95–6. See also Donald S. Carlisle, 'Geopolitics and Ethnic Problems of Uzbekistan and Its Neighbours', in this volume.
11. *Barnomai hizbi islomi – Hidoyat*, (n.p., Feb. 1992).
12. *Barnomai sozmoni Rastokhez – Junbishi mardumii Tojikiston*. Typewritten edition (n.p., n.d.), p. 1.
13. 'Program of the Democratic Party of Tajikistan'. Typewritten edition (n.p., n.d.), p. 1.
14. Program of the Socialist Party of Tajikistan (*Narodnaia gazeta*, 15 Oct. 1991), published as a draft to be adopted after discussion at the second stage of the 22nd Congress. Simultaneously it was underscored that the name of the party would be chosen at a later date. However, developments took such a turn that the second stage of the Communist Party Congress was not convened.
15. Ibid.
16. Program of the Democratic Party of Tajikistan, p. 2.
17. *Barnomai sozmoni Rastokhez*, p. 6.
18. Sh. Abdullaev, 'Musulmane li my?', *Javononi Tojikiston*, 27 June 1990. This article, written by a historian of Islam, was viewed in the republic as the manifesto of the nascent Islamic political movement.
19. *Barnomai hizbi islomi*.
20. *Barnomai sozmoni Rastokhez*, p. 13.
21. Program of the Democratic Party of Tajikistan, p. 2.
22. Program of the Socialist Party of Tajikistan.
23. Ibid.
24. *Barnomai sozmoni Rastokhez*, p. 14.
25. In 1979, the proportion of Tajiks employed in industrial production was only 10.9 per cent of the industrial work force. The figure for Russians was 29 per cent. The situation

was identical in construction, where Tajiks comprised 6.2 per cent and Russians, 17.2 per cent. – R. Narzikulov, 'Dvulikii Ianus v serdtse Azii: nekotorye itogi 70-letnego razvitiia sredneaziatskikh respublik v sostave SSSR', *Vostok. Afro-aziatskie obshchestva: istoriia i sovremennost'* 5 (1991), p. 125.

26. *Oinnomoi hizbi islomi – Hidoyat* (n.p., Feb. 1992).
27. *Barnomai hizbi islomi.*
28. *Barnomai sozmoni Rastokhez*, p. 10.
29. Ibid.
30. Interview with Sh. Iusupov (Yusuf), 'Realii nashikh dnei trebuiut glubokogo osmysleniia', *Narodnaia gazeta*, 29 Jan. 1992.
31. *Barnomai sozmoni Rastokhez*, pp. 10–11.
32. Program of the Socialist Party of Tajikistan.
33. *Barnomai hizbi islomi.*
34. Ibid.
35. Program of the Socialist Party of Tajikistan.
36. *Barnomai hizbi islomi.*
37. S. Olimova and M. Olimov, 'Obrazovannyi klass Tadzhikistana', pp. 100–101.
38. Cf., in particular, A. Malashenko and V. Moskalenko, 'Proigralo li religioznoe dvizhenie v Tadzhikistane?', *Nezavisimaia gazeta*, 31 Jan. 1992; A. Malashenko and A. Niiazi, 'O Tadzhikistane bez pristrastiia. Kto s kem voiuet v respublike?', *Nezavisimaia gazeta*, 3 March 1993.
39. N. M. Nazarshoev, *Intelligentsiia Tadzhikistana v 1965–1985 gg.* (Dushanbe, 1989), p. 204.
40. See Note 3.
41. Nazarshoev, *Intelligentsiia Tadzhikistana.*
42. Cf. *Ozhidaniia i nadezhdy liudei v usloviiah stanovleniia gosudarstvennosti (Opyt sotsiologicheskikh issledovanyi v Tadzhikistane, Kazakhstane, Rossii i na Ukraine)* (Moscow, Russian Academy of Management, 1992), pp. 29–43. See also Note 44 below.
43. In 1979, 54.3 per cent of Tajiks were employed in agricultural production, as against 2.8 per cent of the republic's Russian population – R. Narzikulov, 'Dvulikii Ianus v serdtse Azii', p. 125.
44. Cf. *Ozhidaniia i nadezhdy liudei v usloviiah stanovleniia gosudarstvennosti*, pp. 29–43.
45. *Narodnaia gazeta*, 14 April 1992.
46. In the 1939, 1959, 1970 and 1979 censuses, the Tajiks comprised less than 60 per cent of their republic's total population. Only in 1989 did they exceed that number, with 62.3 per cent.
47. Here the reference is in the first place to the *avlod* – the clan that united living and dead relatives on the paternal side. To this day the *avlod* although somewhat modified, plays a leading role, remaining the main form of social stratification. – V. I. Bushkov, 'Tadzhikskii avlod tysiacheletiia spustia', *Vostok. Afro-aziatskie obshchestva: istoriia i sovremennost'* 5 (1991), pp. 72–81.
48. Such as the population of Gorno-Badakhshan.
49. E.g., Lali Badakhshon.
50. S. Olimova and M. Olimov, 'Obrazovannyi klass Tadzhikistana', pp. 99–102.
51. I. Rotar, 'Vzorvetsia-li Sredniaia Aziia? Nabrosok etnosotsial'nogo portreta regiona', *Nezavisimaia gazeta*, 21 Jan. 1993.

8

A Year of Rule by the Popular Front of Azerbaijan

ARYEH WASSERMAN

The Popular Front of Azerbaijan (PFA), which became the main political force in Azerbaijan after the fall of the pro-communist regime in May 1992[1] and the election in June of the Front's leader Abulfaz Elçibey as President, had one of the most democratic programs of all socio-political movements in the former USSR. There was no reason to doubt the sincerity of Elçibey's intentions and promises to build a Western-style society in Azerbaijan[2] and to integrate the new state into the international community as an equal partner.

Under the PFA government Azerbaijan took its first steps towards democracy. New laws on political parties and the mass media established principles of civil rights. The strong and uncompromising opposition was able to operate freely. Between July 1992 and early 1993, 24 parties were licensed[3] and more than 500 periodicals published.[4]

In a special address commemorating International Human Rights Day (11 December 1992), Elçibey said:

> The Azerbaijan Republic... adopts the principles of defence of human rights and freedom as a basic principle of its statehood...We have to affirm, at the parliamentary level, the precedence of the norms specified in international treaties and other documents on human rights and freedom over national legislation.[5]

But in a society lacking democratic traditions, where authoritarianism was deeply embedded in the national culture, the seeds of democracy had difficulty taking root.

Moreover, the new rulers behaved inconsistently, not infrequently violating democratic norms. Maintaining the principle 'whoever is not with us is against us', the PFA placed its own representatives and supporters in all key areas and positions, irrespective of their professional qualifications, experience and abilities. So, on all levels there was, in effect, a monopoly of one political force, whose accession to power was not the result of a democratic process. The only legal, democratically-elected power was the President. But in fact Elçibey voiced the views and ideology of the Popular Front.

The opposition parties did not recognize the legitimacy of the Milli Mejlis, to which, they stressed, the Supreme Soviet had handed over legislative power only temporarily during the previous regime.[6] They demanded new parliamentary elections, but the authorities delayed holding them, apparently fearing defeat. These parties, which covered a wide political spectrum, including former leaders and adherents of the PFA, and radicals and supporters of ex-communist rulers Aiaz Mutalibov and Geidar Aliev,[7] stepped up their criticism of the PFA regime, as the internal situation in Azerbaijan deteriorated and the republic suffered severe military defeats at the hands of Armenian forces.

The difficult situation in Azerbaijan was caused by objective circumstances. The Popular Front had inherited an economy which for several years had suffered a deep recession. The interruption of normal economic ties with former parts of the USSR, resulting from the breakup of the Soviet Union, as well as economic pressure by Russia, had very grave consequences for the republic. Moreover, the PFA's rule coincided with the most difficult period of the Azerbaijan-Armenian war, when not only Nagornyi-Karabakh but also other areas of Azerbaijan were occupied by Armenian forces.

The crisis situation was further aggravated by the new leaders' lack of experience and incompetence in carrying out policy. PFA leaders admitted that power had fallen to them unexpectedly, and that they had not yet worked out a plan of action.[8] In the economic sphere, the government delayed initiating a process of reform, and when some reform laws were finally adopted, such as that on privatization, no mechanism was prepared for their implementation. As a result, the economic crisis deepened and living standards continued to fall during the PFA's 15-month rule.

The selection of officials on the sole basis of political loyalty and personal devotion[9] was one of the weakest points of the government and caused protests even among some leaders of the PFA.[10] Elçibey himself noted that corruption during the PFA's rule was becoming a great danger.[11]

As a consequence of all this, the euphoria and enthusiasm which accompanied the PFA's accession to power gave way after several months to disappointment among the population, and a little later, to large-scale animosity towards the ruling Front and indifference to its fate.

This chapter will focus on the PFA's policy on the nationalities question and related topics during its 15-month rule. In this sphere important tendencies of the PFA's domestic and foreign policies and ideology intersected, strikingly demonstrating the contradictory nature of the PFA's rule, especially between its ideas, declarations and policy implementation.

The nationalities question had appeared as an important component of political life in Azerbaijan with the beginning of the socio-political crisis that developed in Azerbaijan in the late 1980s. It became one of the central problems of the PFA government, as the worsening situation in the republic and grievous defeats in the war with Armenia led to manifestations of a separatist mood among some of the country's national minorities. There seemed to be a danger that Azerbaijan might actually disintegrate. With the important exception of the Armenian population of Nagornyi-Karabakh, this had not previously been in the cards.

There are many nationalities and ethnic minorities in Azerbaijan,[12] but for several decades the problem of national minorities had not existed either for politicians or for researchers. The study of the nationalities question in Azerbaijan was limited to glorifying the 'Leninist nationalities policy' and to the quest for new ways of 'further strengthening the friendship of the peoples'. National minorities were not even mentioned in textbooks on Azerbaijan's history.

Following the establishment of Soviet power in Azerbaijan in 1920, the local authorities conducted a policy of 'absorbing' some of the national minorities, beginning with such indigenous groups as the Talysh, Lezgins, Tats and Kurds; most were officially labelled Azerbaijanis. At the same time, books and newspapers were published in national languages, teaching in primary schools was conducted in 24 languages, and national theatres and cultural societies flourished – until the end of the 1930s, when all such activity was abruptly stopped in all Soviet republics.[13]

In the decades that followed it seemed that the public had forgotten about the existence of national minorities in Azerbaijan and on the surface there was no friction between them and the Azerbaijanis. With the rise of Azerbaijani nationalism, Russians began emigrating from Azerbaijan and their percentage in the republic decreased from 13.6 in 1959 to 5.6 in 1989.[14] The smaller minorities suffered less than the Russian-speaking population from the rising ambitions of the growing indigenous élite. Of the 93.8 per cent of all administrators in the republic in 1989 registered as Azerbaijanis,[15] quite a few were representatives of these peoples.

Azerbaijanis looked on some of these peoples as kindred nations.

So, while Azerbaijanis had one of the lowest rates of intermarriage of the USSR republics,[16] marriages with representatives of these ethnic groups were not rare. Azerbaijanis have particularly broad kinship relations with the biggest minority group – the Lezgins. About 40 per cent of the Azerbaijani Lezgins are related to Azerbaijanis. Lezgins also play an important role in the scientific life of the republic: 12 per cent of research workers of the local Academy of Sciences are Lezgins, and 14 per cent of the lecturers at Baku University.[17]

Although these peoples were designated as Azerbaijanis, they maintained their traditions and customs. In spite of all the efforts of the Azerbaijani authorities to change the demographic situation in the territories of compact residence of ethnic minorities, in some regions they constituted the majority or a large minority of the population: for example, the Lezgins in northern *raions* such as Kusary where they constituted 70 per cent,[18] the Talysh in Lenkoran Raion, the Ingeloians – in the *raions* bordering Georgia. There was latent antagonism between these groups and the Azerbaijanis. The Azerbaijanis were disparaging about some of these peoples, speaking of the 'stubborn Lezgi', the 'rude, unsophisticated Kurd' and the 'primitive Talysh'.

Representatives of the indigenous minorities were not for the most part appointed to important governmental positions. But there were exceptions. For instance, in the 1960s, Mamed Iskenderov, a Kurd, officially registered as an Azerbaijani, occupied the post of chairman of the Presidium of the Azerbaijan Supreme Soviet.

The gradual rise of national consciousness among the smaller minorities coincided approximately with the growth of Azerbaijani nationalism and, in some respects, was a reaction to it. One of the main causes was a significant increase in the educational level and the size of the intelligentsia among these ethnic groups.

The process of seeking a national identity accelerated among these peoples from the mid-1980s with the democratization of Soviet society and the beginning of the national movement in Azerbaijan in 1988. At first representatives of national minorities took an active part in this movement. Many of them became members of the Popular Front and even part of its leadership. One thousand Lezgin volunteers joined the small, newly formed Azerbaijan army.[19]

At the same time, however, representatives of these peoples began to voice strongly their own problems, including the need to develop their cultures and languages. They demanded to receive at least some of the rights for which the Azerbaijanis had struggled and which they were beginning to enjoy.

Some factors were in their favour: the general weakening of the power structure, the involvement of the Azerbaijanis in the Karabakh crisis and the authorities' reluctance to provoke new national conflicts. The processes which began to develop in the Northern Caucasus, especially among the Lezgins in Dagestan had a great influence on the national minorities in Azerbaijan.[20]

The establishment of public cultural and political organizations of national minorities in Azerbaijan marked a new period. One of the first such organizations was the Lezgin Cultural Centre, Samur, formed in March 1990 and affiliated to the Cultural Foundation of the Azerbaijan Republic. It served as the basis for an independent political organization, the Lezgin National Centre (LNC), likewise designated Samur, and created in 1992. The LNC program stressed the untenability of the continued lack of any 'state or socio-political organization representing and protecting the national interests of the Lezgin people, defending its existence as a single people, a single nation, guaranteeing its socio-political development and welfare and defending the originality of its national culture'.[21]

The main political parties in Azerbaijan began to pay attention to the problem of the national minorities.[22] The Kurdish Equality Party, the Talysh People's Party (formed in 1990 and in 1992 renamed the Party of Equality of the Peoples of Azerbaijan) and the Lezgin Democratic Party (formed in August 1992) came into being. An Institute of Nationality Relations at the Academy of Sciences of Azerbaijan was opened in Baku, to replace the Institute of Friendship of the Peoples. A special department was formed at the Pedagogical Research Institute to prepare a curriculum for the teaching of minority languages in schools.[23]

Already in its early statements in 1989 the PFA had supported the creation of maximal conditions for the preservation and development of the language, culture and national traditions of Russians, Armenians, Lezgins, Talysh, Kurds, Jews, Ingeloians and other national minorities living in Azerbaijan.[24] In the Popular Front program a special section was devoted to the question of ethnic relations, while in the platforms of most of the other parties only a sentence, at most, was given to the problem.[25] In his election platform Elçibey declared: 'It is necessary to recognize the national rights of all people living in Azerbaijan, to fulfill their national needs, and to create conditions for preserving national languages, cultures and customs.'[26]

But the *realpolitik* of the PFA during its rule was shaped by different, often contradictory, factors: on the one hand, the belief of leaders and members of the PFA in democratic principles and tolerance towards other nationalities – though this was significantly weakened with the intensification of Azerbaijani nationalism; on the other, growing nationalistic aggressiveness (under the influence of the

Karabakh war), the ideology of 'Turkism' and the exploitation of inter-ethnic antagonism by political forces inside and outside the republic. The formulation of the PFA's policy on the nationalities question was also influenced by two tendencies in the Azerbaijani national movement, one extremist, the other moderate, which were evident from the movement's very beginning. These were especially manifest in regard to the Armenians. Extremist leaders of the first period of the national movement (1988–89), such as Neimat Panahov[27] and Khatemi Tantekin,[28] demanded the eviction of Armenians from Baku, while moderate leaders and activists of the PFA condemned attacks against them;[29] during the anti-Armenian pogroms in Baku in mid-January 1990 these moderates helped many Armenians to escape[30] and ultimately stopped the slaughter.[31]

Abulfaz Elçibey, in one of his first interviews after his election to the presidency, said: 'The religious and national policy of Azerbaijan will follow the traditions of the Azerbaijan Democratic Republic of 1918–20'.[32] On another occasion he stressed:

> Everyone can speak in whatever language he wants, can open a school in any language; whoever wants to develop his culture, let him develop it. That is to say, we support the autonomy of minorities and the state will help in this matter not only in words, but also in deeds.[33]

On 16 September 1992 Elçibey issued a 'Decree on the defence of the rights and liberties of national minorities, of other minorities and ethnic groups and on rendering state assistance to the development of their languages and cultures'. The decree listed concrete measures to protect these rights and to prevent actions aimed at racial discrimination, national exclusiveness and national pre-eminence, and at stirring up national enmity.[34] Concurrently, a council,[35] and in March 1993, the office of a state adviser on nationalities policy, were created.[36]

The leadership of the republic declared that it was in favour of granting cultural autonomy to national minorities. The teaching of national minority languages was begun in schools.[37] A branch of the Baku teachers' seminary was opened in Kusary to prepare teachers of Lezgin.[38] Books and periodicals were published in Lezgin, Talysh, Kurdish and Tat and there were regular broadcasts in these languages. In April 1993 a Lezgin state theatre was opened in Kusary.[39]

The national minority organizations mostly endorsed the nation-alities policy of the government, and supported the territorial integrity of Azerbaijan. Thus, the main goal of the Lezgin Democratic Party, as stated in its program, was to defend the rights of the Lezgin people within an indivisible and independent Azerbaijan.[40] The other major Lezgin organization, Samur, too, believed that the republican leadership was ready to solve the problems of the Lezgin people, and understood that it could not demand that the government immediately settle all the problems which it had inherited from the previous regime, particularly when the republic was forced to contend with aggression within its borders.

Samur, the most influential Lezgin organization in Azerbaijan, condemned the territorial claims to a republic on the part of the Lezgin organization Sadwal (Unity),[41] an organization formed in neighbouring Dagestan. The main goal of Sadwal was to create a Lezgin state – Lezgistan – which would comprise parts of Dagestan and the territories of Azerbaijan populated by Lezgins.[42] Peoples of the Lezgin language group live in 14 *raions* of the northern zone of Azerbaijan.[43]

Sadwal declared that the time for the disintegration of the 'Azerbaijan empire' had come. In Makhachkala, the third National Congress of the Lezgin People adopted a resolution on the restoration of Lezgin statehood[44] within the Russian Federation, that would include areas in Azerbaijan with large numbers of Lezgins. According to Sadwal, one million Lezgins live in the territory of this future state, 670,000 of them in Azerbaijan, half a million of whom are registered as Azerbaijanis.[45] About 100,000 Azerbaijanis live in Dagestan.[46]

Tensions between Azerbaijanis and Lezgins in both Azerbaijan and Dagestan rose significantly as of spring 1992. There was violence, including ambushes on roads.[47] In Kusary, which is located in the region of Azerbaijan bordering Dagestan. Sadwal organized rallies attended by thousands of Lezgins.[48]

Aggravation of the Lezgin problem was partly a result of Russian measures to introduce strict border control between Azerbaijan and Dagestan,[49] thus minimizing contact between Lezgins on both sides of the border. This was part of Russia's policy of economic pressure on Azerbaijan, which under PFA rule tried to pursue an independent foreign policy. After the authorities in both Azerbaijan and Dagestan protested strongly,[50] Russia agreed to revoke the measure.[51]

To demonstrate Russia's incitement of the Lezgin problem, Azerbaijanis pointed to the visit to Dagestan of Galina Starovoitova, then Russia's presidential adviser on nationality relations, who took part in an anti-Azerbaijani rally in Makhachkala.[52] The republican authorities protested against an increase in arms shipments from Russia to the Lezgin populated areas of Azerbaijan[53] and several 'incendiary' articles on the issue appeared in the Russian press.[54]

Azerbaijan also protested officially to Russia about the interference of Sadwal leaders in the republic's internal affairs and their efforts to destabilize the situation in the republic.[55] Azerbaijan's mass media pointed out that Russia supported Sadwal and its idea of creating

Lezgistan in order to incite a new conflict zone, as in Ossetiia or Transdniestria, and exert influence on Azerbaijan.[56] Indeed, immediately after the nomination of the pro-Russian Geidar Aliev as Acting President of Azerbaijan, Moscow banned the activities of Sadwal in June 1993.

Besides the Lezgins, the most politically active minorities are the Kurds and the Talysh.[57] According to unofficial figures, the Kurdish population in Azerbaijan numbers more than 200,000[58] (although according to the 1989 census, it was only 21,169.[59] Some Kurdish leaders have demanded political autonomy for their people.[60]

Signs of Talysh separatism increased as of the beginning of 1993. Colonel Aliakram Gummatov (or Gumbatov), one of the former leaders of the PFA, who operates from Lenkoran, the *raion* with the heaviest population of Talysh, refused to obey orders from Baku and in June proclaimed a Talysh-Mugan Republic (TMR), which included seven *raions* of Azerbaijan. These seven *raions* include about ten per cent of the population of Azerbaijan.[61] No fewer than 100,000 Talysh live on the Iranian side of the Astara River, which forms the border between Azerbaijan and Iran.[62] Azerbaijan has accused the Iranians of supporting the separatists.[63]

The PFA's policy on the nationalities question was greatly influenced by its ideology of Turkism. Speaking of the Popular Front's ideological tenets – Turkism, Islamism and modernity – Elçibey stressed that first of all 'we are Turks' and secondly Muslims. This is reflected in the tri-coloured Azerbaijani flag, the first colour being blue, which symbolizes Turkism.[64] According to Elçibey, even 'the very idea to create the Popular Front originated from the ideology of Atatürk'.[65]

When the leader of the Pan-Turkist Party of Turkey, Alparslan Türkeş, arrived in Baku in October 1992 he was greeted by enthusiastic crowds and welcomed by Elçibey and leaders of many parties.[66] However, Elçibey, while acclaiming Türkeş as a great Turk, pointed out that he was not a follower of Türkeş's credo.[67] He also denied that he aspired to create a Turanian state.[68]

Adherence to Turkism was proclaimed by almost all political parties in Azerbaijan. The platform of the main opposition group, the Party for the National Independence of Azerbaijan stated: 'We identify Turkism with nationalism since we consider that Turkism forms the basis for national sense in Azerbaijan [i.e., presumably Azerbaijani nationalism]'.[69]

During the PFA's rule, support for the integration of all the Turkic peoples grew considerably. The Popular Democratic Party and the Turan Popular Democratic Party stated in their programs that the

Azerbaijani people could achieve freedom and prosperity only by putting their trust in the spiritual essence, mentality and philosophy of the Turkic people. But their aim was to attain only the moral – not the political – unity of the Turks.[70]

The most blatantly pan-Turkist organization in Azerbaijan is the Turan Association of Free Working People, headed by Panahov,[71] while the best known anti-Turkic party is the Social Democratic Party of Azerbaijan (SDPA). It calls on Azerbaijanis to abandon the illusion that the 'best friend of the Turk is the Turk'.[72]

Although some political figures, like Isa Gambar, one of the leaders of the PFA and head of the Musavat Party, argued that Turkism is a socio-political, not an ethnic, concept,[73] the policy of the turkicization of society caused anxiety, especially among numerous smaller peoples. Their representatives argued that the reaction to the policy of 'turkicization' could be 'lezginization', 'tatization' and 'talyshization'.[74] They sharply criticized the law adopted by the Milli Mejlis on 23 December 1992 renaming the Azerbaijani language Turkic.[75] The chairman of Samur, Ali Musaev, emphasized: 'Lezgins accept the Azerbaijan Republic, the Azerbaijani people and the Azerbaijani language, but do not accept a Turkic republic, Turkic people and Turkic language.'[76] The organ of the PFA, *Svoboda*, wrote on 8 January 1993 that the main mistake in this connection was that 'the renaming of the language occurred without the wish of the people, without a national referendum'.[77] But Elçibey in an interview published in another PFA organ, *Azadlyq*, on 9 January said that 'the name of a language is not determined by referendum, this is science'.[78] Nonetheless, the Front had to confess that the law was inopportune.[79]

Kurds, Talysh, Lezgins and others were inevitably discontented with the change of name of the dominant nationality from Azerbaijani to Azerbaijani Turk. As a compromise, Isa Gambar proposed that in future passports, besides the ethnic entry, there would be an additional entry for nationality origin, where one could register as Turkic, Talysh, Kurdish, Russian and so on, or not fill it in at all.[80]

The growing interest in the nationalities problem and the rising influence of the ideology of Turkism revived the old controversy over the ethnogenesis of the Azerbaijani people, that is, between adherents of the concept of the decisive Turkic role and supporters of the pro-Iranian theory. In the mid-1970s the republican authorities headed by First Secretary Geidar Aliev had resolved the debate by ruling in favour of the Iranian concept. Now, for the first time monographs dedicated to this problem were published.[81] The purely scientific problem of ethnogenesis became a regular theme in the newspapers. The authors of some articles used this discussion to express their opposition to the policy of turkicization. Politicians also intervened in the dispute. The President's adviser on nationalities, Idaiat Orujev, supported the concept according to which Azerbaijan was the homeland of the Oğuz Turks,[82] which obviously meant that he was inclined to accept the theory of the Turkic origins of the Azerbaijani people.

Opponents of the pro-Turkic conception of the ethnogenesis of the Azerbaijani people insist that the Kurds, Talysh, Lakhij and other Persian-speaking peoples are ethnic Azerbaijanis, who had a part from ancient times in the ethnogenesis of the Azerbaijani people, and that all of them share the same Caspian racial type, to which no other Turkic-speaking peoples, not even the Turks themselves, belong.[83]

This debate and the whole process of turkicization troubled the national minorities, and they, as experts pointed out, put a tough question to themselves: were they aliens whom fate had willed to settle on Azerbaijani soil, or an integral component of the Azerbaijani people?[84] The policy of turkicization and the lack of real change in the situation of the national minorities led to growing discontent with the policy of the Popular Front regime among these peoples, and some of their representatives began to favour more radical steps.

At the Congress of the Lezgin Democratic Party of Azerbaijan in late January 1993, even the moderate party leader Fakhruddin Aidaev stressed that the problem of the division of the Lezgin people into two parts must be resolved by the Lezgins themselves without disrupting the territorial integrity of either Russia or Azerbaijan. He demanded free passage across the northern border of Azerbaijan, adoption of a law on dual citizenship and creation of a free trade zone on the territory of Azerbaijan populated by Lezgins. He pointed out the necessity of preparing a state program to solve the nationality question and establishing a government department of nationalities. Under pressure from the radicals the congress decided to exclude the word 'Azerbaijan' from the party's name.[85] However, only two weeks later, after a fierce struggle, the plenum of the party's ruling body decided to retain the name Lezgin Democratic Party of Azerbaijan (LDPA).[86] In any event, the authorities refused to register the LDPA, demanding the exclusion of the word 'Lezgin' from the name of the party, since they opposed the creation of nationalist parties. For the same reason, the Talysh People's Party, which came into existence in 1990, was officially registered only at the beginning of 1993, when it changed its name to the Party of Equality of the Peoples of Azerbaijan (PEPA).[87]

Representatives of national minorities were also worried about the removal of representatives of ethnic minority groups from some state institutions.[88] The chairman of the Baku committee of the LDPA, Iaralii Iaraliev, expressed dissatisfaction with the fact that national minorities were not represented in the legislative and executive bodies of the republic (only in August 1993 did one Lezgin gain Milli Mejlis membership).[89]

Lezgins complained about neglect of their culture. They were indignant at the attitude of the government adviser on nationality policy, Idaiat Orujev, who reacted to their request to return to them their religious and cultural monument, the 12th century mosque in Baku, as follows:

> These Lezgins have raised the question about this mosque so many times now. Why? Are they such believers? And with the return of the mosque to them will all their problems be solved? I wonder why Sadwal refuses to leave us alone.[90]

Ideas of separatism spread increasingly among some national minorities. Lezgin representatives proposed the idea of federalizing Azerbaijan as the only way to solve the nationalities problem. They welcomed the proclamation of the 'Talysh-Mugan Republic'.[91] Iaraliev warned that if the problems of the national minorities could not be resolved, there would be no alternative other than to create a Kurdish republic, a Talysh-Mugan republic, Lezgistan and other autonomous formations.[92] All the non-minority political parties of Azerbaijan, came out resolutely against the idea of federalization.

The attitude of the Russian-speaking population towards the PFA government was positive but distrustful, since it identified the Popular Front with nationalism. Public organizations of the Russian-speaking population – Sodruzhestvo, the Cultural Centre of the Slavs of Azerbaijan, Solidarity, the Azerbaijani-Russian Society and others – supported the government in its nationalities policy and over the Karabakh conflict.[93] But those newspapers which reflected the interests of the Russian-speakers noted with concern that symptoms of 'russophobia' could be felt in Baku.[94]

Under the PFA's rule, use of the Russian language became more restricted. All state institutions, public organizations, and factories were permitted to use only the Azerbaijani language.[95] The authorities in contemporary Azerbaijan have thus gone even further in this direction than their ideological inspirers of three-quarters of a century earlier. Then, the government of the Azerbaijan Democratic Republic, in a decree of 27 June 1918, declared that the state language was Turkic, but that for a transitional period the Russian language could be used too.[96]

In summer 1992 enrolment in Russian sectors of high and vocational schools was considerably curtailed, and in the latter teaching of the Russian language was removed from the curriculum.[97] The process of limiting the use of Russian, manifestations of ultra-nationalism, particularly on the part of some opposition groups, pressure from tens of thousands of refugees (the most vehement guardians of Turkic-Muslim customs and morals who had fled to Baku from Armenia),[98] pessimism about the future, the Karabakh war and an even steeper fall in production and in living standards than in CIS countries[99] – all triggered a mass emigration from the republic. One hundred and fifty thousand people of different nationalities left the republic in 1991 and the first half of 1992.[100] President Elçibey was concerned and stressed that the republican leadership was opposed to the idea of a single nationality state and would do everything to stop this exodus. [101]

The unease of the Russian-speaking population, and particularly of Russians, and fears for their future in the republic rose as a result of anti-Russian propaganda and a deterioration in relations between Azerbaijan and Russia during the PFA regime. Russia's ambassador in Baku, Val'ter Shoniia, stated that under Elçibey's rule there was no policy of forcing out Russians from Azerbaijan. But in the press, in daily life and in the statements of some party leaders the idea prevailed that 'Russia was not treating Azerbaijan too well, favouring another state [that is, Armenia], or was using this other state as a tool to deprive Azerbaijan of its justly attained independence'.[102]

The authorities' concern was understandable, given that the republic was rapidly losing qualified specialists. The proportion of specialists among the non-indigenous-speaking population was higher than among Azerbaijanis: of the total working population in the republic the intelligentsia constituted 30 per cent – 46 per cent of the Russian-speaking population and 28 per cent Azerbaijanis.[103]

The influx of refugees contributed greatly to exacerbating inter-ethnic tensions. By the end of May 1993 there were 233,413 refugees in Azerbaijan, among them 185,519 Azerbaijanis who had been forced to leave Armenia in 1988–89 and 27,550 Meskhetian Turks from Uzbekistan.[104]

The refugees who began arriving from Armenia in February 1988 were a particular source of ethnic tension. With their rapidly growing numbers and miserable conditions, they became a serious de-stabilizing force. In September 1989 the spokesman of the PFA told foreign correspondents that the 100,000 refugees in Baku were 'the source of ethnic unrest. [The situation] is like a powder keg and they could start to murder Armenians any day'.[105] The anti-Armenian pogroms of mid-January 1990 were allegedly carried out mainly by homeless refugees.

The seizure by the Armenian armed forces in 1992–93 of considerable areas of Azerbaijan (by the end of July 1993, 17 per cent of its territory was occupied) and the flight of the population from the occupied regions, created 600,000 displaced persons.[106] Most of them concentrated in Baku, together with thousands of people from the areas bordering the battle-zone. This in turn greatly increased the population of Baku, which rose from 1.6 million in 1989 to 3–3.5 million by autumn 1993.[107] Some of these refugees and displaced people took up residence in hotels, hostels or with relatives. But many settled in apartments that they seized from the Russian-speaking population who had temporarily left their homes, but intended returning as soon as the situation normalized. Hundreds of complaints from these expropriated people were received by Sodruzhestvo in Baku, the National Committee of the Helsinki Civil Assembly and other public organizations; more than 200 such complaints reached the Russian Embassy in Baku. Of the Russian-speaking population, the Russians suffered the most because of Russia's alleged military help to Armenia.[108] This phenomenon, in which local officials participated and to which higher officials turned a blind eye, was one of the main reasons for the ultimate departure of Russian speakers from Azerbaijan.[109]

This exit continued despite reassuring statements by the PFA leaders. A public opinion poll in summer 1992 showed that 56 per cent of Russian speakers were contemplating departure, including six per cent who were ready to leave in the very near future and 26 per cent who kept their suitcases ready, just in case.[110] In 1992, 97,000 Russian-speakers left Azerbaijan.[111] The opposition tried to exploit their discontent. The SDPA, which formed a commission to work with the Russian-speaking population,[112] urged them to become politically active to ensure their future in Azerbaijan.[113]

Of all the Russian-speaking peoples, mention should be made of the treatment of the Jews, who at the end of 1993 apparently numbered just over 20,000.[114] Several public Jewish organizations, set up in the period immediately before Azerbaijan gained its independence (1989–91) or immediately afterwards, operated under the PFA regime. Articles on Jews and Israel were published regularly in the press.[115] President Elçibey included the head of the Azerbaijan Jewish community in the delegation which accompanied him during his official visit to Turkey in November 1992. He also visited one of Baku's synagogues. The PFA resolutely condemned anti-Semitic manifestations.[116]

The attitude of the Azerbaijani authorities towards Jews was based on traditionally good relations between the two nations. For the Azerbaijani leadership, these relations were also instrumental in developing close ties with Israel, which in its opinion could help to change international public opinion on the Karabakh conflict, and also contribute to the establishment of political and economic ties with the

West. Elçibey repeatedly named Israel among the four to five countries to be given priority in Azerbaijan's foreign policy.[117] Preparations were under way at the beginning of 1993 for conclusion of a treaty of cooperation with Israel,[118] but the worsening political situation at home prevented it from being signed.

Since the initiation of the national movement, ties with the Azerbaijani diaspora have grown markedly.[119] Under the PFA government the strengthening of these relations became state policy. It was motivated by feelings of national solidarity, especially with Azerbaijanis in other parts of the former Soviet Union, and by the aspiration to take advantage of the diaspora to advance its foreign policy goals. A Day of Solidarity of Azerbaijanis throughout the World has been celebrated annually since December 1989, when a PFA-led mob destroyed surveillance installations on the Soviet-Iranian border separating the two parts of Azerbaijan.[120] In order to stimulate ties with the Azerbaijani diaspora, a special political party, Yurddash, was formed; it held its constituent convention in February 1993.[121]

According to approximate data of UNESCO, there were 38 million Azerbaijanis living in 68 countries in 1989, including seven million in northern and 21 million in southern Azerbaijan. Another 1.5 million lived in Russia, more than half a million in Georgia and 42,000 in the Ukraine.[122]

The situation of Azerbaijanis in Georgia was the most worrisome. Tensions around them began to mount in 1988. From the beginning of 1989 the authorities in Georgia pursued a policy of changing the demographic situation in the territories of compact Azerbaijani residence by resettling there Svans, the problematic ethnic group from Svanetiia (Georgia). The Georgian authorities ceased to give Azerbaijanis passports or lease them land for building homes and dismissed them from leading positions. Azerbaijani schools and newspapers were closed, hostages were taken, people killed and injured. In the last parliamentary elections in Soviet Georgia in 1991, not a single Azerbaijani was elected to the Supreme Soviet.[123] In 1991–92 no fewer than 100,000 Azerbaijanis left Georgia.[124]

The situation of the Azerbaijanis in Georgia was debated for the first time in the Azerbaijani parliament at the beginning of December 1992 and its speaker Isa Gambar underlined that relations with Georgia depended on the position of the Azerbaijanis there.[125]

The PFA government manifested inconsistencies and discrepancies in its policy on the nationalities question as in most other spheres of its activity. Its decisions were greatly influenced by ideology and often contradicted existing realities.

In the first place, there was a of lack qualified specialists in this field. Secondly, decisions taken were not the result of careful consideration or preparation and their consequences were not calculated.

As a result of all this, in spite of the noble ideas stated in the PFA's programmatic documents and by its government, its actual conduct of nationality policy in fact aggravated the situation and was one of the causes of rising tensions in society.

* * *

The 15-month rule of the PFA concluded the period of 'the people's democratic revolution', about which its leaders had spoken so much. The results of this period were negative: the republic was plunged into a new spiral of crisis, severe internal contradictions and political struggle, which ended with the bloody tragedy in Gandja in June 1993, mutiny and the fall of the PFA regime. This was not fundamentally different from what happened in a number of the USSR's successor states, all of which had to face similar problems and very complex domestic and external circumstances.

Under these circumstances the leaders of the PFA, who were basically idealists or ideologists and not experienced politicians when they came to power, proved to be unfit to govern the state. They did not stand the test of state power and were prone to corruption, demagogy, regionalism and the use of force as a means to political ends. Nor were they assisted by the low cultural level, in particular political culture, of the majority of the population.

The Popular Front has left the political stage. But its role in bringing about qualitative changes in society must not be underestimated. It exerted tremendous influence on the politicization of the masses. As the spearhead of the national movement, the PFA infused it with a democratic spirit. And this was reflected in the programs of all the major political forces in Azerbaijan.

NOTES

1. On 20 Jan. 1990, at the peak of the national foment in Azerbaijan, which had begun early in 1988, Soviet troops were brought to Baku to prevent the opposition from seizing power. Aiaz Mutalibov, until then Prime Minister of the republic, became the new first secretary of the Communist Party of the Azerbaijan SSR. In the elections to the Supreme Soviet of the Azerbaijan SSR, held in Oct. 1990, under conditions of martial law, the opposition gained only 31 seats out of 350 (*Azadlyq*, Baku, 30 Aug. 1991). In the presidential elections in Sept. 1991 Mutalibov was elected President. Yet on 30 Oct. 1991 Mutalibov yielded to the pressure of the opposition and a National Council was formed, which consisted of 50 deputies of the Supreme Soviet, supporters of the president and the opposition on equal footing, and on 26 Nov. 1991 the Supreme Soviet handed over legislative power to the new body – A. Balaev, *Azerbaidzhanskoe natsional'noe dvizhenie: ot Musavata do Narodnogo Fronta*

(Baku, 1992), p. 73. Upon the dissolution of the Soviet Union, the population of Azerbaijan unanimously approved the independence of the republic in a referendum held on 31 Dec. 1991. The disintegration of the USSR and Azerbaijan's defeats in Nagornyi-Karabakh undermined the position of the pro-communist regime and precipitated its fall. The Popular Front of Azerbaijan (PFA), the leading force of the national movement, succeeded in forcing President Mutalibov's resignation in March 1992 after Armenians captured Khojaly, where hundreds of people were killed. After Mutalibov's unsuccessful attempt to regain power in mid-May, the PFA became master of the situation.

2. *Svoboda* (Baku), 11 Dec. 1992.
3. *Molodezh' Azerbaidzhana* (Baku), 6 March 1993.
4. *Azadlyq* (Baku), 28 Jan. 1993.
5. *Bakinskii rabochii* (Baku), 11 Dec. 1992.
6. *Millet* (Baku), 12 Dec. 1992. On 18 May 1992, after Mutalibov's abortive coup, the extraordinary session of the Supreme Soviet passed over all its power to the National Council, which then became known as the Milli Mejlis – FBIS-SOV-92-097, 19 May 1992, p. 50.
7. Aliev had been first secretary of the Azerbaijan Communist Party (1969–82) when he had gone to Moscow to serve in the Politburo. Dismissed from the Politburo by Gorbachev in 1988, he returned to Azerbaijan in 1990 to become chairman of the National Council (later, Milli Mejlis) in the Nakhichevan Autonomous Republic. In Oct. 1993 he was elected President of the Azerbaijan Republic.
8. *Millet*, 19 Sept. 1992.
9. Historian and laboratory assistant in the early stages of the National movement, Panah Huseinov, was nominated to the post of Prime Minister; Minister of Defence Rahim Gaziev was a mathematician and had no military experience; Fahmin Hajiev, who had previously been tried on charges of fraud and larceny, became commander of the interior troops – *Rabochaia gazeta*, Moscow, 11 Sept. 1993.
10. One of the founders and leaders of the PFA, Iusuf Samedoğlu, resigned from the PFA leadership in protest against the appointments policy of the regime – *Millet*, 28 Jan. 1993. The PFA admitted that its policy, particularly such facts as the nomination of a former waiter to the post of deputy chief of executive power in one of the *raions*, evoked great discontent – *Svoboda*, 8 Jan. 1993.
11. *Svoboda*, 5 March 1993.
12. *Bakinskii rabochii*, 19 June 1993, spoke in traditional Soviet style of 115 ethnic groups.
13. Amir Taheri, *Crescent in a Red Sky. The Future of Islam in the Soviet Union* (London: Hutchinson, 1989), p. 121.
14. N. Kiuk and A. Kazatnycky, 'Nationalism – Part of the Solution', *Orbis* 34, 4 (1990), p. 537.
15. *Narodnoe khoziaistvo SSSR v 1989 g.* (Moscow, 1990), p. 67.
16. Ibid., p. 36.
17. *Megapolis-Express* (Moscow), 5 Aug. 1992, p. 13.
18. Ibid.
19. Ibid.
20. Usman Kanberov, 'Lezgistan nakanune buri', *Russkaia mysl'* (Paris), 15 May 1992, p. 6.
21. *Samur. Azerbaidzhan Respublikedin Lezgi gazet* (Baku), Feb. 1993, p. 2.
22. See documents of the most important political organizations: 'Programme of the People's Front of Azerbaijan'. *Central Asia and Caucasus Chronicle* 8, 4 (Aug. 1989), p. 9; *Program of the Party of National Independence of Azerbaijan* (Baku, 1992), p. 3; *Ieni mustaqil Azerbaidzhan ugrunda* (Baku, 1993), p. 12; *Musavat pariasynyn programy* (Ganja, 1993), p. 6.
23. *Azerbaijan* (Baku, in Azerjaibani), 31 Oct. 1992.
24. A. Balaev, *Azerbaidzhanskoe natsional'noe dvizhenie*, p. 42.
25. *Central Asia and Caucasus Chronicle* 8, 4 (1989), p. 918.
26. *Vyshka* (Baku), 12 Sept. 1992.
27. *Meidan* (Baku), 17 Nov. 1992.
28. *Istiqlal* (Baku), 18 Sept. 1992.
29. *Pravda* (Moscow), 8 Sept. 1989.

30. *Krasnaia zvezda* (Moscow), 23 Jan. 1990.
31. T. Dragadze, 'Azerbaidzhan', in Graham Smith (ed.) *The Nationality Question in the Soviet Union* (London, Longman: 1990), p. 174.
32. Bakinskii rabochii, 8 July 1992. The rejection by the leaders of the Azerbaijan Democratic Republic (ADR) of the policy of national exclusiveness may be seen in the composition of the ADR parliament, where in 1919, out of 120 deputies, 84 were Muslims, 27 Armenians and 11 Russians – Lois Massignon (ed.), *Annuaire du monde musulman: Statistique, historique, social et economique, 1954*, 4e édition (Paris, 1955), p. 71.
33. *Azerbaijan* (in Azerbaijani), 31 Oct. 1992.
34. 'Decree of the President of the Azerbaijan Republic on the defence of the rights and liberties of national minorities, less numerous peoples and ethnic groups living in the Azerbaijan Republic and on rendering state assistance to the development of their languages and cultures', Baku, 1992, p. 3.
35. *Bakinskii rabochii*, 14 Oct. 1992.
36. *Bakinskii rabochii*, 16 March 1993.
37. *Bakinskii rabochii*, 3 Nov. 1992; 2 Feb. 1993.
38. *Istiqlal*, 10 Aug. 1993.
39. *Bakinskii rabochii*, 8 April 1993.
40. *Istiqlal*, 19 Feb. 1992.
41. *Vyshka*, 30 March 1993.
42. *Rossiiskaia gazeta* (Moscow), 10 Sept. 1992.
43. Peoples of the Lezgin language group live in the following *raions* of Azerbaijan: Kusary, Khachmas, Sheki, Kuba, Ismaili, Oğuz, Geichai, Kakh, Zakataly, Akhsui, Devechi, Agdash, Balakhany, Shamakhi, and also in Apsheron, in the cities Baku, Sumgait, Mingechaur, Ganja, Ali-Bairamly – *Samur*, Feb. 1993, p. 2, and also in the southern *raions* of Dagestan, as well as in Derbent, Makhachkala and other cities.
44. Leaders of Sadwal meant the state created by Shamil, which united all mountain peoples of Dagestan (not only Lezgins) and which had been eliminated by Russia in 1859. In 1860 the territory populated by Lezgins was divided by tsarist decree into two administrative units separated by the Samur river: Dagestan Oblast and the Baku Governorate.
45. *Rossiiskaia gazeta*, 10 Sept. 1992.
46. *Azerbaijan* (Baku), 7 Nov. 1992.
47. *Bakinskii rabochii*, 14 Aug. 1992.
48. *Bakinskii rabochii*, 16 March 1993.
49. *Samur*, Feb. 1993, p. 2.
50. *Bakinskii rabochii*, 14 Aug. 1992.
51. *Vyshka*, 28 Aug. 1992. For details of this episode, see Moshe Gammer, 'Unity, Diversity and Conflict in the Northern Caucasus', in this volume.
52. *Megapolis-Express*, 5 Aug. 1992, p. 13.
53. *Bakinskii rabochii*, 1 April 1993.
54. See *Nezavisimaia gazeta* (Moscow), 9 and 15 Sept, 1992; *Rossiiskaia gazeta*, 10 Sept. 1992.
55. *Bakinskii rabochii*, 27 March 1993.
56. *Azerbaijan* (in Azerbaijani), 31 Oct. 1992.
57. Talysh – a Persian speaking people. The Talysh Khanate, which existed in the 18th–19th centuries, became a Russian protectorate in 1802, and was finally annexed by Russia in accordance with the Turkmanchai treaty signed by Russia and Persia in 1828. The 'Mugan Republic' was proclaimed and existed for some time on this territory in 1919 – *Istiqlal*, 10 Aug. 1993.
58. *Azerbaijan* (in Azerbaijani), 14 Sept. 1993.
59. *Vestnik statistiki* (Moscow, 1991), No. 1, p. 67.
60. *Azerbaidzhan* (in Russian), 17 June 1993.
61. *Azerbaidzhan*, 17 June 1993.
62. *Vyshka*, 24 Feb. 1993.
63. Radio Moscow, 18 June 1993; FBIS-SOV-93-116-A, 18 June 1993, p. 54.
64. A. Elçibey, *Bu manim taleymdir* (*This is My Fate*) (Baku, 1992), p. 57–8.

65. *Günaydin* (Istanbul), 3 Sept. 1989; FBIS-SOV-89-173, 8 Sept. 1989, p. 32.
66. *Bakinskii rabochii*, 29 Oct. 1992.
67. Elçibey, *Bu manim taleymdir*, p. 177.
68. Elçibey, *Deyirdim ki bu qurulus dagilacaq (I Have Said That This System Would Be Wrecked)* (Baku, 1992), p. 60.
69. *Programme of the Party of National Independence of Azerbaijan*, Baku, 1992, p. 2 (Official English translation).
70. *Bakinskii rabochii*, 9 Nov. 1992.
71. *Meidan*, 31 Dec. 1992.
72. *Istiqlal*, 5 March 1993.
73. *Musavat* (Baku), 25 Feb. 1993. The Musavat Party was formed within the PFA and left it in March 1993 mainly for tactical reasons, but remained closely allied to it.
74. *Azadlyq*, 30 Jan. 1993.
75. *Istiqlal*, 19 Feb. 1993.
76. *Istiqlal*, 20 Jan. 1993.
77. *Svoboda*, 8 Jan. 1993.
78. *Azadlyq*, 9 Jan. 1993.
79. *Svoboda*, 8 Jan. 1993.
80. *Azerbaidzhan* (in Russian), 22 May 1993.
81. G. A. Geibullaev, *K etnogenezu azerbaidzhantsev* (Baku, 1991); A. S. Sumbatzadeh, *Azerbaidzhantsy: etnogenez i formirovanie naroda* (Baku, 1990).
82. *Bakinskii rabochii*, 14 Oct. 1992.
83. *Istiqlal*, 19 Feb. 1993.
84. *Bakinskii rabochii*, 24 Oct. 1992.
85. *Azadlyq*, 30 Jan. 1993.
86. *Istiqlal*, 10 Aug. 1993.
87. *Istiqlal*, 20 Oct. 1993.
88. *Istiqlal*, 10 Aug. 1993.
89. Ibid.
90. *Istiqlal*, 27 July 1993.
91. *Istiqlal*, 10 Aug. 1993.
92. Ibid.
93. See *Vyshka*, 9 July 1992; *Bakinskii rabochii*, 27 Oct. 1992.
94. *Vyshka*, 9 Feb. 1993.
95. Ibid.
96. N. Nasibzadeh, *Azerbaidzhan Demokratik Respublikasy (Magaleler ve sanadlar)* (Baku, 1990), p. 93.
97. *Vyshka*, 12 Sept. 1992. True, some representatives of the Russian-speaking population alleged that there was no restriction on teaching the Russian language in educational establishments. By the beginning of the 1991/1992 academic year there were in the republic 92 Russian schools and in 394 schools the teaching was in two languages – Azerbaijani and Russian – *Vyshka*, 9 July 1992.
98. *Vyshka*, 12 Sept. 1992.
99. Between Jan.–Sept. gross national income in the CIS countries declined by 20.1 per cent and in Azerbaijan by 25.5 per cent. In Azerbaijan in 1992, the rise in consumer prices outstripped income by a coefficient of 2.9, wages by 1.7, pensions by 3.1, student allowances by 2.3. This was one of the worst showings among the republics of the former USSR (*Bakinskii rabochii*, 26 Jan. 1993).
100. *Bakinskii rabochii*, 10 Nov. 1992.
101. *Bakinskii rabochii*, 8 July 1992.
102. *Bakinskii rabochii*, 2 Nov. 1993.
103. *Bakinskii rabochii*, 28 Oct. 1993.
104. *Azerbaidzhan* (In Russian), 28 May 1993. In 1988–90 about 300,000 Armenians left Azerbaijan – *Istiqlal*, 20 Oct. 1992.
105. DPA (Hamburg), 24 Sept. 1989; FBIS-SOV-89-189, 25 Sept. 1989, p. 114.
106. *Azerbaidzhan* (in Russian), 31 July 1993. This number includes the Azerbaijani population of Nagornyi-Karabakh.
107. *Istiqlal*, 20 Oct. 1993.

108. Ibid.
109. Ibid.
110. *Vyshka,* 12 Sept. 1992.
111. *Bakinskii rabochii,* 28 Oct. 1993.
112. *Bakinskii rabochii,* 27 Oct. 1992.
113. *Vyshka,* 12 Sept. 1992.
114. *Bakinskii rabochii,* 4 Jan. 1993. Not all the Jews in Azerbaijan can be included in the Russian-speaking population. For most of the Mountain Jews, who are non-Ashkenazi, the native language is Tat and the second tongue is Azerbaijani.
115. See, for instance, *Bakinskii rabochii,* 1992: 4 and 7 July, 4 Aug., 10 Oct., 4 Nov.; 1993: 10 March, 3 and 22 April, 11 and 13 May; *Vyshka,* 1992: 3 and 9 Sept., 6 and 24 Oct.; 1993: 13 Feb., 18 March, 22 April.
116. See, for instance, the article in the PFA newspaper *Cumhuriyyet,* 7 May 1993, sharply condemning the anti-Semitic character of the newspaper *Islam Duniasy.*
117. See *Bakinskii rabochii,* 8 July 1992; *Nezavisimaia gazeta,* 14 Oct. 1992.
118. *Bakinskii rabochii,* 14 Oct. 1992.
119. The interest of the republican authorities in the Azerbaijani diaspora was already shown in Feb. 1986. In Dec. 1987 a society, Vatan (Motherland), was formed to establish and develop ties with Azerbaijanis living abroad – *Azerbaijan* (in Azerbaijani), 31 Dec. 1993.
120. *Bakinskii rabochii,* 31 Dec. 1992.
121. The leader of Yurddash, Mais Safarli, explained the goal of the party: 'After achieving independence, Azerbaijan must be a moral stronghold for Azerbaijanis all over the world. This is the aim of the party. We shall help to form a strong diaspora abroad, which will influence the foreign policy of the republic' – *Bakinskii rabochii,* 2 March 1993.
122. *Bakinskii rabochii,* 19 June 1993.
123. *Bakinskii rabochii,* 4 Dec. 1992.
124. *Bakinskii rabochii,* 16 March 1993. Most of the Azerbaijanis who left Georgia for Azerbaijan were not registered initially as refugees. Therefore they are not mentioned in the official figures for refugees mentioned earlier.
125. *Bakinskii rabochii,* 4 Dec. 1992.

9

Unity, Diversity and Conflict
in the Northern Caucasus

MOSHE GAMMER

The Caucasus is probably the most varied area in the world with regard to the ethnic and linguistic composition of its population.[1] *In toto* about seventy aboriginal ethnic groups are to be found in the Caucasus, speaking languages belonging to three different linguistic families. The largest number of groups in a single country – thirty – live in Dagestan[2] (see also Table 9.3 for further details). To these must be added the immigrants – Russian and many other nationalities – who settled in the Caucasus during Russian imperial and Soviet rule.[3]

This diversity was clearly reflected in the political and administrative division of the Caucasus during the Soviet period. The area was divided among four union republics – Soviet Socialist Republics (SSRs) in Soviet terminology: the Armenian SSR, the Georgian SSR, the Azerbaijani SSR and the Russian Soviet Federal Socialist Republic (RSFSR). Within the last three were included seven Autonomous Soviet Socialist Republics (ASSRs) and four Autonomous Oblasts (AOs), the nominal nationalities of eight of which (six ASSRs and two AOs) were ethnic groups of the Northern Caucasus: the Abkhaz ASSR and South Osset AO were included within the Georgian SSR; the Dagestan, Checheno-Ingush, North Osset and Kabardino-Balkar ASSRs, as well as the Karachai-Cherkes and Adyge AOs, were part of the RSFSR.[4] (For further details see Table 9.1 and Map 9.1.)

This great linguistic and ethnic diversity notwithstanding, all the inhabitants of the Northern Caucasus, or the 'mountaineers' (*gortsy*) as they were called by their neighbours (mainly the Russians) and consequently came to call themselves, shared the same way of life, traditions, customs and even costume. All these they still share to a great extent. Their common culture has been classified[5] as belonging to the nomadic-patriarchal type, even though the mountaineers were not nomads. This type of society entails the division of the population along patrilineal lines into extended families, clans and tribes. These serve, with different emphases at different levels, as foci of identification and mutual responsibility and provide their members with economic and physical security. Patrilineal divisions thus lie at the basis of the region's political, social and economic structure.

At the same time, this type of society and culture has three major characteristics which operate in the direction of extreme fragmentation: (1) the mountaineers' zealous vigilance over their personal and group freedoms and the strong rejection of any authority external to the kin-group; (2) their being, to use nineteenth-century terminology, a 'martial race' raised from childhood to be warriors; and (3) partly resulting from the above, the vicious blood feuds which may go on for generations and ruin entire communities.

A further, even stronger, unifying factor is Islam. An overwhelming majority of the mountaineers are Sunni Muslims.[6] A great many of them persevered, despite the repressions and persecutions of the Soviet period, in the observance of the precepts of their religion. Most of them succeeded in doing so mainly because of the extensive network of Naqshbandi and Qadiri Sufi *tariqat*, especially among the Dagestanis, Chechens and Ingush.[7] But even for the less religious, Islam remains an important focus of identification and a significant part of their personal and group self-definition. Among mixed (Muslim-non-Muslim) groups, such as the Ossets, the Muslims tend to be 'closer to other Muslims...than to their Christian kinsmen'.[8]

A third unifying factor, connected to the previous two, is the history of the common struggle against Russian conquest and rule. This struggle was led by the *tariqat* under the banner of Islam and was fought in order to preserve the mountaineers' freedom, culture and way of life. Again, not all the ethnic groups participated equally in this struggle – some took no part in it at all – but it still is a strong unifying factor.[9]

Russian imperial and Soviet rule strengthened and added to both diversity and unity among the Caucasian mountaineers. On the one hand, several factors strengthened their solidarity and feeling of unity:

1. The common struggle against Russian and Soviet rule. This did not stop with the conquest of Chechnia and Dagestan in 1859 and the expulsion of the Cherkes in 1864–65. In the eastern part of the Northern Caucasus (Dagestan, Chechnia and Ingushetiia) this struggle was particularly intense, coming to a peak in the uprisings of 1863, 1877–78, the establishment of the short-lived independent 'Mountain Republic' in 1918, and the uprising of 1920–21. Local

uprisings against the Soviet authorities reoccurred in Chechnia and Ingushetiia in the 1930s and 1940s, and the last *abrek* (bandit of honour) fighting the Soviet authorities was killed only in 1979.[10]

2. The shared suffering at the hands of both the Russian imperial and the Soviet authorities (although at different periods of time and in varying degrees, all the mountain peoples experienced assaults on their heritage, way of life and religion: attempts at assimilation and conversion; confiscation of their best lands and the settling of Russians on them; expulsion and wholesale deportation). All these amount, in the view of almost all the mountaineers, and some Western scholars, to attempts at physical and spiritual genocide.[11] On one occasion, this genocide was successful: the entire Ubykh nation fled in 1864 to the Ottoman Empire. The last speaker of Ubykh died in Turkey in October 1992 thus making the Ubykhs an extinct group. The total disappearance of one of the Caucasian peoples had a tremendous effect on the minds of all the mountaineers and was one of the major reasons for the help extended to the Abkhaz.[12]

Common struggle and shared suffering are among the most effective ways of bringing people together. It should not be surprising, therefore, that in the Northern Caucasus they strengthened the feelings of solidarity among the mountaineers. This solidarity was reinforced by another result of the above two factors – namely, the hatred of Russian rule, the Russian authorities and 'Russia' as such, whether imperial or Soviet. This, however, must not be confused with hatred of Russians. A fact-finding mission established, for example, that most Chechens 'distinguish between Russians in the abstract and the present Russian population of Chechnia', and that 'relations between Russians and Chechens on a day-to-day basis appear relatively unstrained'.[13]

On the other hand, the 'divide and rule' policy of the authorities – both Russian imperial and Soviet – was successful in inducing divisions and frictions among the mountaineers. Of particular importance was the division by Stalin of the mountaineers into separate, and on many occasions artificially created, nationalities. Not that they had been unaware before of ethnic and linguistic differences among their ranks.[14]

But Stalin's policy was specifically designed to cut off all connections among the mountaineers. Thus, for example, the establishment of separate autonomies, with only vertical ties to Moscow and no horizontal ties among them at all, meant that any connection on the official level between two local autonomies could only be made through Moscow. Moreover, the transformation of separate vernaculars into literary languages denied the mountaineers a common language.[15]

However, Soviet 'divide and rule' policy did not stop at that. The borders of the different autonomies were delineated in such a way as to prevent the titular nationality from (1) being exclusively concentrated within the borders of its 'national homeland', and (2) forming a solid majority within it. For this purpose, ethnic groups were divided between (or even among) different autonomous units; most autonomies were shared by more than one titular nationality; and a 'quota' of minorities, especially of Russians and other 'loyal' elements, was maintained *inter alia* by the encouragement (sometimes by force) of immigration.[16]

As a result, some Dagestani nationalities inhabiting the southern part of the republic are to be found in great numbers in Northern Azerbaijan – for example, the Lezgins, the Tats and the Tsakhurs; in the latter two instances in larger numbers than in Dagestan (see Table 9.3 and Map 9.1). The wedge between Chechens and Ingush who were 'closely related by their language, way of life and religion' was greatly widened 'because of their different historical backgrounds'.[17] (The Ingush did not take part in the resistance against the Russian conquest, or in the 1920 revolt.) In addition, some seven to eight per cent of the Chechens found themselves within the Dagestani ASSR, while some Ingush territory was annexed in 1944 to the North Osset ASSR and the Ingush could only resettle there – after 1957 – illegally. The Ossets were divided between the RSFSR and the Georgian SSR, being given an autonomous unit in each. The Kabardians, Cherkes and Adyge – all remnants of the tribes collectively known in English as Circassians, who were the original inhabitants of the western half of the Northern Caucasus and the large majority of whom were expelled by the conquering Russians in the 1860s – were divided among three autonomies, despite the fact that they had a common language and self-identification. The Circassians shared two of these autonomies with another titular nationality, the Karachai-Balkars, who likewise had a common language and self-identification.

All these measures, it seems, were fairly successful and seventy years of (not always consistent) application infused life into the new 'states' and nations. How strong these new 'statehoods', patriotisms and nationalisms are is difficult to establish. But they exist and form yet another dimension of the multilateral, multifaceted identity of the mountaineers, as individuals and groups alike. Furthermore, these new identities added new sources of friction between rival nationalisms, between competing 'states', and between nationalisms and 'states'.

To this must be added another divisive factor and source of friction: the 'deportation' of four North Caucasian nationalities (as well as Muslim Ossets) by Stalin in 1943–44, and their rehabilitation by Khrushchev in 1957.[18] The rift between the 'repressed' and the 'non-repressed' mountain peoples has not healed and remains a constant irritant in their relations.[19]

The outcome of all these developments is that the Northern Caucasus is rife with conflict. Many of these conflicts are old, traditional ones, which the Russian imperial and Soviet 'divide and rule' policy barely touched upon, or merely aggravated, without changing their nature. Others are either new conflicts created – whether intentionally or not – by this policy or old ones and which, as a result, developed new dimensions and features. As long as the USSR existed, this situation was considered beneficial by the central authorities;[20] they could use the potential of conflict as a lever against the local authorities and at the same time they were powerful enough to control and contain them. But once the USSR disintegrated the powder keg of the Northern Caucasus was left almost without control. The fact that only three of the many conflicts in the area have so far deteriorated into open warfare is to the credit of the mountaineers and their leaders, who exercised their traditional self-restraint and caution.[21] Indeed, in all three conflicts which flared up into armed clashes, outsiders (that is non-mountaineers) were involved.[22]

The different conflicts in the Northern Caucasus fall into two categories: (1) conflicts between different groups of mountaineers; and (2) conflicts between groups of mountaineers and the central authorities, and between the mountaineers' identites and affiliations and the patriotism and nationalism of the various successor states of the USSR within which these groups are included or on which they border. One should remember, however, that in reality a clear-cut division seldom exists and that most of the conflicts are multifaceted.

Dagestan[23] has witnessed quite a few inter-ethnic tensions, especially between the smaller nationalities and the Avars, who the former feel have been over-represented in positions of power in the republic. The major conflict in Dagestan involves the Chechens, Laks, Kumyks and Avars and is the direct result of the Chechens' deportation by Stalin in 1944. Along with their brethren in Chechnia, the Chechens of the Aki district (which had been included in the Dagestan ASSR) were deported to Kazakhstan. Laks were brought by force from central Dagestan and settled in their stead. In order to prevent the Laks from returning to their homes, their original villages were destroyed. When the Chechens were rehabilitated in 1957 and allowed to return to their homeland, the Aki Chechens found their homes occupied by Laks who had nowhere to go. The problem remained unsettled even after the collapse of the Soviet Union.

In 1992 the Supreme Soviet of Dagestan decided to return to the Chechens all their property and to resettle the Laks in the area of Makhachkala in the lowlands. This was fiercely resisted by the Kumyks. The Soviet policy of resettling the mountaineers in the lowlands (where it would be much easier to control them), which had been carried out in continuous waves during most of the years of Soviet rule in Dagestan, transformed the status of the Kumyks. Once the only native dwellers of the lowlands, they became by the early 1990s a minority of 22 per cent in their own homeland. The Kumyk national front, Tenglik (Equality), thus demanded a separate Kumyk autonomous republic either within Dagestan, or even within the Russian Federation (which would mean separation from Dagestan and attaining equal status to it). This was fiercely resisted by the Avar Narodnyi Front imeni Shamilia (Shamil Popular Front, named after the Avar who was the most famous and successful leader of the mountaineers' resistance to the Russian conquest in the 19th century).

Menaced by a new influx of immigrants as a result of the 1992 Supreme Soviet decision, the Kumyks threatened to resist it by force. The Avars counter-threatened, promising to use force if the Kumyks did, and the Chechens, backed by their brethren across the border, maintained that they would do the same if their problem was not solved soon. Caught in the cross fire, the Laks and their national front, Tsubars (New Star), insisted that it was the responsibility of the authorities to settle their problem. In June 1992, following a dramatic clash between the republican authorities and the Avar national front,[24] martial law was imposed. Russian troops (mainly OMON – Otriady militsii osobogo naznacheniia) were introduced to enforce it. In the following months they managed to defuse the tension and at the beginning of 1993 the Avar national front announced a moratorium on its activity as long as other national movements took no action.

Another internal Dagestani conflict, which, however, has 'external' dimensions also – that is, involves non-mountaineers – is centered on the demands of the Lezgin national front Sadwal (Unity). As mentioned above, over 40 per cent of the Lezgins live in northern Azerbaijan (and according to Sadwal, more than 50 per cent, since many Lezgins – and other Dagestanis – were officially registered by the authorities as Azerbaijanis in the 1920s and 1930s). The fact that they are split has a direct bearing on the status of the Lezgins in Dagestan, because while they are the second largest group (after the Avars) in the Eastern Caucasus, they are only the fourth largest nationality within Dagestan). Sadwal demands the unification of all

Lezgins within one Lezgistan either as part of Dagestan or outside it, as a separate autonomous republic within the Russian Federation. The problem seemed to intensify in October 1992 when the Russian authorities decided to establish a military-regulated border with customs and passport control between the Russian Federation and Azerbaijan. This meant that relatives or friends living astride the border would now need passports and visas whenever they wanted to visit each other. However, as a result of pressure by the Dagestani authorities, Russian-Azerjaibani-Dagestani negotiations led to an agreement on a special arrangement for the residents of the border area on both sides. Although less than satisfactory to the Lezgins (and other groups living on the Russo-Azerbaijani border) it assuaged tensions and averted a conflagration.[25]

The Chechens are involved in three conflicts with their neighbours. One is the above-mentioned problem of the Aki Chechens in Dagestan, which has been kept under control throughout the period under discussion. The second, and by far the most important, is the conflict between the Chechens and Ingush.

> Both peoples recognize their close kinship and use the term [or rather name] Vainakh to cover their common heritage. The languages are mutually intelligible and the folklore and culture almost identical. It is not always clear whether some clans are Chechen or Ingush...They nevertheless feel themselves quite distinct. The Ingush were exposed to the full thrust of the Russian advance in the late 18th century, well before the Chechens...They...were among the last North Caucasian people to embrace Islam.[26]

While in general the Chechens have preferred a united Vainakh state – in fact many Chechens regard the Ingush as one of the Chechen tribes rather than as a separate nationality – the Dudaev government recognized the Ingush right to self-determination and proclaimed in October 1991 a separate Chechen republic, independent of Russia. The Ingush, on their part, chose in a referendum on 30 November 1991 to establish their own republic within the framework of the Russian Federation. In June 1992 the Supreme Soviet in Moscow established a separate Ingush republic. Thus, 'though Chechens consistently express regret that the Ingush have chosen to go a separate way – and many express doubt about the validity of the "choice" process – the issue seems to be more a cause of regret than of rancour or tension'.[27] There remains, however, the question of the border between the two republics, with the main bone of contention being the Sunja district west of Groznyi, the population of which contains Chechens, Ingush and Cossacks. Although so far dormant (at the time of writing in late 1993), this potential conflict may easily be exploited by outside forces – Moscow, or some circles there, has indeed tried to do exactly that (see below) – and may consequently flare up.

These differences notwithstanding, the Chechens have been intensely and emotionally involved on the side of the Ingush in their conflict with the Ossets, making this a third conflict between the Chechens and their neighbours. In the confrontation of October–November 1992 Chechen volunteers fought on the side of the Ingush.

The Ingush-Osset conflict is by far the deepest and most intense 'internal' conflict among the mountaineers and, as of late 1993, the only one which has deteriorated into a war.[28] The friction between the Ossets and other groups of mountaineers goes quite far back in history. Conscious of being different (due also to their linguistic dissimilarity),[29] the Ossets have been 'the odd man out' among the mountaineers. The fact that the majority of the Ossets adopted Orthodox Christianity and chose to side with Russia from the earliest days of its penetration into the Caucasus in the 1770s, – indeed, in the course of time, they became 'the most heavily Sovietized and pro-Russian territory in the Caucasus region'[30] – did not add to their popularity among their neighbours.[31]

The roots of the present conflict, however, go back to the deportation of the Ingush in 1944. The Prigorodnyi district, which until then had belonged to the Checheno-Ingush ASSR, was annexed to the North Osset ASSR and Ossets were settled there in place of the Ingush. When the Ingush were allowed to return to their homes and the Checheno-Ingush ASSR was reinstated, these steps were not reversed. The North Osset authorities 'blocked the efforts of the Ingush to re-establish themselves by discouraging the sale of houses to them and by discrimination against them in education and employment'.[32]

Thus, the Ingush who returned to the Prigorodnyi district – and a Soviet source in 1976 claimed that 'almost all did return'[33] – demanded that the area be annexed to the Checheno-Ingush ASSR, or at least enjoy autonomy within the North Osset ASSR. As the power of the central authorities weakened, both before and after the disintegration of the USSR, the conflict became more intense, with sporadic clashes breaking out in 1991, which were followed by the proclamation in October 1991 of an autonomous Ingush republic within the Russian Federation centred on the Prigorodnyi district. Encouraged by sympathetic proclamations by Eltsin and by the official establishment of the Ingush autonomous republic by Russia's Supreme Soviet in June 1992, and disappointed at the moratorium imposed soon afterwards by Moscow on border changes in the Caucasus, the Ingush intensified their activity, forcibly preventing Osset troops from entering their villages.

In this highly tense atmosphere a small incident on 23 October

1992 was enough to spark off a full-scale war. On 31 October Russian troops were flown in to separate the combatants and by 10 November they occupied in addition to the Prigorodnyi district all of Ingushetiia.[34] As a result of this war, the bulk of the Ingush fled the Prigorodnyi district into Ingushetiia and their villages seem to have been occupied by Osset refugees from South Ossetiia.

In the western part of the Caucasus, the Circassians and the Karachai-Balkars are interested in dividing their joint republics – the Kabardino-Balkar and the Karachai-Cherkes autonomous republics – despite the resistance of the *partocrat* establishments (previous Communist Party *nomenklatura*) of both. There is, therefore, no conflict between these two nations, as each tries to reconstruct its national life and settle the problem of being divided into three (in the case of the Circassians) and two (in the case of the Karachai-Balkars) units. Also, the Karachai-Balkars have yet to fully reconstruct their national life, damaged by the deportation in 1943–44.[35]

The 'external' conflicts involve all three states – Azerbaijan, Georgia and Russia – among which the mountaineers are divided. The conflict involving Azerbaijan is only a potential one at the time of writing, yet the two fierce and bloody disputes involving Georgia gained attention in the Western media. These are the struggles in Abkhaziia[36] and Southern Ossetiia.[37] In both cases local demands for greater autonomy met with Georgian nationalist insistence on greater central control. This led to threats of separation, and union with the Russian Federation, clashes, and a failed Georgian attempt to solve the problem by means of 'ethnic cleansing'. Both conflicts, once fighting erupted, proved difficult to contain and in both – though more so in Abkhaziia – other mountain groups, Russia (at least according to the Georgians) and local Armenians became involved, with Armenia, Turkey and other players being more than interested observers.[38] In both cases the end of large-scale hostilities was achieved through the intervention of Russia.

Two lesser conflicts involving Georgia and its mountain neighbours are on a much smaller scale. One, with Dagestan, is the result of the expulsion from Georgia of Dagestanis – mainly Avars – who have for generations inhabited villages in north-east Georgia, near the Dagestani border. The other, with the Chechens, was caused by the Chechens according refuge to Zviad Gamsakhurdia in Groznyi after the coup against him in Tbilisi.[39] It was aggravated by Chechen support for the Abkhaz, and the participation of Chechen volunteers in the fighting in Abkhaziia. Although both conflicts remained low-key, their mere existence meant that Georgia was in conflict with all its neighbours to the north, and first and foremost with Russia.

In the Caucasus, as in other parts of the former Soviet Union, Russia and Russians have played a crucial role, *inter alia* in conflicts both within and outside the borders of the Russian Federation. In fact, Moscow is still regarded by many as the old empire in a new guise and its intervention in local conflicts – as the acting out of its traditional imperial role.[40] Russia has been involved in conflicts in the Northern Caucasus on four levels, playing a variety of roles.

One level is Russian involvement in the 'external' conflicts between the mountaineers and the two independent states of Azerbaijan and Georgia, which have been described above. This is probably the most sensitive level because it is the only one which involves international politics and relations.

Another level, and an extremely important one, is that of Russia *vis-à-vis* the different North Caucasian nationalities. The declared aim of many – though by no means all – of the national movements of the mountain peoples is to eventually gain full independence from Russia. For the moment, though, only the Chechens have proclaimed their independence of Russia and reject any agreement short of full Russian recognition.

Moscow, on the other hand – apart from a few fringe groups – is not ready to disengage from the Caucasus because of strategic and economic considerations, as well as psychological-emotional reasons. Furthermore, any concession in the Northern Caucasus might create a domino effect in other, perhaps even more important, areas of the Russian Federation.[41]

While the conflict between Russia and the Chechens has been an ongoing one since the beginning of Russian expansion into the Northern Caucasus – the first local resistance movement was led by a Chechen, Shaykh Mansur (1785–91) – the present confrontation started with the events that followed the failed putsch in Moscow on 19–21 August 1991.[42] Taking advantage of the republican party leadership's support of the putsch, the nationalist opposition, united since 1990 in the *ispolkom,* Obshchenatsional'nyi kongress chechenskogo naroda (Executive Committee of the All-National Congress of the Chechen People – OKChN), under the leadership of Johar Dudaev, called for demonstrations in Groznyi demanding the resignation of the *partocrat* leadership. After 18 days of non-stop massive demonstrations, and under pressure from Moscow, the leadership resigned on 6 September.

Power was seized by the *ispolkom* of the OKChN, which also won the elections of 27 October, and Dudaev was elected president. On 1 November, Dudaev proclaimed by presidential decree the 'state sovereignty of the Chechen Republic'.[43] Within less than a year the Chechens, according to an independent fact-finding mission, 'created the framework for an independent republic which impresses the visitor as a distinct political entity'.[44]

Eltsin, who until the elections supported Dudaev, decreed the elections illegal, imposed martial law and on 8 December sent paratroopers into Groznyi, where they were immediately surrounded at the airport by vastly greater numbers of Chechens. However, armed confrontation was avoided and Eltsin – who was criticized by both the Russian Supreme Soviet and the press – backed down. All Russian troops were withdrawn from Chechen territory and with the exception of one incident[45] have not returned (as of late 1993).

Instead, Moscow and Groznyi launched a 'cold war', in which an economic blockade (though never fully implemented), psychological warfare and the manipulation of the media (Western as well as Russian) were the main weapons. A 1992 mission of enquiry

> found the situation in every respect less strained and confrontational than we had anticipated. We uncovered no current trends that seem to be leading irrevocably toward exacerbation of the Russian-Chechen relationship. There are, nevertheless, factors in the situation which – if handled irresponsibly by either side – could have explosive consequences.[46]

A third level, of no lesser importance, is that of Russia *vis-à-vis* the mountaineers *en gros*, as represented by the Confederation of the Mountain Peoples of the Caucasus (CMPC). Formed in October 1991, the CMPC claims to be 'the legitimate heir of the Independent North Caucasian Republic ("The Mountain Republic"), formed on 11 May 1918' (and soon after overrun by the White Army).[47] Representing 15 peoples (in late 1993), it strives for the eventual re-establishment of that republic with its capital in Sukhumi (the capital of Abkhaziia).

The CMPC has many problems. Among the most salient are: (1) not all the mountain peoples have joined it. The Karachai and Balkars, for example, have refused so far to do so; (2) its members are peoples and not republics, which reflects the fact that with the exception of the Chechens, all the other national movements are opposition groups confronting the *partocrat* governments in their republics, or at any rate not in power; (3) the fact that the Chechen republic is the only member state in the CMPC makes it essential to the Confederation, but at the same time creates the danger of Chechen supremacy in the CMPC and consequently of the Confederation becoming a tool of the Chechen regime; (4) internal national and personal quarrels. Of these the Ingush-Osset conflict seems to be less detrimental than the less publicized rift between the 'repressed' and 'unrepressed' nationalities – that is, between those who were deported in the 1940s and those who were not.

Nevertheless the CMPC has proved to be an important factor in the political and military game in the Northern Caucasus. It helped to mobilize volunteers to aid the Chechens in November 1991 and the Abkhaz through the war started on 14 August 1992 by the Georgian move into Abkhaziia.[48] In April 1993 it signed an agreement with the Cossacks of the Caucasus. Furthermore, it has been conducting a restrained and prudent policy, avoiding any hint of provocation. All these have transformed the CMPC into more than a theoretical threat to Moscow's hold on the Northern Caucasus, though one should by no means overestimate it.

To counteract the threat of a united front of the mountain peoples, some Russian circles seem to have been trying to replay again the old 'divide and rule' card by endorsing, and even getting involved in, existing or potential conflicts among the mountaineers. This is the fourth level of Russian involvement in conflicts in the Northern Caucasus. The one that erupted, and demonstrated the danger and disastrous consequences of such a course, was the Ingush-Osset conflict, described above.

The two prevalent interpretations of the Russian military involvement are that it was either pro-Osset, in view of the 'well established dependability of the Ossetians in the eyes of Moscow',[49] or essentially anti-Chechen. A combination of both seems closer to reality, especially in view of the fact that the creation of an Ingush republic by Moscow was designed to drive a wedge between them and the Chechens, and given the widespread Russian suspicion that the Ingush approach to Moscow was merely a tactical move aimed at acquiring the Prigorodnyi district.[50]

Whatever the Russian motives, the intervention caused a backlash. All the mountaineers (with the exception of the Ossets, of course), saw it as another example of Russian 'treachery' and a lesson of what happens to those who try to align themselves with Russia. According to the mountaineers' interpretation, the Russian behaviour was nothing but a cynical exploitation of the Ingush in order to sow discord between them and the Chechens, and once this goal was achieved and there was no more need for the Ingush, they were dropped. The result was the great loss of good will towards Moscow among the mountaineers and their heightened sense of solidarity and unity in opposition to the centre.[51]

Although by the end of 1993 the situation in the Caucasus seemed to have calmed down, the Northern Caucasus remained a potential powder-keg riven with tensions that might explode at any moment. The events in Moscow, the dissolution of the Russian Supreme Soviet in October and then the elections in December, which were a major success for extreme nationalist, even chauvinistic, forces, seemed to have markedly heightened these tensions and advanced the region further down the road towards bloodshed. This, at least, was the feeling shared by most mountaineer leaders and intellectuals, who by the end of 1993 were radiating a great deal of gloom and pessimism. The Chechnia events of summer 1994 only served to intensify these sentiments.

NOTES

1. The only area in the world which rivals the Caucasus in this respect is Papua, New Guinea.
2. See, for example, M. O. Kosven *et al.* (eds.), *Narody Kavkaza* (Moscow: Nauka, 1960); M. O. Kosven and Kh. M. Khashaev (eds.), *Narody Dagestana. Sbornik stat'ei* (Moscow: Nauka, 1955). In English one can consult the appropriate parts of Shirin Akiner, *Islamic Peoples of the Soviet Union* (London: Kegan Paul, 1983, 1986); Alexandre Bennigsen and Enders Wimbush, *Muslims of the Soviet Empire – A Guide* (London: C. Hurst, 1985); Amiram Gonen *et al.* (eds.), *The Encyclopedia of the Peoples of the World* (New York: Henry Holt, 1993).
3. For the changes in the composition of the population before and during Russian imperial rule in the Caucasus, see N. G. Volkova, *Etnicheskii sostav naseleniia Severnogo Kavkaza v XVIII – nachale XX veka* (Moscow; Nauka, 1974); D. I. Ismail-Zade, *Naselenie gorodov zakavkazskogo kraia v XIX – nachale XX v* (Moscow: Nauka, 1991).
4. The term 'Northern Caucasus' is not used here in its purely geographical meaning, which encompasses only the areas north of the main range. Rather, it departs from an ethnographical point of view and thus covers all the area settled by the ethnic groups living mainly north of the main range, as well as in some areas south of it, in two of the autonomous units of Georgia as well as the northern part of Azerbaijan.
5. Lewis J. Luzbetac, *Marriage and Family in Caucasia. A Contribution to the Study of North Caucasian Ethnology and Customary Law* (Vienna:independent publication, 1951).
6. The only exceptions are the Ossets, a majority (at least 70 per cent) of whom are Orthodox Christians, the Abkhaz, 30–50 per cent of whom are Orthodox Christians, and the Tats, the Muslims among whom are Twelver Shi'ites, not Sunnis.
7. For the preservation of religion, 'parallel Islam' and the Sufi *tariqat*, see Bennigsen and Wimbush, *Muslims of the Soviet Empire;* Alexandre Bennigsen and Chantal Lemercier-Quelquejay, *Le Soufi et le commissaire. Les Confréries musulmans en URSS* (Paris: Seuil, 1986); Bennigsen and Lemercier-Quelquejay, 'Lieux saints et soufisme au Caucase', *Turcica* XV (1983), pp. 180–99; Bennigsen and Lemercier-Quelquejay, 'L'Islam paralèle en Union Soviétique. Les organisations soufies dans la République tchetcheno-ingouche', *Cahiers du monde russe et soviétique* XXI, 1 (Jan.–March 1980), pp. 49–63; Chantal Lemercier-Quelquejay, 'Le tariqat au Caucase du Nord', in A. Popovic and G. Veinstein (eds.), *Les ordres mystiques dans l'Islam. Cheminements et situation actuelle* (Paris: EHESS, 1985); Alexandre Bennigsen, 'The Qadiriyah (Kunta Haji) Tariqah in North East Caucasus, 1850–1987', *Islamic Culture* (Hyderabad, India), 2–3 (April–July 1988), pp. 63–78; Fanny E. Bryan, 'Anti-Religious Activities in the Chechen-Ingush Republic of the USSR and the Survival of Islam', *Central Asian Survey* 3, 2 (1984), pp. 99–116. For the role of the *tariqat* in political life, see Michael Rywkin, 'The Communist Party and the Sufi Tariqat in the Checheno-Ingush Republic', *Central Asian Survey* 10, 1–2 (1991), pp. 133–46. For the role of Islam in the national life of the North Caucasian peoples, see Fanny E. Bryan, 'Internationalism, Nationalism and Islam', in Marie Bennigsen-Broxup (ed.), *The North Caucasus Barrier. The Russian Advance towards the Muslim World* (London: C. Hurst, 1992), pp. 195–218.

8. Bennigsen and Wimbush, *Muslims of the Soviet Empire,* p. 206.
9. For the struggle against the Russian conquest, see Alexandre Bennigsen, 'Un mouvement populaire au Caucase au XVII siècle. La *Guerre Sainte* du Shaykh Mansur (1785–1791), page mal connue et controversée des relations russo-turques', *Cahiers du monde russe et soviétique* V, 2 (April–June 1964), pp. 159–205; Moshe Gammer, *Muslim Resistance to the Tsar. Shamil and the Conquest of Chechnia and Dagestan* (London: Frank Cass, 1994); Paul Henze, 'Circassia in the Nineteenth Century. The Futile Fight for Freedom', in Ch. Lemercier-Quelquejay, G. Veinstein and S. E. Wimbush (eds.), *Passé turco-tatar, présent soviétique. Etudes offertes à Alexandre Bennigsen* (Louvain and Paris: Peters and EHESS, 1986), pp. 243–73; Henze, 'Circassian Resistance to Russia', in Marie Bennigsen-Broxup (ed.), *The North Caucasus Barrier,* pp. 62–111; Henze, 'Fire and Sword in the Caucasus: The 19th Century Resistance of the North Caucasian Mountaineers', *Central Asian Survey* 6, 4 (1987), pp. 5–44.
10. No proper study of the 1863 and 1877–78 uprisings, or indeed of the struggle of the mountaineers against Russian rule during the second half of the 19th century, has been published. For the events of the civil war, see Alexandre Bennigsen, 'Muslim Guerrilla Warfare in the Caucasus (1918–1928)', *Central Asian Survey* 2, 1 (July 1983), pp. 45–56; Marie Bennigsen-Broxup, 'The 1920–1921 Uprising', in Marie Bennigsen-Broxup (ed.), *The North Caucasus Barrier,* pp. 112–45. For further uprisings up to the Second World War, see Abdurahman Avtorkhanov, 'The Chechens and the Ingush during the Soviet Period and Its Antecedents', in *ibid.,* pp. 146–94.
11. See, for example, Marie Bennigsen-Broxup, 'Introduction: Russia and the North Caucasus', in Bennigsen-Broxup (ed.), *The North Caucasus Barrier,* pp. 1–17; Avtorkhanov, 'The Chechens and the Ingush during the Soviet Period'.
12. 'The Ubykh are dead. We will not sit back and watch this fate befall the Abkhaz. It simply will not happen', said a Kabardian princess to John Colarusso – quoted in Colarusso, 'Abkhazia', paper presented at the Conference on the Contemporary North Caucasus, School of Oriental and African Studies, University of London (SOAS), 22–23 April 1993, p. 11. This and other papers presented at that conference and quoted here are to be published by C. Hurst, London.
13. International Alert, Fact-Finding Mission to Chechnia (24 Sept.–3 Oct. 1992), *Report* (London, n.d.), p. 32 and *Preliminary Summary Observations* (London, Oct. 1992), p. 4. International Alert, a non-governmental organization based in London, which seeks to help resolve conflicts, was invited by Moscow, with Groznyi's consent, to send a mission to Chechnia.
14. In fact, a sense of separate ethnic identification started to appear before 1917, partly under the influence of Russian imperial administration and ethnography - see Austin Jershild, 'The Making of Ethnicity in Caucasia: Mountaineer *Narody* and Russian Rule', paper presented at the Fifth International Conference on Central Asia, Madison, Wisconsin, April 1993.
15. Until then Arabic had been used throughout the Northern Caucasus as the general literary means of communication, while several Turkic dialects had been *lingua franca.* The adoption of separate alphabets based on the Latin script aimed *inter alia* at dealing another blow at the position of Arabic. See also Isabelle Kreindler, 'Soviet Muslims: Gains and Losses as a Result of Soviet Language Planning', in this volume.
16. In the Chechen-Ingush ASSR, for example, where since its restoration in 1957 the first party secretaries were always Russians, a table indicating the number and percentage of Russians within the republic hung in the secretary's office and was updated daily – private sources.
17. Bennigsen and Wimbush (eds.), *Muslims of the Soviet Empire,* p. 189.
18. The basic work in English for this is still Robert Conquest, *The Nation Killers: The Soviet Deportation of Nationalities* (London: MacMillan, 1970).
19. 'Since our deportation, our relations with the Dagestanis have not been the same; their attitude towards us has changed', is a claim heard frequently in Chechnia when people are asked about their attitudes to, and relations with, neighbouring groups.
20. This is true of other areas of the USSR as well. Thus, for example, both the outbreak of the conflict in Nagornyi-Karabakh and the inter-ethnic clashes in Central Asia in 1989–90 were regarded by many as instigated by the centre – e.g., Audrey L. Alstadt,

'Nagorno-Karabkh – "Apple of Discord" in the Azerbaijan SSR', *Central Asian Survey* 8, 4 (1989), pp. 63–78; Yaacov Ro'i, 'Central Asian Riots and Disturbances 1989–90: Causes and Context', *Central Asian Survey* 10, 3 (1991), pp. 21–54.

21. It is in this spirit that the dagger – *kinjal* – so characteristic of the mountaineers has always been tied extremely tightly to the hip. Indeed, it makes good sense that there are far fewer warmongers among people who are experienced in warfare and therefore know better its costs and the sacrifices demanded by it.

22. Two of the three conflicts – in Abkhaziia and in Southern Ossetiia – are between mountaineers and outsiders, namely Georgians. The third – between the Ingush and the Ossets, both mountaineer groups, escalated because of the involvement of outsiders – Russian troops in this case – who, according to some reports initiated the fighting; e.g., 'Ethnic Cleansing Comes to Russia', *The Economist* (28 Nov. 1992), p. 38.

23. For the situation in Dagestan, see Robert Chenciner and Magomedkhan Magomedkhanov, 'Dagestan Avoids Violence', paper presented at the Conference on the Contemporary North Caucasus.

24. Following the arrest of several front members in Khasavyurt on charges of illegal possession of weapons, the front took both the city and the republic prosecutors as hostages, demanding the release of its arrested members.

25. For the Azerbaijani perspective on the Lezgin problem, the Lezgins' activities and position in Azerbaijan, as well as the policies and attitudes of Azerbaijani political forces toward them, see Aryeh Wasserman, 'A Year of Rule by the Popular Front in Azerbaijan', in this volume.

26. International Alert, Fact-Finding Mission to Chechnia, *Report*, p. 34.

27. Ibid.

28. For the Ingush-Osset conflict, see Julian Birch, 'Ossetia: A Caucasian Bosnia in Microcosm', paper presented at the Conference on the Contemporary North Caucasus. See also International Alert, *Report*, pp. 34–6.

29. The Osset language belongs to the Iranian group of the Indo-European family of languages, while all their neighbours speak languages belonging to the Caucasian linguistic family.

30. Birch, 'Ossetia: A Caucasian Bosnia in Microcosm', p. 1.

31. The lack of sympathy towards the Ossets was clearly demonstrated by the failure of other mountain groups and of the Confederation of the Mountain Peoples of the Caucasus (see below) to unequivocally take the Ossets' side in their conflict with Georgia.

32. Birch, 'Ossetia: A Caucasian Bosnia in Microcosm', p. 19.

33. Birch, 'Ossetia: A Caucasian Bosnia in Microcosm'. The number of Ingush in the Prigorodnyi district was estimated in the early 1990s at about 60,000.

34. While occupying Ingushetiia, the Russian force entered Chechen territory and faced a Chechen force, but eventually, once it had become clear that they had indeed transgressed on Chechen territory, retreated to agreed borders.

35. For further details, as well as historical and other background, see Riecks Smeets, 'Circassia', paper presented at the Conference on the Contemporary North Caucasus.

36. For the conflict in Abkhaziia and its background from various points of view, see: B. George Hewitt, 'Abkhazia: A Problem of Identity and Ownership', *Central Asian Survey* 12, 3 (1993), pp. 267–323; John Colarusso, 'Abkhazia'; The Unrepresented Nations and Peoples Organization (UNPO), 'Report of a UNPO Mission to Abkhazia, Georgia and the Northern Caucasus', *Central Asian Survey* 12, 3 (1993), pp. 325–45; International Alert, *Georgia on the Path to Democracy and the Abkhaz Issue. A Report of an International Alert Mission, 22 Nov.–Dec. 1992* (London, January 1993). For the official Abkhaz version, see N. Akaba, 'Regarding International Alert's Mission Report on their Visit to Abkhazia and Georgia' (n.p., n.d.) (attached to the above-mentioned International Alert Report); Stanislav Lakoba, 'Abkhazia is Abkhazia', presented at the Conference on the Contemporary North Caucasus. For the regional and international dimensions and implications of the conflict, see Paul B. Henze, 'Caucasian Madness', RAND Corporation, n.d. [early 1993].

37. For a scholarly description of the conflict in Southern Ossetiia, its background and causes, see Julian Birch, 'The Georgian/South Ossetian Territorial and Boundary Dispute', paper submitted to the conference on 'Transcaucasian Boundaries', SOAS,

University of London, June 1992; Birch, 'Ossetia. A Caucasian Bosnia in Microcosm', pp. 13–17.

38. For an analysis of the regional and international dimensions and consequences of the conflict in Abkhaziia, see Colarusso, 'Abkhazia', pp. 13–17.

39. Dudaev, the Chechen president, admitted in private conversation that the presence of Gamsakhurdia in Groznyi was extremely inconvenient, but he could not violate the Caucasian code of hospitality. Thus, while he could, and would, say nothing to Gamsakhurdia personally, he said in private that 'were I in his place, I would have left long ago, so as not to embarrass my host' – private sources.

40. Russia's internal and foreign defence policies as such concerning the territory of the previous USSR and their formulation are outside the scope of this chapter. It should be observed, however, that there appears to be no single clear-cut policy. Dmitry Trofimov and Gia Djanjgava, for example, claim that:

> As regards Russia, nowadays we are witnessing *no less than three or four Russian foreign/domestic policies* (with two co-existing and sometimes competing layers – central and regional): that of the president and his local representatives, the Supreme Soviet and local Soviets, the Ministry of Defense and semi-independent field commanders of various local subunits, and last but not least – central and regional security service regiments. *None of these is united or integral*, although the two following quotations might be cited as suggesting unification: 1) 'Russian frontiers will forever remain unchanged' (Boris Eltsin, October 1991); 2) 'The North Caucasian military district is becoming the principal one' (Pavel Grachev, Russian Minister of Defence, March 1993).

'Some Reflections on Current Geo-Political Situation in North Caucasus' [sic.], paper presented at the Conference on the Contemporary North Caucasus [emphasis is in the original]. Cf. also Paul B. Henze, *Conflict in the Caucasus*, RAND Corporation, July 1993 (P-78307), pp. 15–18.

41. Like the Middle Volga-Ural basin (Tatarstan) and Siberia (Iakutiia).

42. For the situation in the Chechen republic and its confrontation with Moscow, from the Chechen point of view, see Dalkhan Khozhaev, 'The Contemporary Chechen State – Imagination or Reality?' paper submitted to the Conference on the Contemporary North Caucasus. For an example of Moscow's point of view, see Yuri Zakharovich, 'Breakaway Dancing', *Time* (15 March 1993), pp. 34–5. Also see the International Alert reports (note 13 above); Marie Bennigsen-Broxup, 'After the Putsch, 1991', in Bennigsen-Broxup (ed.), *The North Caucasian Barrier*, pp. 219–40; Flemming Hansen, 'The Chechen Revolution: Moscow's Response', to be published in *Central Asian Survey*.

43. One should not forget that the term 'sovereignty' has a different interpretation in Soviet terminology. As an independent fact-finding mission reported: 'In discussing these issues, we were struck over and over again by the lack of understanding on the part of many Chechens of the pragmatic meaning of sovereignty and independence, and of international law and procedure affecting their status' – International Alert, *Preliminary Report*, p. 8.

44. International Alert, *Report*, p. 15.

45. See note 34 above.

46. International Alert, *Preliminary Report*, p. 5.

47. 'Treaty on the Confederation Union of the Mountain Peoples of the Caucasus', Article 1 (see Appendix).

48. The CMPC's involvement in the Abkhaz conflict helped to cover the embarrassment of the Ingush-Osset war.

49. 'Ossetia: A Caucasian Bosnia in Microcosm', pp. 29–32.

51. 'In the view of specialists in the Caucasian section of the Institute of Ethnology and Anthropology of the Russian Academy of Sciences in Moscow, Ingush interest in separate political status is based not on grievances against the Chechens, but on their overwhelming desire to regain the Prigorodnyi *raion*' – International Alert, *Report*, p. 35.

52. According to recent visitors to the Caucasus, these feelings were prevalent also among many officials – all '*partocrats*'.

TABLE 9.1 THE NORTH CAUCASIAN AUTONOMOUS UNITS AND THEIR
ETHNIC COMPOSITION IN 1989 ACCORDING TO THE 1989 CENSUS

Name and Affiliation	Area in sq. kms.	Population (in rounded thousands)		Per-centage
Dagestan ASSR (RSFSR)	50,300	Dagestanis –	1,600[1]	78.8
		Total Muslims –	1,755	86.4
		Russians	236	11.6
		Total	2,030	100.0
Checheno-Ingush ASSR (RSFSR)	19,300	Chechens	735	57.8
		Ingush	164	12.9
		Russians	294	23.1
		Total	1,271	100.0
North Osset ASSR (RSFSR)	8,000	Ossets	214	49.3
		Ingush	33[2]	7.6
		Russians	152	35.0
		Total	434	100.0
Kabardino-Balkar ASSR (RSFSR)	12,500	Kabardians	363	48.2
		Balkars	101	13.4
		Russians	241	32.0
		Total	753	100.0
Karachai-Cherkes AO (RSFSR)	14,100	Karachai	129	31.2
		Cherkes[3]	40	9.6
		Russians	176	42.5
		Total	414	100.0
Adyge AO (RSFSR)	7,600	Adyge	95	22.0
		Russians	294	68.0
		Total	423	100.0
South Osset AO (Georgian SSR)	3,900	Ossets	66	66.0
		Georgians	30	30.0
		Total	100	100.0
Abkhaz ASSR (Georgian SSR)	8,600	Abkhaz	91	17.3
		Georgians	242	46.2
		Armenians	77	14.6
		Russians	74	14.2
		Ukrainians	11	2.2
		Total	524	100.0

1. For details, see Table 9.2.
2. In 1993 their number was estimated at c. 60,000, see note 33.
3. Including Abazins.

TABLE 9.2 ETHNIC COMPOSITION OF DAGESTAN ACCORDING TO THE 1989 CENSUS

	(rounded thousands)	(%)
Avars	524[1]	25.8
Dargins	314[2]	15.5
Kumyks	249	12.3
Lezgins	231[3]	11.4
Laks	98	4.8
Tabasaranians	94	4.6
Nogai	32[4]	1.6
Rutluls	19	0.9
Aguls	18	0.9
Tats	11[5]	0.5
Tsakhurs	7[6]	0.3
Total Dagestanis	1,600[7]	78.8
Azerbaijanis	84	4.1
Chechens	62	3.0
Tatars	6	0.3
Ossets	2	0.1
Total Muslims[8]	1,755	86.4
Russians	236	11.6
Ukrainians	9	0.4
Armenians	9	0.4
Georgians	2	0.1
Jews	20	1.0
Grand Total	2,030	100.0

1. Within the Avars the following groups are included: Akhvakhs, Andis, Archinians, Bakgulals, Botlykhs, Chamals, Didoians, Godoberians, Kapuchinians, Karatains, Khunzalians, Khvarshinians, Tindians.
2. Within the Dargins the following groups are included: Kaitaks, Kubachinians.
3. These constituted less than half the total number of Lezgins, a great number of whom lived in the Azerbaijani SSR.
4. These constituted less than half of the total number of Nogai. An equal number lived in the Stavropol *krai* of the RSFSR, and the rest in the Chechen Republic.
5. These constituted less than 40 per cent of the Tats. A far greater number lived in the Azerbaijani SSR.
6. These constituted about a third of the Tsakhurs, two-thirds of whom were living in the Azerbaijani SSR.
7. The five 'Shahdagh' peoples – Jeks, Kryz, Khaputs, Budakhs and Khainalugs – as well as Udins – are not included here, since practically all their population lived in the Azerbaijani SSR.
8. Only some of the Tats and the Ossets are Muslims, but they consider themselves 'mountaineers' and are accepted, at least to a certain degree, as such by their neighbours.

TABLE 9.3 MAJOR ETHNIC GROUPS IN THE NORTHERN CAUCASUS IN 1993 –
A RUSSIAN ESTIMATE[1]

Group	No. (in thousands)	% of whom live in their Titular Republic
DAGESTANIS:		
Avars[2]	665	87
Lezgins[3]	508	49 (41 in Azerbaijan)
Dargins[4]	406	86
Kumyks	309	89
Laks	126	83
Tabassarians	110	96
Nogai	83	42 (42 in Stavropol *krai)*
Tats	35	33 (39 in Azerbaijan)
Rutuls	24	96
Tsakhurs	24	34 (63 in Azerbaijan)
Aguls	22	95
VAINAKHS:		
Chechens	1,060	81
Ingush	264	75
Ossets	623	65 in Russia; 30 in Georgia
ADYGE:		
Kabardinians	430	95
Adyge	125	79
Cherkes	55	73
Abazins	36	82
KARACHAI-BALKARS:		
Karachai	168	83
Balkars	101	91
Abkhaz	106	92

1. Based on Dmitry Trofimov and Gia Djanjgava, 'Some Reflections on [the] Current Geo-Political Situation in the Northern Caucasus', paper presented at conference on the Contemporary North Caucasus, The School of Oriental and African Studies, University of London, 22-23 April 1993. The figures for some groups are probably much larger, first because members of some ethnic groups were officially registered as belonging to others and second, because some groups have large diasporas outside the former USSR. For these groups there can be no reliable estimate, only guesses.
2. Within the Avars the following groups are included: Akhvakhs, Andis, Archinians, Bakgulals, Botlykhs, Chamals, Didoians, Godoberians, Kapuchinians, Karatains, Khunzalians, Khvarshinians, Tindians.
3. The five 'Shahdagh' peoples – Jeks, Kryz, Khaputs, Budakhs and Khainalugs – as well as the Udins living only in Azerbaijan – are not included.
4. Within the Dargins, the following groups are included: Kaitaks, Kubachinians.

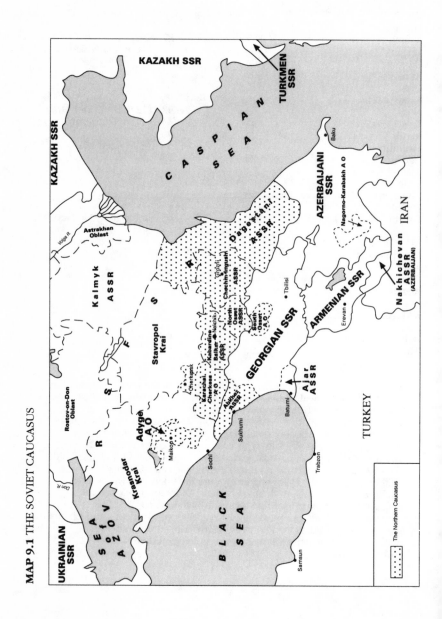

MAP 9.1 THE SOVIET CAUCASUS

APPENDIX 9.1 TREATY ON THE CONFEDERATIVE UNION OF THE
MOUNTAIN PEOPLES OF THE CAUCASUS

We, plenipotentiary representatives of the Abazinian, Abkhazian, Avar, Adygian,
Aukhov-Chechen, Dargwa, Kabardian, Lak, Ossetian (of North and South
Ossetia), Cherkes, Chechen, Shapsagh peoples, sensing our ethno-cultural
kinship and the common character of our ecological surroundings and historical
fate, which have found their confirmation at every heroic and tragic stage in the
history of our common struggle for self-preservation:

taking into account the inalienable right of each nation to self-determination;
aspiring on the basis of the Universal Declaration of Human Rights and of
other generally recognized international-legal acts to create all conditions for
satisfying the interests of each nationality, to guarantee equal rights for all
peoples, ethnic groups and each person;
convinced that unity and collaboration between our fraternal peoples, at the
separation of whom were directed the politics of both the tsarist autocracy
and the totalitarian regime of the former Soviet Union, will facilitate the self-
preservation and survival of the Mountain Peoples of the Caucasus;
recognizing as unacceptable any infringement of the interests of individuals
by race, religion or other factor and as contrary to natural law any attempts
to achieve one's own freedom at the expense of the oppression of others;
considering it our sacred duty by every means to facilitate the return to the
Homeland of our fellow-nationals, [whose ancestors were] forced into exile
during the period of the Russo-Caucasian war;
firmly determined to oppose any action designed to inflame inter-ethnic
enmity, and ready with united forces to face up to any aggression;
entrusting to democratic methods, in particular to people-diplomacy, which
has a multi-century tradition and which has not lost its power in the
Caucasus today, an exceptional role in settling vexed questions and disputes
in inter-ethnic relations;
inspired by the prospects of showing to the whole world through the
example of the multi-ethnic Caucasus, a region unique on the ethno-cultural
plane, our sincere striving for the establishment of brotherly relations
between peoples on the basis of the principle of equality of rights and close
collaboration in the settling of socio-economic and cultural problems,

have decided to conclude the following

TREATY
Article 1
The 3rd Congress of the peoples of the Caucasus, in continuation of the work
begun by the 1st Congress of the united mountain-peoples of the Caucasus (1
May 1917, Vladikavkaz), announces the start of the process of restoring the
sovereign statehood of the mountain-peoples of the Caucasus and declares the
Confederation of the Mountain Peoples of the Caucasus (CMPC) to be the
legitimate heir of the independent North Caucasian Republic ('The Mountain
Republic'), formed on 11 May 1918.

Article 2
The subjects of the Treaty are the mountain-peoples of the Caucasus existing as
the historically independent ethnic communities who have expressed in their
national congresses (conferences) and their executive committees their desire to

enter the Confederation and whose plenipotentiary delegates drew up and recognized the present Treaty.

Article 3
The Treaty partners declare that they will act in the spirit of fraternity, friendship and cooperation with the aims of further developing and strengthening political, socio-economic and cultural ties between the mountain-peoples of the Caucasus, following the principles of respect for state-sovereignty, cooperation, mutual help and non-interference in the internal affairs of the republics which they represent.

Article 4
The Treaty partners recognize the need for (i) the coordination of forces for mutually agreed management of socio-political processes in the republics and national-territorial formations of the region, (ii) the formation of a highly developed and optionally functioning inter-republican socio-economic complex, (iii) the creation of conditions for the transition to a market economy, (iv) the effective and rational use of natural resources and their conservation, (v) the development and strengthening of the artificially interrupted ties between our peoples, (vi) the raising of the standard of living of the population of the republics and of the region in general, and with this aim to go with proposals for the concluding of bilateral and multilateral treaties on cooperation and mutual assistance to the highest leading organs of the republics and national territorial formations.

Article 5
The subjects of the Confederation have equal rights within the limits of the association irrespective of the number of their peoples. They can differ according to the size and structure of the powers delegated by them to the Confederation.

Article 6
The formation of confederative organs is produced by national congresses (conferences) to the Congress of the Mountain-Peoples of the Caucasus by means of delegating their plenipotentiary representatives. The Congress itself forms and confirms the confederative organs according to this very principle on a basis of parity. However, it is proposed that with the appearance of necessary conditions the Caucasian Confederation will pass over to the conducting of direct elections of delegates to the Congress of Mountain Peoples of the Caucasus.

Article 7
The President, Presidential Council, Chairman of the Court of Arbitration, the Caucasian Parliament (Caucasian Assembly), the Chairman of the Committee of Caucasian Associations and the Coordinator for the business of the CMPC chosen by the supreme organ of the CMPC will with unconditional priority for the legislative and executive organs of the republics fulfil their plenary powers by discussion, decision and control for the realization of each and every problem and question touching upon the interests of the peoples united in the Confederation.

Article 8
The organs of the CMPC are built according to the principle of the division of powers between the legislative, the executive and the judiciary, and they function, in accordance with the 'Statute concerning the leading organs of the CMPC', ratified at the 3rd Congress of the Mountain Peoples of the Caucasus, and with regard to the laws of the republics of the region.

Article 9
The Caucasian Parliament (Caucasian Assembly) is elected directly by the plenipotentiary representatives chosen at the congresses of the participating peoples of the CMPC and is not dependent on national parliamentary institutions but at the same time effects a direct link with them through persons who are simultaneously deputies of the Caucasian and national parliaments.

Article 10
The Committee of Caucasian Associations – the executive organ of the Confederation – consists of leading employees of the ministries, departments and public organizations of the republics heading the various specialist associations.

Article 11
The Committee of Caucasian Associations in the person of the President, his First Deputy, the Chairman of the various specialist associations and the Coordinator for the business of the CMPC on the basis of treaties in a variety of directions will draw up a general plan for the socio-economic and cultural cooperation of the republics, and after agreement in the institutions of the Caucasian Parliament and Presidential Council they will distribute it to the national parliaments and governments of the republics.

Article 12
Particularly acute and complex questions within and between the subjects of the Confederation and also between them and the Confederation will with agreement of the parties be examined in the Confederation's Court of Arbitration. Decisions of the Court convey a recommendatory character and are effected through the influence of the authority of the general opinion of the united peoples.

Article 13
With the aim of resolving inter-ethnic conflicts and of guaranteeing stability in the region, the 3rd Congress of the Mountain Peoples of the Caucasus charges the Caucasian Parliament with drawing up a special Statute on the status and functions of established forces for regional security.

Article 14
The subjects of the Confederation have the right to unite among themselves and with other subjects in any associations if their goals are not directed against the interests of the Confederation they have created.

Article 15
The Treaty is open for new subjects to join. An act of union with it will be effected by a special Agreement, confirmed by the Parliament of the Confederation or by the next Congress of the Mountain Peoples of the Caucasus.

Article 16
Withdrawal from the Confederation is achieved by decision of a national congress (conference) of the subjects of the Treaty and will be considered by the Parliament of the CMPC.

Article 17
The Statutes of the present Confederative Treaty can be abolished, altered or supplemented at the request of the subjects by decision of the Parliament of the Confederation with subsequent confirmation by the Congress of the Mountain Peoples of the Caucasus.

Article 18
The participants of the Confederative Treaty commit themselves to observe its conditions and to bear responsibility before their own peoples and the commonwealth of Caucasian peoples as a whole for their actions according to the commitments they have taken upon themselves.

Article 19
The parties to the Treaty have chosen as place of residence for the leading organs (headquarters) of the CMPC the city of Sukhumi, capital of the Abkhaz Republic.

Article 20
The Treaty comes into effect from the moment of its recognition (i.e., from 2 November 1991). It is subject to ratification in the national congresses (conferences) or parliaments of the peoples who have created the CMPC. Documents of ratification will be deposited with the Presidential Council of the CMPC.

Source: B. George Hewitt, 'Abkhazia: A Problem of Identity and Ownership', *Central Asian Survey* 12, 3 (1993), pp. 304-8. Translation by Hewitt.

10

Soviet Muslims: Gains and Losses as a Result of Soviet Language Planning

ISABELLE T. KREINDLER

> If you confirm a people's language by giving it any kind of writing, leading it to school and to church, you confirm it as a people which will value its own particularity (*samobytnost'*).
>
> Tsarist official attacking a system of education which relied on the mother tongue (1869).[1]

To begin with, a clarification of the terms 'gains and losses' in the title is necessary. 'Gains' are usually considered as positive and 'losses' as negative. But from whose point of view? If one result of Soviet language planning is the 'gain' of a modern intelligentsia, is that positive or negative? To Nazif Shahrani, the well-known anthropologist and expert on Central Asia, for example, this Soviet-created intelligentsia represent 'larvae of locusts' blocking the return to a genuine Islam. Guy Imart, on the other hand, sees them as the only safeguard keeping Islamic militancy in check.[2] This chapter will examine the gains and losses chiefly from the point of view of the Soviet Muslim peoples as nations seeking to modernize, and as ethnic groups wishing to preserve their distinct cultures and traditions.

MUSLIMS OF THE RUSSIAN EMPIRE IN 1917

On the eve of the revolution, the close to 20 million Muslims were a disparate group scattered geographically over vast expanses, ranging from nomadic through semi-nomadic to settled populations and speaking a variety of dialects, mainly Turkic, but also Iranian and Ibero-Caucasian and even Chinese (the Dungans had come from China between 1876–81). The overwhelming majority were illiterate –

only among the Volga Tatars did the literacy rate reach about 30 percent; among the Azerbaijanis, it was under five per cent, and in Central Asia it was no more than three per cent. Among the Tajiks of Turkestan proper, for example, the literacy rate was only 2.3 per cent and it dropped even lower to one in 200 among those living in eastern Bukhara.[3] In 1906 *Vestnik vospitaniia* (*Bulletin of Education*) estimated that given the current rate of development it would take 4600 years for men and 3260 for women to achieve universal literacy in Central Asia.[4]

By the end of the 19th century traditional Muslim education had sunk to a low level. The medium of instruction was a foreign tongue, Arabic or Persian. In the lower schools, most of the time was spent on learning passages from the Qur'an by heart, while the texts studied in the upper schools were the same as those used in the 12th century or even earlier. While undoubtedly there were some exceptions, 'much of what was taught in the elementary school (*maktab*) and *madrasa* became dysfunctional'.[5] The few government Russian-native schools, though of extreme importance in increasing the ranks of the new secularized Muslim intelligentsia (the other sources were the 'new method', *jadid*, schools and education abroad) could hardly affect these statistics.

This largely pre-literate society, used the Arabic script and the three traditional literary languages, Arabic, Persian or Chagatay, when writing (according to Isaev, 16 peoples were using the Arabic alphabet before the revolution).[6] The fact that language was not a serious issue can be explained by the prevailing mass illiteracy. After all, as Rustow comments, 'it doesn't matter in which language you cannot read or write'.[7] However, the often presented picture of an undifferentiated, pluralistic, multilingual, tolerant community united by a common faith is, as Muriel Atkin points out, too neat. Muslim unity had not prevented 14 centuries of constant warfare in Central Asia. Nor were the Tajiks, for example, unaware of the difference in their language from that of their Turkic neighbours, or of their special connection to Persian culture.[8]

Some communities were in fact developing into nations with their own literary languages. By the end of the 19th century, the Volga Tatars, the group in longest contact with Russians and with a relatively high literacy rate, were clearly emerging as a nation with a literary language based on spoken Tatar; so too were the Azerbaijanis and the Crimean Tatars. Even in Central Asia, the three traditional literary languages of Arabic, Persian and Chagatay were beginning to be replaced by Kazakh, Turkmen and Uzbek.[9] Among the Kazakh intelligentsia, who were battling against the strong cultural influence of both the Russians and the Tatars, the association of language and nation was especially developed. As Ahmed Baytursunov, the editor of a popular Kazakh newspaper and future Kazakh commissar of education wrote in 1913,

> for the preservation of our national identity we must proceed toward enlightenment and develop our own literary language. It should never be forgotten that only that people which creates a literature in its own native language has a right to independent existence.[10]

By the beginning of the 20th century, the trend was certainly in the direction of linguistic and national differentiation. Gaspralı's reform movement, which aimed to modernize Muslim education and to promote unity through a common Turkic language, was generally much more successful in its first aim. In fact, the two aims were to some extent contradictory; for, with education came appreciation for one's own language (especially since the language of instruction in the first grades in *jadid* schools was the vernacular rather than Arabic). While many seemed to favour Gaspralı's common Turkic in theory, only those whose own language was very close to it favoured the language in practice. The Volga Tatars, with a growing literature in their own tongue, would have preferred Tatar to become the common language. The Kazakhs were consciously perfecting their own literary language and showed little interest in the common Turkic. The general atmosphere, including that in Turkey itself, was to return to the language spoken by the people. The decisions by the early Muslim congresses (1905–6) to rely in the first grades on the vernacular and to shift in upper grades to the common Turkic language were not very effective. The fact that the Muslim peoples were still a largely un-differentiated mass was not an indication of Islamic uniqueness but largely a reflection of the retardation in modernization, the result, as Wheeler put it, of 'centuries of foreign domination and invasion'.[11] With the spread of education and modernization, this would begin to change. Indeed a contemporary analyst of national movements among Russian Muslims confidently predicted that the Muslim community would in the future divide into separate nations.[12]

FROM 'NATIONAL IN FORM, SOCIALIST IN CONTENT' TO 'RUSSIAN AS THE HALLMARK OF THE SOVIET PEOPLE'

The 70 or so years of Soviet language planning fall into three quite distinct periods. The first (1917–1930s) and last (late 1950s–1985) were both very active but largely at cross purposes with each other. These two periods were separated by a hiatus of about twenty years (1930s–1950s) where little language planning activity took place.

THE MOTHER TONGUE TAKES CENTRE STAGE (1917–1930s)

Lenin's generous linguistic policy, which formed the core of his nationality policy, derived from a rather narrow view of non-Russian nationalism. He saw it largely as a reaction to 'Great Power chauvinism', and considered the chief grievance of the nationalities to be the disrespect shown for their national languages. Lenin therefore stressed the need to guarantee 'the most complete equality of nationalities and their languages', and specifically insisted that Russian should not be a state language or a compulsory subject in non-Russian schools. To ensure true national equality, Lenin promoted a broad program of 'development of languages and literatures of the formerly repressed nationalities' so that these languages could take their rightful position in schools and in local administration. It was on Lenin's initiative that special commissions to study languages were formed, that work on alphabets for peoples with no writing began and that the Turkestan State University (now University of Tashkent) was established in 1918.[13]

Of course, there was also a practical reason for developing and using the various vernaculars. According to Lenin, there could be no politics without literacy and, undoubtedly, the easiest and quickest way to promote literacy was through the mother tongue. It was the message of communism rather than its linguistic form that Lenin was seeking to impart. Taking a leaf from a Kazan missionary acquaintance of his father, whose system of education had been described as 'Orthodox in content, national in form', Lenin insisted on the use of the native languages no matter how few their speakers or un-developed their language. Like the missionary educator, N. I. Il'minskii, he wanted to reach out to the people and the most effective way to do that was in the language spoken by them.[14]

This populist approach explains many seemingly utopian practices in early Soviet language planning. There were enormous investments in language development work for languages with few speakers, and often separate literary languages were created for closely related dialects. 'It is not easy', as Simon Crisp writes, 'to recapture the heady atmosphere of those days, when contemporary sources speak of the almost limitless possibilities for development of even the smallest languages and of the inherently revolutionary nature of the Latin alphabet.'[15] The early period of language planning appears rather more confused than 'planned and deliberate' as has sometimes been suggested.[16] While the basic Communist Party program as proclaimed by the 1920 and 1923 party congresses unequivocally supported the national languages, often there were disagreements between the centre and the regions or even within their respective bureaucracies.

Nor was there uniformity of opinion among the individual language planners, who may have represented pan-Turkist, Arabist or tsarist colonial views.[17]

The first few years appear especially inconsistent. Initially, the Bolsheviks treated the Muslims as a single community. In spite of the stress on the mother tongue, 'Turkic' was proclaimed the official tongue of the Turkestan Soviet Socialist Republic, though recognition was also extended to Kazakh and Kyrgyz. In Dagestan, the local languages were to gain recognition only after 1928. Dagestani Bolsheviks had at first turned to Arabic as the chief language of communication, then from 1923 to 1928 to Azerbaijani adding for a brief period in 1928 also Kumyk (both Turkic languages).[18] The Idel-Ural project, which was to include not only the Bashkirs but also non-Muslim nationalities such as the Chuvash and Maris, with the Tatars obviously playing the dominant role, had Stalin's backing. It was largely wrecked by fellow-Muslim Bashkirs, who under Zeki Validov's leadership began to assert their national individuality.[19] By 1920 when the Bolsheviks began moving towards a federal system, they had no clear policy concerning the various peoples and their languages.

The creation of national literary languages, which went hand in hand with the creation of national territories, is often presented as artificial and deliberately calculated for purposes of 'divide and rule'. However, literary languages are, as Hobsbawm writes, 'almost always semi-artificial constructs'. In Europe, too, in the case of the new nations of the 19th to early 20th century, language was 'the main factor in the creation of national consciousness'.[20] Certainly the Bolsheviks had many enthusiastic nationals in the language construction work.

The guiding principle in the 'delimitation' was as far as possible language. The strange borders or the seemingly illogical divisions which often resulted were more the outcome of the complexity of the task – intermingled, illiterate populations, unstudied dialects – rather than a deliberate policy to weaken the Muslim peoples. Also, the influence of local leaders should not be ignored. As Donald Carlisle has, for example, shown in this volume, Greater Uzbekistan was largely the product of the Bukhara *jadids*.

Bennigsen's proposed division of Central Asia into only three units, Kazakh-Kyrgyz, Uzbek-Tajik and Turkmen, does not seem to be a great improvement over the Soviet division into the six units of Kazakh, Kyrgyz, Uzbek, Tajik, Turkmen and Karakalpak.[21] One wonders how long Kazakh-Kyrgyz relations would have remained friendly under the joint arrangement, especially when one considers the tensions which have existed even between the northern and southern Kyrgyz. And would the Uzbek-Tajik state have escaped such language problems as those of Belgium, for example? Or would the Tajiks have peacefully assimilated with the more numerous Uzbeks? Even the Karakalpak national unit was not completely 'artificial'; their dialect, although close to Kazakh, was nevertheless different.

Certainly the communists were aware of and wished to discourage the movements of pan-Turkism and pan-Islam, and yet this does not negate the fact that the principle of language and culture was uppermost. The differences were not created by the Bolsheviks, they were only used by them. In fact, if divide and rule was indeed the main concern, many additional subdivisions could have been easily engineered to produce smaller, weaker units. Perhaps a contributing factor to the present problem of Tajikistan is that the differences between the North and South were ignored and that so many different clans and even peoples and languages were put together in one unit. Uzbekistan, too, could have been easily divided further – there were, for example, proposals for creating three separate Uzbek languages.[22] Moreover, alphabet changes in this period do not seem to have been pre-planned or primarily designed to promote disunity. At first, attempts were made to reform the Arabic alphabet. In fact, quite a number of nationalities received their first alphabet in Arabic, among them the Adyge (1918), the Karachai-Balkars (1920), the Bashkirs (1923), the Karakalpaks and the Kyrgyz (1924).[23] Nor was Latinization, which was first proposed by the Azerbaijanis, primarily motivated by a desire to cut off the people from their Islamic past or to introduce an alphabet which would not obscure linguistic differences in closely related Turkic languages as Arabic did (although no doubt this was not unwelcome!). In the 1920s, the Latin alphabet was viewed as the alphabet of the revolution and it was expected that Russian too would adopt it shortly. Many non-Muslim peoples who had been using the Russian script, were forced to shift to the Latin alphabet. The Latin alphabet was indeed easier to learn and mass literacy grew rapidly after its adoption. Even among the Volga Tatars, where the opposition to abandoning the Arabic alphabet was the strongest, the Latin alphabet caught on easily.[24]

This first period of Soviet language planning yielded most of the significant gains in individual language development and in the development of various cultural and state institutions which were staffed at least partly by the native people (this was the period of *korenizatsiia*). It was during this era that languages were standardized and provided with reformed or totally new alphabets. They were also developed to meet the demands of functioning in schools and other institutions. Language corpus planning, in this period was viewed as an integral part of state construction. The magazine *Sovetskoe stroitel'stvo* (*Soviet Construction*) often carried articles devoted to language construction (*iazykovoe stroitel'stvo*). Languages were developed into efficient means of communication and in the case of the larger nationalities prepared for functioning in most domains of human endeavour. It was the language policy that breathed the autonomous units into life by producing a cultural élite which staffed the local institutions and became well rooted in its home territory. The program captured the enthusiasm of both the leaders and the people – it was after all their language! The thrill of seeing one's language emerge as a literary tongue can be felt even through the stilted double translation of a poem by a Kumyk poetess:

> We too, have our language!
> How long ye little peoples, have ye sought
> Your hidden lost language in vain,
> Like a birthmark upon a woman's cheek
> That beneath the *chadra* has lain.
>
> We lived long under a bitter yoke,
> And our sacred mother-tongue
> From her slumber never awoke
> Till the spell that roused her was sung.
>
> Now the yoke is consumed
> By revolt, the mighty fire;
> And our minds are illumed
> And knowledge new we acquire
> We learn to speak, to read, and to write
> The tongue that we love as our mother bright![25]

Nonetheless, there were also losses. The abandonment of the Arabic alphabet caused a break with both the Muslim past and with fellow Muslims beyond the borders, though not with Turkey, since it too shifted to the Latin alphabet in 1928. Moreover, choosing the language spoken by the people as the base for the literary language meant a departure from the élite tradition of earlier scholarship and culture. Basing literary Tajik on popular speech, for example, made it more distant from literary Persian.[26]

It was also in this period that the Volga Tatars, though making progress – in the 1920s Tatar-language textbooks were prepared not only for primary and secondary schools, but also for many university level courses – were losing their leading position among the Muslims of Russia. In 1917 they had enjoyed first place with 139 newspapers, while the Uzbeks were in second place with only 39 newspapers. By 1935, though the number of Tatar-language newspapers had increased to 203, they had slipped into second place and the decline was to continue.[27]

RUSSIAN RETURNS (1930s–1950s)

It is difficult to pinpoint with accuracy the shift toward Russian and away from the national languages. Actually, an undercurrent favouring Russian was always present, but attacks on national languages could easily be beaten back as manifestations of 'Great Power chauvinism'. As Stalin himself put it in 1930, 'is it not evident that those who advocate one common language within the borders of the USSR are in essence striving to restore the privileges of the formerly predominating language, namely the Great Russian language?'.[28] Some change in atmosphere can be detected already in the late 1920s accompanied in several cases by purges (such as among the Crimean and Volga Tatars).[29]

In the 1930s, amidst growing centralism and a revival of Russian patriotism, the Russian language was making its comeback.[30] Nineteen thirty-four apparently marks the year when the tide turned against the Latin alphabet, as was signalled by the attacks on I. Khansuvarov's book, which had praised Latinization as an instrument of Leninist policy. But the clearest indication of the new emphasis on the Russian language was the March 1938 decree which, in direct violation of Lenin's injunction, decreed Russian as a compulsory subject in all non-Russian schools. This was followed shortly by an abrupt shift to the Russian script, justified on the grounds of making the study of Russian easier.[31] The new Russian alphabets were much more divisive for no attempt was made to unify them as was tried with the Latin alphabets. Furthermore, the languages were now directly open to Russian influence.

The greatest setback for the national languages, however, was not the re-emergence of Russian by their side but the physical elimination of the native intelligentsia in the Stalin purges. Writers, linguists and literary scholars were especially vulnerable to the charge of bourgeois nationalism. Many Russians, too, among them the famed Turkologist E. D. Polivanov, lost their lives in the purges. The purges cast a pall on all cultural activities. The field of linguistics became especially inactive as the accusation of 'wrecking on the language front' could cost a linguist his life. All creative language planning stopped as the only safe language work became 'enrichment' from Russian. This usually involved not only wholesale borrowing from Russian but also introducing Russian calques and verbal phraseology as well as the outright setting aside of native terms and replacement with Russian ones. In the first year of glasnost, Chingiz Aitmatov was to vent his deep resentment at such terms as the title of a Kyrgyz newspaper — *Naryn pravdasy* — as if Kyrgyz had no words for 'truth' or 'justice'.[32]

And yet, there was 'no wholesale abandonment of the earlier

commitment to the national languages as an essential means of socialist construction in a multinational state'.[33] No new justifying theory was put forth to change the status of Russian among the non-Russians. Soviet nationality theory was still firmly based on the 'national in form, socialist in content' formula, which theoretically assured the position of the national languages.

Indeed, there was no drastic drop in either the number of languages used in schools or in publishing. In 1938–39 over 70 languages were in use as media of instruction; 22 languages were in use in Uzbekistan alone, 20 in Dagestan.[34] Most languages held their position and most non-Russian children still continued to receive a great part of their schooling in the mother tongue. Even during the grimmest years of Stalin's regime, while native language writers and linguists, teachers and actors were being swept away in the purges, while the languages were subjected to a crude russification and there was a virtual freeze on creative language development, literacy in the national languages continued to grow.

RUSSIAN AS THE HALLMARK OF THE SOVIET PEOPLE (1950s–1985)

As the Stalin period began to thaw under Khrushchev, the Soviet cultural scene came alive and linguistics and socio-linguistics, as the Soviet linguist Avrorin put it, 'got back on their feet'.[35] Crude russification of languages, though not completely abandoned, was now much more difficult to enforce. Serious linguistic research, including work on dialects was revived. In spite of the emphasis on the so-called 'common lexical fund' for all Soviet languages, many Muslim linguists and writers began to bring back native terms, which were usually based on Arabic or Persian. Even languages that were being phased out as media of instruction in school, such as numerous languages of the Northern Caucasus, were again lovingly studied and became subjects of scholarly articles and monographs.[36]

However, it was also under Khrushchev that the Russian language was officially thrust onto centre stage. In line with his claim of the approaching victory of communism, the Soviet Union was supposed to have 'solved its nationality problem' and to have achieved 'an unprecedented unity of peoples' with Russian as its 'language of inter-nationality communication'. All this was soon to be encapsulated in the new formula of Soviet nationality policy as 'the Soviet people: a new historical community', with the Russian language being one of its basic hallmarks (*priznak*).[37]

The new theory found its practical application in the education reform laws of 1958–59 which swept aside the unequivocal right to an education in one's mother tongue, a right that was anchored in all previous Soviet legislation and party documents. (Even the 1938 decree which had made Russian a mandatory subject, had expressly cautioned that this should not be construed as setting aside the mother tongue as the medium of instruction!) Now parents were allowed to choose the language of instruction, and whether or not their children would study their mother tongue as a subject. The national language was thus reduced to the category of 'this or that language of choice'. This 'free choice' provision gave rise to vigorous opposition in several republics, including Azerbaijan (but not in the other Muslim republics), and until abrogated by the various union republic language laws in the late 1980s, it was to be the chief target of national protest movements.[38]

The Russian language promotion campaign, first launched under Khrushchev, continued to accelerate under Brezhnev. As it became more and more obvious that communist ideology, which Khrushchev had tried to revive, had become largely irrelevant, the Party leadership seized on Russian as its chief instrument for unity. The last decades of the Soviet regime, as I have pointed out elsewhere, strongly resemble those of the tsarist regime in this desperate seizure of language as the 'cement' of empire. (The term 'cement' was used in both periods.) However, the glorification of the Russian people and their language went far beyond anything attempted in tsarist times. Beyond its role as instrument of inter-nationality communication and as the language of culture and science, Russian was now endowed with the unique attributes of the language of Lenin, October and the communist future. The Russian language was now seen as an all-Soviet treasure which helped develop all nationalities and which was becoming 'an integral part of their culture'. All non-Russians were now alleged to have a 'craving' (*tiaga*) for the Russian language which, as originally coined by Khrushchev, had become for them 'a second mother tongue'.[39]

Party leaders and government functionaries in Islamic areas, above all the Uzbek party leader Sharaf Rashidov, distinguished themselves as especially zealous propagandists of Russian.[40] The Russian language was now upheld for all nationalities as 'an inner need', 'a source of spiritual growth', 'an important factor in the formation of a personality with a specific ideology and moral qualities'.[41] Russian language lessons often became Russian value lessons, for their aim, as two educational specialists explained, was to promote 'the gradual merging (*sblizhenie*), and ultimately also integration, within the framework of a common socialist culture'.[42]

Though the censuses continued to record a very high language loyalty among the Muslim peoples (mostly well over 90 per cent), there is no question that this last period led to losses, especially among the below-union republic nationalities. Between 1961 and 1982 for example, 31 languages in the Russian Federation were totally phased out as media of instruction, among them Adyge, Balkar, Checheno-Ingush, Karachai. But even among the ten or so Islamic nationalities that still retained the mother tongue as language of instruction through secondary school, including the six union-republic nationalities which also continued it through higher education in some disciplines, the trend was towards the expansion of Russian media education and increasing the hours devoted to teaching Russian. By 1982, for example, 70 per cent of pupils in Kazakhstan were studying in Russian language schools; and the Kazakh language continued to retreat in the school as elsewhere. In 1990, the Kazakh writer Anuar Alimjanov complained that almost 40 per cent of Kazakh children did not speak Kazakh.[43] While Uzbeks were on the whole more successful in retaining their language as a medium of instruction, about 17 per cent of school-time in Uzbek language schools was devoted to the study of Russian.[44]

In publishing the picture was similar. In the Caucasus, Wixman has found 'a general decline in the average number of titles published per year in the North Caucasian languages', while according to Bennigsen and Quelquejay the Dagestani literary languages were rapidly becoming 'semi-literary'. Among the Karachai, a nationality that had suffered from Stalin's deportation policy, one book was published per 2.6 Karachai in 1959, dropping to one book per five in 1970 and even further down to one book per ten in 1979, or only 0.1 book per Karachai per year.[45] Among the Tatars, the decline was not only relative but absolute: in 1985 only 183 titles were published, 157 fewer than in 1913.[46] In the union-republics, especially Kirgiziia and Kazakhstan, native language publications were also in retreat and in the field of science and technology were almost phased out. For example, in the decade 1967–77, 93–95 per cent of scientific publications in the Kirgiz republic were in Russian.[47]

Although the Leninist theory of language equality was never repudiated and national languages were not directly attacked, the emphasis on Russian engendered an unhealthy atmosphere for the national languages. In 1978, the Kyrgyz linguist A. Orusbaev could already foresee 'in the none too distant future the mother tongue being confined to the domain of custom (*byt*) and Kyrgyz national culture', leaving all other domains to Russian.[48] As the languages lost prestige and narrowed in function, the national élite, especially in the cities, began to know Russian better than their own language. Also, more and more prominent national authors, among them, Chingiz Aitmatov

(Kyrgyz), Timur Pulatov (Uzbek), Olzhas Suleimenov (Kazakh), Fazil Iskander (Abkhaz), were writing in Russian. This growing mass phenomenon gave rise to a new branch of literary criticism and to heated discussion regarding the legitimacy of non-Russian writers writing in Russian and the literature, Russian or native, to which such works should be assigned.[49]

Language interference, the invasion of foreign words and strange constructions leading to what was later described as the '*makaronizatsiia*' of language, became a serious problem. The massive campaign for Russian did not result in the very effective teaching of Russian. Instead of bilingualism, the outcome was often 'semilingualism – not knowing either language properly'.[50] All languages, including Russian, were harmed.

As to the chief goal, that of integration, the campaign for Russian proved to be largely counter-productive. As Joshua Fishman has pointed out, a language's very decline may become the rallying force for a national revival campaign.[51] This is exactly what happened in the last decades of the Soviet regime. The association of language with nation had become so strong, that when the future of the language was placed in doubt, the future of the nation was also seen as under threat. 'And if tomorrow my language disappears', proclaimed the Avar poet Rasul Gamzatov, 'then I am ready to die today.'[52] Or, as Uzbekistan President Islam Karimov, no great speaker of Uzbek himself, expressed it in prose:

> A people is its language. The years that the Uzbek language in its own territory was a language of secondary importance and non-compulsory, were the very years when an Uzbek felt his unworthiness, his dependence on the elder brother.[53]

LANGUAGE AND THE RISE OF NEW STATES

The Russian language continued to be the focus of official attention in the first years of perestroika, in spite of the fact that glasnost had blown the linguistic scene wide open and the initiative was rapidly passing to the nationalities. While the centre and the local party leadership continued to sound the old slogans about the importance of Russian and the 'democratic' principle of free choice in language, the national cultural élite, eloquently articulating the pent-up language grievances, had captured the support of the youth and eventually of the broad public. Almost every mass protest, beginning with that of Alma-Ata in December 1986, contained a significant linguistic component. The first informal organizations such as the Tatar Public Centre or the Foundation for the Tajik Language, were formed around the language issue. The first concrete manifestations of national self-assertiveness in virtually every republic were the language laws, later to be followed by declarations of sovereignty and ultimately by declarations of independence. Indeed, as a Soviet commentator put it in 1989, 'the language issue has become the detonator calling forth an explosion of emotions'.[54] With independence, however, the language issue, as Fierman points out in this volume, has become much less pressing.

With the exception of the Uzbeks who would be the chief beneficiaries from a resurrected Turkestan, there have been few recent proponents of Muslim or Turkic reunification. On the contrary, not only are the Bashkirs, Kyrgyz or Karakalpaks now confirmed individual nations, but such closely related peoples as the Karachai and Balkars have made no move to unite, while the Chechen and Ingush have actually separated from each other. Even the estimated 300,000 Siberian Tatars of north-west Siberia who have always used the Volga Tatar literary language for writing and in schools, and who have been counted in all the post-1926 censuses as Volga Tatars, are now asserting their self-identity and demanding the construction of a literary language of their own.[55]

Today, the 58 million or so Muslims of the former Soviet Union are divided into over 30 separate nationalities, six of which are now recognized independent states. As a legacy of the Soviet regime, most of them have a literary language and near universal literacy, and all have a modern élite still able to communicate in the mother tongue with its people. Most of the nationalities are endowed with a network of schools, with many reaching tertiary level, as well as a plethora of cultural institutions, including an Academy of Sciences in the case of the six former union republics. In spite of economic difficulties, the recent trend has been to expand both education and publishing in the mother tongue, with Russian retreating.

But there were also losses, including the irreparable one of spiritual and cultural leaders in the purges. Amidst modern cultural development there was also an oppressive stultification of spiritual and cultural national life. In the last decades of the regime a growing threat to the viability of national languages was added as a result of the massive Russian language promotion campaign. But all this is now rapidly changing. After being largely cut off from their Islamic past, the cultural élite and people are both energetically turning to their roots. The current popular revival of Islam and scholarly efforts to recapture historical and cultural traditions are now leading to the restoration of some of the lost elements of the spiritual content of national identity. Linguistically, this has manifested itself in moves to purify the language by dropping Russian accretions and restoring native terminology, as well as in a renewed interest in the Arabic language and alphabet. However, so far, no nationality has plans to return to the Arabic alphabet. With the Azerbaijanis in the lead again, most are returning instead to the Latin script. Nor is Arabic particularly prominent in language enrichment. 'Overall, in print especially', as Eden Naby reports, 'Russian words and phrases are being discarded in favour of English words (especially economic terminology, but not confined to this field) as well as Turkic and Iranian words and phrases.'[56]

The Muslim peoples in the newly-established states face tremendous problems in the wake of the unmitigated disaster of communist rule. But the problems are not essentially different from those faced by the non-Muslim peoples of the former Soviet empire. Certainly, culturally, they are now far better prepared to meet the challenges than they were in 1917.

NOTES

1. *Sbornik dokumentov i stat'ei po voprosu ob obrazovanii inorodtsev* (St. Petersburg: MNP, 1869), p. 16.
2. Nazif Shahrani, 'The Lessons and Uses of History', *Central Asian Monitor* 1 (1993), p. 27; Guy Imart, *From 'Roots' to 'Great Expectations': Kirgizstan and Kazakhstan between the Devil and the Deep Green Sea* (Bloomington: Indiana Univ. Press, 1990), p. 7.
3. E. I. Ubriatova, 'Obshchie svedeniia o tiurkskikh iazykakh', in E. A. Bokarev and Iu. D. Desheriev (eds), *Mladopis'mennye iazyki narodov SSSR* (Moscow/Leningrad: Akademiia Nauk SSSR, 1959), p. 38; M. I. Isaev, *Sotsiolingvisticheskie problemy iazykov narodov SSSR* (Moscow: Vyshaia shkola, 1982), p. 69; G. Wheeler, *The Modern History of Soviet Central Asia* (London: Weidenfeld and Nicolson, 1964), p. 198; B. S. Asimova, *Iazykovoe stroitel'stvo v Tadzhikistane 1920–1940* (Dushanbe: Donish, 1982), p. 14.
4. R. I. Khashimov, 'Razvitie turkmenskogo iazyka', in A. N. Baskakov and V. Iu. Mikhal'chenko (eds.), *Razvitie natsional'nykh iazykov v sviazi s ikh funktsionirovaniem v sfere vysshego obrazovaniia* (Moscow: Nauka, 1982), p. 215. This estimate was often quoted by Soviet authors on tsarist education as a wonderful foil for Soviet achievements.
5. M. Mobin Shorish, 'Traditional Islamic Education in Central Asia prior to 1917', in Ch. Lemercier-Quelquejay *et al.* (eds.), *Passé turco-tatar, présent soviétique. Etudes offertes à Alexandre Bennigsen* (Louvain/Paris: Peters and EHESS, 1986), pp. 317–41.
6. M. I. Isaev, *Iazykovoe stroitel'stvo v SSSR* (Moscow: Nauka, 1979), p. 41.
7. D. A. Rustow, 'Language, Nations and Democracy', in J. G. Savard and R. Vigneault (eds.), *Multilingual Political Systems: Problems and Solutions* (Quebec City: International Center for Research on Bilingualism, 1973), p. 56.
8. Muriel Atkin, 'Religious, National and Other Identities in Central Asia', in Jo-Ann Gross (ed.), *Muslims in Central Asia: Expressions of Identity and Change* (Durham: Duke Univ. Press, 1992), pp. 46–72.
9. Wheeler, *The Modern History of Soviet Central Asia*, p. 275.
10. Quoted in S. A. Zenkovsky, *Pan-Turkism and Islam in Russia* (Cambridge: Harvard Univ. Press, 1967), p. 66. For the Kazakh national awakening, see also Isabelle T. Kreindler, 'Ibrahim Altynsarin, Nikolai Il'minskii and the Kazakh National Awakening', *Central Asian Survey* 2, 3 (Nov. 1983), pp. 99–116, and a recent study by Kemal H. Karpat, 'The Roots of Kazakh Nationalism: Ethnicity, Islam or Land?', in Marco Buttino (ed.), *In A Collapsing Empire* (Milano: Fondazione G. Feltrinelli, 1992), pp. 313–33.

11. Wheeler, *The Modern History of Soviet Central Asia*, p. 29.
12. K. Zalevskii, 'Natsional'nye dvizheniia', in L. Martov *et al.* (eds.), *Obshchestvennoe dvizhenie v Rossii v nachale XX-go veka* (St. Petersburg: Obshchestvennaia pol'za, 1911), p. 237.
13. Kreindler, 'The Changing Status of Russian in the Soviet Union', *International Journal of the Sociology of Language* 33 (1982), pp. 7–8; Khashimov, 'Razvitie turkmenskogo iazyka', p. 220; D. S. Baktygulov, *et al.*, *K voprosu gosudarstvennogo stroitel'stva Kirgizstana*, (Frunze: Kyrgyzstan, 1974), p. 10.
14. Kreindler, 'A Neglected Source of Lenin's Nationality Policy', *Slavic Review* 36, 1 (March 1977), pp. 86–100.
15. Simon Crisp, 'Soviet Language Planning 1917–53', in Michael Kirkwood (ed.), *Language Planning in the Soviet Union* (London: Macmillan, 1989), p. 27.
16. For example, Ronald Wixman, 'Applied Soviet Nationality Policy: A Suggested Rationale', in Ch. Lemercier-Quelquejay *et al.* (eds.), *Passé turco-tatar, présent soviétique.* pp. 449–68.
17. Crisp, 'Soviet Language Planning', p. 40. Stephen Blank shows, for example, how Narkompros and Narkomnats worked at cross purposes – Stephen Blank, 'The Origins of Soviet Linguistic Policy 1917–1920', *Russian History* 15, 1 (1988), pp. 71–92.
18. William Fierman, 'Language Development in Soviet Uzbekistan', in Isabelle Kreindler (ed.), *Sociolinguistic Perspectives on Soviet National Languages* (Berlin: Mouton de Gruyter, 1985), pp. 206–7; Alexandre Bennigsen and Ch. Lemercier-Quelquejay, 'Politics and Linguistics in Daghestan', in Kreindler (ed.), *Sociolinguistic Perspectives*, pp. 134–5.
19. Zenkovsky, *Pan-Turkism and Islam in Russia*, pp. 180, 196.
20. E. J. Hobsbawm, *Nations and Nationalism since 1780* (Cambridge: Cambridge Univ. Press, 1990), p. 54; Hugh Seton-Watson, *Nations and States: An Enquiry into the Origins of Nations and the Politics of Nationalism* (Boulder: Westview Press, 1977), p. 9.
21. A. Bennigsen and Ch. Quelquejay, *The Evolution of the Muslim Nationalities of the USSR and Their Linguistic Problems* (London: Central Asian Research Centre, 1961).
22. William Fierman, *Language Planning and National Development: The Uzbek Experience* (Berlin: Mouton de Gruyter, 1991), p. 74.
23. Isaev, *Iazykovoe stroitel'stvo v SSSR*, pp. 90, 99, 105, 107, 188. Already in the 19th century, the Azerbaijani playwright Mirza Fath Ali Ahundzade (1812–78) had devised an alphabet based on Cyrillic and Latin letters, but neither the authorities in Istanbul nor in Tehran were prepared to back his project.
24. T. Dawletschin, *Cultural Life in the Tatar Autonomous Republic* (New York: Research Program on the USSR, 1953), p. 11.
25. Quoted in Fanina Halle, *Women in the Soviet East*, tr. from German (New York: Dutton, 1938), p. 214.
26. Asimova, *Iazykovoe stroitel'stvo v Tadzhikistane*, pp. 25–6.
27. A. Bennigsen and Ch. Lemercier-Quelquejay, *La presse et le mouvement national chez les musulmans de Russie avant 1920* (Paris/The Hague: Mouton, 1964), pp. 283–4.
28. Quoted in Elliot R. Goodman, *The Soviet Design for a World State* (New York: Columbia Univ., 1960), p. 273.
29. Alan Fisher, *The Crimean Tatars* (Stanford: Hoover Institution Press, 1978); Edward Lazzerini, 'Crimean Tatar: The Fate of a Severed Tongue', in Kreindler (ed.), *Sociolinguistic Perspectives*, pp. 109–24; Azade-Ayse Rorlich, *The Volga Tatars* (Stanford: Hoover Institution, 1986).
30. For an excellent analysis of the changing atmosphere, see Gerhard Simon, *Nationalism and Policy toward the Nationalities in the Soviet Union*, tr. from German (Boulder: Westview Press, 1991), especially Ch. 6.
31. Kreindler, 'The Non-Russian Languages and the Challenge of Russian', in Kreindler (ed.), *Sociolinguistic Perspectives*, pp. 352–4.
32. *Literaturnaia gazeta*, 13 August 1986.
33. Crisp, 'Soviet Language Planning', p. 39.
34. Kreindler, 'The Changing Status of Russian', p. 10.

35. V. A. Avrorin, *Problemy izucheniia funktsional'noi storony iazyka* (Leningrad: Nauka, 1975), p. 178.
36. See, for example, the solid collection under the general editorship of V. V. Vinogradov, *Iazyki narodov SSSR*, 5 vols.(Moscow: Nauka, 1966–68), or conference proceedings such as S. M. Basieva and N. Kh. Kulaev, *Materialy piatoi regional'noi nauchnoi sessii po istoriko-sravnitel'nomu izucheniiu ibereisko-kavkazskikh iazykov* (Ordzhonikidze, 1977).
37. Kreindler, 'Soviet Language Planning since 1953', in Michael Kirkwood (ed.), *Language Planning in the Soviet Union*, pp. 47–8.
38. Yaroslav Bilinsky, 'The Soviet Education Laws of 1958–1959 and Soviet Nationality Policy', *Soviet Studies* (October 1962), pp. 138–57.
39. Kreindler, 'Soviet Language Planning', pp. 52–3.
40. See, for example, Sh. Rashidov, *Iazyk druzhby i bratstva* (Moscow: Pravda, 1977), or his *Iazyk nashego edinstva i sotrudnichestva* (Moscow: Pravda, 1979).
41. *Russkii iazyk v kirgizskoi shkole*, 4 (1979), p. 2; K. Kh. Khanazarov, *Reshenie natsional'no-iazykovoi problemy v SSSR* (Moscow: Politizdat, 1982), p. 197; *Russkii iazyk v natsional'noi shkole* 2 (1986), pp. 61–2.
42. *Russkii iazyk i literatura v kirgizskoi shkole* 1 (1982), p. 16. On the cultural approach to teaching Russian, see Kreindler, 'Forging a Soviet People: Ethnolinguistics in Central Asia', in William Fierman (ed.), *Soviet Central Asia: The Failed Transformation* (Boulder: Westview Press, 1991), pp. 219–31, and 'Teaching Russian Esthetics to the Kirgiz', *The Russian Review* 40, 3 (1981), pp. 333–8.
43. *Russkii iazyk v natsional'noi shkole*, 6 (1982), p. 38; *Literaturnaia gazeta*, 11 April 1990, p. 3.
44. Fierman, 'Language Development in Soviet Uzbekistan', in Kreindler (ed.), *Sociolinguistic Perspectives*, pp. 220–22. Considering the tremendous costs and often unsatisfactory results, a Western scholar has argued that economically the massive Russian teaching program made little sense – Toussaint Hocevar, 'Economic Costs of Linguistically Alternative Communication Systems: The Case of Uzbek', *Nationalities Papers* X, 1 (1982), pp. 55–64.
45. Ronald Wixman, *Language Aspects of Ethnic Patterns and Processes in the North Caucasus* (Chicago: Univ. of Chicago, 1978), p. 160; Bennigsen and Lemercier-Quelquejay, 'Politics and Linguistics in Daghestan', in Kreindler, *Sociolinguistic Perspectives*, p. 135; Alf Grannes, 'A Note on Publishing in a Small Minority Language – Karacaj: A Quantitative Analysis', *Nordic Journal of Soviet & East European Studies* 4, 2 (1987), pp. 45–7.
46. *Pechat' SSSR v 1985 godu* (Moscow: Finansy i statistika, 1986), p. 25; Nadir Devlet, 'A Specimen of Russification: The Kazan Turks (Tatars)', *Central Asian Survey* 2, 3 (1983), pp. 79–88.
47. *Pechat' SSSR v 1979 godu* (Moscow: Finansy i statistika, 1980), p. 108.
48. *Russkii iazyk v kirgizskoi shkole*, 3 (1978), p. 6.
49. See, for example, M. V. Oreshkina, 'Tiurkskie leksicheskie zaimstvovaniia v sovremennoi russkoiazychnoi poezii i v russkikh perevodakh', in N. G. Mikhailovskaia (ed.), *Kul'tura russkoi rechi v usloviiakh natsional'no-russkogo dvuiazychiia* (Moscow: Nauka, 1985), pp. 119–32, where the author complains that non-Russians often violate the norms of the Russian language. For a broader discussion of the subject, see Chingiz Guseinov, 'O dvuiazychnom khudozhestvennom tvorchestve: istoriia, teoriia, praktika', *Voprosy literatury* 9 (1987), pp. 79–112, or Nafi Dzhusoity, 'Chto eto takoe rodnoi iazyk pisatelia?' *Voprosy literatury* 7 (1988), pp. 29–57. Also the work by Andzhei Dravis, originally published in 1981 in London, 'Ne tol'ko russkaia literatura', *Voprosy literatury* 8 (1990), pp. 28–44.
50. Michael Kirkwood, 'Russian Language Teaching Policy in Soviet Central Asia 1958–1986', paper presented at Second European Seminar on Central Asian Studies, 7–10 April 1987.
51. Joshua Fishman, *Language in Sociocultural Change* (Stanford: Stanford Univ. Press, 1972), pp. 58–9.
52. Quoted in I. B. Dzhafarov, *Russkii iazyk – iazyk druzhby i bratstva* (Baku: Azerbaidzhanskoe gosizdat, 1982), p. 18.

53. *Literaturnaia gazeta*, 14 August 1991, p. 3.
54. *Literaturnaia gazeta*, 6 Sept. 1989, p. 3.
55. B. Valeev and S. Iskhakova, 'Iazykovye problemy zapadno sibirskikh Tatar', in V. M. Solntsev *et al.* (eds.), *Iazykovaia situatsiia v Rossiiskoi Federatsii: 1992* (Moscow: Rossiiskaia Akademiia Nauk, 1992), pp. 78–82.
56. Eden Naby, 'Publishing in Central Asia,' *Central Asian Monitor* 1 (1993), p. 29.

11

Independence and the Declining Priority of Language Law Implementation in Uzbekistan

WILLIAM FIERMAN

In October 1989, Uzbekistan's Supreme Soviet adopted a law 'On the State Language of the Uzbek SSR' (henceforth LSL).* This law was an important symbol of the dynamics in relations between Uzbekistan and Russia, and the pre-eminence of Uzbek culture in Uzbekistan. Four years after the LSL's adoption, there have been many changes in the language situation in Uzbekistan, but they fall far short of those promised in the LSL. This is especially striking in view of the fact that the law was adopted when Uzbekistan was just one of fifteen republics in a centralized political system, whereas in 1993 Uzbekistan is a country with a two-year history of independence.[1]

The LSL was drafted in March or April 1989, and reviewed on 18 May by Uzbekistan's Supreme Soviet presidium; this body adopted a decree requiring publication of the draft as the beginning of a republic-wide discussion.[2] For reasons little related to language, the 'discussion period' was a critical turning point in the history of Uzbek politics. Within days after the decree, bloody riots erupted in the Fergana Valley. Some weeks later, when the violence had quietened down, First Secretary of the Uzbekistan Communist Party Rafiq Nishanov was replaced by Islam Karimov. The former, who had served for only a year and a half, had been widely perceived as an outsider to Uzbekistan politics, and someone imposed by Moscow to represent

* The author would like to express his gratitude to the International Research and Exchanges Board for a travel grant which allowed him to go to Tashkent in the summer of 1992 and conduct some of the research used in this chapter.

the centre's interests.[3] Islam Karimov, in contrast to his political foe Nishanov, had never been 'exiled' from the republic by Brezhnev-era leader Sharaf Rashidov; thus, he did not have the the the stigma of 'outsider'. In the same manner as 'reformed' communist leaders throughout the Soviet Union in the late 1980s, Karimov quickly adopted many 'nationalist' positions. In Uzbekistan, these had been promoted in the preceding months by the opposition group Birlik.

In the case of language, Karimov's shift meant that in late summer 1989 he began to support a stronger version of the draft language law; unlike the spring version whose title referred to 'languages' (in the plural – that is, the Uzbek and Russian languages), the new version which Karimov eventually endorsed was entitled 'On the State Language' (singular). Although Karimov's new position on the language law distinguished him from his predecessor, it is unlikely that he embraced the new version with great enthusiasm. Indeed, it appears likely that he adopted Birlik's platform less out of conviction than from a sense of *realpolitik*; moreover, this shift was almost certainly accomplished with Moscow's permission if not encouragement.[4]

In the two years that followed Uzbekistan's adoption of the language law, debate continued throughout the Soviet Union over such fundamental questions as delegation of powers to the republics, sovereignty and the shape of the future union or confederation. During this period, implementation of the LSL served to emphasize Uzbekistan's sovereignty over its own affairs and the primacy of the Uzbek people in the republic. Though hardly at the top of the political agenda, measures to carry out the LSL were the subject of frequent articles in the press of the republic.

One might have expected the collapse of the Soviet Union and Uzbekistan's achievement of national independence to have accelerated implementation of the LSL. Indeed, since independence, Uzbekistan has continued to carry out relatively inexpensive symbolic measures which represent Uzbekistan sovereignty and the dominant role of the Uzbek people. However, the government seems to have slowed down implementation of more substantive measures which involve greater material cost and which are more disruptive in the short term. Today's press carries many articles on symbolic aspects of language policy, but few treat the more substantive issues.

One of the most obvious signs of retreat on LSL implementation concerns a set of corrections that were being finalized in the summer of 1992 to bring the 1989 law into accordance with Uzbekistan's status as an independent country. At that time some of the officials who were working on the revisions reported that it was planned to submit the changes to the country's legislature for consideration at its autumn session.[5] This, in fact, did not happen. An interview with Prime Minister Abdulhashim Mutalov on the third anniversary of the law (October 1992) suggests that the country's leadership was having second thoughts. Although Mutalov told a correspondent about amendments that would soon be submitted to the Supreme Soviet, his answers were very vague.[6] As it turned out, the amendments did not reach the legislature for consideration at all in 1992, or in 1993.

The following study examines implementation of Uzbekistan's LSL in the context of other developments between 1989 and 1993. After a brief overview of some provisions of the law and organizations relevant to implementation, it looks at some of the results of the law and the constraints on implementation. Then it analyzes some of the broader problems in independent Uzbekistan which seem likely to affect language law implementation; in particular, it considers why implementation of substantive language change, especially expanding the role of Uzbek, seems to have become a low priority on the agenda of the country's government. Finally, this study looks at some similarities between Uzbekistan and the other newly independent Central Asian states in the area of language change.

It is impossible in a brief chapter to examine all of the important dimensions of language policy in Uzbekistan. Thus, while it focuses on the capital city and communications at the republic level, it largely ignores the effect of the law in other areas of Uzbekistan, in particular rural regions. (Most of Uzbekistan's population lives in rural areas, which are much more 'Uzbek' – ethnically and linguistically – than urban areas.[7]) Likewise, the present discussion will not address the very important problem of languages of non-Russian minorities in Uzbekistan.

Before proceeding, it is important to present some basic facts about Uzbekistan's population. Uzbeks and Uzbek speakers have constituted the dominant majority of Uzbekistan's inhabitants throughout the republic's history. By 1989, Uzbekistan's population was over 71 per cent Uzbek, almost all of whom claimed Uzbek as their native language. The second largest ethnic group, the Russians, accounted for eight per cent, while Tajiks, in third place, accounted for under five per cent.[8] Kazakhs (about four per cent) along with Tatars and Karakalpaks (about two per cent each) were the only other groups with more than one per cent of the total. (The overwhelming majority of all of these groups claimed their nationality language as their native tongue in the 1989 census).[9]

Many of Uzbekistan's Uzbeks speak Russian as a second language, but the number is difficult to ascertain. Although 14.5 per cent of Uzbekistan's Uzbeks claimed fluency in Russian in the 1970 census, in 1979 Rashidov produced figures claiming that the share had risen to just under one half.[10] The 1989 census showed a decline from the 1979 figures and indicated that less than a quarter of Uzbekistan's Uzbeks spoke fluent Russian.[11]

Most of Uzbekistan's Russians and other native Russian speakers live in urban areas; only a very small percentage of them know Uzbek.[12] This is true above all in Uzbekistan's capital Tashkent and certain industrial and mining towns. The importance of the Russian-speaking population in the capital city is especially great given the concentration of power in Soviet political institutions.

THE LANGUAGE SITUATION AND THE LSL

The Law on the State Language of the Uzbek SSR consists of a preamble and thirty articles.[13] Most of the articles concern the spheres of use of Uzbek and other languages in Uzbekistan. There is scant mention of language corpus issues, and problems of implementation are dealt with only in very general terms.

Prior to the LSL, Uzbek had no official status within the Uzbek Soviet Socialist Republic (UzSSR). This, of course, was the same with all other non-Russian national languages except for Georgian, Armenian and Azerbaijani. The LSL changed this by making Uzbek the single state language (Article 1). (It also, however, provides for Russian as the 'language of cross-national communication'.)

Many of the articles in the LSL were designed to expand the role of Uzbek in public life. Article 3, for example, guarantees inhabitants of Uzbekistan the right to address state and public organizations and enterprises in Uzbek and to receive responses in the same language. (It also guarantees the right to address communications in Russian or other languages and to receive responses in Uzbek or Russian.) The law further states (Article 4) that managers (and workers, in the law's Russian text) are obliged to learn Uzbek to the extent necessary to fulfil their job responsibilities. The same requirement also applies to those whose work involves serving the population.

Articles 5 through 12 and Article 22 raise the status of Uzbek in public meetings, provide for use of Uzbek in the preparation and adoption of the republic's laws, and enhance the role of Uzbek in office work, accounting and financial documentation in enterprises, establishments and organizations. They also establish the role of Uzbek in the legal system and in notarial procedures, and provide that such documents as birth and death certificates, marriage registration and personal identity documents be issued in Uzbek. (Nevertheless, many of these same articles explicitly preserve a substantial role for Russian. For example, Article 12 – which deals with personal identity and certain other documents – indicates that along with the Uzbek text these papers should carry a Russian translation.)

Although Articles 13, 14 and 17 of the LSL provide for choice of language of instruction in UzSSR schools at various levels, it is obvious that their primary intention is to strengthen the position of Uzbek. Article 15 provides for the study of the state language as part of the curriculum for students receiving their education in languages other than Uzbek (and for the study of Russian by children studying in Uzbek and non-Russian minority groups). Article 16, which provides for the study of the Arabic-based script in all Uzbek-language groups in primary and secondary schools, adds a new dimension to Uzbek-language education. (This script was used for Uzbek until the late 1920s.) Article 18 provides for the use of the state language in scholarship, including the presentation and defence of dissertations.

It should be kept in mind that even in 1988–89, 77.1 per cent of Uzbekistan's children were in classes with Uzbek as the language of tuition (to be abbreviated below as 'ULG' for 'Uzbek language group'); 14.8 per cent attended classes with Russian as the language of tuition ('RLG' for 'Russian language group').[14] Although RLG pupils did indeed 'study' Uzbek, the language was treated as an unimportant subject, and most non-Uzbek children completing their education in RLGs had weak Uzbek skills or none at all. In universities, institutes and the Academy of Sciences too Uzbek had a much less central role than in primary and secondary education.

The expansion of Uzbek envisioned in the LSL, of course, implied the need for the creation of new terminology. The use of Uzbek in higher technical education has always been quite limited, so such measures as the publication of many Uzbek-language textbooks were contingent on this development. This question is addressed in Article 19; this article also deals with the study, dissemination and translation of the Uzbek heritage. Article 20 states that books, newspapers and journals in the UzSSR shall be printed 'primarily' in Uzbek, with the same provision for radio and television broadcasts.

Names are the subject of two separate LSL articles. Article 24 states that names of towns, villages, streets and other geographical referents shall be rendered only in Uzbek, and the following article gives all citizens the right to write their names 'in accordance with national-historic traditions'.

Among the law's other provisions, Article 27 prohibits responsible authorities from refusing petitions, complaints or proposals under the pretext that they do not know Uzbek (or Russian). The law charges the managers of state and other organizations with personal responsibility for observance of the law within their areas of jurisdiction (Article 28). The last article places responsibility for verification (*kontrol'*) of implementation on the republic's Supreme Soviet and its Standing Commission on Language.

Twenty-three of the LSL's articles were to go into effect immediately upon the law's adoption, on 21 October 1989. Seven others, however, were to be introduced gradually, over a period of up to eight years. Most importantly, up to eight years were to be allowed for implementing Article 4 (concerning knowledge of Uzbek by various categories of employees) and Articles 7 and 8 (concerning office work and statistical/financial documentation).

PARTICIPANTS IN IMPLEMENTATION

The 21 October 1989 resolution of the Uzbekistan Supreme Soviet 'On the Procedure for Implementing the Law "On the State Language of the UzSSR"' obliged the republic's Council of Ministers to adopt a state program on the law's realization within six months.[15] This program assigned responsibilities to a wide variety of organizations for tasks related to implementation, and designated very broad periods in which work was to be accomplished (generally a particular year or several years). Naturally, much of the work of implementation fell to the Ministry of Education and the Ministry of Higher and Secondary Specialized Education. Other tasks were assigned to the Ministries of Culture, Finance and Communications, the Academy of Sciences, the State Committee on Television and Radio, and the State Planning Committee.[16]

To oversee the implementation of the LSL the Council of Ministers established a thirty-five-member commission. Although the commission was supposed to convene twice monthly,[17] it appears to have met much less frequently.[18] Many of the meetings have been devoted to the implementation of the law in particular institutions, such as the Ministry of Communications, Ministry of Justice or the national airline.[19] This Council of Ministers' commission is replicated at lower levels of administration and, it appears, in many large institutions, especially in urban areas.[20]

Another establishment with an important role in LSL implementation has been the Terminological Committee. Although the Council of

Ministers' decree establishing the committee in December 1989 assigned it only matters concerning terminology,[21] in fact its activities have been much broader, including general supervision of language law implementation.[22]

Another potentially important body is the Uzbekistan Supreme Soviet's Committee on Matters of Cross-National Relations, Language and Culture. However, this organization has a staff of only four, plus twenty-four deputies who serve on it. As of 1992 this committee was meeting five or six times a year. Its primary function with regard to the LSL is to verify implementation and to identify violations. It is not, however, responsible for measures to correct them.[23]

Before the collapse of the Soviet system the Communist Party, of course, played a very important role in language policy implementation. Since the decline of the Communist Party and the shift of many functions from party to state organs, much of the policy making and *kontrol'* related to language policy has no doubt shifted to the presidential apparatus and the state apparatus at lower levels. On paper, a recently organized public organization known as the 'Uzbek Language Society' might also seem to be a key organization in this area. In fact, however, its importance is probably minimal.[24]

IMPLEMENTATION

Although Uzbekistan's Law on the State Language is important as a legal document, it is only one of many factors affecting language processes in Uzbekistan. Even without the law, for example, demographic developments would have an impact of their own. Therefore, as we turn to the matter of implementation, it is critical to view the law as only a single, albeit major, component in a broader environment.

As noted above, under Islam Karimov's leadership Uzbekistan's government has shown far greater enthusiasm for implementing symbolic over substantive change. One of the most visible indications of symbolic change has been the implementation of the law's provisions on toponyms. The scale of the renaming activity is suggested by a single decree of Tashkent city's executive committee in February 1991 which all at once changed the names of 171 streets. By September 1992 the name change had affected over 500 streets in the capital city.[25] The process is not, of course, limited to Tashkent. In the Fergana Valley town of Namangan, over fifty street names were changed in the first ten weeks of 1993.[26] In harmony with these name changes, as of mid-1993 many public signs in Tashkent were only in the Uzbek language. Moreover, it appeared that this symbolic implementation was continuing at a rapid pace.

Though they are also significant as symbols, most other aspects of the language law are potentially more substantive; their implementation can affect citizens' lives in more tangible ways and require far greater expenditure. One such key area has been increased instruction in the Uzbek language, especially in the schools. Efforts in this area are apparent in the greater number of hours which began to be devoted to Uzbek following adoption of the LSL. Thus, for example, prior to the language law, children in ULGs were supposed to spend 2,346 hours in Uzbek language and literature classes in the course of their full primary and secondary education. Following the adoption of the language law, this was raised by about 15 per cent to 2,720 hours; this latter total was equal to the number of hours in the curriculum devoted to Russian language and literature for Uzbekistan's RLG children.[27]

Given the finite number of hours in the school day, the increase in Uzbek-language study had to be compensated for by decreases in time for other subjects. Some of the gains for Uzbek have been achieved at the expense of the number of hours devoted to Russian language and literature. Before the adoption of the LSL, Russian language and literature consumed 1,598 hours of school-time for students completing secondary school in ULGs. Following the law's passage this was cut to 1,258. A year after Uzbekistan's independence, that is, for the 1992–93 school year, it was scheduled to drop further to around 900 hours.[28]

Just as the quantity of hours devoted to Russian in the ULG has dropped, the number of hours devoted to Uzbek language in the RLG curriculum of Uzbekistan has grown. Before the law's passage, the curriculum for children in Uzbekistan's RLGs included only 544 hours of instruction in Uzbek; by September 1990, the school plan called for an increase to 884 hours.[29] In part, the hours were 'found' by introducing Uzbek at an earlier stage, during the second half of the first grade.[30]

Teaching the Uzbek language as a subject is related to another very important educational issue – the change in the language of tuition in schools following the adoption of the Law on State Language. Without additional information regarding migration and population growth it is difficult to assess the full significance of available data. However, as noted above, in 1988–89, 77.1 per cent (3,414,927) of Uzbekistan's school children were in ULGs; moreover, by 1991–92 the number had already grown to 79 per cent (3,641,343). Most of the remaining children in both years attended RLGs, but whereas in 1988–89 these accounted for 14.8 per cent (657,171), by 1991–92 the number had declined to 12.1 per cent (556,876). At first glance, this shift seems quite small; however, a drop of over two per cent out of only 14.8 per cent is proportionally quite large.[31]

The general trend for the republic appears to hold true in the capital. Whereas in 1988–89, 142,450 children (45 per cent) in Tashkent attended ULGs, by the beginning of the 1991–92 school year the number had jumped to 165,088, or almost 51 per cent. Available data do not permit an analogous measurement of the shift of specialized secondary and higher education from Russian to Uzbek. Nevertheless, fragmentary evidence suggests that although a considerable movement toward uzbekization of higher and specialized secondary education has been under way since 1988 or 1989, it has proceeded very unevenly. Citing anecdotal evidence, interlocutors in Tashkent in 1992 and 1993 almost unanimously felt that more subjects were being offered in Uzbek and that a proportionally larger number of slots had been opening up in higher education for students entering Uzbek groups. However, these and other interlocutors felt that even in 'Uzbek' groups, Russian language was often still playing a major role, and that the quality of education was often better in Russian-language institutions.

Between 1989 and the collapse of the USSR the Communist Party quite openly supported expansion in the use of Uzbek and sharply criticized those whom it considered were dragging their feet. Published statistics claim that whereas in 1989 only 14 *raion* party committees conducted office work in Uzbek, by February 1990 the number had grown to 29.[32] By the summer of 1991, 57 *raion* party committees are reported to have been conducting their office work only 'in the language of the indigenous population' (*tub millet tilida*), while 45 *raion* and city committees were reported to be using Russian only, and 87 raion and city committees were using both Uzbek and Russian.[33] An official's report in February 1990 boasted that the party was responding to all correspondence using the language most convenient for the intended recipient[34] (presumably the language of the original letter). In the first half of 1991, over 85 per cent of *oblast* party committee responses to letters are reported to have been in Uzbek.[35]

In accordance with the law, measures were taken to train cadres to operate in an Uzbek environment. By 1990, sixteen vocational schools had opened courses to prepare secretaries and stenographers. Towards the same goal, such Uzbek-language instructional materials as a typing book and a manual on office procedures were also produced.[36]

It is impossible to judge how much impact such measures have had on the language of oral and written communication in government offices. The degree of shift to Uzbek seems to vary greatly from institution to institution. It is reported that as of late 1992, many republic offices still conducted 60–70 per cent of their paper-work in Russian.[37] Among the institutions paying least attention to the language law have been the Ministry of Finance, the State Committee on Statistics and the State Bank. The former two were reportedly still operating in Russian in the autumn of 1992, by which time the State Bank had not even managed to issue a directive on implementing the language law.[38] As of mid-1992, the Tashkent railroad office was still conducting all of its work in Russian.[39] The state airline apparently also relied on Russian for most of its office work. When investigated in 1992, it was discovered that although the airline had established a commission on LSL implementation, most members did not even know the state language.[40] The Main Medical Center of the Ministry of Internal Affairs was reported in the autumn of 1992 to be holding all of its meetings in Russian.[41] Significantly, since late 1992 the Uzbekistan press has given much less attention to these kinds of matters than in the pre-independence era.

The uneven shift to Uzbek for internal use in meetings and office work is also reflected in public services. One of the successes is the announcement of stops on Tashkent's subway, which are no longer bilingual, but only in Uzbek. Some non-Uzbek speakers have cited this as a violation of the language law, where Article 22 provides for oral announcements to be given in Uzbek as well as in translation. Despite the situation on the subway, in the summer of 1992, most signs in Tashkent's Northern railway station were reportedly still in Russian only; although some of the signs in the kiosk next to the station where tickets were sold had been translated into very poor Uzbek, almost everything else – from the menu in the café to the employment announcements – were still only in Russian. Moreover, some of the ticket sellers could not communicate in the state language.[42]

Lack of relevant data makes it impossible to provide a full assessment regarding the implementation of Article 20 mandating publication of all types of periodical literature and books 'primarily in the state language'. In some sense, this was already being carried out in 1989, when 122 of the republic's 140 *raion* newspapers were in Uzbek, as were nine of the 19 city papers, ten of the 24 *oblast* papers, and eight of the 18 republic ones. Likewise, 69 per cent of the republic's television and 76.5 per cent of the radio transmissions were in Uzbek.[43] Perhaps a still larger share of all of these media are now in

Uzbek. However, at least in the case of print, the absolute number of publications and often their size has dropped drastically.

In the area of terminology, scholars in many fields have compiled vocabularies and dictionaries; moreover, the Terminological Committee has published its own lists of approved terms. Nevertheless, to date there seems to have been little progress toward standardization. To judge from the press, any 'success' in this area is limited to official government documents and press reports of Uzbekistan's news agency, UzTAG.

CONSTRAINTS

We will briefly examine some of the constraints on fuller implementation of the LSL, in particular, on the greater use of Uzbek. The categories used below unavoidably overlap; however, they provide a useful classification to illustrate some of the obstacles in language law implementation.

Attitudes. Attitudes about language have been the most intractable problem undermining efforts to implement the LSL. Four years after passage of the LSL, one still frequently hears non-Uzbeks in Uzbekistan describe the state language as 'backward' and 'underdeveloped', and a language which there is little reason to want to learn. There are numerous reports suggesting that many people signed up for courses to learn Uzbek only under duress, and that fear of negative consequences was the primary factor motivating them to enrol.[44] Monolingual russophones appear to see few positive incentives to become fluent in the state language. Russophone Uzbeks with weak Uzbek language skills seem to share the attitudes manifested by Russians and other Russian-speaking minorities.

Although in less direct fashion, the impatience and overenthusiasm of Uzbeks who want to rush with 'uzbekization' may also be a serious obstacle to implementation. For example, non-Uzbek speakers forced to 'take part' in meetings held exclusively in Uzbek may not be at all encouraged to learn the new state language. Rather, because they may perceive the power games which are being played out at such events, they may dig in their heels even more stubbornly in opposition to language law implementation.

Financial, Material and Personnel. Many of the problems are more 'objective' than the attitudes described above. Underlying almost all of them is the question of money. Uzbekistan's severe economic problems in the period of independence have made it extremely difficult to find funds for anything but the most essential and immediate needs. This problem affects virtually all institutions.

One of the ways that Uzbekistan's financial problems affect language law implementation relates to the publishing industry. The rising cost of paper has had a drastic effect on the number, size and runs of books, periodicals and newspapers. Even the Terminological Committee's bulletin has been appearing more infrequently and its size has been cut. The paper shortage has also prevented the publication of desperately needed terminological dictionaries.[45]

Although paper is one of the key 'material' bottlenecks in implementing the LSL, there are also many others. They include the small number of meeting rooms with the equipment needed to provide simultaneous translation,[46] the inability of the central teletype to handle texts in Uzbek, and the shortage of typewriters with Uzbek letters.[47] Limited Uzbek language skills among Russians and many of the Uzbek élite are also an 'objective' bottleneck.[48] Less direct, but perhaps most important, the cost of transition and the (at least) short-term inefficiency incurred – for example, when teaching new disciplines in higher education in Uzbek – also impede LSL implementation.

Problems of Teaching the Uzbek Language. Besides the attitude problem mentioned above, efforts to teach Uzbek have been plagued by poor methods and a lack of qualified teachers. Uzbek lessons were long treated as a low priority in RLGs, and the available textbooks were unsatisfactory.[49] The requirement for 'Uzbek language teachers' to teach RLG students has often been 'satisfied' by having teachers of other subjects (with no training in language pedagogy) teach Uzbek.[50] When no one can be found to teach Uzbek lessons, the classes may simply not take place.[51] The situation with teachers and materials for adult Uzbek classes does not appear to be any better.

Lack of Standardization. The lack of standardized terminology has been another serious obstacle to implementation of the language law. It has sometimes delayed or prevented publication of Uzbek language materials, or else interfered with their comprehension. For example, in order to accommodate Uzbek students, Tashkent's Higher Police School attempted to introduce Uzbek language instruction. However, 'the experiment in conducting lectures and holding seminars in Uzbek was unsuccessful specifically due to the underdeveloped state of legal terminology in the Uzbek language'.[52] The failure of the Terminological Committee to lay down clear and consistent principles, and the committee's own low authority have also impeded progress in the area of standardization.

It should be added here that the anarchy in Uzbek terminology is only one of a number of areas plagued by instability. Another important area is orthography. There are, for example, at least four distinct spellings for the word 'Europe' – all different from the formerly standard one which was identical to the Russian.[53]

Organizational and Legal. Finally, one other important factor impeding the LSL's implementation has been the lack of any organization with the authority (not to mention resources) to supervise and coordinate measures related to the law. This function has not been performed by the Supreme Soviet's Committee on Cross-National Relations, Language and Culture, by the Terminological Committee, or by the Council of Ministers' Commission on Implementing the Law on the State Language.[54] The organizations which do exist are very poorly staffed, and most of their members are unpaid workers who serve ex-officio. Their recommendations are easily ignored, above all, because there is no legal framework to ensure compliance with the LSL. Thus, although Article 28 states that managers bear personal responsibility for observing the requirements of the law in the spheres under their authority, as of late summer 1992, not a single manager had ever been made to answer for violations.[55]

Of course, the Uzbekistan Supreme Soviet's failure to adopt amendments to the 1989 LSL has aggravated this situation. Moreover, the absence of an authoritative version of the law for post-Soviet Uzbekistan makes it much easier for individuals or institutions to improvise in ways that reflect their own preferences.

THE BROADER CONTEXT OF LANGUAGE POLICY

The most remarkable fact about implementation of the LSL between 1989 and 1993 is its apparent decline in importance on the agenda of Uzbekistan's political leadership. In 1989 language was a major political issue in Uzbekistan. Realizing its salience, the Communist Party adopted Birlik's platform on language, and permitted relatively frank discussion of language issues on the pages of Uzbekistan's press. As reflected in the LSL, the country's leadership seemed to be making a commitment to take measures to achieve not only symbolic changes, but more substantive ones as well.

As of 1993, Uzbekistan's leadership is still extremely supportive of the symbolic measures. However, there are mixed signals concerning the more substantive areas. There seems to be a momentum for the uzbekization of education, especially at the lower levels and in non-technical areas. In time, this will have a major impact on the language used in a wide variety of spheres throughout the republic. However, for the moment the government seems less concerned about ensuring that all institutions pursue rapid linguistic uzbekization.

Before concluding, we will consider some of the major trends and forces which have been shaping Uzbekistan's political development over the last four years, and which seem especially relevant to the implementation of language law. Three of these – the economic situation, relations with Russia and the desire to maintain stability – seem to be of primary importance. However, other phenomena also play significant roles. Among them are the Uzbek leadership's manipulation of symbols, expectations of demographic development, the current style of policy making and implementation and the policy towards Islam.

Economic Crisis. Uzbekistan's financial crisis in the post-Soviet era has had a profound impact on all of President Karimov's policies, including those related to language. In some important ways today's situation is very different from that of 1989 when the LSL was adopted. Then, Uzbekistan and all other Soviet republics were still seeking more control over economic affairs within their own borders. Nevertheless, by and large their leaders expected this to happen within the context of a single Soviet state. Islam Karimov's remarks at the 28th Congress of the CPSU in July 1990 emphasized greater rights for the republics and the republican communist parties; but he also demanded consideration of Uzbekistan's *startovoe polozhenie* (starting position) in the process of economic reform. In essence, this was a request that the centre provide something of a social net to the disadvantaged republics, including Uzbekistan.[56].

The Soviet economy did not improve during the thirteen months between Karimov's speech and the August putsch attempt, nor did the centre or Russia demonstrate a willingness to help Uzbekistan and other Central Asian republics solve their economic problems. The collapse of the entire Soviet structure in 1991 made it even clearer that as an independent state, Uzbekistan would have to solve its own problems, especially the economic ones.

Although some Uzbeks – pointing to gold, other natural resources and the diligent work habits of the people – claimed to see a bright economic future for their country, the immediate economic outlook upon independence was most unfavourable. As with other former union republics, many of Uzbekistan's previous sources of supply and markets were disrupted; among the other most serious problems affecting the economy were the ecological crisis and growing over-population and unemployment.

Rather than receive help from Russia or any 'centre', Karimov has been obliged to search for his own way to deal with Uzbekistan's economic crisis. Above all, and most acutely, he has needed to continue certain food and fuel subsidies, and to keep the population employed. This serious situation seems unlikely to change substantially in the foreseeable future.

Karimov and other members of Uzbekistan's leadership probably view the costs of rapid and consistent language law implementation as too high. Although in October 1989 Karimov placed a price tag of 1.5 billion rubles on the implementation of the language law,[57] it is highly unlikely that this was based on any realistic calculation of the costs. Even in 1989 prices, a total of only 75 rubles per capita would have been a very small sum to cover all of the measures required by the LSL. Today, of course, Uzbekistan is less able to afford the costs than at the time that the LSL was adopted. Independence has reduced overt interference from outside in Uzbekistan's language politics. At the same time, however, it has also brought an economic crisis which makes it extremely difficult for the country to take the measures required to implement even the law adopted during the Soviet era.

Independence and Relations with Russia. Despite formal independence, Uzbekistan is still very much tied to Russia. President Karimov has demonstrated a recognition of the need to maintain good relations with Russia and the rest of the Commonwealth of Independent States. Moreover, despite his obvious annoyance with Russia over monetary policy, Karimov was reluctant to remove his country from the ruble zone and introduce a national currency. Likewise, although Uzbekistan established its own army, it has maintained close links with Russia's military and cooperated with Russia in supporting the 'reformed communist' forces against the 'Islamic militants' in Tajikistan.

Uzbek leaders are certainly aware of the concerns of Russian politicians in the Russian Federation about discrimination against their fellow ethnics in Central Asia. Karimov knows that discrimination against Uzbekistan's Russian speakers will complicate relations with Moscow, especially if Russia's leaders perceive that the Uzbek government sanctions these measures. Russia has already had difficulty accommodating the Russian ethnic and other refugees who have come 'home' from various parts of the once sprawling empire, and would certainly not welcome an increased and disorganized flood of more Russians, let alone of other Russian-speaking minorities.

With the relations among members of the Commonwealth of Independent States still in flux, the degree and nature of future military, economic, political and/or other spheres of integration among former Soviet republics is still unclear. At the moment, Karimov seems to favour continued strong ties with Russia. In part this may be due to the support he requires in order to maintain his own domestic political position; but for geographical and historical reasons, it is likely relations with Russia will remain an important element in any future Uzbek leader's policy. To the extent that integration continues or expands, the Russian language in Uzbekistan seems likely to retain a higher status than simply one of the 'other' foreign languages, and thus it may slow down the progress of linguistic uzbekization .

Political and Social Stability. In 1989 Uzbekistan was ruled by a centralized communist party which was controlled (though to a diminishing extent) from Moscow. The dominant political figure in the republic was the first secretary of the republic's communist party. Today, independent Uzbekistan has no party called 'communist', and the president does not derive his power from his status in any political party. For all of these changes, however, there has hardly been a social, political or economic revolution in Uzbekistan. The former élites are still in control; in many ways they have changed little but their titles.

If it had been implemented fully and quickly, the 1989 LSL would have produced a social revolution in Uzbekistan. Rapid implementation, however, was contrary to the interests of many within the country's political élite. On the whole, in the late Soviet era Uzbekistan's ULGs – even in urban areas – provided a standard of education that was considerably lower than the Russian ones. Moreover, it appears that a disproportionately high number of 'special' schools (with enriched training in foreign languages, maths, physics, etc.) also operated in Russian. Not surprisingly, most of the Uzbek urban élite sent their children to RLGs. Their choice of Russian-language education for their young children was often shaped by the belief in the superior quality of training in RLG's and the opportunities which were open only to individuals with superior Russian skills. Study outside Uzbekistan in the USSR's best central educational institutions, of course, required Russian. Some Uzbeks selected RLGs for their children because insistence on Uzbek-language education could be interpreted as an expression of 'nationalism' and 'anti-Russian feeling'. Such matters could have had negative consequences on the parents' employment.

Whatever the reasons, RLG education left many Uzbek children with weak skills in reading and writing Uzbek. If they had even a smattering of Uzbek from their family, these children derived little, if any, benefit from the Uzbek-language classes offered by their schools. In some cases, especially when the RLG pattern was followed for two generations, Russian partly or even fully displaced Uzbek as the language of the home.

As for most ethnic Russians, for élite ethnic Uzbeks with a weak knowledge of 'their native Uzbek' language, the prospect of full implementation of the language law is very threatening. It would be difficult for them to learn quickly to write reports, keep records or speak at meetings in the state language. Moreover, the opportunities of their children who are completing higher education in Russian-language groups would also be severely limited.

Even with the limited implementation of the LSL that has been pursued under Karimov, most of these élite Uzbeks (and members of other nationalities) with poor Uzbek skills have no doubt experienced discomfort. Given that today's Uzbekistani political and economic élites include a large number of Russian speakers with much to lose from a radically enhanced status for Uzbek, it is likely that their lack of enthusiasm has also been a powerful brake on the pace of LSL implementation.

Symbols of Independence. Even though Uzbekistan has not adopted a revised version of the LSL, Karimov has attempted to use language to emphasize Uzbekistan's existence as an independent state and the homeland of the Uzbeks. The constitution of 1992 simply states that Uzbek is the state language, without reference to any language of cross-national communication. Toponyms and personal names are still being changed, and many public signs even in the capital have been 'uzbekized' even further than mandated in the language law by the elimination of Russian translations. As noted above, the same is true – even in violation of the language law – in the case of announcements on the Tashkent subway.

This is very much in keeping with Karimov's broader policy concerning symbols and legitimacy. Realizing that in the short term he has very limited resources to satisfy the population, the president is trying to enhance his legitimacy through symbolic demonstrations that Uzbeks are the masters of their homeland. This is embodied, for example, in the transformation of Tashkent's Lenin Square into what is now Independence Square. The flag of independent Uzbekistan is a very common symbol in Tashkent today. Many of the city's street cars have been painted in their likeness with bands of blue, white and green divided by red stripes. Uzbekistan's history is now being rewritten with special attention to those events which reflect the country's independence and now crystallizing identity, rather than to events and individuals which brought Uzbeks inexorably closer to Russia.

These symbols on their own, of course, will not support any regime indefinitely without economic improvements taking place. But they are relatively inexpensive; they are also perhaps better tolerated by non-Uzbeks than measures which threaten educational and job opportunities. The implementation of symbolic measures related to the Uzbek language seems to be part of the strategy to find affordable measures to enhance the regime's legitimacy among the majority of the country's population. These symbolic measures, however, do not redistribute educational and professional mobility opportunities among sectors of the population according to a new set of linguistic criteria.

Demography and Time. Many Uzbeks, even among the more nationalistically-minded, probably realize that demographic momentum is on their side. They may therefore see less need to rush ahead with language shift. In 1989, Uzbeks constituted about 71 per cent of the republic's population, and Slavs slightly over nine per cent. More telling than the absolute numbers, however, are the trends and the ratio of Uzbeks to Slavs. In 1959, when Slavs accounted for 14.6 per cent of Uzbekistan's population, the Uzbeks comprised just over 62 per cent. This means that in that census, the number of Uzbeks was about 4.2 times the number of Slavs. The proportion had changed significantly in 1989, when Uzbeks were found to outnumber Slavs by a ratio of 7.8 to 1. Although thus far the shift in the capital city is much less dramatic (1959 = one Uzbek for every 1.2 Slavs; 1989 = one Uzbek for every 0.85 Slavs), this is also a major change and it seems likely to accelerate.[58]

It is possible that over the last few years the number of Uzbek births has dropped. However, the number of children born to Russians has also fallen, and the decline has been accentuated by an increasing outmigration. Most importantly, however, the proportion of Uzbeks to Russians in the younger population is even higher than in the population at large. Consequently, even if the next generations of Uzbeks and Russians have birth rates identical to one another (a possibility which seems extremely remote), the republic will be substantially more Uzbek in the year 2010 than it is today.

Theoretically, even in an Uzbekistan with a larger percentage of its population belonging to the titular nationality, the present level of use of Russian might be preserved. However, given the trends which seem to be at work regarding language of education at all levels, the majority of the next generation of Uzbeks will almost certainly speak the Uzbek language. Thus, in light of the country's severe economic crisis, the promotion of Uzbek in the immediate future may seem a luxury that even proponents of linguistic uzbekization are willing to forego.

In passing, it should be noted here that language policy in turn has a potentially major impact on at least one aspect of demographic development – migration. No reliable figures are available for the numbers of non-Uzbek speakers who have left Uzbekistan in recent years. Nevertheless, numerous conversations with residents of Tashkent suggest that language is one of the primary concerns that has encouraged many non-Uzbek speakers to consider leaving, or to actually depart, from the city. Russian parents of primary and secondary schoolchildren in Tashkent tell of their anxiety that their children (who do not know Uzbek) will be denied entry into higher educational institutions, and eventually denied the best jobs. (Some parents, however, see language more as a pretext that will be used to legitimize denial of entry, which will in fact be based rather on nationality criteria.) A major factor moderating the outmigration from Uzbekistan has been the unattractiveness of job opportunities that are open to new arrivals in Russia, Belarus and Ukraine.

The Style of Current Uzbek Politics. The fate of Uzbekistan's LSL can be seen as an example of the nature of interest articulation, aggregation, legislation and law enforcement in Uzbekistan over the last four years. The adoption of the LSL occurred at the beginning of a brief, relatively democratic, interlude in Uzbekistan's history. During this period, which lasted until the early months of 1992, Uzbekistan's periodical press was relatively open to the exchange of new and contradictory opinions. These months witnessed the registration of the Birlik Popular Movement and the Erk Democratic Party; in December 1991 a contested election was held for the Uzbekistan presidency. Since the spring of 1992, however, the political atmosphere in Uzbekistan has become more repressive as censorship of the official press has tightened, the opposition press has been closed down, and opposition leaders have been subjected to harassment and beatings. Uzbekistan has adopted a democratic-sounding constitution, but civil rights in the country are routinely violated. A new cult of personality has emerged around Uzbekistan's President Karimov, as the newspapers are filled with testimonies describing how his speeches and writings provide answers to the major challenges facing the country.[59]

In the days when the language law was discussed and adopted, the press carried a fairly lively debate on language issues. Not only did citizens read and write letters about language, but in 1988 and 1989 many went out onto the streets to demonstrate their feelings on this vital matter.[60] Moreover, the debate was not merely about the symbolic language issues. It included conflicting ideas about language status in education, government and the economy.

The general political clampdown in Uzbekistan has had a chilling effect on the debate about language. As in all other areas, no public criticism of the government's language policy or its effects is tolerated. Increasingly, the press avoids discussion of language status issues, especially when it points to conflict among individuals or groups. There is no discussion of such sensitive problems as how institutions adjudicate on the numerous disputes which are inevitably part of implementation of a language law.

Uzbekistan's failure to adopt an amended version of the LSL makes it impossible to carry out language policy in accordance with any clear legal standard. Many provisions of the old language law are inapplicable, but the Karimov regime has evidently decided that the problems involved in providing clear rules are more trouble than they are worth.

This does not mean that the advancement of Uzbek as the state language will always suffer. Over the past few years monolingual Russian-speaking inhabitants of Tashkent have frequently complained about cases of individuals in positions of authority who exceeded the limits of the law in promoting Uzbek. Such actions may promote faster uzbekization, but not implementation of the LSL or any other law. This, however, is the general pattern of politics in Uzbekistan today. It does not appear likely that the 'lawlessness' with regard to language will change until a much more fundamental shift in Uzbek politics occurs.

Islam. The overt role of Islam in Uzbek society has altered radically since Karimov rose to the leadership of his republic's communist party. Despite the CPSU's efforts, Islam remained a powerful force in Uzbekistan even in the pre-Gorbachev days. Although the CPSU's policy towards religion in general and Islam in particular had already changed by the middle of 1989, since that time the number of officially operating mosques has grown dramatically, and major Islamic celebrations are now state holidays in independent Uzbekistan. Parallel with the treatment of Orthodoxy in Russia, under Karimov, Islam has been treated as an inalienable part of Uzbek culture.

Although Karimov has publicly identified himself as the leader of a country with a primarily Muslim population by taking the oath of office with his hand on a Qur'an and by travelling to the holy sites in Saudi Arabia, his relation to Islam is not simple.[61] The official Islamic Establishment in Tashkent is subject to substantial government influence, but much, if not most, Islamic activity in Uzbekistan does not take place in institutions under the official spiritual directorate's command or through religious leaders whom it designates.

Especially since the civil war in Tajikistan began in 1992, Karimov has stressed the danger of religious 'fundamentalism' to stability in the region. It is unclear what the real danger of 'fundamentalism' is in Uzbekistan. In any case, even if Karimov's fear has more to do with opposition political forces united under an Islamic banner than with fundamentalism per se, Karimov has frequently reiterated the importance of Uzbekistan becoming a secular state on the Turkish model.

In this regard it is significant that Uzbekistan proceeded with the introduction of courses to teach the Arabic script to children in ULGs.[62] The alphabet, of course, is not tantamount to Islam, but it is perceived as a symbol of Islam by the Uzbek masses. Although the Arabic alphabet is being taught in schools, now that Uzbekistan has officially announced its intention to shift to the Latin alphabet,[63] there is little chance that without a political revolution writing will revert to Arabic letters. Indeed, a year before the legislature's adoption of the Latin script, discussion about the Arabic script seemed to have tapered off.

The trends in vocabulary also seem to reflect the tendency not to allow Uzbekistan to become too closely linked to its Islamic past at the expense of ties with other parts of the world. The case of the word for 'republic' is a good example. Initially, at the end of the 1980s, the Arabic-based word *jumhuriyat* made substantial inroads, replacing the Russian word *respublika* which had been used in Uzbek since the 1930s. One of the early bulletins of the Terminological Commission, published in 1990, gave both *respublika* and *jumhuriyat* as the Uzbek equivalents of the Russian *respublika*. However, in April 1992, the commission issued a new list of words in which 'republic' was rendered in only one 'Uzbek' form, *respublika*.[64] Islam seems to be of minor importance in the area of language status policies, but it is probably a major factor affecting language corpus decisions.

UZBEKISTAN: A 'BEST CASE' SCENARIO FOR LANGUAGE CHANGE IN CENTRAL ASIA?

The factors discussed above are not unique to Uzbekistan. All of the newly independent countries of Central Asia have encountered many of the same problems in implementing laws adopted in 1989 and 1990 to raise the status of their titular nationality languages.[65] Thus, for example, the unfavourable attitudes toward the language of the titular majority among Uzbekistan's monolingual Russian-speakers are largely shared in other republics of the region. Moreover, nowhere in Central Asia do the new state languages enjoy high prestige among the non-indigenous nationalities. Reflecting this fact, in the 1989 census fewer than five per cent of the non-Central Asian nationality population throughout the region claimed fluency in a Turkic language or Tajik.[66] All of the other republics also share the personnel, equipment, textbook and other shortages described above. Moreover, all of the Central Asia state languages lack standardized sets of terminology for new fields where their use is now being encouraged; and everywhere the standardization process is impeded by conflicting tendencies of purification and 'internationalization'.[67]

There have been many ups and downs in Russia's role in Central Asia in 1992 and 1993, but everywhere Russia looms as a very large force. Among other things, geography may make Kazakhstan the most vulnerable to Russian pressure which could be exerted to prevent 'extreme' measures in raising the status of the state language. But ever since the start of Tajikistan's civil war, Uzbekistan and other states of the region have seemed more accommodating to Russia's interests.

While the above factors are largely shared, in a number of ways Uzbekistan seems to be in a stronger position than its neighbours with regard to raising the status of its state language. One of the most important reasons is the proportion of the population belonging to the titular nationality: Uzbeks are in a much more dominant position than titular groups in Kazakhstan and Kyrgyzstan. True, the proportions are changing rapidly, but as late as 1989 Kazakhs comprised only about 40 per cent of Kazakhstan's population, while in Kyrgyzstan the analogous figure for Kyrgyz was slightly over half. The significance of this fact is magnified by the preponderance of other nationalities (primarily native Russian speakers) in the capital city: over three-quarters of the population of Almaty and Bishkek (then still Alma-Ata and Frunze) were respectively non-Kazakhs and non-Kyrgyz in 1989.[68]

At least in the cases of Kazakhstan and Kyrgyzstan, the demo-graphic and related linguistic statistics are reflected in much less communication in the native language in government and public services. Beyond this, however, in the case of higher education, Uzbek seems to have enjoyed greater use than any of the other indigenous languages. This applies not only to Kazakh and Kyrgyz, but to Tajik and Turkmen as well. Although in the late Soviet period many scientific and technical specialities were available in Uzbekistan only through Russian-language education, many other higher educational students – especially in disciplines of the humanities, agriculture, and in pedagogical institutes – received much of their training in Uzbek. This is probably a major reason why a relatively large proportion of the Uzbek intelligentsia (certainly in comparison with Kazakhstan and Kyrgyzstan) appears to have a spoken and written mastery of its own native language. Likewise, because Uzbek has been used for a broader range of communications, it appears to have a more comprehensive set of terminology than the other languages.

Their relatively large population in absolute terms may be a 'plus' for the Uzbeks. Inasmuch as they are by far the most numerous of the Central Asian nationalities and Uzbekistan is the most populous republic, language law implementation in Uzbekistan is likely to enjoy an economy of size. Thus, for example, the per capita costs for developing Kyrgyz-, Turkmen- or Tajik-language textbooks for university disciplines will be much higher than for Uzbeks.

It is still difficult to judge the relative economic prospects for the Central Asian republics. However, as of now, Turkmenistan with its abundant natural resources and small population seems to be in a more favourable situation than the other states. From this perspective Turkmenistan may be in a stronger position to overcome some of the other problems impeding implementation of language law in Uzbekistan. As indicated above, however, the economy is only one of many factors, and not always the decisive one.

On the whole, the experience of Uzbekistan and all of the other Central Asian states demonstrates that language was a very important issue symbolizing the declining role of Russia and Russians in the last years of Soviet power. Moreover, in all republics, language status change continues to have the potential to affect profoundly the status and mobility of all strata of society. However, everywhere in the region language policies are closely linked to a complex array of other issues confronting these societies, and these in turn limit the range of choices open to their governments. For the moment, the leaders of all the Central Asian countries seem to have placed a low priority on substantive language change. It should not be excluded that future governments with different priorities – and perhaps more nationalist programs – might once again place a stronger emphasis on major language status shift. This, however, depends on the general political paths which the newly independent states will take over the coming years. At the moment it is too early to discern where these paths might lead.

NOTES

1. Some of the material in this chapter also appears in an article prepared for an upcoming issue of *Nationalities Papers* under the title 'Problems of Implementing Uzbekistan's Language Law'. The present chapter focuses on the political context of the shift in priority of language law implementation; the piece in *Nationalities Papers* focuses on the language situation and the practical problems of implementation.
2. *Komsomolets Uzbekistana*, 20 June 1989, reprinted in JPRS-UPA-89-048, 28 July 1989, p. 5.
3. Nishanov had spent much of his career outside Uzbekistan. For a discussion of the shift in leadership, see Donald S. Carlisle, 'Power and Politics in Soviet Uzbekistan', in *Soviet Central Asia: The Failed Transformation*, William Fierman (ed.), (Boulder: Westview Press, 1991), pp. 115–17; also Carlisle, 'Geopolitics and Ethnic Problems of Uzbekistan and Its Neighbours', in this volume.
4. Subsequent references by Karimov to the language question illustrate his restrained position on this issue. See, for example, *Pravda vostoka*, 7 Oct. 1989; also *Pravda vostoka*, 5 June 1990, reproduced in JPRS-UPA-91-010, 19 Feb. 1991, p. 34.
5. In July 1992 the author was shown a copy of the draft which was being prepared.
6. *Ozbekistan avazi*, 22 Oct. 1992.
7. The rural population of Uzbekistan in 1989 accounted for 59 per cent of the total population. Yet no less than 83 per cent of the republic's Uzbeks lived in rural areas – see Mark Tolts, 'Modernization of Demographic Behaviour in the Muslim Republics of the Former USSR', in this volume.
8. These figures relate only to those Tajiks officially registered as such. The number of Tajiks residing in Uzbekistan and registered as Tajiks is thought by Tajiks in Tajikistan to be much higher.
9. Of course, some Uzbeks (not to mention members of other nationalities) respond that their native language corresponds to their nationality even though they know very little of that 'native' language; on the whole, however, the vast majority of Uzbeks learn to speak Uzbek first and indeed know it better than any other language.
10. See Gerhard Simon, *Nationalism and Policy toward the Nationalities in the Soviet Union* (Boulder: Westview Press, 1991), Table A8; Kh. Khanazarov, 'Sud'ba russkogo iazyka v Uzbekistane', *Russkii iazyk v SSSR* 11 (1991), pp. 5–9.
11. *TsSU SSSR, Itogi Vsesoiuznoi perepisi naseleniia 1970 goda*, (Moscow: Statistika, 1973), Vol. IV, p. 202; *TsSU SSSR Chislennost' i sostav naseleniia SSSR po dannym Vsesoiuznoi perepisi naseleniia 1979 goda* (Moscow: Finansy i statistika, 1984), pp. 110–11; manuscript of census materials, *Gosudarstvennyi komitet po statistike, Natsional'nyi sostav naseleniia* (Moscow: Finansy i statistika, 1989), p. 64.
12. At the time of the 1989 census, fewer than 5 per cent of Russians living in Uzbekistan claimed to be fluent in Uzbek – *Natsional'nyi sostav naseleniia* (Moscow: Finansy i statistika, 1989), p. 64.
13. For a more detailed discussion of the law itself readers are referred to the author's forthcoming article in *Nationalities Papers* (cited in note 1), or Michael Lenker, 'The Politics of Language Policy: A Case Study of Uzbekistan', in Alfred J. Lieber and and Alvin Z. Rubinstein (eds.), *Perestroika at the Crossroads* (Armonk, NY: M. E. Sharpe, 1991), pp. 264–77.
14. Statistics provided to the author by the Uzbekistan Ministry of Education in summer 1992. Because many schools had both Russian and Uzbek language groups, neither

the term 'Russian language schools' nor 'Uzbek language schools' includes all 'RLGs' or 'ULGs'. A total of less than 10 per cent of Uzbekistan's children were taught in other languages – Karakalpak, Tajik, Kazakh, Turkmen and Kyrgyz.

15. G. Abdumazhidov, *Komentarii k Zakonu Uzbekskoi SSR o gosudarstvennom iazyke* (Tashkent: Uzbekistan, 1990), p. 37.
16. 'Ozbekistan SSRning davlat tili haqida'gi qanuni amalga ashirishning davlat programmasi' (mimeograph copy).
17. *Pravda vostoka*, 13 Feb. 1990.
18. One report of inactivity is contained in an interview with Adil Yaqubov – *Turkistan*, 15 Aug. 1992.
19. *Turkistan*, 15 Aug. 1992.
20. For a description of the work of the commission at Samarkand State University, see *Ma'rifat*, 12 Aug. 1992.
21. *Ozbekistan Sovet Sotsialistik Jumhuriyati Vazirlar kengashi huzuridagi jumhuriyat Atamashunaslik qomitasi, Ozbek tili atamashunasligi akhbarat (Oz. tili atamashunasligi)* 3–4 (1990), pp. 5–8.
22. *Turkistan*, 15 Aug. 1992.
23. Communication from Sergei Zinin, deputy chairman of the Uzbekistan Supreme Soviet's Committee on Matters of Cross-National Relations, Language and Culture, summer 1992.
24. The head of the organization is Iristay Qochqartayev – *Ozbekistan adabiyati va san'ati*, 19 July 1992.
25. *Ozbekistan avazi*, 19 Sept. 1992.
26. *Khalq sozi*, 11 March 1993. For a few other examples of articles concerning renaming, see *Yash leninchi*, 1 Nov 1991; *Ozbekistan adabiyati va san'ati*, 29 Nov 1991; *Ozbekistan avazi*, 7 Jan. 1992.
27. *Oqituvchilar gazetasi*, 1 Sept. 1990.
28. Following the law's passage, when Uzbekistan's curriculum maintained 1,258 hours for Russian language, this was still 340 hours more than the minimum recommended by the USSR State Committee on Education – *Oqituvchilar gazetasi*, 1 Sept. and 24 Nov. 1990. The figure of 900 was provided in a personal communication from Sergei Zinin in July 1992.
29. *Oqituvchilar gazetasi*, 1 Sept. 1990 and 24 Nov. 1990.
30. *Sovet Ozbekistani*, 26 Aug. 1990.
31. It is quite possible, of course, that the shift began even before the adoption of the LSL.
32. *Pravda vostoka*, 8 Feb. 1990. A report in a less authoritative source – an interview in the republic Komsomol paper – indicates much more uzbekization of office business; according to it, 57 of 142 *raion* committees already conducted office work in Uzbek in late 1989 – *Komsomolets Uzbekistana*, 4 Oct. 1989.
33. *Sovet Ozbekistani*, 10 Aug 1991.
34. *Pravda vostoka*, 8 Feb. 1990.
35. *Sovet Ozbekistani*, 10 Aug. 1991.
36. *Ozbekistan adabiyati va san'ati*, 28 July 1990.
37. *Tashkent aqshami*, 1 Jan. 1993. This statistic, unfortunately, is of limited use, since it is not known what proportion of the work had been in Uzbek previously, nor even how much of the remaining 30–40 per cent of the work might have been generated in Russian and then translated (or recorded as 'translated') to fulfil some sort of target.
38. *Khalq sozi*, 29 Oct. 1992.
39. *Ozbekistan avazi*, 30 July 1992.
40. *Ozbekistan avazi*, 5 May 1992.
41. *Ozbekistan avazi*, 19 Sep. 1992.
42. *Ozbekistan avazi*, 30 July 1992.
43. *Pravda vostoka*, 13 Feb. 1990.
44. See, for example, *Ma'rifat*, 6 May 1992 and *Khalq sozi*, 12 Feb. 1993.
45. *Oz. tili atamashunasligi* 7–8 (1992), pp. 12–13. In June 1992, Anvar Jabbarov reported that the paper shortage was holding up publication of fourteen terminological dictionaries.

46. At the time the law was passed, not even the halls of the Uzbekistan Communist Party Central Committee or the Komsomol Central Committee had such equipment; or did the Writers' Union, Tashkent's major ballet and opera (Navoi) theatre, or the House of Knowledge. The latter institution was a major site for public lectures on a wide variety of popular issues.

47. *Ozbekistan avazi*, 17 Dec. 1991; *Sovet Ozbekistani*, 10 Aug. 1991.

48. According to quite a few informants, even President Karimov's language capabilities limit his effectiveness in public speeches in Uzbek.

49. *Komsomolets Uzbekistana*, 28 Feb. 1989.

50. *Oqituvchilar gazetasi*, 8 Jan. 1991; *Ma'rifat* 30 Jan. and 16 Dec. 1992.

51. *Ma'rifat*, 15 Aug. 1991.

52. B. Mirenskii, 'Gde izuchat' iazyk zakona', *Maktabda ozbek, rus tillari va adabiyati* 7 (July 1991), p. 44.

53. *Oz. tili atamashunasligi* 7–8 (1992), p. 28.

54. Adil Yaqubov, chairman of the Terminology Committee has referred to this problem – *Turkistan*, 15 Aug. 1992.

55. *Turkistan*, 1 Aug. 1992.

56. *Pravda vostoka*, 6 July 1990.

57. *Pravda vostoka*, 7 Oct. 1989.

58. 'Demograficheskie protsessy v Kazakhstane i Uzbekistane', in *Tsentral'no-Aziatskoe obozrenie (istoriia, politika, ekonomika)* (Alma-Ata/Tashkent: Sotsiologicheskii Tsentr 'Ekspert', 1993), pp. 102, 104.

59. For an explanation of these developments, see Donald S. Carlisle, 'Geopolitics and Ethnic Problems of Uzbekistan and Its Neighbours', in this volume.

60. One of the first open demonstrations concerning language to take place in Tashkent occurred in December 1988 – *Yash leninchi*, 13 Jan. 1989.

61. See Martha Brill Olcott, 'Islam and Fundamentalism in Independent Central Asia', in this volume.

62. Instruction in the Arabic alphabet appears to be a regular part of the curriculum in most ULGs today. One sign of the rapid introduction of the script was a textbook to teach the Arabic letters to third- and fourth-grade pupils. This book was published in 1991 in an edition of 550,000 copies – M. Qadirov and M. Hakimjanov, *Alifbe* (Tashkent: Oqituvchi, 1991). Posters obviously intended to teach Uzbek children the Arabic letters were for sale in kiosks in Tashkent in the summer of 1992.

63. *Khalq sozi*, 12 Oct. 1993.

64. *Oz. tili atamashunasligi* 3–4 (1990), p. 64 and 7–8 (1992), p. 7.

65. The first of the Central Asian language laws, in Tajikistan, was adopted in July 1989. Kazakhstan and Kyrgyzstan adopted theirs in Sept. 1989, while Turkmenistan's law was not adopted until May 1990. Of course, in many cases, Uzbekistan's experience in language law implementation resembles developments not only among its immediate neighbours, but also in other former Soviet republics and other states that have sought to legislate language change.

66. *Natsional'nyi sostav naseleniia* (Moscow: Finansy i statistika, 1989), pp. 64, 68, 87, 90, 94.

67. In fact, the picture is much more complex than merely 'purification' or 'internationalization'. Once decisions are made, for example to eliminate a word borrowed from or through Russian, there are often various candidates competing from Turkic sources, and in some cases from Persian and/or Arabic.

68. Mikhail Guboglo, 'Demography and Language in the Capitals of the Union Republics', *Journal of Soviet Nationalities* 1, 4 (Winter 1990–91), p. 7.

12

Modernization of Demographic Behaviour in the Muslim Republics of the Former USSR

MARK TOLTS

The Muslims are the fastest growing population group in the former USSR.[*] However, the consistently high rate of growth conceals the ongoing processes of demographic modernization among them. Changes in demographic behaviour (first of all in marriage patterns and marital fertility) are a very important part of general modernization, and these can be measured according to available data, whereas many other aspects of modernization are conjecture or are apparent. Analysis of demographic processes can be very useful for understanding the level of modernization as a whole among the Muslim populations of Azerbaijan and ex-Soviet Central Asia including Kazakhstan, and can offer a perspective on the development of the newly independent Muslim states. The present chapter aims, within the space available, to make such an analysis.[1] The traditional approach to an analysis of demographic processes in the former USSR would compare the populations of the Muslim and non-Muslim republics.[2] However, for a better understanding of ex-Soviet Muslim demographic indicators, it is more useful and appropriate to compare them with the Muslim populations of the Middle East and Northern Africa, and this is the approach we have chosen.

[*] This article could not have been completed without the help of Dr. Evgeny Andreev and Dr. Leonid Darsky, who supplied statistical data and copies of important material. Prof. Michael Zand advised on the ethnography of Azerbaijan and former Soviet Central Asia. Mrs. Judith Even read and edited an earlier draft. The author is grateful to all of them. Responsibility for the content of the paper is, of course, the author's alone.

231

In contrast to the situation in many other Muslim countries, there are voluminous statistical data on the demography of ex-Soviet Muslims in the last decade. We have detailed here data from the 1979 and 1989 censuses as well as data from the official 1985 micro-census. We also have an extensive series of vital statistics. But the serious problem for our analysis is the accuracy of these data.[3] We may assume that the fertility data for the 1980s are accurate enough. However, even over the last decade, the mortality data – and especially infant mortality data – have been far from precise for Azerbaijan and the republics of former Soviet Central Asia, and today are probably even less so.

The populations of Muslim origin form the majority of the total populations in these republics with the exception of Kazakhstan, where in 1989 Muslims constituted only 47 per cent of the whole population. At this time, 72 per cent of the population was of Muslim origin in Kirgiziia and in the four other republics (Azerbaijan, Tajikistan, Turkmeniia and Uzbekistan) this population group made up between 87 per cent and 90 per cent of the total. Of course, the percentage of the titular nationality group in each republic is lower (sometimes much lower) than the percentage of the population of Muslim origin as a whole (Table 12.1).

In the urban population of Azerbaijan and the republics of former Soviet Central Asia, the percentage of the population of Muslim origin is lower than that of the total populations of these republics: in 1989, one-third of the urban population in Kazakhstan was of Muslim origin, one-half in Kirgiziia, from 70 per cent to 74 per cent in Tajikistan, Turkmeniia and Uzbekistan, and 80 per cent in Azerbaijan.

The structure of the rural population is more homogeneous. Only in two republics did non-Muslims constitute a considerable part of the rural populations: in 1989, they comprised one-third in Kazakhstan and 15 per cent in Kirgiziia. The percentage of the population of Muslim origin is as high as 99 per cent among the rural populations of the three other former Soviet Central Asiatic republics (Tajikistan, Turkmeniia and Uzbekistan), and about 96 per cent in rural Azerbaijan. Thus, the rural populations of these four republics can be considered as almost entirely Muslim and their indicators should be very useful in our analysis.

From the above, we see that only several sources of data on different groupings (the titular nationalities of the former union republics, and the rural populations of the four republics just noted, but not the total or urban ones) can give a complete and rather precise picture of the modernization of demographic behaviour among Muslims in Azerbaijan and former Soviet Central Asia.

TABLE 12.1 PERCENTAGE POPULATION OF MUSLIM ORIGIN AND MUSLIM TITULAR
NATIONALITY, BY TOTAL, URBAN AND RURAL POPULATION OF THE FORMER UNION
REPUBLICS, 1979 AND 1989

Republic	Total population		Urban population		Rural population	
	1979	1989	1979	1989	1979	1989
	Percentage population of Muslim origin					
Azerbaijan	82	87	72	80	95	96
Kazakhstan	43	47	27	33	61	67
Kirgiziia	66	72	43	51	81	85
Tajikistan	86	90	62	70	99	99
Turkmeniia	84	88	68	74	99	99
Uzbekistan	86	89	68	74	98	99
	Thereof: Percentage titular nationality					
Azerbaijan	78	83	68	77	89	90
Kazakhstan	36	40	21	27	54	57
Kirgiziia	48	52	23	30	63	66
Tajikistan	59	62	43	51	67	68
Turkmeniia	68	72	48	54	87	87
Uzbekistan	69	71	48	54	83	83

Sources: 1979 and 1989 censuses

OVERALL ASSESSMENT OF FERTILITY DECLINE

Many different demographic indicators are necessary for an overall
assessment of fertility dynamics. Among these is the average number
of children ever born to women at various ages; these figures were
computed originally from the 1979 and 1989 Soviet censuses.

Comparison of the 1979 and 1989 census results shows that in
Muslim titular nationalities this indicator fell for all ages 20–44 (Table
12.2). In many cases this decrease was very pronounced. For example,
at ages 30–34 the average number of children ever born to Azerbaijani
and Kazakh women decreased by one child, at ages 35–39 by 1.7
children for Kazakh women and 1.4 for Azerbaijani women, 1.2 for
Kyrgyz women, and by one child for Turkmen and Uzbek women.

Completed fertility, which is usually measured at ages 45–49, also
fell among Azerbaijanis and Kazakhs, but in 1989 was still higher
among all other nationalities than it had been in 1979. However, this
rise was caused by an increase in marital fertility in Soviet Central Asia

in the 1960s.[4] The women aged 45–49 in 1989 were at their most fertile in the 1960s. This indicator is dependent, at each age, on the fertility history of that particular cohort. Thus it does not characterize the recent situation.

TABLE 12.2 AVERAGE NUMBER OF CHILDREN EVER BORN TO WOMEN OF MUSLIM TITULAR NATIONALITIES OF THE FORMER UNION REPUBLICS[a], 1979 AND 1989

Nationality	Age of Women in Respective Census						
	15–19	20–24	25–29	30–34	35–39	40–44	45–49
Azerbaijanis							
1979	0.02	0.61	2.19	3.51	4.76	5.32	5.46
1989	0.03	0.57	1.58	2.54	3.38	3.97	4.65
Kazakhs							
1979	0.02	0.66	2.16	3.71	5.52	6.22	6.23
1989	0.03	0.63	1.70	2.75	3.80	4.75	6.09
Kyrgyz							
1979	0.03	0.98	2.88	4.58	6.37	7.00	6.50
1989	0.04	0.88	2.30	3.75	5.14	6.21	7.32
Tajiks							
1979	0.04	1.21	3.44	5.30	6.79	7.43	7.41
1989	0.03	1.01	2.78	4.60	6.24	7.30	7.85
Turkmen							
1979	0.02	0.83	2.90	4.63	6.41	7.12	7.11
1989	0.02	0.54	2.18	3.98	5.42	6.38	7.20
Uzbeks							
1979	0.04	1.04	3.00	4.67	6.13	6.67	6.68
1989	0.04	0.96	2.52	3.98	5.16	6.00	6.71

(a) Inside respective former union republic
Sources: 1979 and 1989 censuses

The actual dynamics for each age-group during the last decade can be found by comparing age-specific birth rates for the end of the 1970s and the end of the 1980s. These rates show a drop in the fertility of all the nationalities (other than the Tajiks) aged 25–29 and older (see Appendix 12.1). The indicators for rural Azerbaijan, Tajikistan, Turkmeniia and Uzbekistan (where almost the entire population is, as noted above, Muslim) show a decline even from ages 20–24 (see Appendix 12.2).

The noted reduction was, in all cases, more pronounced among the more advanced fertile ages. From 1978–79 to 1988–89 the number of births per 1000 women aged 40–44 fell by as much as 2.4–3 times among the Kazakhs, Kyrgyz and Uzbeks, and by more than two times among the Turkmen. During the same period, this indicator declined by more than four times for ages 45–49 in rural Azerbaijan, Turkmeniia and Uzbekistan, and by more than two and a half times in rural Tajikistan.

To attain an overall assessment of the fertility level for a given year, demographers use the total fertility rate (TFR). This indicator is the summary of all the age-specific fertility rates for the given year, and it signifies the average number of children that a woman would bear in her lifetime, on condition that the current fertility level remain constant throughout her fertile period (usually from 15 to 49).

During 1978–79 to 1988–89, the TFRs fell among all analyzed Muslim nationalities – for their total, urban and rural populations – except among the total and rural Tajiks (Table 12.3). The drop was as much as 1.0–1.1 children on average per each Azerbaijani and Kazakh woman, and about two children per each rural Kyrgyz, Turkmen and Uzbek woman.

For an assessment of the overall level of their demographic modernization by the end of the 1980s, we compared the TFRs of former Soviet Muslims with those of Middle Eastern and North African populations for the same period.[5] In 1988–89, the TFR was 2.9 for Azerbaijanis and 3.6 for Kazakhs; there are no such low levels in the Muslim countries which we compared. Even in the well-known examples of Muslim demographic modernization the TFRs were higher: in 1986–90, 3.8 in Turkey and 3.9 in Tunisia.

The TFR for Kyrgyz, Turkmen and Uzbeks was 4.7–4.9 children, which is very close to Egypt's level of 4.5 and about the same as Morocco's level of 4.8, but noticeably less than that of Algeria: 5.4. The Tajiks had a TFR of 5.95; but at the same time Iraq had a rate of 6.2, Iran, 6.5, and Syria's TFR reached 6.7 children.[6]

Whereas the TFR for Tajiks was higher than for all other former Soviet Muslim titular nationalities in 1988–89, data show that this was not the case in 1978–79, and this contrast demands attention. The 1978–79 Tajik data for total and rural population can be shown to be implausibly low for this ethnic group in comparison with others – Kyrgyz, Turkmen and Uzbeks.[7]

TABLE 12.3 TOTAL FERTILITY RATE OF MUSLIM TITULAR NATIONALITIES OF THE FORMER UNION REPUBLICS,[a] 1978–79 AND 1988–89

Nationality	1978–79	1988–89	1988–89 as % of 1978–79
		Total population	
Azerbaijanis	3.93	2.94	75
Kazakhs	4.68	3.58	76
Kyrgyz	6.67	4.83	72
Tajiks	5.71	5.95	104
Turkmen	6.55	4.90	75
Uzbeks	6.22	4.66	75
		Urban population	
Azerbaijanis	3.16	...	...
Kazakhs	3.74	3.03	81
Kyrgyz	4.30	3.34	78
Tajiks	4.84	4.42	91
Turkmen	5.58	4.66	84
Uzbeks	4.29	3.72	87
		Rural population	
Azerbaijanis	4.77	...	...
Kazakhs	5.21	4.07	78
Kyrgyz	7.35	5.45	74
Tajiks	6.03	6.56	109
Turkmen	7.08	5.05	71
Uzbeks	7.09	5.12	72

(a) Inside respective former union republic

Sources:
E. M. Andreev, L. E. Darskii, T. L. Khar'kova, *Naselenie Sovetskogo Soiuza: 1922–1991* (Moscow: Nauka, 1993), p. 90.
G. A. Bondarskaia and L. E. Darskii, 'Etnicheskaia differentsiatsiia rozhdaemosti', *Vestnik statistiki*, 12 (1988), p. 19.
L. E. Darsky and N. B. Dworak, *Fertility Indicators and Characteristics of the Potential Market for Modern Contraception* (Washington, DC: The Futures Group, 1993), Vols.: Kazakhstan, p. 12, Kirgiziia, p. 12, Tajikistan, p. 12, Turkmeniia, p. 12, Uzbekistan, p. 12.

The TFR for rural Tajiks for 1978–79 has been estimated as only 6.0. However, at the same time, the TFR for the total population of rural Tajikistan was as high as 7.7. Given the known percentages of Tajiks and non-Tajiks in this population (according to the data of the 1979 census – 67 per cent and 33 per cent, respectively) for these figures to be logical, non-Tajiks would have had a TFR of more than 11 children, which is most improbable.

We may assume that the above cited TFR for rural Tajiks in 1978–79 is a result of under-registration of births and/or a difference between the coverage of the population by nationality in the 1979 census and time-related vital statistics. We may also note that during the period from 1978–79 to 1989, the TFR for the total population of rural Tajikistan fell by 1.6. The actual TFR dynamics for rural Tajiks were probably analogous to this figure. At the same period the TFR fell by 1.4 in rural Azerbaijan, by 1.8 in rural Turkmeniia and by 2.1 in rural Uzbekistan.[8]

CHANGES IN MARRIAGE PATTERNS

A decrease in overall fertility can be caused by changes in marriage and marital fertility. In fact, in some Arab countries most of the fertility decrease has been attributed to later age at first marriage.[9] We shall now analyze the changes in marriage patterns.

The primary demographic characteristics of marriage patterns are age at first marriage and the extent of final celibacy. There are various different approaches to estimate mean age at first marriage. For purposes of comparison, this mean age is often measured according to census data, and the indicator arrived at by this method has been named the singulate mean age at marriage (SMAM). Recently this has become the most commonly used indicator of mean age at first marriage.[10]

Traditionally among Muslims, women's age at first marriage has been low. But since men marry for the first time considerably later, the age gap between spouses was very pronounced. Thus, according to the data of the 1897 census, in Tsarist Central Asia, the mean age at first marriage was 17.7 for females and 27.4 for males.[11] That is, the difference in mean age of brides and grooms was about ten years.

By the 1970s and 1980s, the situation was changing dramatically. According to the data of the 1989 census, mean age at first marriage was as high as 23.6 for Kazakh women and 23.9 for Azerbaijani women (Table 12.4). These ethnic groups reached the low limit (23–24 years) of what is demographically termed the 'European marriage pattern'.[12]

At the same time, in the Middle East and North Africa there was only one Muslim country with such a high age at first marriage for women: in 1984, in Tunisia it was 24.3. In all the other Muslim countries of the region the mean age at first marriage for women was 21–22 or younger.[13]

According to the 1989 census data the mean age at first marriage was 20.9 for Tajik women. Thus, Tajik women still cling to the 'non-European marriage pattern', whose upper limit is below 21 years.[14] Uzbek women are around the same level, with SMAM 21.0.

TABLE 12.4 SINGULATE MEAN AGE AT MARRIAGE (SMAM) OF MUSLIM TITULAR NATIONALITIES OF THE FORMER UNION REPUBLICS,[(a)] 1979 AND 1989

Nationality	Males		Females		Difference in SMAM of males and females	
	1979	1989	1979	1989	1979	1989
	Total population					
Azerbaijanis	26.2	25.8	23.5	23.9	2.7	1.9
Kazakhs	25.1	25.2	22.8	23.6	2.3	1.6
Kyrgyz	23.6	24.0	21.3	21.8	2.3	2.2
Tajiks	23.2	23.1	20.3	20.9	2.9	2.2
Turkmen	23.3	23.8	21.5	22.9	1.8	0.9
Uzbeks	23.1	23.1	20.9	21.0	2.2	2.1
	Urban population					
Azerbaijanis	...	26.4	...	23.7	...	2.7
Kazakhs	...	25.4	...	24.7	...	0.7
Kyrgyz	...	24.9	...	24.0	...	0.9
Tajiks	...	23.9	...	21.5	...	2.4
Turkmen	...	24.2	...	23.0	...	1.2
Uzbeks	...	23.8	...	21.6	...	2.2
	Rural population					
Azerbaijanis	...	25.2	...	24.2	...	1.0
Kazakhs	...	25.1	...	22.5	...	2.6
Kyrgyz	...	23.7	...	20.8	...	2.9
Tajiks	...	22.8	...	20.6	...	2.2
Turkmen	...	23.5	...	22.8	...	0.7
Uzbeks	...	22.7	...	20.7	...	2.0

(a) Inside respective former union republic
Sources: 1979 and 1989 censuses

Between the 1979 and 1989 censuses, mean age at first marriage rose among women of all the nationalities analyzed here, except

Uzbeks among whom it remained almost constant. The rise in age was steepest among the Turkmen women (1.4 years over the decade), and their SMAM reached 22.9, which is very close to the already noted low limit of the 'European marriage pattern'. According to the data of the 1989 census, the mean age at first marriage for Kyrgyz women was 21.8, a medium level. However, the rural Kyrgyz women, as well as rural Tajik and Uzbek women have SMAMs under 21 years and they still act according to the 'non-European marriage pattern', whereas the urban Kyrgyz, Azerbaijani and Kazakh women have already attained the low limit of the 'European marriage pattern': 24 years.

According to the data of the 1989 census, the mean age at first marriage for men was 25–26 years for Azerbaijanis and Kazakhs, and 23–24 years for all other Muslim titular nationalities of the former union republics. In all of these populations, the difference in mean age of brides and grooms reached a moderate level of about two years or less. This is far from the pronounced difference of 4–7 years which was registered recently in most Muslim countries of the Middle East and Northern Africa.[15]

In demography the proportion of those never married at age 45–49 (which coincides with the upper limit of the woman's reproductive ages) is usually regarded as an indicator of the extent of final celibacy. Despite the noted dramatic rise in women's mean age at first marriage, this indicator has remained at a definitely low level: according to the data of the 1989 census it was 2.2 per cent for Azerbaijani women and 1.3 per cent for Kazakh women. For all other Muslim titular nationalities of the former union republics it was very low: 0.4 per cent, and 0.5 per cent among Tajik women.

At the same time, in the urban populations, at ages 45–49 there were 2.3 per cent never-married among Azerbaijani and Kazakh women, 0.8 per cent among Kyrgyz women, and only 0.7 per cent among the others. In the rural population of the same age, the proportion of never-married was 2.1 per cent among Azerbaijani women, 0.8 per cent among Kazakh women, 0.4 per cent among Tajik women, and as low as 0.3 per cent among the others.

Another important characteristic of marital structure is the proportion of females currently married at given ages. Fertility is, of course, linked to these proportions. Demographers use a special indicator to give an overall assessment of these proportions, namely the average number of years spent in married status within the fertile ages.[16] This indicator for the entire fertile period from 15 to 49 years can be broken down into two parts: from 15 to 29, and 30 to 49 years.

According to the data of the 1989 census, for women of all Muslim titular nationalities, the average number of years spent in married status in the fertile ages had decreased in comparison with the data from all preceding post-war censuses (Table 12.5). This decrease was largely caused by the dynamics at ages 15–29, that is, the result of the above-mentioned increase in age at first marriage.

TABLE 12.5 AVERAGE NUMBER OF YEARS IN MARRIAGE IN FERTILE AGES AMONG FEMALES OF MUSLIM TITULAR NATIONALITIES OF THE FORMER UNION REPUBLICS,[a] 1959, 1970, 1979 AND 1989

Nationality	1959	1970	1979	1989
	At ages 15 – 49			
Azerbaijanis	23.7	24.8	23.7	23.4
Kazakhs	25.5	25.4	24.0	23.3
Kyrgyz	27.2	27.2	26.1	25.1
Tajiks	27.3	28.3	28.0	27.2
Turkmen	26.3	27.4	26.5	25.1
Uzbeks	27.0	27.7	27.1	26.8
	Thereof: at ages 15 – 29			
Azerbaijanis	8.7	7.9	6.5	6.5
Kazakhs	9.5	8.0	6.9	6.7
Kyrgyz	10.7	9.4	8.3	7.9
Tajiks	10.5	10.0	9.4	8.8
Turkmen	10.5	9.4	8.2	7.0
Uzbeks	10.1	9.5	8.7	8.7
	Thereof: at ages 30 – 49			
Azerbaijanis	15.0	16.9	17.2	16.9
Kazakhs	16.0	17.4	17.1	16.6
Kyrgyz	16.5	17.8	17.8	17.2
Tajiks	16.8	18.3	18.6	18.4
Turkmen	15.8	18.0	18.3	18.1
Uzbeks	16.9	18.2	18.4	18.1

(a) Inside respective former union republic
Sources: 1959, 1970, 1979, and 1989 censuses

As opposed to the low findings for ages 15–29 from the 1989 census, the same source showed a consistent rise for ages 30–49 from the 1959 census, a less consistent rise from the census of 1970, and even the decrease from the 1979 census was moderate. However, at precisely these ages the above-noted drop in age-specific fertility rates occurred, and has intensified. Thus, we must seek another explanation as to the primary reason for the fertility drop among Muslims in Azerbaijan and former Soviet Central Asia.

DECREASE OF MARITAL FERTILITY

According to data from the 1989 census, the average number of children ever born to currently married women in Soviet Central Asia was lowest at ages 25–29 and over, among Kazakhs, and highest at ages 20–24 and over, among Tajiks (Table 12.6). At the same time, the data indicated large discrepancies between the urban and rural populations.

TABLE 12.6 AVERAGE NUMBER OF CHILDREN EVER BORN TO CURRENTLY MARRIED WOMEN OF MUSLIM TITULAR NATIONALITIES OF THE FORMER UNION REPUBLICS,[a] 1989

Nationality	Age in the 1989 census						
	15–19	20–24	25–29	30–34	35–39	40–44	45–49
	Total population						
Kazakhs	0.40	1.15	2.12	3.14	4.16	5.09	6.40
Kyrgyz	0.33	1.31	2.65	4.09	5.46	6.53	7.63
Tajiks	0.26	1.33	3.03	4.82	6.45	7.55	8.09
Turkmen	0.36	1.09	2.44	4.14	5.60	6.62	7.47
Uzbeks	0.35	1.32	2.75	4.18	5.36	6.23	6.95
	Urban population						
Kazakhs	0.41	1.06	1.87	2.66	3.35	3.93	4.91
Kyrgyz	0.34	1.11	2.18	3.24	4.11	4.73	5.25
Tajiks	0.30	1.24	2.69	4.06	5.16	6.07	6.67
Turkmen	0.36	1.10	2.25	3.62	4.82	5.54	6.38
Uzbeks	0.37	1.26	2.44	3.56	4.41	5.02	5.72
	Rural population						
Kazakhs	0.39	1.22	2.31	3.50	4.72	5.83	7.05
Kyrgyz	0.33	1.37	2.81	4.38	5.88	7.06	8.11
Tajiks	0.25	1.36	3.16	5.13	6.98	8.15	8.62
Turkmen	0.36	1.09	2.54	4.43	6.03	7.21	7.98
Uzbeks	0.34	1.35	2.87	4.48	5.83	6.88	7.53

(a) Inside respective former union republic
Source: 1989 census

Expectedly, the urban population began its fertility decline earlier, and by the end of the 1980s had reached a more advanced stage of modernization of fertility behaviour. Completed marital fertility, measured by the indicator at ages 45–49, was clearly lower in the urban than in the rural population: by 1.6 children among Turkmen, by 1.8 among Uzbeks, by 2.0–2.1 among Kazakhs and Tajiks, and by as much as 2.9 among Kyrgyz.

Data from the censuses show a decline in marital fertility. For example, in the decade 1979–89, the average number of children ever born to currently married Tajik women aged 30–34 fell from 4.5 to 4.1 in the urban population and, among the rural population, from 5.6 to 5.1 (see Table 12.6).[17] These figures confirm our previously stated conclusion regarding a decrease in Tajik fertility.

These indicators do not characterize the recent situation generally, but rather the history of the marital fertility of a particular cohort. The actual dynamics for each age-group during the last decade can be seen by comparing the age-specific marital birth rates for the end of the 1970s with those for the end of the 1980s.[18] These rates show a fertility drop among all the titular nationalities of Soviet Central Asia from ages 25–29 and over – except, again, the Tajiks, whose data for 1978-79 we consider to be defective (Appendix 12.3). In all cases, the decline in fertility was greater among more advanced fertile ages. A comparison of the percentage drop of the age-specific birth rate (Appendix 12.1) with that of the age-specific marital birth rate (Appendix 12.3) shows that they are very similar in most cases. Thus, we see that the dynamics of marital fertility were the main reason for the overall fertility decline.

This conclusion is further confirmed by data on rural Azerbaijan, Tajikistan, Turkmeniia and Uzbekistan (Appendix 12.4, which data should be compared with the data of Appendix 12.2). From 1978–79 to 1989, at ages 45–49, the number of births per 1000 married women fell by as much as 4–4.5 times in rural Azerbaijan, Turkmeniia and Uzbekistan, and by 2.6 times in rural Tajikistan.

A decomposition of the decrease in TFRs of the rural population of these republics[19] shows that most of the decrease was caused by marital fertility, and only a smaller part is due to marriage change: in rural Uzbekistan 95 per cent and 5 per cent, in rural Azerbaijan 89 per cent and 11 per cent, in rural Tajikistan 85 per cent and 15 per cent, and in rural Turkmeniia 76 per cent and 24 per cent, respectively.

The 1985 micro-census data clearly show a decrease in the average number of children expected (including those already born) when we compared currently married women of younger ages with women at a more advanced age (Table 12.7). At ages 20–24, the number expected was only 3.4–3.5 children among all married Azerbaijani and Kazakh women, and even less than three among the urban married women of these nationalities.

TABLE 12.7 AVERAGE NUMBER OF CHILDREN EXPECTED (INCLUDING ALREADY BORN) BY CURRENTLY MARRIED WOMEN OF MUSLIM TITULAR NATIONALITIES OF THE FORMER UNION REPUBLICS, 1985

Nationality	Age of married women				
	20–24	25–29	30–34	35–39	40–44
	Total population				
Azerbaijanis	3.44	3.59	4.02	4.39	4.93
Kazakhs	3.48	3.71	4.24	4.83	5.65
Kyrgyz	4.98	5.15	5.85	6.42	6.98
Tajiks	5.44	5.85	6.61	7.43	7.47
Turkmen	5.91	6.03	6.49	7.12	7.13
Uzbeks	5.11	5.28	5.80	6.29	6.52
	Urban population				
Azerbaijanis	2.97	3.11	3.42	3.65	3.89
Kazakhs	2.97	3.06	3.45	3.73	4.44
Kyrgyz	3.84	3.92	4.36	4.60	5.09
Tajiks	4.42	4.51	4.97	5.72	6.17
Turkmen	4.81	4.88	5.43	5.78	5.88
Uzbeks	4.05	4.16	4.60	5.05	5.29
	Rural population				
Azerbaijanis	3.97	4.28	4.98	5.59	6.20
Kazakhs	3.78	4.13	4.75	5.50	6.21
Kyrgyz	5.36	5.64	6.37	7.05	7.37
Tajiks	5.78	6.40	7.29	8.18	8.02
Turkmen	6.33	6.45	6.88	7.55	7.48
Uzbeks	5.52	5.76	6.38	6.96	7.13

Source: V. A. Borisov (compiler), *Naselenie mira: Demograficheskii spravochnik* (Moscow: Mysl', 1989), pp. 43–4.

All Tajik and Kyrgyz married women at ages 20–24 expected two children less than did the 40–44 age group, and this drop by age group was even stronger among Kazakh married women: 2.2 children.

All these changes in marital fertility occurred despite the new pro-natalist policy adopted by the Soviet government in the early 1980s on a national level.[20] This unique and strange experiment obviously did not stop the modernization of demographic behaviour among the Muslim populations of former Soviet Central Asia and Azerbaijan.

DIFFICULTIES AND OBSTACLES

In the past decade the demographic dynamics of the Muslim popula-tions of Azerbaijan and former Soviet Central Asia have been characterized by some serious difficulties and obstacles. First of all, the growth rates rose or were rather constant despite the above-noted demographic changes. These rates were caused by crude birth rates (the annual number of births per 1000 population), which are heavily dependent on changes in age structure.

In 1989, the number of births was between 37 and 39 per 1000 Kyrgyz, Turkmen and Uzbeks, and 43 per 1000 Tajiks, but only 29 and 31 per 1000 Azerbaijanis and Kazakhs, respectively. In all cases but the Kyrgyz and Uzbeks, these rates were higher than in 1979 (Table 12.8). This was caused by the rapid growth in the number of females of fertile age. For example, between 1979 and 1989, the number of women of the titular nationalities in the Central Asian republics aged 20–29 rose by 1.6–1.8 times, and the number of women of this group aged 30–39 more than doubled.

In the Middle Eastern and North African countries, during the period 1976–80 and 1986–90, the crude birth rates per 1000 population fell: notably from 45 to 35.5 in Algeria, 39 to 36 in Morocco, 39 to 35 in Egypt, 36 to 29 in Tunisia, and from 32 to less than 30 in Turkey. In other, Muslim countries of this region there was no such decline, and this rate was, for 1986–90, as high as 40 in Iraq, 43 in Iran and 44 in Syria.[21] That is, only the birth rate of the Tajiks approaches the highest cited indicator. On the other hand, the rates for Azerbaijanis and Kazakhs were about as low as those in Tunisia and Turkey. Also, only peculiarities of age structure can explain the higher levels of crude birth rates among the urban, as opposed to rural, populations, as seen from the 1989 data on Kazakhs and Turkmen.

In the case of rural Tajiks this rate was very high: 46 per 1000 population. If we take into consideration the demographic tensions resulting from over-population, we have at least a partial explanation for the serious political and economic disorder in Tajikistan as compared with other newly independent states of former Soviet Central Asia.

TABLE 12.8 BALANCE OF CRUDE BIRTH AND DEATH RATES OF MUSLIM TITULAR NATIONALITIES OF THE FORMER UNION REPUBLICS (PER 1000 POPULATION), 1979 AND 1989[a]

Nationality	Birth rate		Death rate		Balance	
	1979	1989	1979	1989	1979	1989
Total population						
Azerbaijanis	27.5	28.9	6.3	5.8	21.2	23.1
Kazakhs	30.3	31.1	6.6	6.3	23.7	24.8
Kyrgyz	38.4	38.3	7.7	6.3	30.7	32.0
Tajiks	42.1	42.9	7.7	6.1	34.4	36.8
Turkmen	38.1	38.6	7.2	7.6	30.9	31.0
Uzbeks	38.6	37.4	6.6	5.9	32.0	31.5
Urban population						
Azerbaijanis	26.7	26.7	5.4	4.9	21.3	21.8
Kazakhs	32.2	32.0	6.4	5.5	25.8	26.5
Kyrgyz	41.0	35.4	4.5	3.8	36.5	31.6
Tajiks	36.5	35.6	6.4	4.6	30.1	31.0
Turkmen	36.6	40.6	6.2	7.0	30.4	33.6
Uzbeks	30.6	32.2	5.5	5.2	25.1	27.0
Rural population						
Azerbaijanis	28.2	31.2	7.1	6.7	21.1	24.5
Kazakhs	29.5	30.6	6.7	6.7	22.8	23.9
Kyrgyz	37.8	39.1	8.4	7.0	29.4	32.1
Tajiks	43.9	45.6	8.1	6.6	35.8	39.0
Turkmen	38.9	37.6	7.8	7.9	31.1	29.7
Uzbeks	41.7	39.7	7.0	6.2	34.7	33.5

(a) Inside respective former union republic

Source: Goskomstat SSSR, *Demograficheskii ezhegodnik SSSR, 1990* (Moscow: Finansy i statistika, 1990), pp. 184–7.

A unique feature of Soviet Central Asia was the stagnation of urbanization everywhere but in Tajikistan and Turkmeniia, where there was even ruralization (decrease in percentage of urban population). This took place in spite of the fact that some rural areas were reclassified as urban, further muddling the statistics of these dynamics.[22]

Towards the end of the Soviet period, indeed up to the end of 1991, ruralization began spreading everywhere, except Kazakhstan.[23] This trend seems to have continued after independence, at least in certain republics. There were no similar dynamics in the Muslim countries of the Middle East or Northern Africa, except Egypt.[24]

This structural factor is a further obstacle to any decrease in the crude birth rate of ex-Soviet Central Asia's population. According to the data of the 1989 census, the urban percentage among the population of Muslim origin was 50 in Azerbaijan, 38–39 per cent in Kazakhstan and Turkmeniia, 34 per cent in Uzbekistan, but only 27 per cent in Kirgiziia and 25 per cent in Tajikistan. The percentage of urbanization among titular nationalities in many cases was even lower (Table 12.9).

TABLE 12.9 PERCENTAGE URBAN DWELLERS AMONG POPULATION OF MUSLIM ORIGIN AND MUSLIM TITULAR NATIONALITY, BY FORMER UNION REPUBLICS, 1979 AND 1989

Republic	Muslim population		Titular nationality	
	1979	1989	1979	1989
Azerbaijan	46	50	46	50
Kazakhstan	33	39	31	38
Kirgiziia	25	27	18	22
Tajikistan	25	25	25	26
Turkmeniia	38	38	33	34
Uzbekistan	32	34	29	31

Sources: 1979 and 1989 censuses

One of the most serious limits to modernization of demographic behaviour in ex-Soviet Central Asia and Azerbaijan is the high level of infant mortality. For many years all pertinent statistical information was kept secret; however, recently published statistical data do not show the true dimensions of the problem. Even according to an official statement by the former Soviet Central Statistical Administration, the level of infant mortality rates in rural Central Asia is actually 1.5–2 times higher than the registered rate, which was about 50 for every 1000 newborn.[25]

The high levels of infant mortality have been exacerbated by the health service crisis and the ecological crisis in the region.[26] But behavioural characteristics are another important factor: traditional, primitive infant care, that is, with relatively low hygiene standards, compounded by the frequent untimely delay in the necessary search for medical help prevent a decrease in infant mortality.[27]

Although there are some contradictions in the estimates of the level of infant mortality,[28] we may assume that the actual level among the Muslims of this region in the latter half of the 1980s was higher than that in Egypt and Turkey: 65 and 68 for 1000 newborn, respectively.[29]

The recent drop of this published indicator in ex-Soviet Central Asia is actually a mere reflection of the worsened coverage of the vital statistics. The existence of high infant mortality has been an obstacle to further fertility decrease. From all the above, we can see that the demographic development in the area has been rather inconsistent.

CONCLUDING REMARKS

From our analysis we see that in the 1980s, despite all the difficulties and obstacles, modernization of demographic behaviour among the Muslims in Azerbaijan and former Soviet Central Asia progressed. However, various ethnic groups reached different stages of demographic modernization. Marriage and fertility data show that the Azerbaijanis and Kazakhs belong to the vanguard of demographic modernization in the Muslim world, whereas other nationalities are still at the less advanced stages of this process, especially the Tajiks.

The example of Iran shows that with strong islamicization, demographic modernization can be delayed or even reversed.[30] And the question arises: can such a reversal occur in Azerbaijan and former Soviet Central Asia? The majority of even the least advanced Muslim populations attained in the Soviet period a stage of modernization of demographic behaviour which was more advanced than that in pre-revolutionary Iran.

The recent economic and political crisis in the newly independent Muslim states is a serious danger to health services, whose decline began already in the last years of the Soviet era. This must also be taken into account in any discussion of the prospects of demographic development in the region, together with the possible effects of apparent islamicization.

NOTES

1. The author based his research first of all on the data of the 1979 and 1989 Soviet censuses, which have been published only in part.
2. See, for example, A. Blum, 'La transition démographique dans les Republiques orientales d'URSS', *Population* 42, 2 (1987), pp. 337–48.
3. See M. Tolts, 'Nedostupnoe izmerenie', in A. G. Vishnevskii (ed.), *V chelovecheskom izmerenii* (Moscow: Progress, 1989), pp. 334–40.
4. About this and its reasons see R. I. Sifman, *Dinamika rozhdaemosti v SSSR.* (Moscow: Statistika, 1974), p. 73; A. J. Coale, B. A. Anderson and E. Harm, *Human Fertility in Russia since the Nineteenth Century* (Princeton, N.J.: Princeton University Press, 1979), p. 91; V. A. Belova, G. A. Bondarskaia and L. E. Darskii, 'Sovremennye problemy i perspektivy rozhdaemosti', in A. G. Volkov (ed.), *Metodologiia demograficheskogo prognoza* (Moscow: Nauka, 1988), p. 53.
5. All non-Soviet TFRs drawn from United Nations, *World Population Prospects: The 1992 Revision* (New York: United Nations, 1993), Table A.19.
6. According to another estimate for the early 1990s, this TFR was 7.1 – A. R. Omran and F. Roudi, 'The Middle East Population Puzzle', *Population Bulletin*, 48, 1 (1993), p. 13. In various sources there are also some other contradictions to cited indicators for other countries; see for example, Population Reference Bureau (PRB). *World Population Data Sheet* (Washington, DC, 1993), Middle East and North African data.
7. This has already been noted by some scholars. They suggested that the reason for the low Tajik TFR was simple miscomputation (B. A. Anderson and B. D. Silver, 'Demographic Sources of the Changing Ethnic Composition of the Soviet Union', *Population and Development Review* 15, 4 (1989), p. 653, note 29). However, one author of the published figures states that he regards the Tajik data as accurate (personal communication between myself and Dr. Leonid Darsky, April 1994, Jerusalem).
8. All TFRs for rural populations of the republics drawn from: Goskomstat SSSR, *Demograficheskii ezhegodnik SSSR, 1990* (Moscow: Finansy i statistika, 1990), pp. 310–11, 314–15.
9. Ph. Fargues, 'The Decline of Arab Fertility', *Population* (English selections) 1 (1989), p. 159.
10. SMAM is computed by using census data which give the proportions of the never-married by age – see, for example, United Nations, *Manual X: Indirect Techniques for Demographic Estimation* (New York: United Nations, 1983), Annex 1, pp. 225–9.
11. M. S. Tolts and A. G. Vishnevskii, 'Evoliutsiia brachnosti i rozhdaemosti v sovetskii period', in L. L. Rybakovskii (ed.), *Naselenie SSSR za 70 let* (Moscow: Nauka, 1988), p. 79.
12. See J. Hajnal, 'European Marriage Patterns in Perspective', in D. V. Glass and D. E. C. Eversley (eds.), *Population in History* (London: Edward Arnold, 1965), p. 108.
13. United Nations, *Patterns of First Marriage: Timing and Prevalence* (New York: United Nations, 1990), pp. 69, 174.
14. See Hajnal, 'European Marriage Patterns', p. 108
15. United Nations, *Patterns of First Marriage*, pp. 297, 310.
16. This indicator is computed from census data on the proportions of the currently married, by age – see, for example, United Nations, *Urban-Rural Differences in the Marital-Status Composition of the Population* (New York: United Nations, 1973) p. 26. It has been standardized by age, and disregards mortality.
17. Cf. E. B. Babin, 'Differentsiatsiia brachnoi rozhdaemosti v SSSR po dannym Vsesoiuznoi perepisi naseleniia 1979 goda', in G. P. Kiseleva (ed.), *Problemy demograficheskogo razvitiia SSSR* (Moscow: Institute of Sociology, USSR Academy of Sciences, 1988), pp. 45, 47.
18. Estimated rates (Appendices 12.3 and 12.4) were obtained by dividing age-specific birth rates (Appendices 12.1 and 12.2) by the corresponding proportion of currently married according to the 1979 and 1989 census data. Rates obtained include illegitimate births.

19. For the method used to determine decomposition see: R. D. Retherford and J. R. Rele, 'A Decomposition of Recent Fertility Changes in South Asia', *Population and Development Review* 15, 4 (1989), pp. 744–5.
20. Concerning this policy see V. A. Borisov (compiler), *Naselenie mira: Demograficheskii spravochnik* (Moscow: Mysl', 1989), pp. 324–7; E. Jones and F. W. Grapp, *Modernization, Value Change and Fertility in the Soviet Union* (Cambridge: Cambridge University Press, 1987), pp. 270–5.
21. United Nations, *World Population Prospects: The 1992 Revision* (1993), Table A.19.
22. See N. Lubin, 'Implications of Ethnic and Demographic Trends', in W. Fierman, (ed.), *Soviet Central Asia: The Failed Transformation* (Boulder: Westview Press, 1991), p. 51.
23. Statkomitet SNG, *Strany-chleny SNG: Statisticheskii ezhegodnik, 1992* (Moscow: Finansovyi Inzhiniring, 1992), pp. 90, 208, 249, 371, 409, 447. (New York: United Nations, 1993)
24. United Nations. *World Urbanization Prospects: The 1992 Revision* (1993), Table A.1.
25. Goskomstat SSSR, 'Novaia informatsiia: Mladencheskaia smertnost' ', *Vestnik statistiki* 4 (1990), p. 63.
26. See, for example, M. Feshbach and A. Friendly, Jr., *Ecocide in the USSR: Health and Nature under Siege* (New York: Basic Books, 1992), pp. 76–82.
27. E. M. Andreev, 'Sotsial'naia determinatsiia smertnosti, demograficheskaia politika i prognozy prodolzhitel'nosti zhizni', in A. G. Volkov, *Metodologiia demograficheskogo prognoza*, pp. 126–7; V. M. Dobrovol'skaia, 'Etnicheskaia differentsiatsiia smertnosti', in A. G. Volkov (ed.), *Demograficheskie protsessy v SSSR* (Moscow: Nauka, 1990), p. 160.
28. See B. A. Anderson and B. D. Silver, 'Trends in Mortality of the Soviet Population', *Soviet Economy* 6, 3 (1990), pp. 224–7; N. Ksenofontova, 'Trends in Infant Mortality in the USSR', in W. Lutz, S. Scherbov and A. Volkov (eds.), *Demographic Trends and Patterns in the Soviet Union before 1991* (London/New York: Routledge, 1994), pp. 372, 376.
29. United Nations, *World Population Prospects: The 1992 Revision* (1993), Table A.19.
30. See A. Aghajanian, 'Population Change in Iran, 1966–1986: A Stalled Demographic Transition?' *Population and Development Review* 17, 4 (1991), pp. 710–13.

APPENDIX 12.1 AGE-SPECIFIC BIRTH RATES OF KAZAKHS, KYRGYZ, TAJIKS, TURKMEN, AND UZBEKS (PER 1000 WOMEN), 1978-79 AND 1988-89(a)

Age group	Kazakhs			Kyrgyz			Turkmen			Uzbeks			Tajiks		
	1978-79	1988-89	1988-89 as % of 1978-79	1978-79	1988-89	1988-89 as % of 1978-79	1978-79	1988-89	1988-89 as % of 1978-79	1978-79	1988-89	1988-89 as % of 1978-79	1978-79	1988-89	1988-89 as % of 1978-79
15 – 19	19.5	30.6	157	37.9	40.9	108	16.3	15.7	96	35.6	43.1	121	36.9	37.6	102
20 – 24	222.0	232.0	105	297.9	296.1	99	271.5	223.8	82	307.6	312.5	102	348.7	316.2	91
25 – 29	252.5	208.2	82	281.5	261.3	93	360.7	323.1	90	339.9	272.5	80	369.1	314.4	85
30 – 34	201.4	140.1	70	314.1	186.8	59	300.1	225.4	75	270.1	176.8	65	171.1	251.1	147
35 – 39	142.9	75.8	53	231.9	114.8	50	209.1	128.7	62	177.8	88.8	50	118.2	167.2	141
40 – 44	79.4	26.8	34	134.3	55.5	41	122.3	55.9	46	92.8	33.9	37	75.1	86.8	116
45 – 49	14.6	2.9	20	31.3	9.6	31	25.8	6.9	27	17.0	4.1	24	18.4	14.6	79
50 – 54	2.9	…	…	4.1	…	…	4.9	…	…	2.7	…	…	4.1		

(a) Inside respective former union republic

Sources: Bondarskaia and Darskii, 'Etnicheskaia differentsiatsiia rozhdaemosti', p. 17.
Darskii and Dworak, *Fertility Indicators*, Vols: Kazakhstan, p. 13, Kirgiziia, p. 13, Tajikistan, p. 13, Turkmeniia, p. 13, Uzbekistan, p. 13.

APPENDIX 12.2 AGE-SPECIFIC BIRTH RATES OF RURAL POPULATION OF AZERBAIJAN, TAJIKISTAN, TURKMENIIA, AND UZBEKISTAN (PER 1000 WOMEN), 1978–79 AND 1989

Age group	Azerbaijan			Tajikistan			Turkmeniia			Uzbekistan		
	1978-79	1989	1989 as % of 1978-79	1978-79	1989	1989 as % of 1978-79	1978-79	1989	1989 as % of 1978-79	1978-79	1989	1989 as % of 1978-79
15 – 19	15.8	30.7	194	38.2	38.6	101	15.0	15.3	102	38.4	42.1	110
20 – 24	219.5	212.0	97	357.0	331.7	93	277.2	224.0	81	341.8	325.4	95
25 – 29	288.5	208.8	72	375.5	323.0	86	379.5	315.1	83	366.0	280.1	77
30 – 34	215.5	123.4	57	328.6	257.9	78	334.6	228.2	68	305.8	182.9	60
35 – 39	128.5	54.1	42	256.8	172.7	67	223.4	129.6	58	202.3	93.3	46
40 – 44	53.7	19.2	36	141.1	84.0	60	141.8	55.9	39	108.4	37.1	34
45 – 49	7.8	1.8	23	37.0	14.2	38	30.4	7.4	24	20.7	4.9	24

Source: Goskomstat SSSR, *Demograficheskii ezhegodnik SSSR, 1990*, pp. 310–11, 314–15.

APPENDIX 12.3 AGE-SPECIFIC MARITAL BIRTH RATES OF KAZAKHS, KYRGYZ, TAJIKS, TURKMEN, AND UZBEKS (PER 1000 MARRIED WOMEN), 1978–79 AND 1988–89[a]

Age group	Kazakhs			Kyrgyz			Turkmen			Uzbeks			Tajiks		
	1978-79	1988-89	1988-89 as % of 1978-79	1978-79	1988-89	1988-89 as % of 1978-79	1978-79	1988-89	1988-89 as % of 1978-79	1978-79	1988-89	1988-89 as % of 1978-79	1978-79	1988-89	1988-89 as % of 1978-79
15 – 19	...	528	...	...	405	...	...	403	...	...	395	...	...	321	...
20 – 24	432	449	104	442	463	105	415	468	113	430	428	99.5	432	424	98
25 – 29	308	271	88	319	316	99	388	368	95	370	304	82	392	351	90
30 – 34	229	169	74	344	215	63	318	242	76	287	192	67	179	270	151
35 – 39	161	90	56	255	131	51	224	140	63	190	97	51	125	179	143
40 – 44	93	32	34	150	64	43	134	62	46	101	37	37	80	94	118
45 – 49	18	4	22	37	12	32	30	8	27	19	5	26	21	16	76
50 – 54	4	...	...	5	...	...	6	...	...	3	...	...	5	...	...

(a) Inside respective former union republic

Sources: Appendix 12.1; 1979 and 1989 censuses

APPENDIX 12.4 AGE-SPECIFIC MARITAL BIRTH RATES FOR RURAL POPULATION OF AZERBAIJAN, TAJIKISTAN, TURKMENIIA, AND UZBEKISTAN (PER 1000 MARRIED WOMEN), 1978–79 AND 1989.

Age group	Azerbaijan			Tajikistan			Turkmeniia			Uzbekistan		
	1978-79	1989	1989 as % of 1978-79	1978-79	1989	1989 as % of 1978-79	1978-79	1989	1989 as % of 1978-79	1978-79	1989	1989 as % of 1978-79
15–19	293	394	134	294	322	110	246	373	152	323	379	117
20–24	447	421	94	430	427	99	409	446	109	446	432	97
25–29	359	286	80	395	353	89	402	352	88	393	308	78
30–34	241	150	62	342	272	80	349	239	68	322	196	61
35–39	142	62	44	269	182	68	237	138	58	215	100	47
40–44	54	22	41	150	90	60	154	61	40	117	40	34
45–49	9	2	22	41	16	39	35	8	23	23	6	26

Sources: Appendix 12.2; 1979 and 1989 censuses

253

13

The Economies of Central Asia: The Socialist Legacy

ALASTAIR McAULEY

The territory and peoples of what are now Uzbekistan, Tajikistan, Kyrgyzstan and Turkmenistan were ruled by Russia for almost one hundred and fifty years, first by the tsarist regime and then by the communists.[1] This relationship has had a significant impact on all aspects of social and cultural life in the area.[2] It has affected perceptions of national identity; it has shaped social and cultural attitudes. Equally if not more important, it has determined the boundaries of successor states and influenced their economic structure. These factors will continue to have an effect on the political and economic development of the region for decades to come. It could be argued, indeed, that the socialist legacy of the region will play as important a role in future developments as the continuing relationship with Russia or the new relationships with regional powers like Turkey or Iran.

It is not possible to deal with all of these issues adequately in a single chapter. Therefore, three features of post-Soviet Uzbekistan which appear to be consequences of the so-called socialist legacy of the country will be discussed. It will be suggested that the political institutions inherited from socialism are incomplete; that the economic structure is distorted; that social and economic expectations are out of line with the capacity to satisfy them. Although the focus is on Uzbekistan, it is apparent that the other Central Asian republics suffer from similar if not the same weaknesses. Indeed, there is some evidence to suggest that certain aspects are common not only to the republics of the former Soviet Union but also to the ex-socialist states of Eastern Europe.

As suggested above, the experience of being part of the Soviet

255

Union, with its planned economy and state-socialist political institutions, has not left the economies of Central Asia ready for independence and statehood. Soviet-style socialism has resulted in a number of institutional weaknesses in Uzbekistan – and, so far as can be ascertained, in other republics. In particular, the overcentralization of both political authority and administrative structures means that élites in individual republics have little experience of routine policy making in many areas of government. Furthermore, there is no institutional structure, inherited from the socialist past, with responsibility for such matters. As a result, governments in the new states are inexperienced if not incompetent in many areas. This weakness is accentuated by the political isolation imposed upon republics of the former Soviet Union by Russian paranoia if not by the constraints of the Cold War. New governments and their administrators are ignorant of the way in which most international institutions work.

Second, incorporation into the planned economy has resulted in the development of distorted economic structures. On the one hand, industrial capacity has been located with very little regard to the republic's boundaries. This has resulted in excessive trade dependence. On the other, plants are often large, inefficient and technologically obsolete. Furthermore, all economies in the region reflect the anti-services bias that was generated by the Soviet version of socialist doctrine. As a result, productivity is low and the economy's ability to satisfy consumers' expectations is limited in all republics.

Third, these expectations themselves are in part a product of the experience of socialist society. Despite the formally federal structure of its political institutions, the USSR operated in many respects as a unitary state. In particular, the authorities in Moscow attempted to pursue a common cultural and social policy. The educational system displayed many features that were common to all union republics. There was a common health service – although facilities were certainly better in some regions than in others. There was a unified social security system. These union-wide institutions resulted in expectations that, in Central Asia at least, bear little relationship to the region's 'ability to pay'. This is a source of potential political dissatisfaction; it constitutes a constraint on government's freedom of action.

INCOMPLETE POLITICAL INSTITUTIONS

The republics of Central Asia and, apparently, all the other republics of the former Soviet Union were less well-prepared for independence than the former colonies of Britain or France. In part, this was because the gaining of independence in 1992 was unexpected; there had been no extended period of preparation for the handing over of power.[3] More fundamentally, it was a consequence of the nature of the Soviet (or possibly the state-socialist) political system. There appear to be four features of the political institutions of Soviet-style socialism which have resulted in the creation of a state structure in Uzbekistan that is ignorant of the outside world and its institutions, inexperienced in political decision making and, in some respects, technically incompetent.

The first of these is the centralization of political authority. This means that the new republics have neither the institutions nor the experience of policy making in many crucial areas. This problem of overcentralization works on at least two levels. The fact that so much power was focused on the Party in Moscow means that the local party – and hence the post-independence political élite – is relatively inexperienced in policy making. For example, the Uzbek party had little or no experience of foreign affairs before 1991. In addition, the fact that so much political power was centralized in the hands of the Party means that republican political institutions are often not designed to undertake the discussion and formulation of policies; in the past, they were limited to a fairly straightforward executive role. For example, it has been suggested that labour market policy in Uzbekistan is not articulated and developed in the Uzbek Ministry of Labour. It is not even formulated in the Council of Ministers. Policy initiatives come primarily if not exclusively from the President and his advisers. It is here that one finds the successor to the Politburo.[4]

This centralization has three consequences: since it limits the number of participants in any particular policy debate, it reduces the range of policy options explored. Furthermore, since it tends to exclude specialists, it reduces the sophistication of the policy options that are discussed. Second, because there are relatively few presidential advisers, and they must, inevitably, focus upon what are perceived to be the major political problems of the day, it reduces the system's flexibility. Finally, centralization results in the over-politicization of policy making. If areas of government responsibility only attract attention when they are the source of political problems, responses – and new policy initiatives in particular – will be formulated as much for their political impact as for their technical (or social) consequences.

The centralization of political authority in the Soviet system was accompanied by centralization of administrative responsibility. This means that republican (and local) institutions have had little experience of many of the 'normal' functions of government. This centralization did not only affect politically sensitive issues; it extended to whole areas of public policy. For example, the Ministry of Education in Moscow was responsible for curriculum development for secondary schools throughout the USSR. It was also substantially responsible for the commissioning and publishing of school textbooks. As a result, the ministry in Uzbekistan had little or no experience in this area. It does not possess the appropriate divisions and will take time to develop them. Nor does the economy possess the appropriate capacity to produce the necessary pedagogical materials.[5] But this is easier to rectify.

Under Stalin, a conscious attempt was made to isolate the USSR from the capitalist world that encircled it. Attempts were made to reduce Soviet autarky under Khrushchev and his successors. But the process of opening the country up to the outside world was controlled. Soviet borders remained more or less closed. Decisions on whom to admit were taken in Moscow. The same was true about whom to allow abroad. Much of Central Asia remained substantially off-limits to west (and even east) Europeans; similarly, Uzbeks and others from the region were not given a high priority in the allocation of *komandirovki* (business trips) to the West. Insofar as official contact was encouraged, they were used to foster Moscow's relations with the Third, and particularly the Islamic, world.

At the same time, central planning and the foreign trade monopoly meant that economic contact with the outside world was mediated by Soviet foreign trade organizations. These were located almost exclusively in Moscow – and staffed by Russians or other Europeans. At best, Central Asians were permitted to engage in limited cross-border trade. All of this means that the new republics of Central Asia have neither the experience nor the personnel to operate international activities – particularly the more technical ones involving foreign currency. They are also ignorant of the way in which international trade institutions function.

Finally, the Russian (and, indeed, the Soviet) obsession with security means that all republics have had little prior experience with the organization and operation of military services. The Soviet Army was a unified structure with no 'national' units. Its officer corps was overwhelmingly European – indeed Russian. Its geographical command structure paid little if any attention to republican boundaries. As a result, none of the new republics has inherited an institutional framework that would secure civilian control of the military; they have had to improvize. Equally, none has inherited ready-made military structures with their associated logistical services.

This has meant that security policy and the creation of both appropriate forces and structures has been of considerable concern to the new regimes.

DISTORTED ECONOMIC STRUCTURE

Uzbekistan was incorporated into the Soviet planned economy, as were all the other republics of the Soviet Union. Uzbekistan's economy was planned and administered from Moscow. In fact, the Soviet economy was administered as a single entity, with little or no regard for republican boundaries, and with little respect paid to the formal powers possessed by republican governments. This state-socialist approach to economic administration resulted in the development of distorted economies in the new states that emerged out of the former Soviet Union. These distortions are, perhaps, the most negative component of the so-called socialist legacy. At all events, they have been the focus of most attention on the part of Western governments and international agencies like the IMF or the European Bank for Reconstruction and Development (EBRD).

Analytically, it is possible to distinguish between three sorts of distortion from which the economies of the republics of Central Asia suffer. First, because it was a centrally planned economy, the USSR lacked the institutions necessary to ensure stability once planners' control was relaxed and private or cooperative enterprises were permitted to operate. It lacked a well-developed banking system. It lacked a capital or money market. It lacked an effective fiscal system: it could not call upon a corps of well-trained and experienced tax-collectors operating according to a clear code of tax law. What was true of the system as a whole was equally true of its parts – the former union republics like Uzbekistan or Kirgiziia: they lacked the instruments necessary for the formulation and implementation of effective macro-economic policy.

Second, because the planned economy was based upon public ownership, production was very inefficiently organized. Enterprises were provided with inputs by planners; planners guaranteed to dispose of what was produced. Managers were thus under no economic compulsion to reduce costs below those of competitors. In the jargon of the economist: socialist enterprises were faced by soft budget constraints; as a result, they were characterized by high levels of x-inefficiency.[6] Furthermore, virtually all prices were set by the state; no attempt was made to use the price system to convey information about opportunity costs. Thus, the economy also suffered from allocative inefficiency.[7] Again, what was true of the Soviet economy as a whole was certainly true of the economies of the Central Asian republics: they suffered from substantial micro-economic inefficiency.

These macro- and micro-economic shortcomings of the state-socialist economy have received a great deal of attention from Western analysts in the last few years. Their nature and consequences are fairly well understood and will not be discussed in this chapter. Rather, it will focus upon the third feature of the economic legacy of socialism: structural distortion. There are three aspects to this: the consequences of locational policy; the consequences of Soviet development policy – or the lack of it; and the consequences of planners' preferences. Each is examined at greater length below.

As has already been pointed out, decision making in the USSR was very centralized. This was particularly true of the economy. Decisions about which plants to build and where they should be sited were made by the so-called industrial ministries; these were located almost exclusively in Moscow. This had definite – and mostly unfortunate – consequences for the development of the economies of individual republics. There were certain general policies on location, designed to ensure a degree of regional self-sufficiency and to economize on the use of transport. These were the responsibility of the All-Union and republican planning committees (*gosplans*). These bodies were responsible for drawing up annual and five-year plans. In practice, however, these policies were often ignored. Gosplan proved to be weaker, in this respect at least, than the industrial ministries.[8] Rather, it appears that an important if not the primary consideration was control: ministries – and, indeed, planners generally – preferred to deal with a few large plants rather than large numbers of small ones. The logic of planning thus reinforced all the other forces in favour of so-called gigantomania. As a result, the Soviet economy was characterized by an excess of large plants and a dearth of small or medium-sized ones in comparison with other economies at similar levels of development.

The prevalence of large plants has two consequences for the structure of individual republican economies. First, it means that within individual republics, concentration ratios are likely to be high.[9] Second, it is important to recognize that such plants existed within an All-Union network: their supplies often came from plants subordinate to the same ministry but located in other republics; similarly, their output was often shipped disproportionately to other plants under the same 'head ministry'. In consequence, as the figures in Table 13.1

show, the economies of Soviet republics like Uzbekistan appear to be extremely trade dependent. In 1989, for example, probably the last 'normal' year for the economy, imports amounted to as much as 45 per cent of GDP; even in 1991, when the central planning system had more or less collapsed, they still amounted to more than a third of national income. Moreover, as a result of the micro-economic distortions referred to above, there is no guarantee that this pattern of production was more efficient than one which might have paid more attention to republican balance. Thus, as a result of the way in which locational decisions were made under central planning, Uzbekistan and the other republics of Central Asia have inherited economies whose production structures are ill-suited to the pattern of domestic demand. At the very least, this means that they are susceptible to terms of trade shocks. In other words, changes in the value of the exchange rate between the currencies of individual Central Asian republics and those of the rest of the world, will result in significant changes in the volume of exports needed to acquire a given quantum of imports. These will have substantial effects on the standard of living.

TABLE 13.1 THE SHARE OF IMPORTS AND EXPORTS IN GROSS DOMESTIC PRODUCT (GDP): UZBEKISTAN, 1989-1991 (IN PERCENT OF GDP)

	1989	1990	1991
Exports:			
to countries outside the FSU*	5.2	3.5	3.9
to former Soviet republics	27.8	25.2	30.9
Imports:			
from countries outside the FSU	6.4	7.1	6.4
from former Soviet republics	39.2	36.6	29.5

*FSU – Former Soviet Union
Source: EBRD Review: current economic issues, July 1993, p. 170.

The second type of structural distortion that will be discussed here is a consequence of Soviet development policy.[10] In the 1920s, the economies of what were to become the republics of Central Asia were dominated by peasant agriculture. The same was true of Russia and most of the rest of the USSR. Economic development that occurred after 1928 involved the differentiation and specialization of production. This is normal. But, in the planners' conception of the future Soviet economy, Central Asia – and particularly Uzbekistan –

261

was to become the major supplier of raw cotton for the USSR as a whole. As a result, agriculture continues to dominate the economy of the region.

The position is worse than that: the Uzbek economy is dominated by cotton monoculture. In the late 1980s cotton accounted for almost a half of cultivated area; it absorbed considerable quantities of scarce water and resulted in substantial environmental pollution.[11] This cotton was not used to underpin the development of a local textile industry; the vast bulk of it was exported to the RSFSR. In return, Russia provided grain, energy and manufactures of all types. In this sense, the development gap between Central Asia and the European areas of the Soviet Union is larger now than in the 1960s. It can even be argued that, despite sixty years of Soviet development, living standards in Central Asia are not much higher than in other countries of the so-called northern tier – Iran and Turkey.[12]

Finally, the economies of the Central Asian republics, in common with the rest of the socialist bloc, have suffered distortion as a result of planners' preferences between forms of activity and opportunities for investment. The structure of all of the socialist economies of Eastern Europe, including that of the USSR, was characterized by the overdevelopment of the primary and secondary sectors of production and the underdevelopment of the so-called tertiary sector when compared with capitalist economies at similar levels of development. What this means is that, first, too many people were employed in agriculture or manufacturing and not enough were involved in services. Second, there was little innovation (or investment) in those service enterprises that did exist. The sector was undercapitalized and inefficient.

The overdevelopment of primary and secondary sectors of production under socialism has complex roots. To some extent, it is a reflection of the Marxist distinction between productive and unproductive labour. Because services were not included in net material product, planners had less incentive to commit resources to their development. Further, many traditional service-sector activities were associated with the life-style of the pre-revolutionary exploiting classes: hotels and restaurants, theatres, pubs, bars and cabarets; indeed banks and insurance companies, were all condemned as wasteful if not immoral by socialist puritans.[13] It will not be easy to modify this.

Also, the underdevelopment of the services sector is partly a statistical artifact. Under socialism, the enterprise provided its work force with a range of services that would have been supplied by separate organizations in a market economy. For example, many Soviet enterprises ran – and still run – their own pre-school child-care facilities. They possessed their own clinics. They owned and operated housing; they operated rest homes and sanatoria. Many of those employed at these facilities would be classified as working in manufacturing.

This structure for the provision of services has had another consequence. There has been little competition between various service outlets; rather, each has been involved in catering to its own captive population. As a result, there has been little or no incentive to innovate, and little concern to study and respond to the preferences of customers.

In a modern market economy, the services sector includes more than hotels and restaurants. It also contains elements of transport and communications, financial intermediaries, information technology and so on. The ex-socialist economies are deficient in all of these areas. In part, this is because such institutions were unnecessary in a planned economy. In part, particularly as it affects the failure to develop information technology, it reflects the CPSU's obsession with political censorship; but it also reflects much incompetence.

In conclusion, the republics of Central Asia embark upon an independent existence with severely distorted economies. They lack the institutions necessary to maintain macro-economic equilibrium in a mixed economy; their leaders also have little experience of formulating and implementing the necessary policies. The legacy of planning and public ownership means that there is much economic inefficiency. Finally, there are structural distortions: the services sector is underdeveloped; industry and particularly agriculture are hypertrophied. In my opinion, it is only in this last respect that the four republics differ from the rest of the CIS.[14] All the other distortions form part of the common legacy of state socialism.

UNREAL SOCIAL EXPECTATIONS

The socialist legacy that Central Asia received from the USSR comprises not only political and economic institutions, physical capital and a polluted environment; it also includes elements of the social psychology of the population. It is inevitable that attitudes towards politics and ethnic identity and towards social relations, will have been affected by the population's experience in the last seventy (or even one hundred and fifty) years' contact with Russia and through Russia with Europe. Incorporation into the USSR will also have influenced social expectations. This proposition raises a very large number of issues that cannot be discussed adequately in a single chapter. Therefore only a few observations will be made about social expectations and social policy.[15]

As part of the Soviet Union, Uzbekistan and the other republics of Central Asia acquired a state-socialist welfare system. The intellectual origins of the Soviet system of social policy are to be found in late nineteenth-century and early twentieth-century European social-democratic thought (although specific policies were adapted to meet the reality of state socialism and a centrally planned economy). After the Second World War, the Soviet government provided its citizens with a welfare system similar to that found in other European states. Soviet citizens were protected from loss of income in sickness and old age through state pensions, sick pay and disability benefits. Families received some financial assistance in bringing up their children through a program of child allowances (and, after 1974, through the institution of a family-income supplement for those whose per-capita income fell below the semi-official poverty line).[16] Finally, an array of goods and services were provided either free of charge or at subsidized prices. These include cheap housing and virtually 'free' utilities; heavily subsidized medicine; free education and so on. After almost fifty years, the population has come to accept many features of this system as rights; the benefits it provides are seen as part of the 'natural order' of things. This causes problems.

This state-socialist welfare system was predicated on levels of productivity achieved in the European part of the USSR; the republics of Central Asia did not achieve these levels. While they were part of the USSR, their 'welfare states' were supported by subsidies from the central budget. With independence these have ceased. It was sometimes claimed that Soviet pricing favoured Russia and 'exploited' the republics of Central Asia. The experience of 1991–92 does not bear this out, or at least suggests that the picture was more complex. In 1991, Uzbekistan found that it was unable to sell its cotton on the world market for as much as it would have received from the former Soviet Union – indeed, the Uzbek crop was so large that the attempt to sell it resulted in a weakening of the world market price. Russia has not yet tried to charge the world market price for the energy that it ships to the region. It is unlikely that the republics of Central Asia will be compensated by a windfall gain in their terms of trade for the loss of budgetary transfers from Moscow.[17] There is no alternative: the new governments must find ways of reducing expenditure in line with reduced revenue.

In fact, they must trim expenditure on traditional social welfare programs even more sharply. The structure of what may be called the Soviet welfare state was attuned to the institutions of a planned economy. This means that, first, it failed to furnish protection against some of the main risks that confront members of a market economy. Sooner or later, resources must be found, for instance, to provide for unemployment insurance. Second, the extensive subsidies granted under the old Soviet system of price controls resulted in an irrational structure of relative prices which contributed to the significant inefficiency in the allocation of resources that characterized state socialism. This too must change. The shifts in prices will force people to recognize the full costs of their patterns of consumption; it will lead to modifications in the composition of household expenditure. It will also lead to feelings of dissatisfaction since real consumption will fall.

The Soviet educational system was also imposed on the republics of Central Asia. This was designed, on the one hand, to invest in human capital and thus to increase both output and productivity in the region. But it was also intended to inculcate a set of cultural values that derived from the secular rationalism of nineteenth-century Europe. These values differ from those that characterized the traditional Muslim and peasant cultures of the region. In particular, they propose a very different social role for women. They downgrade, if they do not deny, the importance of religious authority. They emphasize the power of reason. The Soviet educational system was not noted for its success in creating the new Soviet man, but it did, apparently, have an influence on the consciousness, personal beliefs and social attitudes of the population of Central Asia.[18] This, too, is part of the legacy of socialism.

CONCLUSION

What has been the legacy that the republics of Central Asia have inherited from state socialism? This chapter has only managed to scratch the surface of this enormous topic. But three areas have been identified that deserve closer study. First, it is suggested that as a result of their incorporation into the centralized Soviet state, the republics acquired independence with an incomplete set of political institutions. Union republic governments lacked the administrative capacity and the experience to handle a range of routine tasks; their structures were also ill-suited to the development of a framework for policy making.

This lack of competence was to be found particularly in the economy. The absence of both institutions and experienced personnel makes it difficult if not impossible for the new governments to operate effective macro-economic policies. Equally, state ownership and central planning mean that there is a great deal of economic inefficiency. This is perhaps particularly true in agriculture where *sovkhozy* and *kolkhozy* continue to operate in almost wilful disregard of economic efficiency. More generally, prices do not reflect costs; technologies have been chosen with little regard to the scarcity of resources. There is much waste.

Some of these problems may be alleviated by privatization and the introduction of a market economy. But some are more deep-seated. They are embodied in the structure of the economy and will be eliminated only with time – and perhaps substantial investment. Enterprises are almost always too large. They are sometimes ill-suited to their markets: they produce the wrong goods using inappropriate technologies. As far as Uzbekistan is concerned, too much effort was devoted to the production of raw cotton. The state and collective farm system did not provide incentives to use resources efficiently; it did not encourage individual farmers to seek ways of improving yields or reducing costs. Also, in Uzbekistan too little was done to encourage the development of the services sector.

The socialist legacy was not confined to political and economic institutions, however. Socialism also influenced social expectations. On the one hand, having been part of an essentially European welfare state for about half a century, the population has come to take its benefits for granted. But these benefits have been provided to a considerable extent on the basis of transfers from Moscow which, with independence, have ceased. The population is now poorer than it was. It will find it difficult to adapt to its new reduced circumstances. (Since the introduction of a market economy is likely to result in an increase in inequality, the reduction in the standard of living will bear particularly heavily on the least skilled.) On the other hand, it is important to recognize that the socialist legacy is not wholly negative. The Soviet educational system has encouraged the spread of secular rationalism. More simply, it has created a literate and relatively skilled population. On the whole, this must be an asset for the new states contemplating an independent future.

NOTES

1. This relationship appears to have been much more clearly 'colonial' than that between Moscow (or St. Petersburg) and the Ukraine or Belorussia. The colonial character of Russian rule was quite explicit under the tsars. Since many features of Russian rule persisted across the revolution, as it were, it continued to be colonial, however it was described in Soviet ideology – see Ralph Clem, 'The Frontier and Colonialism in Russian and Soviet Central Asia' and L. Schwartz, 'The Political Geography of Soviet Central Asia: Integrating the Central Asian Frontier', in Robert Lewis (ed.) *Geographic Perspectives on Soviet Central Asia* (London: Routledge, 1992), pp. 19–36, 37–73, respectively. But this is not an argument that will be pursued in this chapter. For present purposes, it does not matter how the relationship between Moscow and its former Central Asian territories is described.

2. It also seems to have affected both the public status of religion and the nature of religious belief within the population. But this topic will not be explored any further in this chapter.

3. Up until August 1991, the hand-over had been contested everywhere. The Minsk and Alma-Ata Declarations of autumn 1991 foresaw a privileged position for the ruble in the new states and this logically entailed a special status for the Russian Central Bank, although this was not fully recognized by those who signed these declarations. In some republics, particularly the Baltic states, the power contest continued even after independence.

4. Overcentralization of political institutions is a problem not only in the fomer Soviet Union; it also affects the ex-socialist states of Eastern Europe. As one commentator has written: '...the structure of central government has not changed and still largely mirrors the old planned, nationalized economy...[N]o democratic equivalent has been found for the strong centralizing, supervising and co-ordinating authority of the Communist Party — once exercised through the Politburo and the Secretariat of the Central Committee' – Z. Pelczynski, *An Account of the Polish Experience with Public Administration Reform since 1989*, mimeo, Oxford, June, 1993, p. 1.

5. On this theme, see William Fierman, 'Independence and the Declining Priority of Language Law Implementation in Uzbekistan', in this volume.

6. X-inefficiency is a concept introduced by the American economist Harvey Liebenstein. It refers to situations where a firm produces at a point *inside its production function*. That is, it uses more resources than 'necessary' to produce its output. Hence costs are higher. Liebenstein suggests that a degree of monopoly power is necessary if x-inefficient firms are to survive. But, the socialist experience suggests that any system which provides firms with soft budget constraints will also result in x-inefficient production. See McAuley, 'The Political Economy of Privatisation', in L. Somogyi, *The Political Economy of the Transition Process in Eastern Europe* (Aldershot: Edward Elgar, 1993), pp. 190–6, for a full discussion.

7. Allocative efficiency is the traditional concern of the neo-classical microeconomist. It is characterized by coincidence between marginal rates of substitution in production and marginal rates of transformation. It is, supposedly, ensured by competitive markets. See McAuley, 'The Political Economy', for further discussion of this point.

8. See V. V. Kistankov, *Territorial'naia organizatsiia proizvodstva* (Moscow: Ekonomika, 1981); A. T. Khrushchev, *Geografiia promyshlennosti SSSR* (Moscow: Mysl', 1979).

9. The 'concentration ratio' is defined as the proportion of the output (or employment) of an industry accounted for by its largest firms. In Western practice, one encounters most commonly either three-firm or five-firm concentration ratios. They are used to provide an empirical analogue to monopoly power.

10. For a fuller analysis of the consequences of Soviet development policy on the economic structure and living standards in Central Asia, see McAuley, 'Soviet Development Policy in Central Asia' in R. Cassen (ed.), *Soviet Interests in the Third World* (London: Sage, 1985); and 'Central Asian Economy in Comparative Perspective', in M. Ellman and V. Kontorovich (eds.), *The Disintegration of the Soviet Economic*

System (London: Routledge, 1992).

11. *Strany-chleny SNG: statisticheskii ezhegodnik* (Moscow, 1992), p. 457.
12. McAuley, 'Central Asian Economy'.
13. Maurice Dobb, *Soviet Economic Development since 1917*, 5th ed. (London: Routledge & Kegan Paul), 1960.
14. In many respects Kazakhstan can be numbered with the four republics that the Soviet Union included in the region of Central Asia. But it is not clear that agriculture in Kazakhstan was overdeveloped relative to industry.
15. Some of the other issues raised here are discussed in McAuley, 'Soviet Development Policy'; 'Nation and Nationalism in Central Asia', in C. Keeble, *The Soviet State: The Domestic Roots of Soviet Foreign Policy* (London: Gower, 1984).
16. McAuley, *Economic Welfare in the Soviet Union* (Madison: Univ. of Wisconsin Press, 1979), p. 282–5.
17. McAuley, 'The Economic Consequences of Soviet Disintegration', *Soviet Economy* 7, 3 (July–Sept. 1991) pp. 189–214.
18. This is an important topic that has not been studied sufficiently by Western specialists. But it is mentioned by Violet Conolly, *Beyond the Urals: Economic Development in Soviet Asia* (Oxford: Oxford University Press, 1967); Gregory Massell, *The Surrogate Proletariat: Moslem Women and Revolutionary Strategies in Soviet Central Asia, 1919–1929* (Princeton: Princeton University Press, 1974); Geoffrey Wheeler, *The Modern History of Soviet Central Asia* (London: Weidenfeld and Nicholson, 1964).

14

Roots of Diversity and Conflict: Ethnic and Gender Differences in the Work Force of the Former Republics of Soviet Central Asia

MICHAEL PAUL SACKS

The successor states of the former USSR are far from stable democracies moving steadily toward market economies. Instead, there is great diversity among these states, and the political and economic outcomes are as yet unclear. In former Soviet Central Asia there are particularly acute struggles to establish or sustain stable political systems and growing economies. New structures must rest upon a foundation of demographic and employment patterns continuing from the Soviet period and even earlier. This chapter assesses some important patterns revealed by recently released data from the Soviet censuses of 1979 and 1989 and the continuities made clear from a look back at the census of 1926.

INTRODUCTION

Central Asia is here defined as including the four former republics of Uzbekistan, Kirgiziia, Tajikistan and Turkmeniia.[1] Uzbekistan is by far the largest, with a population in 1989 of 19.8 million. Kirgiziia had 4.3 million, Tajikistan had 5.1 million, and Turkmeniia had 3.5 million.[2]

All of the Central Asian republics are extremely multi-ethnic. Table 14.1 shows only those groups that comprised at least four per cent of the total population. The ethnic groups in the table represented from 79 to 92 per cent of each republic's population.

There is no denying the strength of ethnic identification and the extent to which individuals perceive their own standing as tied to the relative position of their ethnic group in society. Central Asian states are named for the ethnic group which is currently the majority within their boundaries. A quarter to nearly a half of the population of each state comprises minority ethnic groups. For decades the federal structure of the USSR fostered the development of powerful indigenous élites within the republics.[3] Whichever indigenous ethnic group controlled the political system acquired far greater importance in the independent states. The collapse of the Soviet centre has further shifted political contention to the periphery. As the civil war in Tajikistan and the repression of opposition groups in Uzbekistan illustrate, there are deep intra-ethnic political and religious divisions.

Drawing on evidence from a wide diversity of multi-ethnic states in transition, Donald Horowitz saw the political system to be a key arena for 'struggles over relative group worth'.[4] The affirmation of status could take on far greater importance than material gain:

> The fear of ethnic domination and suppression is a motivating force for the acquisition of power as an end....Fundamental issues, such as citizenship, electoral systems, designation of official languages and religions, the right of groups to 'special position' in the polity, rather than merely setting a framework for politics, become the recurring subjects of politics. Conflicts over needs and interest are subordinated to conflicts over group status and over the rules to govern conflict. Constitutional consensus is elusive, and the symbolic sector of politics looms large.[5]

But there is more at stake than just symbols. Political and economic resources do not always correspond. Independence has strengthened the control of the eponymous group over the state, while in recent decades the population of eponymous ethnicity has tended to grow the fastest. Yet an increase in the share of the population or of political power has not readily translated into an increase in the group's share of the economy. Several minority groups have long shown high achievement;[6] some have the added support of powerful nearby states. Russians are the largest minority group in Central Asia as a whole. Uzbeks greatly outnumber all other ethnic groups in Central Asia. They are also the largest minority group in Tajikistan and the second largest minority in Kyrgyzstan and Turkmenistan.

The severe clashes between Uzbeks and Kyrgyz in the Osh Oblast of Kirgiziia in June 1990 illustrates problems that can arise. The incidents stemmed in part from resentment by Kyrgyz that Uzbeks dominated retail trade, public dining and the taxi service – jobs which 'provide considerable opportunities for satisfying consumer demand in

TABLE 14.1 URBANIZATION AND ETHNIC COMPOSITION OF THE CENTRAL ASIA REPUBLICS, 1970–89

Republic and ethnicity	Percentage residing in cities			Percentage increase in the urban population		Percentage of the republic's urban population			Percentage of the republic's total population		
	1970	1979	1989	1979-89	1970-89	1970	1979	1989	1970	1979	1989
UZBEKISTAN											
Uzbeks	23.0	28.6	30.5	42.9	143.2	41.1	48.1	53.7	65.5	68.7	71.4
Russians	*89.1*	*93.4*	*94.8*	*0.8*	*19.5*	*30.4*	*24.8*	*19.5*	*12.5*	*10.8*	*8.3*
Tajiks*	25.2	37.0	32.3	36.8	166.9	2.6	3.5	3.7	3.8	3.9	4.7
Kazakhs	27.5	34.9	39.6	48.1	144.2	3.0	3.4	4.0	4.0	4.0	4.1
Tatar	73.4	82.0	88.1	-22.5	-2.2	9.7	8.5	5.1	4.9	4.2	2.4
Total population	36.6	40.8	40.6	28.0	86.1	86.9	88.3	86.1	90.7	91.6	90.9
KIRGIZIIA											
Kyrgyz	14.5	18.3	21.8	57.1	160.9	16.9	22.9	29.9	43.8	47.9	52.4
Russians	*65.9*	*68.6*	*69.9*	*2.5*	*13.6*	*51.4*	*46.4*	*39.5*	*29.2*	*25.9*	*21.5*
Uzbeks	36.1	36.2	37.5	33.9	72.2	10.9	10.9	12.7	11.3	11.3	12.9
Total population	37.4	38.3	38.2	20.4	48.0	79.3	80.2	82.0	84.3	85.1	86.8
TAJIKISTAN											
Tajiks	25.5	25.2	26.4	48.4	101.0	38.6	42.8	50.5	56.2	58.8	62.3
Russians	*93.8*	*94.1*	*93.9*	*38.7*	*54.8*	*30.0*	*28.3*	*22.0*	*11.9*	*10.4*	*7.6*
Uzbeks	21.9	18.6	18.9	-1.9	13.0	13.5	12.4	13.6	23.0	22.9	23.5
Total population	37.1	34.6	32.5	25.8	53.7	82.2	83.5	86.2	91.0	92.1	93.4
TURKMENISTAN											
Turkmen	31.7	33.0	33.8	37.4	90.8	47.6	47.6	53.8	68.4	68.4	72.0
Russians	*95.7*	*96.5*	*96.9*	*-4.0*	*8.0*	*25.7*	*25.7*	*20.3*	*12.6*	*12.6*	*9.5*
Uzbeks	54.6	53.4	51.6	31.1	67.0	9.5	9.5	10.3	8.5	8.5	9.0
Total population	47.9	47.4	45.2	21.5	53.9	82.9	82.9	84.4	89.5	89.5	90.5

*The especially high growth of Tajiks in Uzbekistan is surely inaccurate, because the 1979 census results seriously underreported the number of Tajiks - A. A. Il'khamov, 'Uzbekistan: etnosotsial'nye problemy perekhodnogo perioda'. Sotsiologicheskie issledovaniia 8 (1992), pp. 12–17.

Sources: Tsentral'noe statisticheskoe upravlenie pri sovete ministrov SSSR (TsSU), Itogi vsesoiuznoi perepisi naseleniia 1970 goda, Vol. 4: natsional'nyi sostav naseleniia SSSR, soiuznykh i avtonomnykb respublik, kraev, oblastei i natsional'nykb okrugov (Moscow, 1973), Tables 11, 22, 24, 27; Gosudarstvennyi komitet SSSR po statistike (Goskomstat SSSR), Itogi vsesoiuznoi perepisi naseleniia 1979 goda, Vol. 4: Natsional'nyi sostav naseleniia SSSR, Part I, Book 2 (Moscow, 1989), Tables 19, 21, 24; Statisticheskii komitet Sodruzhestva Nezavisimykh Gosudarstv. (Statkom SNG), Itogi vsesoiuznoi perepisi naseleniia 1989 goda, Vol. 7: Natsional'nyi sostav naseleniia SSSR, Part 2 (Minneapolis: East View Publications, 1993), Tables 9, 20, 22, 25.

a general environment of consumer scarcity'.[7] A survey of the population showed that this situation 'generated a feeling among the Kyrgyz population, especially young people, of wounded pride and deprivation in their own land', while Uzbeks were angered at their underrepresentation in the *oblast* government, the police and trade unions.[8]

Privatization provides new types of opportunities, but a prior advantageous economic position may help a group to sustain or advance its lead over others. If the state is weakened, lacks sufficient resources or is opposed to intervention on ideological grounds, it may be more difficult than in the Soviet past to effectuate policies that reduce group differences in occupational attainment. Huskey notes that 'the ethnic Kyrgyz will be especially vulnerable in the transition to a market-oriented economy. As a group, they have neither the education and skills nor the commercial traditions of the Uzbeks or the Koreans living in Kyrgyzstan.'[9]

EARLY ETHNIC STRATIFICATION

Current ethnic group differences have strong roots in the past. The census of 1926 was particularly valuable for examining these roots, as it included very detailed occupational data by ethnicity. This section examines evidence for Uzbekistan alone, but it points to patterns that were present throughout Central Asia.[10]

As is true today, in 1926 Uzbekistan's indigenous ethnic groups (about two-thirds were recorded as Uzbeks and one-sixth as Tajik) were far more concentrated in agriculture than were the Russians and Ukrainians. Among those aged 20–59, Russians and Ukrainians comprised eight per cent of the population but 43 per cent of the nonagrarian work force.

Slavic and indigenous ethnic groups differed substantially in the type of nonagricultural work they did. Among all the 141,000 workers and employees of indigenous ethnicity employed outside agriculture, 40 per cent of the males and 92 per cent of the females worked in small-scale and handicraft production. This compared with only seven to eight per cent in this type of production among Russians and Ukrainians. The Slavs were far more likely to be in more modern, large-scale, institutional settings.

Metallurgy, a male occupational preserve, is an excellent illustration. The typical Slavic metalworker was employed in a factory; nearly two-fifths worked as fitters (machine assemblers), who were almost exclusively of Slavic ethnicity. The indigenous metal workers were employed primarily (59 per cent) as blacksmiths. They worked in small-scale production either alone or with members of their family.

Experience in cottage industry did not serve as a bridge to employment in the growing modern sector of the economy. When indigenous male workers were employed outside a family setting, over two-thirds were categorized as unskilled manual labour. Only one-fifth of Slavic males working outside a family setting were listed as unskilled.

For women of indigenous ethnicity there were very limited opportunities for employment outside agriculture. Under two per cent of women of indigenous ethnicity between the ages of 20 and 59 worked outside agriculture as compared with 11 per cent among the men. Nearly all women employed outside agriculture (87 per cent) fell into two categories: textile workers and seamstresses.

There were lasting consequences to the severe limitations on female labour and the concentration of men in cottage industry or in unskilled labour when they worked in factories. With the expansion of cities and industrialization, the Slavic groups had a clear advantage over the indigenous ethnic groups, and females continued to lag behind men in their occupational advancement. As is shown below, these early patterns also fostered important gender differences among ethnic groups.

ETHNIC DIFFERENCES IN EMPLOYMENT

By 1989 Russians were still very underrepresented in agriculture and overrepresented in industry and many other sectors of the labour force. In 1989 Russians comprised 11 to 12 per cent of the employed population in Uzbekistan, Tajikistan and Turkmeniia. They comprised less than one per cent of the workers in the agricultural branch of the economy but were over one-fifth of the workers in industry. In Kirgiziia, Russians were a quarter of the work force, with nearly seven per cent of those employed in agriculture and over two-fifths of those employed in industry.[11]

In 1977 in each of the Central Asian republics, the eponymous ethnic group comprised 58 to 67 per cent of agricultural workers.[12] The group's share among industrial workers ranged from a low of 15 per cent in Kirgiziia to between 34 to 38 per cent in the other three republics. There were substantial increases by 1988. The share of the eponymous group among industrial workers rose to 25 per cent in Kirgiziia and 48 to 53 per cent in the other republics.[13] There can be no question that the indigenous ethnic groups in Central Asia were clearly being drawn into modern sectors of the labour force.

Unfortunately, the only Soviet census publications to provide detailed data on the ethnic composition of the labour force were those for 1926. To go beyond these few figures for branch of the economy, one must rely on indirect measures and on extrapolating from data on population composition.

Given the concentration of Soviet industry in urban areas, the degree of urbanization is a rough indicator of economic development. In 1989 the Central Asian republics varied from 33 per cent urban in Tajikistan to 45 per cent urban in Turkmeniia. Due largely to the higher birth rates in rural areas, the Central Asian republics were actually less urban in 1989 compared with 1979, or even with 1970 in the cases of Tajikistan and Turkmeniia. Russia, by contrast, was 62 per cent urban in 1970, 69 per cent urban in 1979 and 74 per cent urban in 1989.

Within each republic, there are sharp differences among ethnic groups, and these again must reflect differences in group presence in the modern sector of the economy. Few Russians lived outside the cities (figures for Russians are italicized in Table 14.1). The only exception is Kirgiziia where Russians have a longer history of settlement in rural areas.[14] In 1989, 70 per cent of Russians in Kirgiziia were urban; in the other republics Russians varied between 94 and 97 per cent urban. In 1989 only one-fifth to one-third of the eponymous ethnic group was urban.

Uzbeks were among the top three ethnic groups in Kirgiziia, Tajikistan and Turkmeniia. In all of Central Asia in 1989 there were 16.2 million Uzbeks, by far the largest ethnic group in the region. Within the territory of the former USSR, there were 2.6 million Uzbeks living outside Uzbekistan, over two million of whom were located in Central Asia. This population dispersion stemmed from the way republic boundaries were drawn in 1924.[15]

Uzbeks in Kirgiziia and Turkmeniia were far more urban than the titular ethnic groups. This too reflects early ethnic stratification. For example, in Kirgiziia in 1926, when almost all Kyrgyz dwelt in the countryside, nearly half the Uzbeks lived in cities. Russians and Ukrainians comprised half the nonagricultural labour force, over one-fifth were Uzbek and only ten per cent were Kyrgyz.[16]

As expected from their growth among workers in industry, between 1979 and 1989 the eponymous ethnic group increased substantially in the cities and became a majority of the urban population in Uzbekistan, Tajikistan and Turkmeniia. Their urban growth greatly outpaced Russians as well as Uzbeks outside Uzbekistan (see Table 14.1, columns 4 and 5). In Kirgiziia the rise in the proportion of Kyrgyz was especially dramatic, but the urban areas were still less than a third Kyrgyz even by 1989. The Russian share of the population has been falling in all four former republics. Reversing the trend over many decades, in the 1980s and 1990s there has been a net outmigration of Russians from Central Asia.[17]

Between 1970 and 1989 the cities of Russia grew by one-third. Table 14.1, column 5 shows that during the same period the urban population of eponymous ethnicity in Central Asia rose between 91 per cent (in Turkmeniia) to 161 per cent (in Kirgiziia). It is clearly important to distinguish between urban growth (increase in size of the urban population) and urbanization (growth in the proportion of the population living in cities). A major problem for the region is to deal with this enormous total population increase combined with insufficient expansion of employment opportunities.

AGRICULTURE AND GENDER DIFFERENCES

Though the population continued to be predominantly rural, most of the employed population in Central Asia worked outside agriculture. Agriculture, of course, remained very important and a key indicator of the low level of the region's economic development and the inequality among groups. The number working in agriculture was surely greater than needed for the most efficient production.[18] Gleason argues that during the Brezhnev years concern about the possibility of high unemployment contributed to a policy of limited mechanization of cotton production. The failure to modernize could only temporarily defer both population and economic problems.[19]

In Russia only eight per cent were employed in agriculture in 1989, down from 14 per cent in 1970 (see Table 14.2). In Central Asia in 1989 the force employed in agriculture ranged from 19 per cent in Kirgiziia to a high of 35 per cent in Tajikistan. Far from stagnating over this period, the proportion in agriculture had declined appreciably in both Kirgiziia and Uzbekistan; Tajikistan and Turkmeniia lagged behind.

All groups did not benefit equally from the expansion of other areas of the economy. In Russia the number of women employed in agriculture fell from 4.7 million in 1970 to 2.1 million in 1989. Among the employed population, by 1979 fewer of the women than of the men worked in agriculture. This was a particularly positive development given the very arduous nature of female agrarian labour and the limited opportunities for upward mobility for women in the countryside.[20] In Central Asia, except for Kirgiziia, females were far more likely to be working in agriculture than were men. Between 1979

275

TABLE 14.2 PERCENTAGE EMPLOYED IN AGRICULTURE IN CENTRAL ASIA
AND RUSSIA, 1979–1989

	Republic				
	Russia	Uzbekistan	Kirgiziia	Tajikistan	Turkmeniia
ALL WORKERS					
1970	14.1	35.9	29.0	39.0	33.2
1979	10.5	33.8	27.0	40.3	34.6
1989	7.5	25.3	18.8	34.6	31.5
FEMALES					
1970	14.6	44.4	33.5	48.3	41.4
1979	9.6	42.5	30.7	53.9	44.1
1989	5.6	28.7	18.3	43.7	38.6
MALES					
1970	13.6	28.1	24.8	31.4	26.3
1979	11.4	25.7	23.6	27.8	26.0
1989	9.4	22.5	19.3	27.9	25.7
DIFFERENCE BETWEEN FEMALES AND MALES					
1970	1.0	16.2	8.7	16.9	15.1
1979	-1.8	16.8	7.2	26.1	18.1
1989	-3.8	6.2	-1.0	15.8	12.9

Sources: TsSU, *Itogi vsesoiuznoi perepisi naseleniia 1970 goda*, Vol. 6:
Raspredelenie naseleniia SSSR po zaniatiiam (1973), Tables 3, 6, 13, 14, 16, 19,
22, 29, 30, 32.
Goskomstat SSSR, *Itogi vsesoiuznoi perepisi naseleniia 1979 goda*, Vol. 9:
Raspredelenie naseleniia SSSR i soiuznykh respublik po zaniatiiam, Part 2
(1993), Tables 3, 6, 13, 14, 16, 19, 22, 29, 30 32.
Statkom SNG, 1993. *Itogi vsesoiuznoi perepisi naseleniia 1989 goda*, Vol. 11:
Zaniatiia naseleniia SSSR, Part 1: Tables 2, 3.

and 1989 the proportion of employed women in agriculture fell sharply in Uzbekistan and Kirgiziia, while the gender gap and the proportion of employed women in agriculture remained much higher in Tajikistan and Turkmeniia.

Young workers benefited far less from the shift away from agriculture than did older workers.[21] The highest proportion in agriculture in 1979 was among those in their forties and early fifties. This was especially true in the more developed republics of Kirgiziia and Uzbekistan. But by 1989 the young were at a distinct disadvantage. They had not gained as much from the change as had those aged 40–54. For example, in Uzbekistan the proportion of the employed population in agriculture among those aged 40–49 fell to 24 per cent in 1989 from 38 per cent in 1979. Among those aged 20–29, 26 per cent were in agriculture in 1989, down from 31 per cent in 1979. In Tajikistan and Turkmeniia those aged 20–29 were slightly more likely to be employed in agriculture in 1989 than they were in 1979.

Demographic changes shaped the differences in the opportunities of the young and old. Between 1979 and 1989 the number of persons in their forties declined by ten to 21 per cent in the Central Asian republics. Over the same period the number aged 20–29 grew by 55 per cent in Tajikistan, 43 per cent in Uzbekistan, 40 per cent in Turkmeniia and 27 per cent in Kirgiziia.[22] In 1979 there had been under two persons aged 20–29 for every one person aged 40–49; in 1989 there were about three persons aged 20–29 to every one person aged 40–49. The younger cohort faced dramatically increased competition in schools and employment. The older cohort would find increased demand for their labour not only as a consequence of the small size of their cohort but also of the overall expanded economy and population.

The pressure on young people was manifested in decreased labour force participation rates. In 1979 labour force work rates were almost as high in Central Asia as they were in Russia. For example, among those 20–29 years old, work rates varied from 88 to 90 per cent in Central Asia compared with 90.7 per cent in Russia. In the 30–39 age group, the rates were 97.3 in Russia and between 94 and 96 in Central Asia. These figures for the whole population indicate that women's work rates must have been very high; one should not overestimate the restraints on women imposed by a Muslim heritage although, as we shall see, many rural women worked in the home or in agriculture in a solely female environment.[23]

By 1989 work rates had fallen most sharply among those aged 20–29, ranging from a drop of under six percentage points in Kirgiziia to nearly 12 points in Tajikistan. Among those 30–39 years old, in Tajikistan rates dropped by 7.8 points and by almost five points in Uzbekistan and Turkmeniia. As appears to be the case in recent years, women may have been more adversely affected than men, but data are available only for the total population.

URBAN AND RURAL EMPLOYMENT

There are valuable census data on differences between urban and rural employment. With the extreme concentration of Russians in cities, rural data isolate the indigenous population. In 1989 Russians comprised 13 per cent of the employed population in rural Kirgiziia but only about one per cent in the other three republics. Russians constituted 43 per cent of the urban employed population in Kirgiziia and 24 to 28 per cent in the other republics.[24]

Data on rural/urban differences reveal important gender variations between Russians and indigenous groups. Table 14.3 shows female representation in four areas of employment (actually branches of the economy grouped together) for 1970, 1979 and 1989. Russia is included in order to help in discerning the likely ethnic Russian pattern of labour deployment.

In line with the ethnic makeup of the regions, the largest differences are between rural Russia and rural Central Asia (see Table 14.3, columns 4 to 6). Rural Russia differs least from rural Kirgiziia because of the larger Russian presence in the Kyrgyz countryside.

Rural/urban differences in female representation are quite small in Russia. In the area of public health, education, etc., the percentage of females is actually higher in rural areas than in urban areas. By contrast, female representation in rural areas is far below that in urban areas in Tajikistan and Turkmeniia; this is true to a somewhat lesser degree in Uzbekistan.

The higher female representation in cities must be due to the presence of large numbers of Russian women. In the countryside, women's work outside farming is far more circumscribed due to both heavy family responsibilities and Muslim traditions – a situation that was common in the Middle East until at least well into the 1970s.[25] Men in rural areas had to make up for this shortage in female labour supply by entering many occupations which elsewhere in the former Soviet Union were staffed by women. In cities Russian women could provide much of the requisite female labour. Geographic segregation permitted overlapping employment of Russian women and indigenous men without members of one group interacting with the other.

TABLE 14.3 PERCENTAGE FEMALE BY BRANCH OF THE ECONOMY, 1970–1989

Branch and Republic	Urban areas			Rural areas			Urban minus rural		
	1970	1979	1989	1970	1979	1989	1970	1979	1989
Industry, construction, transportation, communication									
Russia	42.1	41.4	39.1	35.8	36.8	34.0	6.3	4.6	5.1
Uzbekistan	37.0	36.7	34.1	19.9	18.5	24.2	17.1	18.2	10.0
Kirgiziia	39.4	38.2	38.8	30.9	30.7	28.6	8.5	7.5	10.2
Tajikistan	37.0	36.5	34.0	12.7	15.6	17.4	24.3	21.0	16.6
Turkmeniia	32.9	33.8	30.0	25.2	15.1	16.0	7.7	18.8	13.9
Trade, public catering, marketing, procurement									
Russia	79.0	79.9	76.0	72.3	77.8	75.1	6.8	2.1	0.8
Uzbekistan	52.2	55.0	50.0	29.2	34.8	34.0	23.0	20.2	16.0
Kirgiziia	68.4	68.0	63.0	57.0	62.3	56.6	11.4	5.7	6.4
Tajikistan	50.1	51.9	48.6	13.4	17.9	21.1	36.7	34.0	27.6
Turkmeniia	58.6	60.6	56.9	24.4	28.1	37.4	24.2	32.6	19.5
Municipal housing, consumer services, administration									
Russia	49.8	51.2	49.7	43.3	50.2	50.6	6.4	1.0	-0.9
Uzbekistan	43.2	46.5	41.9	27.7	26.6	26.5	15.6	19.9	15.4
Kirgiziia	45.6	44.1	43.2	37.2	43.2	39.5	8.3	0.9	3.7
Tajikistan	45.4	47.5	42.9	17.3	19.0	18.0	28.1	28.5	25.0
Turkmeniia	41.8	44.1	41.6	20.4	21.8	21.8	21.5	22.3	19.8
Public health, education, science, art									
Russia	72.0	72.7	72.5	74.5	76.0	76.9	-2.5	-3.4	-4.4
Uzbekistan	69.3	72.0	72.8	47.5	55.2	63.2	21.8	16.8	9.5
Kirgiziia	71.8	73.2	73.1	63.6	65.8	69.0	8.1	7.4	4.1
Tajikistan	67.1	69.7	71.2	33.4	38.3	44.1	33.7	31.4	27.1
Turkmeniia	66.4	71.5	72.2	40.8	43.8	53.7	25.5	27.7	18.6
Total employed population (including agriculture)									
Russia	50.8	50.7	49.7	49.2	47.5	44.3	1.6	3.2	5.4
Uzbekistan	46.0	47.8	45.9	49.1	49.2	45.0	-3.0	-1.4	0.9
Kirgiziia	48.9	47.8	48.4	48.1	48.2	44.6	0.8	-0.4	3.8
Tajikistan	45.6	46.6	45.2	44.6	48.3	40.4	1.0	-1.7	4.8
Turkmeniia	43.3	45.8	44.1	48.0	49.1	45.6	-4.7	-3.3	-1.5

Sources:
TsSU, *Itogi vsesoiuznoi perepisi naseleniia 1970 goda*, Vol. 5: *Raspredelenie naseleniia SSSR po obshchestvennym gruppam* (1973), Tables 16, 23, 24, 26.
Goskomstat SSSR, *Itogi vsesoiuznoi perepisi naseleniia 1979 goda*, Vol. 8: *Raspredelenie zaniatogo naseleniia SSSR i soiuznykb respublik po otrasliam narodnogo khoziaistva: Statisticheskii sbornik* (1990), Table 2.
Statkom SNG, 'Roots of Republic Differences in Central Asia: A Comparison of the Labor Force and Population of Kyrgyzstan and Uzbekistan', *Post-Soviet Geography* 34, 1 (1993), pp. 29–32, Table 1.

Change over time is somewhat mixed, but in areas such as public health and education and in those such as trade and public catering, female representation rose in rural areas in Uzbekistan, Tajikistan and Turkmeniia. These are areas that were three-quarters female in Russia already in 1970.

Women of indigenous ethnicity appeared to be taking a growing share of jobs in the nonagrarian sector as a whole. This was especially true in Uzbekistan: in rural areas the percentage of women among those employed outside agriculture rose to 40.5 per cent in 1989, up nearly seven points from 1970. In 1989 in rural Tajikistan women comprised about a quarter of those outside agriculture and in Turkmeniia a third; in these republics there had been a two to three percentage point rise from 1970.

Widely dispersed male employment may now be limiting female work opportunities. Elsewhere in the USSR far more occupations would be reserved for women, that is, defined as 'women's work'. In rural Central Asia men may have viewed female entry into these same jobs as a threat. Segregating women from men may have been more important to indigenous men given the patriarchal values within the culture. Russian female employment in cities may have been a factor which discouraged migration of indigenous ethnic groups to urban areas. Only in Kirgiziia was rural/urban gender segregation less likely due to the far more pervasive Russian influence. In rural Kirgiziia women comprised 45 per cent of those employed outside agriculture in 1970 and 48 per cent in 1989 – well above the other Central Asia republics.

AGGREGATE GENDER SEGREGATION

Detailed occupational data can be used to explore further the extent to which men and women are employed in different jobs. If there is overlap in male and female employment as a consequence of the ethnic patterns described above, one would expect that occupational data combining rural and urban areas would show lower segregation of men from women in Central Asia (except Kirgiziia) than in Russia. Aggregate gender differences in the nonagrarian labour force can be summarized using the commonly applied index of dissimilarity.[26] This measure is equal to half the sum of the absolute differences between the distribution of males and females. It can be interpreted as the proportion of either men or women who would have to change jobs in order for women to be equally represented in all occupations.

TABLE 14.4 AGGREGATE GENDER OCCUPATIONAL SEGREGATION IN
RUSSIA AND CENTRAL ASIA, 1970–1989 (EXCLUDES AGRICULTURE)

Republic	(N = 87)			(N = 95)		(N = 106)
	1970	1979	1989	1970	1979	1989
Russia	52.6	54.5	55.5	54.3	56.8	59.4
Uzbekistan	40.4	49.1	46.7	40.8	49.6	47.6
Kirgiziia	52.5	55.3	50.9	53.4	56.4	53.0
Tajikistan	45.4	54.7	51.3	45.7	55.5	52.7
Turkmeniia	51.9	55.3	53.7	52.3	55.9	54.8

Source: Same as Table 2

The more the number of occupational categories, the greater the segregation likely to be revealed. A category with equal representation of men and women may actually contain sub-categories which are exclusively male and exclusively female. Because occupational classifications vary across censuses, it is not possible to match all categories over time. Eighty-seven categories could be matched for comparison across all three census years. Comparing just 1970 and 1979 (both in the 1979 census publication) yields 95 categories. The most detailed data, 106 categories, are available for 1989 only.[27]

All three sets of data are shown in Table 14.4. Because of the random fluctuation likely in smaller populations, Uzbekistan may provide the most accurate information on gender segregation. In 1989 there were 2.5 million women working outside agriculture in Uzbekistan. In Tajikistan and Turkmeniia there were far fewer: 435,000 and 394,000, respectively, and 665,000 in Kirgiziia. Uzbekistan consistently had the lowest level of segregation. The most detailed data, those for 1989 (see the last column), show a measure of 47.6 for Uzbekistan, nearly 12 points below Russia; the other republics were also clearly below Russia.

Segregation may have risen between 1970 and 1979. The evidence of decline between 1979 and 1989 is based on the smallest number of categories. Caution is warranted here, as workers in categories that are dropped fall into one broad residual category. Obviously the larger the residual category, the more male/female differences are concealed.

MEN IN RUSSIA AND IN UZBEKISTAN

An indirect method of discerning ethnic differences in the division of labour between men and women is to compare male employment in Uzbekistan and Russia. This comparison entails calculating for each occupation the ratio of the number of men employed in Uzbekistan to the number of men employed in Russia. Assuming that Russian men in Uzbekistan were likely to have employment patterns similar to men in

TABLE 14.5 OCCUPATIONS WITH A HIGH NUMBER OF MALES IN UZBEKISTAN AS COMPARED WITH THE NUMBER OF MALES IN RUSSIA

Occupation	Males, 1989 Number Russia	Males, 1989 Number Uzbekistan	Ratio*	Percentage Female Russia 1989	Percentage Female Uzbekistan 1989	Uzbekistan compared with Russia** 1970	Uzbekistan compared with Russia** 1979	Uzbekistan compared with Russia** 1989
Agronomists and zootechnicians	211466	29739	14.1	46	17	-30	-33	-29
Agents and expediters	61989	9594	15.5	67	21	-39	-49	-46
Managers in department stores	71289	21992	30.8	76	25	-33	-48	-51
Leaders in educational institutions	51306	9034	17.6	54	26	-19	-26	-28
House painters, plasterers	215148	53879	25.0	73	27	-18	-41	-46
Miscellaneous trade, public dining personnel	162200	34747	21.4	71	35	-36	-43	-36
Communal and everyday service workers	46320	8951	19.3	70	36	-21	-26	-34
Record-keepers	19663	6982	35.5	86	37	-52	-54	-50
Bakers, confectioners, candy makers	16415	13845	84.3	93	37	-62	-56	-56
Hairdressers and manicurists	5670	10011	176.6	96	38	-63	-64	-59
Dentists	16035	2864	17.9	72	45	-30	-37	-27
Postal workers	20221	6524	32.3	89	47	-49	-46	-42
Cooks and culinary specialists	91144	58061	63.7	91	50	-37	-41	-41
Merchandisers	21248	7529	35.4	91	56	-25	-34	-35
Booth and buffet managers, sales assist.	72991	54570	74.8	95	57	-42	-35	-38
Primary and secondary school teachers	406654	171471	42.2	78	59	-31	-26	-19
Physician assistants and midwives	27159	12123	44.6	91	60	-32	-33	-32
Misc. planning and accounting personnel	68446	57948	84.7	96	62	-26	-30	-34
Misc. cultural-enlightenment workers	14373	1886	13.1	82	63	-23	-18	-19

TABLE 14.5 (CONTINUED)

Occupation (cont.)	Males, 1989 Number		Ratio*	Percentage Female		Uzbekistan compared with Russia**		
	Russia	Uzbekistan		Russia 1989	Uzbeki-stan 1989	1970	1979	1989
Cashiers	14846	7543	50.8	97	69	-22	-24	-28
Economists and statisticians	63623	13449	21.1	93	70	-17	-19	-22
Pharmacists	3263	1945	59.6	97	77	-21	-24	-20
Telephone operators	7169	1804	25.2	92	78	-9	-11	-15
Misc. sewing machine operators	5940	1221	20.6	91	81	-12	-3	-10
Winding machine operators (textiles)	6463	1576	24.4	86	85	-5	0	-1
Waiters	14284	781	5.5	84	86	-7	0	1
Secretaries and other office personnel	19680	4427	22.5	97	88	-10	-5	-9
Heads of libraries, librarians	11748	3038	25.9	95	89	-10	-6	-6
Weavers	1678	4408	262.7	98	89	-20	-11	-9
Spinners	2036	758	37.2	97	91	-7	-4	-6
Typists and stenographers	2206	1547	70.1	99	94	-4	-3	-5
Managers and educators in children's homes	23161	7674	33.1	98	95	-1	-2	-4
Nurses	14839	6048	40.8	99	96	-3	-3	-2
Total employed population	39701126	4259411	10.7	48	45	-2	-1	-3
Total nonagrarian workers	35988781	3301083	9.2	49	43	-8	-8	-6

*The ratio of males in Uzbekistan to males in Russia times 100.
**The percentage of female in Uzbekistan minus the percentage of female in Russia.

Source: Same as Table 2.

Russia,[28] it follows that men of indigenous ethnicity were most likely to be in those occupations where the Uzbekistan/Russia ratio was high.

A high ratio was defined as double the ratio for the nonagrarian labour force as a whole. In 1989 there were 9.2 men in the nonagrarian labour force of Uzbekistan for every 100 men in the nonagrarian labour force of Russia. Occupations with a ratio of 18.4, thus, were labelled high for 1989. Table 14.5 includes any occupation that had a high ratio in any one of the three census years. Very few occupations had a ratio below 18.4 for 1989 (see column 3).

The occupational categories have been sorted according to the percentage of females in Uzbekistan in 1989 (column 5). These categories included 19 per cent of the nonagrarian male work force in Uzbekistan but only five per cent in Russia. The last three columns show the difference between the percentage female in Uzbekistan and the percentage female in Russia for 1970, 1979 and 1989. A negative figure indicates that the percentage female is lower in Uzbekistan. The columns are clearly filled with largely negative figures. Only the bottom rows show occupations which were overwhelmingly female in both Russia and Uzbekistan. The pattern of change over time is mixed across occupations, but the gap between Russia and Uzbekistan remained large. Overall, the data support the argument that males of indigenous ethnicity in Central Asia are much more likely to be employed in jobs which in Russia would be labelled 'women's work'.

CONCLUSION

Ethnic tensions are exacerbated by the weak economy and expanding population entering the work force in Central Asia. Population growth also manifests itself in a very youthful age structure. Aspirations are fuelled by greater exposure to the mass media and rising educational attainment, but, as the situation of those aged 20–29 compared with those aged 40–49 shows, the young are likely to feel a growing sense of both relative and absolute deprivation.

Just as Russians have sustained their advantage in entering the modern sectors of the economy, men continue to have an advantage over women. Women of indigenous ethnicity are far more likely to be found in agriculture than are men. While their employment rates are high despite patriarchal cultural traditions and heavy child care responsibilities, occupational opportunities for indigenous women probably remain quite limited. Revived Muslim traditions may further undermine gender equality; in fact, developments adverse to women have become widespread throughout the former USSR.[29] Gender segregation increased in the 1970s; it is less clear what occurred in the 1980s. Part of what may today be restricting female employment is a long extant pattern of male presence in jobs which elsewhere are female-dominated. This indigenous male employment pattern may have made contact with Russians more conflict-ridden and provoked indigenous men to be more patriarchal.

There are important differences between the states of Central Asia. Independence has surely spurred further differentiation. Tajikistan and Turkmenistan have particularly low levels of economic development and large differences among men and women. Russian influence has been most marked in Kyrgyzstan, where the Kyrgyz have again become a majority in their own state (from the 1940s until the 1980s the Kyrgyz had to adapt temporarily to being a minority). The Uzbeks have had a far different experience. The much larger proportion of Uzbeks in Uzbekistan and the considerable number of Uzbeks in border states shape its politics and economy.

Data on ethnic differences in the labour force of post-independence Central Asia are limited. This is probably due to the politically volatile nature of the issue and/or to post-Soviet government censorship.[30] Particularly lacking are data which distinguish among indigenous ethnic groups. This information is essential to trace shifts in ethnic, gender and regional inequality that affect the potential for solving the region's political and economic problems.

NOTES

1. It is now more common to include Kazakhstan as part of Central Asia. This is not done here, in part because of the ethnic composition of the republic and the fact that the indirect measures of labour force ethnic differences depend upon data for the republic as a whole. Unlike all the other former republics, the eponymous ethnic group comprises less than the majority of the population in Kazakhstan (Kazakhs are outnumbered by Russians and Ukrainians taken together). Kazakhs predominate in the southern part of Kazakhstan, but unfortunately data do not appear separately for this region, which should most clearly be treated as part of Central Asia.
   In accordance with the rule explained in the Note on Orthography, Kyrgyzstan and Turkmenistan are used for the post-independence period and Kirgiziia and Turkmeniia, as they were then called, for the Soviet period.
2. Gosudarstvennyi komitet SSSR po statistike (Goskomstat SSSR). *Demograficheskii ezhegodnik SSSR: 1990* (Moscow: Finansy i statistika, 1990), Table 1.5
3. Phillip G. Roeder, 'Soviet Federalism and Ethnic Mobilization', in Rachel Denber (ed.), *The Soviet Nationality Reader: The Disintegration in Context* (Boulder: Westview Press, 1992), pp. 147–78. See also D. Carlisle, 'Geopolitics and Ethnic Problems of Uzbekistan and Its Neighbours', and D. Vaisman, 'Regionalism and Clan Loyalty in the Political Life of Uzbekistan', in this volume.

4. Donald L. Horowitz, *Ethnic Groups in Conflict* (Berkeley: University of California Press, 1985), p. 185.
5. Ibid., p. 187.
6. Robert A. Lewis, Richard H. Rowland and Ralph S. Clem, *Nationality and Population Change in Russia and the USSR: An Evaluation of Census Data, 1897–1970* (New York: Praeger, 1976), pp. 333–42.
7. Aynur B. Elebayeva, 'The Osh Incident: Problems for Research', *Post-Soviet Geography* 33, 2 (1992), p. 81.
8. Ibid.
9. Gene Huskey, 'Kyrgyzstan: The Politics of Demographic and Economic Frustration', in I. Bremmer and R. Taras (eds.), *Nations and Politics in the Soviet Successor States* (Cambridge: Cambridge Univ. Press, 1992), p. 411.
10. This section is based on data from Tsentral'noe statisticheskoe upravlenie SSSR, sekstsiia perepisi (TsSU), *Vsesoiuznaia perepis' naseleniia 1926 goda* (Moscow: Izdanie TsSU Soiuza SSSR, 1929), Vols. 15 and 49. For more detailed information, see Michael Paul Sacks, 'Ethnic, Gender and Regional Differences in the Soviet Work Force in 1926: A Comparison of Russia, the Urals, and Kazakhstan and Uzbekistan', paper presented at a conference entitled, 'The Making of the Soviet Working Class', Michigan State University, 9–11 Nov. 1990.
11. Iu. V. Arutiunian, L. M. Drobizheva, M. N. Kuz'min, N. S. Polishchuk and S. S. Savoskul, *Russkie: Etnosotsiologicheskie ocherki* (Moscow: Nauka, 1992), pp. 95, 100.
12. This set of data pertains only to workers and employees, i.e., it excludes collective farm workers as well as those engaged solely in private agriculture. According to Rapawy and Heleniak, in Central Asia in 1979 there were 1.24 million workers and employees in agriculture (state farm workers) as compared with 1.75 million collective farm workers – Stephen Rapawy and Timothy E. Heleniak, 'Annual Average Employment of the Socialized Sector in Soviet Central Asia, 1970–1985', *Research Note* (July) (Washington, DC: Soviet Branch, Center for International Research, US Bureau of the Census, 1987).
13. Goskomstat SSSR, *Trud v SSSR: statisticheskii sbornik* (Moscow: Finansy i statistika, 1988), p. 22.
14. See Sacks, 'Roots of Republic Differences in Central Asia: A Comparison of the Labor Force and Population of Kyrgyzstan and Uzbekistan', *Post-Soviet Geography* 34, 1 (1993), p. 30.
15. James Critchlow, *Nationalism in Uzbekistan: A Soviet Republic's Road to Sovereignty* (Boulder: Westview Press, 1991), p. 11.
16. Sacks, 'Roots of Republican Differences', pp. 30–1.
17. Anatolii V. Topilin, 'Vliianie migratsii na etnonatsional'nuiu strukturu', *Sotsiologicheskie issledovaniia* 7 (1992), pp. 38–40.
18. Peter R. Craumer, 'Agricultural Change, Labor Supply, and Rural Out-Migration in Soviet Central Asia', in Robert A. Lewis (ed.), *Geographic Perspectives on Soviet Central Asia* (London: Routledge, 1992), pp. 132–80.
19. Gregory Gleason, 'Marketization and Migration: The Politics of Cotton in Central Asia', *Journal of Soviet Nationalities* 1, 2 (Summer 1990), pp. 66–98.
20. Sue Bridger, 'Women and Agricultural Reform', in Mary Buckley (ed.), *Perestroika and Soviet Women* (Cambridge: Cambridge Univ. Press, 1992) pp. 39–53; Sacks, *Women's Work in Soviet Russia: Continuity in the Midst of Change* (New York: Praeger, 1974).
21. The data on age differences in the remainder of this section are based on Statisticheskii komitet Sodruzhestva Nezavisimiykh Gosudarstv. (Stat.kom. SNG), *Itogi vsesoiuznoi perepisi naseleniia 1989 goda.* Vol. 10: *Raspredelenie zaniatogo naseleniia SSSR po otrasliam narodnogo khoziaistva* (Minneapolis: East View Publications, 1993); Goskomstat SSSR (1990), Table 1.5; Goskomstat SSSR, *Itogi vsesoiuznoi perepisi naseleniia 1979 goda.* Vol. 9: *Raspredelenie naseleniia SSSR i soiuznykh respublik po zaniatiiam*, Part 2 (Moscow: Goskomstat, 1990).
22. By contrast, between 1979 and 1989 the number aged 20–29 in Russia shrank by ten per cent. These figures are calculated from Goskomstat SSSR (1990).
23. It is not possible to know, however, what proportion of the women work only part-time or part of the year. Such work was very limited in the former Soviet Union as a

whole, although it may have been more common among the large families of Central Asia. Women have been doing work at home in the folk-art and sewing industries – William Moskoff, *Labour and Leisure in the Soviet Union* (New York: St. Martin's Press, 1984), pp. 26–33.

In figures for average annual employment on collective farms (but not on state farms), those who work as little as one day are counted as being employed for the whole month – see Rapawy and Heleniak, 'Annual Average Employment of the Socialized Sector', pp. 10–11. The census figures come from a different source: the occupation and type of work for which the respondent reports earning money (excluding labour in the private economy) – Goskomstat SSSR (1979), p. 4.

24. Arutiunian *et al.*, *Russkie: Etnosotsiologicheskie ocherki*, p. 95.
25. Nadia Haggag Youssef, *Women and Work in Developing Societies*, Population Monograph Series, No. 15 (Berkeley: Institute of International Studies, University of California, 1974), p. 37.
26. Gregory Williams, 'Trends in Occupational Differentiation by Sex', *Sociology of Work and Occupations*, III, 1 (1976), pp. 38–62.
27. Occupational segregation is also concealed by the fact that categories containing very low female representation were often omitted from published census tables – Sacks, *Work and Equality in Soviet Society: The Division of Labor by Age, Gender and Nationality* (New York: Praeger, 1982).
28. Cf. Arutiunian *et al.*, *Russkie: Etnosotsiologicheskie ocherki*, p. 99.
29. R. G. Ianovskii, 'Zhenshchina i obshchestvo: sotsial'no-politicheskii aspekt', *Sotsiologicheskie issledovaniia* 5 (1992), pp. 33–7.
30. For Russia, by contrast, detailed occupational data have been released which show gender difference for forty different ethnic groups – Gosudarstvennyi komitet Rossiiskoi Federatsii po statistike (Goskomstat Rossii), *Professional'nyi sostav naseleniia korennykh i naibolee mnogochislennykh natsional'nostei Rossiiskoi Federatsii* (Moscow: Respublikanskii informatsionno-izdatel'skii tsentr, 1992).

15

The Russians in Central Asia and Kazakhstan

VALERY A. TISHKOV

After acquiring their independence unexpectedly with little, if any, preparation, the states of the Central Asian region (Kazakhstan, Uzbekistan, Kyrgyzstan, Tajikistan and Turkmenistan[1]) have entered a transitional period in their histories.* This period is characterized by a search for new formulae and socio-political foundations of national development and for their own niche in the new geopolitical space. Inasmuch as the disintegration of the USSR took place under the slogan of the doctrine of ethnic nationalism, it is only natural that the proclamation of so-called 'national states' within the borders of the former union republics should be made on behalf of the 'titular' ethno-nations: the Kazakhs, Uzbeks, Kyrgyz, Turkmen and Tajiks.

These nations are mainly socio-cultural constructs of the Soviet period. However, in the past 70 years they have undergone an extremely intensive process of 'nation-building', with the regional, religious and dynastic-clan identities of the past giving way to a new ethnicity based on the concept of the 'socialist nation'. This new ethnicity was closely bound to the 'national-state delimitation' that was

*Use has been made in this paper of the results of ethno-sociological surveys conducted in Uzbekistan in 1991 and Kyrgyzstan in 1992 by a group from the Institute of Ethnology and Anthropology of the Russian Academy of Sciences (IEA, RAS) composed of A. I. Ginzburg, L. V. Ostapenko, S. S. Savoskul and I. A. Subbotina, as well as materials provided by another member of the same institute, O. I. Brusina. The author wishes to express his profound gratitude to them.
For an outline of the research of the above group and some of its results, see S. S. Savoskul (ed.), *Russkie v novom zarubezhe: Sredniaia Aziia. Etnologicheskii ocherk* (Moscow: IEA, RAN, 1993).

determined from above and the protracted sway of the republics' Communist Party élite, or *nomenklatura*, through which the Union centre exercised its rigidly centralized rule in Central Asia and Kazakhstan. The nation-building process was attended by radical changes: economic modernization, promotion of mass education and the establishment of prestigious institutions of 'national statehood' based on a new powerful stratum – the administrative, creative and scientific-technical intelligentsia. Finally, the 1960s–80s saw a noticeable shift of the demographic balance in favour of the 'titular nations', which now became the majority in all states except Kazakhstan.[2]

It is precisely these 'successes' of Soviet nationalities policy, and not just the crimes of the Soviet regime and the persisting centralization and ideological and cultural control of the Russian-speaking centre, that contributed to, in fact made possible, the powerful thrust of the Central Asian periphery toward national self-determination. Yet the old tenacious doctrine of ethno-nationalism incorporated in the Marxist-Leninist theory of nationalities and the nationalities question has also generated a major problem that the new post-Soviet states have to tackle in developing their statehood, namely the status and fate of the non-titular population, which is a sufficiently numerous component in these states (from 30 to 50 per cent). Central to this problem is the fate of the Slav, primarily the Russian, population.

DEMOGRAPHIC BACKGROUND

According to the 1989 USSR census, the Russian population in the region numbered 9,500,000 and constituted 19.3 per cent of the overall population. Russians accounted for 21.5 per cent of the population in Kirgiziia, 7.6 per cent in Tajikistan, 8.4 per cent in Uzbekistan, 37.8 per cent in Kazakhstan and 9.5 per cent in Turkmeniia. Many of the Russians were old-timers. Back in 1917 there were 1,500,000 Russians in the region making up almost ten per cent of the population of Turkestan. Slightly less than half of the Russians had settled in rural areas; the rest were urban dwellers. The newcomers from Russia had played a major part in the development of agricultural production, in irrigation, and the expansion of arable land, in building railroads and towns, and in the emergence of heavy and mining industries. This was true especially regarding northeastern Kazakhstan, which was part of the Orenburg Governorate and afterwards, up to 1936, part of the RSFSR.

Under Soviet rule, the influx of migrants from Russia increased, owing mainly to the Soviet government's doctrine of accelerated industrialization, in which the new arrivals – specialists and workers – were largely instrumental. The Engineers and technicians, scientific and medical personnel, professionals in education and the arts arrived in the cities of Central Asia and Kazakhstan. In the 1930s, settlements of deported populations from Russia and Ukraine were formed in different regions, mainly in Kazakhstan. During the war of 1941–45 a great number of factories complete with personnel were evacuated to Central Asia. Ninety large factories and about 1,000,000 people were moved to Uzbekistan alone. Many of those people stayed there after the war was over. In the postwar decades the stream of immigrants continued. In Uzbekistan, for instance, they accounted annually for eight–nine per cent of the urban population growth.[3] In large measure the influx to the cities and industrial regions was generated by extensive industrial development and housing construction (especially in Tashkent) and the workforce recruiting campaign for the new industries. The 1950s also saw a mass resettlement in Kazakhstan's 'virgin lands' of people from Russian rural areas (the Volga, Central Russia, Western Siberia).

It was only in the 1970s that the Russian population stopped growing. In the past two decades the absolute number of Russians and their share in the overall population have been steadily decreasing in Uzbekistan, Tajikistan and Turkmeniia, whereas in Kazakhstan and Kirgiziia they increased only slightly in absolute terms. Compared with the 1960s, the migration balance for the five republics was clearly negative in the 1980s (Table 15.1). According to the 1989 data, slightly less than half the Russians living in the region were born there (from 43.3 to 48.3 per cent for different republics), and about 30 per cent of the newcomers had lived there for more than ten years.[4]

TABLE 15.1 BALANCE OF MIGRATION (IN THOUSANDS).

	1961–1970	1979–1989
Kazakhstan	431	-789
Central Asia	4	-84
Uzbekistan	257	-507
Kirgiziia	126	-157
Tajikistan	70	-102
Turkmeniia	457	-850

The changes in the population pattern since the 1970s were primarily the result of the high birth rate of the 'titular', as distinct from the European, population, particularly in Uzbekistan and Tajikistan (where crisis symptoms generated by the uncontrolled population growth were discernible), the growing migration of people of local nationalities from the countryside to the cities, and the outflow of the Russian-speaking population from the region. The Russian rural population was dwindling the fastest, leaving for other parts of the USSR and for the region's industrial centres. Today, Russians and people of other European nationalities live mainly in the urban areas. The proportion of Russians who are urban dwellers varies from 70 per cent in Kyrgyzstan and 77 per cent in Kazakhstan, to 94–97 per cent in Tajikistan, Uzbekistan and Turkmenistan (as against 20.5 per cent, 38.5 per cent, 26.5 per cent, 28 per cent, and 34 per cent of the titular population, respectively). Only in Kazakhstan and Kyrgyzstan is the proportion of Russians living in the countryside still considerable: approximately 20 and 10 per cent in 1989.

THE SOCIO-ECONOMIC SITUATION

When the USSR existed, the Russians in Central Asia and Kazakhstan were employed primarily in the development of industry, transport and urban construction. Their social and professional pattern is basically different from the employment pattern of the local nationalities. Indeed, traditionally, it was mostly Russians who worked in industry, transport, construction and communications where their share exceeded their proportion in the working population many times over. Among the intelligentsia they comprise the majority of the specialists in technical fields and in the exact sciences.[5] Only in Kazakhstan and Kyrgyzstan is the percentage of Russians employed in agriculture still high; they work mainly as machine operators and agricultural and animal husbandry specialists. In contrast, people of the titular nationalities are predominantly employed in agriculture. In the cities, Russians work mostly in trade and the services; among white-collar workers they comprise the majority of managerial personnel, cultural workers and the professional intelligentsia (Table 15.2). According to the 1979 data, the share of Russians employed in industry ranged from 22.4 to 32.6 per cent of the entire working population in Uzbekistan, Kirgiziia, Tajikistan and Turkmeniia, and in construction, from 12.2 to 18.2 per cent. For the titular nationalities the respective figures were from 9.2 to 11.1 per cent in industry and from 4.8 to 8.4 in construction. The proportion of Russians working in agriculture was 10.2 per cent in Kirgiziia, and from 2.7 to 3.4 per cent in the other republics, while the figures for the titular nationalities were from 52.6 to 56.9 per cent.[6] According to the 1989 data, 22.4 per cent of the Kazakh population and 52.6 per cent of the Russian population of Kazakhstan were employed in ·industry. The share of Russians engaged in agriculture was steadily decreasing and in 1989 stood at 17.7 per cent in Kazakhstan, 6.8 per cent in Kirgiziia, 0.6 per cent in Uzbekistan, and 0.7 per cent in Turkmeniia and Tajikistan. However, Russians accounted, respectively, for 20.4 per cent, 13.9 per cent, 4.2 per cent, 5.9 per cent, 3.9 per cent of farm managers and agricultural specialists and 26.8 per cent, 17.5 per cent, 1.3 per cent, 2.1 per cent, 2.2 per cent of machine operators.[7]

TABLE 15.2 DYNAMICS OF THE PERCENTAGE OF RUSSIANS AMONG SPECIALISTS, SENIOR MANAGERS AND HIGHLY SKILLED WORKERS 1979–1989. URBAN POPULATION. PARTICIPATION INDEX*

Republic	Specialists and senior managers		Highly skilled workers	
	1979	1989	1979	1989
Uzbekistan	128	121	115	113
Tajikistan	125	122	108	107
Turkmeniia	128	129	101	101
Kazakhstan	98	99	107	105
Kirgiziia	107	106	100	99

The table was compiled on the basis of the USSR censuses of 1979 and 1989.
* The participation index is calculated by the formula:

$$\frac{\text{Percentage of Russians in this category of manpower}}{\text{Percentage of Russians in the gainfully employed population}} \quad \text{x} \quad 100.$$

The higher the participation index, the greater the Russian representation in the given category. The value of the index below 100 shows that Russian representation in the given category is lower than in the gainfully employed population.

The social and professional differentiation along ethnic lines was and remains greater than in other regions of the former USSR. The local population is keeping within its traditional village-agrarian economy niche, although in the past few decades it made a dramatic breakthrough into the more prestigious spheres of management, public education, public health and law, and quite recently also into trade and commerce, light industry and urban services. The Russians have not expanded their social and professional profile in the 1990s but they have increased their share in the heavy industry work force and in the industrial and technical intelligentsia.

Even before the dramatic changes of the perestroika era began, then, the employment pattern of the Central Asian republics was marked by undercurrents of ethnic conflict, and the 'Russian problem' existed, although it had not surfaced. It was reflected in a major way in the inadequate Russian representation both in the service sector (teachers, doctors, lawyers, the non-scientific intelligentsia) and in the power structure, especially in the courts of law, the militia and republican and local level administration. The peculiarities of the Russians' social and professional composition, that previously made for their comparatively high living standard, have become definitely negative over the past few years, in view of the economic-sectoral and production reorientation: a reduction in heavy industry enterprises, including the military-industrial complex, a general crisis in government-subsidized spheres and an upsurge of commercial, broker and financial activity.

The Russians have been faced with the serious problem of finding a new niche in the changing economic and socio-cultural situation. The results of a sociological survey conducted in 1992 in Kyrgyzstan by staff of Moscow's Ethnology and Anthropology Institute show that the prospect of reorientation towards employment in the food and light industries, in agriculture, trade and the services is acceptable to them. However, for the Russians to actually implement this reorientation, namely, to change their profession, sphere of activity and even forms of property (from state and cooperative to private) is no simple matter in this region of tenacious labour traditions. The Russians in Kyrgyzstan who wish to work in trade and the services, as middlemen or in finance are three times as numerous as those already employed in these fields. Yet their prospects of 'ousting' representatives of the titular nationality, who are even now predominant in these occupations and are desirous of increasing their representation in them in the future (Table 15.3), are dim indeed.

More active involvement of Russians in free enterprise could provide a partial solution to the problem. However, the prospects for such an involvement are limited as a result of insufficiently developed market relations and shortage of initial capital, which as a rule is accumulated illegally or in trade, coupled with misgivings regarding the status of Russians in the newly emerged states. According to the

TABLE 15.3 BREAKDOWN OF RUSSIANS AND KYRGYZ BY
EMPLOYMENT BRANCH: REAL AND PREFERRED* IN PERCENTAGE OF
URBAN POPULATION).

Industry	Russians		Kyrgyz	
	Real	Preferred	Real	Preferred
Heavy industry	34.0	12.9	20.1	9.3
Light and food industries	8.9	12.5	9.8	16.2
Construction, transport, communications	20.5	9.5	22.6	12.3
Public health, education, science, culture, the arts	16.9	14.1	20.9	11.6
Trade, services, brokering, finance	10.5	32.0	14.2	36
Agriculture	2.1	12.9	8.1	13.9

* The real branch breakdown was calculated on the basis of the 1989 USSR census. The preferred breakdown was calculated on the basis of a 1992 ethno-sociological survey undertaken in Kyrgyzstan on the basis of answers to the question: "In what branch of the economy would you prefer to be employed?"

above-mentioned survey, only 16 per cent of Russian urban dwellers in Kyrgyzstan would like to become owners of private enterprises, while the number of such people among the Kyrgyz is twice as high. Many Russians are pessimistic about their chances of acquiring property in Kyrgyzstan (land or an enterprise in the sphere of production or in the service sector, a house, an apartment or shares) and nearly a quarter think that, given a future process of privatization, their chances are worse than those of the Kyrgyz.

The situation is especially complicated for those of the Russian intelligentsia whose work involves contacts with the local population and use of the language of the titular nationality. Insufficient knowledge of the language of the titular nationality is a formidable obstacle for Russians working in public health, education, culture and administrative work and a principal argument in favour of their dismissal. Such a state of affairs may further reduce the already insignificant number of Russian teachers, doctors, lawyers, writers and journalists, which would be detrimental to the entire Russian-speaking population, including people of the titular nationalities close to Russian culture.

A resurgence of Muslim traditions in some of the Central Asian countries instills in the younger generation and introduces into everyday culture and the arts, traditions which are far removed from European canons, and will only complicate the activities of Russian educationalists and cultural workers. The spread of Islam may also affect the attitude of the population to female labour. The situation where women work as managers or practise technical professions, which is normal for Russians, may evoke a negative reaction on the part of zealous Muslims and adversely affect job opportunities for Russian women. The problem of employment is very acute for Russian women as it is. In all the republics they are the first to be fired. Russian women living in an alien ethnic environment constitute the most vulnerable stratum because they are more widely employed in public health, education, office work, and in general as white-collar workers; the percentage of women among skilled blue-collar workers is small. Russian women, moreover, are even less familiar than Russian men with the language of the titular nationality.

The problem of employment, education and professional training is no less acute for young Russians living in the former Soviet non-Russian republics. Starting with the 1960s and up to the end of the 1980s, the number of Russian university and college students declined steadily in all the republics. The curtailment in the past few years of Russian-language tuition in technical schools and institutes of higher learning, can be expected to exacerbate this trend.

What solutions can be offered? What are the employment prospects for Russians who have suddenly found themselves living in a new state? Much will depend on the economic and political orientation of the former union republics, the rate of development of market relations within these countries, and the steps that will be taken to solve the problems of the non-titular population and to improve inter-ethnic relations.

Judging by the results of the ethno-sociological survey in Kyrgyzstan, the majority of the local Russian population is at a parting of the ways and is not taking any decisive steps to change jobs, profession, or place of residence. And this is probably the case in the other Central Asian states. A solution may be gleaned from the answers of respondents to the question of how they would advise young Russians to make their way in life. Significantly, only 14 per cent of Russians would advise them to leave Kyrgyzstan, while a much larger proportion (31 per cent) suggested that young Russians should study

Kyrgyz and Kyrgyz culture and become full-fledged citizens of the country with equal opportunities for social advancement. Very significantly, 60 per cent of the Kyrgyz chose the latter variant for young Russians and only 12 per cent suggested that they should leave the republic.

On the whole, Russians are highly qualified, possess organizational potential, technical skills, and extensive professional contacts in various regions of the Soviet Union and beyond its borders. Their chances to reconstruct their lives and find appropriate jobs both inside their republic and outside it are still quite good. The most favourable situation seems to obtain today in Kazakhstan, where the influence of Islam is weaker, economic reorganization is more intensive and Russian skilled workers, who constitute a considerable portion of the Russian population, are already widely employed both in those branches of heavy industry that are changing their profile and in other spheres of the economy. In Uzbekistan, Tajikistan and Turkmenistan the development of market relations is marking time for a number of reasons. The signs are that the going will be harder for the local Russian population in these republics: most of them are white-collar workers or employed in heavy industry, and as such have experienced a greater psychological shock from the loss of their social status, in addition to differing more sharply from the titular nationality regarding their spheres of employment. The large share of people – as compared with the titular population – employed in these types of work has changed for the Russians in the present post-communist period from a positive feature, from the point of view of their social status, to a negative one, for precisely these fields of employment have been subject to the greatest depression.

THE ETHNO-CULTURAL SITUATION

In the former USSR Russians enjoyed for decades the comfortable status of a people dominating all the major socio-cultural areas. The Russian language and culture were reference points for all culture that was transmitted forcibly from the centre to the periphery via the educational system, the mass media, party and government structures, and especially via the system of training managerial and intellectual élites, and military service. Under these circumstances, Russians residing in the union republics had no overwhelming motivation to learn the languages of the titular nationalities and integrate into the non-Russian ethno-cultural environment.

Apart from the socio-political and language situation that was comparatively favourable for the local Russians, possibilities for meeting their wider cultural requirements also existed in Central Asia and Kazakhstan up until the USSR's disintegration. All levels of education were available in Russian, and the media and cultural activities (cinema, theatre, libraries, etc.) were predominantly Russian. Russian was the language of office work and the social services.

As a result, in Central Asia and Kazakhstan Russians (about half of whom were first generation settlers) basically retained their cultural profile, even though influenced to an extent by some of the local population's values. As far back as the 1970s, for instance, analysts noted that Russians in Central Asia married at an earlier age than in other regions, especially as compared with the Baltic republics. This undoubtedly was influenced by the marriage behaviour of the local nationalities.[8]

Although there were intensive inter-ethnic contacts and a high level of linguistic russification in all former Soviet republics, in this region the Russians and the titular population kept a cultural distance from one another and were in effect isolated communities with their own social niches and circles of everyday contacts. Mixed marriages between Russians and people of the local nationalities were and remain rare.[9] Marriages between Russians and Ukrainians, Germans, Tatars and Koreans are much more frequent. The percentage of Russians with a free command of the titular nationality's language is insignificant, from 4.5 per cent in Uzbekistan to 0.9 per cent in Kazakhstan, as compared with 38 and 34 per cent, respectively, in Lithuania and Armenia.

Russians have preserved their traditional culture in everyday life, rites and behaviour (especially in rural areas). The Orthodox churches that exist in the towns and some villages are an important rallying factor for the Russian population. Most Russian folk traditions and rites are performed strictly within their own communities and their Muslim neighbours often do not even know of their existence. At the same time, especially in areas where Russians do not comprise more than a small percentage of the overall population, many traditions connected with popular holidays have disappeared and many religious festivals are on the way to oblivion.[10] Among the Russian population some of the descendants of those who came to live in the region before the revolution or before the war comprise a group unto themselves. They are better acquainted with the language, culture and everyday life of the indigenous peoples, and are less condescending. More often than not they see Central Asia or Kazakhstan, where they or their parents or even grandparents were born and many of their relatives are buried, as their 'little homeland'.[11] Yet both Russian old-timers and recent migrants have an increasingly keen ethnic consciousness and are worried by the disregard of the state authorities for their national, cultural and religious requirements and by growing islamicization and traditionalism in official circles.

The vigorous manifestation of sovereignty in the realm of language, which has been a major instrument in the titular group's assertion of its dominant political and socio-cultural status, has proved an especially sensitive issue for the local Russians. In reply to the question concerning the law on the state language, the overwhelming majority of Russians in Tashkent (79 per cent) said they would prefer to have two state languages: Uzbek and Russian. The Russian population is deeply worried by the speed with which the law has been implemented – signboards in public transport (in the Underground, as well as in above-ground transport), timetables, street signs and office work in public institutions (the medical, educational and industrial establishments) are now only in Uzbek.[12]

In Kyrgyzstan, too, the Russian population is greatly concerned over the status of the Russian language following the adoption of the language law. Over two-thirds of those polled (68 per cent) said the law had changed the position of the Russians. Just one-fifth said the law had not in fact changed anything, and the rest were either undecided or refused to answer. Most of those polled said the law had first and foremost had an adverse effect on the Russians' social status, that is, it made it more difficult to enter institutions of higher education (24 per cent), limited job and promotion opportunities (17 and 16 per cent, respectively), and increases the chances of being sacked (12 per cent). Sixteen per cent said the law had created difficulties in everyday communication with the Kyrgyz. Only seven per cent said that making Kyrgyz the state language had diminished the quantity of information available in Russian. Fifteen per cent of the Russian respondents found positive aspects in the law, namely, that it made Russians realize the need to study Kyrgyz.

The survey of the Russian urban population in Kyrgyzstan testifies to their overwhelming concern lest there no longer be full use of the Russian language in education, culture and the media. Over 80 per cent of the respondents favoured the preservation of higher and specialized secondary educational establishments in Russian, 80 per cent were for the preservation of the Russian theatre, and 90 per cent for television broadcasting in Russian.

Over a quarter of those polled in Tashkent (27 per cent) said it was necessary to have more Russian-language theatres, one third believed that opportunities for receiving higher education in Russian must be augmented, over two thirds (68 per cent) said that the television broadcasting time in Russian should be increased. A vast majority (92 per cent) favoured resuming broadcasts of the Russian TV channel discontinued in August 1991.

At the same time, concern over the fall in status of the Russian language and Russian culture does not mean that the Russian population of Central Asia is unwilling to master the languages of the titular nations. There is, indeed, a growing awareness among Russians that, if they want to stay in the newly emerged, sovereign states of Central Asia, they must know their languages much better than they do now. This is corroborated by the answers given by Russians living in Tashkent to the question: what is the preferable way of improving inter-ethnic relations in Uzbekistan today – that Russians learn Uzbek or that Uzbeks learn Russian better? Thirty-six per cent favoured the first against half that figure who favoured the second. True, over one third of the respondents were unable to decide one way or the other.

Most of the Russians in Tashkent and Russian urban dwellers in Kyrgyzstan assess realistically the negative consequences of their inadequate knowledge of the language of the titular nationality. Only slightly more than a quarter of the respondents found it difficult to answer what negative consequences their inadequate knowledge of Uzbek or Kyrgyz might have or said they personally did not see why they should learn these languages. The rest of the Russians polled in Tashkent said it complicated communication in the social sphere and in everyday life (54 per cent), created career difficulties (26 per cent), limited opportunities of receiving higher education (8 per cent). The question 'Do Russians need the Kyrgyz language?' was answered by the Russian urban population of Kyrgyzstan in Table 15.4. In other words, the most weighty argument in favour of knowing the language of the titular nationality is the threat of loss in social status, on the one hand, and the difficulties encountered in adapting to cultural and everyday life, on the other.

TABLE 15.4
Without knowing Kyrgyz it is difficult to:

	Per cent
Keep one's job	27
Receive education	15
Communicate in public transport, shops, market, etc.	27
Integrate in the local culture	17

POLITICAL STATUS AND INTER-ETHNIC RELATIONS

The deterioration of inter-ethnic relations in Central Asia and Kazakhstan in recent years has been caused mainly by the upsurge in ethnic nationalism among the representatives of the titular groups and by inter-clan and inter-regional disputes that climaxed in a series of ethnic conflicts and even, in the case of Tajikistan, in a devastating civil war. Ethnic minorities deported to the region in an earlier period (such as the Meskhetian Turks in Uzbekistan) and groups of the autochthonous population living outside their own native republics (like the Uzbeks in Osh Oblast in Kirgiziia) were the main victims of this violence. Even the civil strife in Tajikistan has clear ethnic overtones in that it hits hardest at representatives of the indigenous small groups of Gorno-Badakhshan.

Except for the 1990 events in Dushanbe, violence was not targeted at Russians. However, one of the features of the present-day social climate is that the blame for past injustices and crimes committed by the centre is now projected on the Russians, the dominant ethnic group in the former Soviet Union. Even after independence, the worsening economic situation and political instability are often blamed on the Kremlin's pernicious legacy and Russia's current actions, which serves to keep anti-Russian sentiments alive. These sentiments are often fanned by politicians and ethnic activists in order to rally and consolidate the 'indigenous nations', rent as they are by internal dissension.

At the same time, the social transformations taking place in the region, with their comcomitants of economic crisis, unemployment and inflation which aggravate the situation primarily of the Russian urban population, are seen by the Russians as manifestly directed at 'ousting' them from prestigious jobs and 'forcing' them out of the republics in which they live. The enactment of the laws on language and citizenship, the shrinking of opportunities for children to get schooling in their mother tongue, anti-Russian nationalistic rhetoric and the actions of local radicals and fundamentalists affecting the Russians' everyday affairs evoke a painful psychological reaction among the Russians. The situation is further aggravated by occasional threats against 'Europeans' and rumours about such threats that one hears ever more frequently. The alarmist rhetoric of Russia's media and the official orientation of certain government departments concerning the inevitable 'exodus' of Russians from Central Asia also have a negative impact on the Russians' mood and behaviour.

The results of the ethno-sociological research in Uzbekistan and Kyrgyzstan have confirmed that the situation surrounding the Russian community in Central Asia has enormous potential for conflict. The Russian and the titular population are divided, for instance, in their assessment of the role Russians played in the life of the peoples of the USSR. The greater part of the Russian urban population in Kyrgyzstan (78 per cent) believe that Russians always played a progressive role in the relations between the two peoples and in general helped other peoples. Just one-third of the Kyrgyz respondents from among the urban population share this opinion. On the other hand, the view that Russians have always been bent on dominating other peoples is held by only three per cent of the Russians and more than a quarter (29 per cent) of the Kyrgyz. The view that Russians have not played a significant role in the life of the other peoples of the USSR is supported by seven per cent of the Russians and 17 per cent of the Kyrgyz. Notable is the discrepancy, although less marked than in the previous case, between Russians and Krygyz regarding whether a policy of russification was carried out in Kyrgyzstan, with 31 per cent of the Russians and almost half (49 per cent) of the Kyrgyz answering in the affirmative and 43 per cent of the Russians and 17 per cent of the Kyrgyz in the negative. The numerous – but in the views of the Russians, fundamentally negative – changes in the situation of the Russian population in the countries bordering on Russia, which resulted from the dissintegration of the USSR and the independence of the former union republics, led to significant shifts in attitude towards that population both on the part of the titular nationality as well as of the ruling institutions of the new states. The survey of the Russian population of some of the Central Asian republics leaves no doubt as to the Russian opinion on that score. In Tashkent, for instance, more than two thirds of the Russians believe that over the past few years the attitude of the local authorities to them has changed for the worse. Only seven per cent are of the opinion that it has improved, while 12 per cent see no change. In Kyrgyzstan's urban centres the same opinion is held, respectively, by 48 per cent, 11 per cent and 33 per cent of the Russians. The clearly divergent views on the question expressed by Russians in Uzbekistan and Kyrgyzstan stem from the essentially differing overall policy pursued by these countries and from their policy *vis-à-vis* the local Russian population. Approximately the same correlation exists among Russians in Tashkent and in Kyrgyzstan's urban centres in their assessment of the change in inter-ethnic relations on the everyday life level, the only difference being that the proportion of those who said these relations had improved or that there was no change was smaller than in the assessment of the situation on the official level.

One of the concrete manifestations of the negative turn in inter-ethnic relations is that people feel that their national pride is being affronted. Over half of the Russians in Tashkent said that they had experienced this recently and only about one third said that they had not felt this. The respective figures for the Russians in Kyrgyzstan's urban centres were 27 and 42 per cent. The proportion of respondents who could name concrete circumstances, instances, etc., that aroused such a feeling (in comparison with those who said they felt their national dignity was being trampled upon), in general was somewhat smaller. A large portion of the respondents (38 per cent in Tashkent and 13 per cent in Kyrgyzstan's urban centres) linked such situations in the main to depersonalized episodes in commercial enterprises, at the market, in public transport, etc. Comparatively few people said they had experienced this on the part of colleagues at work or during their studies or when addressing state institutions.

Significantly, only a small proportion of Russians – ten per cent in Tashkent and 17 per cent in Kyrgyzstan – expect inter-ethnic relations in their respective republics to get better, while more than half (56 per cent in Tashkent and 52 per cent in Kyrgyz urban centres) believe they will get worse.

It is only natural that in this situation the Russian population should feel defenceless. As many as 72 per cent of the Russians living in Kyrgyzstan's urban centres said that the Russians in the republic must be protected. Over half of the respondents think that this should be the responsibility of Kyrgyzstan's organs of power. Less than a third believe that the responsibility lies with Russia. A far smaller percentage of those polled named other states or international institutions and public movements as the bodies that should take the responsibility of protecting the interests of the new Russian diaspora (Table 15.5).

TABLE 15.5

Who must defend the interests of the Russian inhabitants of Kyrgyzstan? *

	Per cent
Supreme Soviet and Government of Kyrgyzstan	56
Supreme Soviet and Government of Russia	31
World community, UN	15
Russian troops	9
Orthodox Church	8
Russian public movements in Kyrgyzstan	17
Russian public movements in Russia	13
Mass media	11

*The answers were not mutually exclusive, and respondents were free to give several alternatives; as a result, the total percentage exceeds 100.

The assessment of the role of the Russian army as a potential protector of the local Russian population was considerably lower than in response to the question: 'Will the position of the Russians in Kyrgyzstan change if Russian troops pull out?' Two per cent said that it would get a little worse and 17 per cent that it would get much worse.

Russia is expected to uphold the interests of the Russians primarily in the political, legal and economic fields (Table 15.6).

TABLE 15.6

*What actions can Russia take to protect the Russians in Kyrgyzstan?**	Per cent
To insert a provision about their protection in bilateral agreements with Kyrgyzstan	47
To resort economic and political sanctions if the rights of the Russians are violated	22
To help those wishing to leave Kyrgyzstan	24
To back the public movement of Kyrgyzstan's Russian population	12

* The answers were not mutually exclusive, and respondents were free to give several alternatives; as a result, the total percentage exceeds 100.

The appraisal of Russian policy on the part of the new Russian diaspora with respect to Russians in the newly emerged states, including those of Central Asia, is influenced by a number of factors. One of the most important of these is the stand taken by Russia on the ultimate destiny of the USSR. A sizable percentage of the Russians in the newly emerged states disapprove of the Belovezhskaia Pushcha agreements that comprised the decision to dissolve the USSR and create the Commonwealth of Independent States (CIS). The ethnocratic trends in the policy of these states serve to strengthen the negative view that their Russian inhabitants take of the USSR's disintegration and their opinion that the leadership of the new Russia is mainly responsible for this. Russia's inability, in view of its own economic difficulties, to properly absorb those of its nationals who would like to leave the former constituent republics also serves to reinforce in the mass consciousness the notion that Russia does not need them and has betrayed them. These sentiments presumably explain Eltsin's low rating as against other CIS leaders, which polls of Russian urban dwellers in Uzbekistan and Kyrgyzstan have shown. Fourteen per cent of the Russians in Tashkent said they fully trusted Eltsin, as against Karimov and Nazarbaev who each got 26 per cent.

Eltsin is mistrusted by 33 per cent, Karimov by 16 per cent, and Nazarbaev by eight per cent. The rating of CIS leaders with urban Russians living in Kyrgyzstan is found in Table 15.7.

TABLE 15.7 ATTITUDE TO LEADERS (PER CENT)

Leaders	Trust		Mistrust	Undecided
	Fully	To some extent		
Akaev	33	40	18	8
Eltsin	19	34	32	13
Nazarbaev	48	21	5	11
Karimov	9	22	21	48
Kravchuk	7	21	47	23

In the geopolitical and ethno-political situation obtaining after the demise of the USSR and the formation of the new sovereign states, it would be unreasonable for the Russian leadership to ignore the problems of the Russian population and the rest of the Russian-speaking population in the 'new abroad'. Unquestionably, a balanced policy *vis-à-vis* these groups requires at least an idea of what measure of support they are likely to give it. Specifically, our information on the ethno-political orientation of the Russian population of Uzbekistan and Kyrgyzstan shows that the preservation of ties among the former union republics, both multilateral, within the framework of the CIS, and bilateral – between Russia and the other sovereign successor states – will doubtless enjoy the support of the Russian population in Central Asia.

The overwhelming majority of the Russians polled in Tashkent (96 per cent) favoured Uzbekistan's joining the CIS (the poll was taken when the CIS was forming). They linked the preservation of the CIS with the stability of their own position. A third (33 per cent) of the respondents believed that the situation of the Russian population would improve if Uzbekistan joined the CIS, and more than half of them hoped it would at least remain as it was. Seventy-six per cent of the respondents said that if Uzbekistan stayed out of the CIS, the situation of the Russians would worsen, while 18 per cent believed there would be no appreciable change.

Opinion samples taken among Kyrgyzstan's urban dwellers revealed a similar ethno-political orientation. About half of those polled (44 per cent) favoured developing Kyrgyzstan's foreign ties primarily within the CIS, 20 per cent came out for a principally

Russia-oriented policy and 14 per cent preferred a trilateral alliance between Kyrgyzstan, Russia and Kazakhstan.

Dual citizenship – that of their country of residence and Russian – is seen by many Russians and people of associated nationalities as a way to stabilize their status. As many as 74 per cent of Russians in Tashkent said they would like to have dual citizenship when asked what citizenship – Uzbekistan, Russian or dual – they would prefer. Russian citizenship was chosen by ten per cent and Uzbekistan by five per cent. The rest were undecided. Opinions were almost equally divided in answering the question that followed: 'What citizenship would you prefer if you cannot get dual citizenship?' Forty-two per cent favoured Russian citizenship and 41 per cent Uzbek. In Kyrgyzstan the picture was somewhat different. Dual citizenship was also favoured by a majority, although by a considerably smaller one than in Uzbekistan – 58 per cent. Fifteen per cent opted for Russian citizenship and the same exactly for that of Kyrgyzstan.

The answer to the question of what they believe to be their homeland – the former USSR as a whole, the republic in which they live or Russia – is also an indication of the ethno-political orientation of the Central Asian Russian population. The response of those polled in Tashkent was 50 per cent, 20 per cent and 15 per cent, respectively, and in Kyrgyzstan's urban centres 52 per cent, 28 per cent, and 12 per cent. The rest gave no answer or were undecided. All this shows that the overwhelming majority of the Russian population in the Central Asian republics, where opinion samples were taken, identify themselves with the USSR, an entity which has now become past history. It is clear that such an ethno-political orientation cannot but breed ethno-conflict situations, even though these have not yet surfaced.

All this means that the new socio-cultural and political status of the Russians in the former Central Asian republics has led a considerable share of them to adopt ethno-political positions that are significantly at variance with the stand taken by the leadership of the republics in which they live and by a large proportion of the titular nationalities. Judging by all the signs, the overwhelming majority of the Russians living in the newly emerged independent countries are unprepared and unwilling to accept the status of an ethnic minority. Apparently, the Russian population, hoping that their position will stabilize and reluctant to exacerbate their relations with the authorities and population of the titular nationality, is willing to adapt to the new socio-cultural and ethno-political conditions up to a certain point. But who can say beyond what point most Russians in the newly emerged states will refuse to go? The steadfast negative attitude of most Russians in the former constituent republics, apart from Russia, to the Russian leadership (for which there were and are objective reasons) further complicates their ethno-political situation. Only a resolute, unambiguous and basically consistent policy, comprehensible to Russians living in the territory of Russia's new neighbouring states, could dispel such sentiments.

The position of the Russians largely depends on the new states' current policies, which in turn are impacted by the economic situation in Russia. The governments of Kazakhstan, Turkmenistan, Kyrgyzstan and lately Uzbekistan realize full well that the exodus of Russians will lead to a tangible decline in their manufacturing and extraction industries and have taken a number of steps to quell the fears of their Russian population, ensure its safety and raise obstacles in the path of Russian emigration.

In Kyrgyzstan, for instance, a Slav University was opened in 1992. Moreover, in summer 1991 President Askar Akaev 'vetoed' the article in the Land Law which proclaimed that the land was the 'property of the Kyrgyz people', having it replaced by a statement that the land was the property of all the republic's citizens. Organized activity of the Russians in Central Asia in defence of their rights and safety is weak, which reflects the general behaviour of the Russian population in most of the non-Russian regions of the former Soviet Union.

Two, relatively minor, socio-political movements among the Russian and other Russian-speaking (primarily non-titular) population in the region are the Social Democratic Party and the Unity Movement (Edinstvo) in Kazakhstan, both of which champion civil equality and democratic reforms.

The Russian population of Uzbekistan has no organization of its own and is hardly interested in the Uzbek opposition. However, a few years ago, in 1989, a numerically small Intersoiuz organization was formed, which was a reaction of the Russian-speaking population to the growth of Birlik. The creation of Intersoiuz was in a way initiated by the authorities in Moscow and Tashkent and it was oriented towards the preservation of the Union. Yet at the beginning of 1990, these same authorities took repressive actions against it, its activity declined dramatically and by 1992 it no longer existed.[13]

Apart from the above-mentioned movements for civil rights and democracy, there are others in the region which, with various degrees of emphasis, have propounded the Russian nationalist idea, but they do not enjoy any appreciable support. Movements of this kind are the Vozrozhdenie (Rebirth) association and the Ural Cossack Host in Kazakhstan. The principal goal of the Cossacks is the conservation of their own ethnic group identity and the struggle for Cossack autonomy. In Kyrgyzstan, a Slav Foundation has been officially registered. Initially, in 1990, its main concern was the status of the Russian language and it emphasized its non-political character. There is also a *Landsmannschaft* of Kyrgyzstan Cossacks which in 1992 had just a few dozen members. It is a conservative group which supported the State Emergency Committee (GKChP) during the abortive coup of August 1991.

In May 1992, an attempt was made to set up a 'Russian Community' in Turkmenistan but it was blocked by the authorities as unconstitutional.[14] Such a 'Russian Community' in fact exists in Tajikistan. Its program and main goals are typical of most of the organizations of the Russian-speaking population: they orient themselves towards the Russian government (previously, they as a rule supported the All-Union government), calling upon it to protect all Russians in the newly emerged states, promote the introduction of dual citizenship, continue economic ties with the region, support industrial enterprises where the work force is predominantly Russian, and declare its responsibility for the fate of the Russians in Central Asia.[15]

The political inertia of the Russians in Central Asia is largely a result of their loss of hope regarding the prospects of their continued presence in the region. Emigration sentiments are preponderant every-where except among the Russian-speaking inhabitants of most of Kazakhstan. In the past few years the outflow has sharply increased. The overwhelming majority of Russians have already left Tajikistan. In 1989–91, 145,000 Europeans moved from Kyrgyzstan, although a third have returned.[16] In Turkmenistan, the negative migration balance in 1986 was 3,400 people and in the first six months of 1992 alone it exceeded 8,000.[17]

Russians prefer to go to those Russian industrial or agricultural regions, where it is relatively easy to get a job and rent or buy housing, or where they have relatives. Their main destinations are the southern regions of European Russia, Krasnodar and Stavropol *krai*; and, to a lesser extent, Central Russia, especially Voronezh and Belgorod Oblasts. Many move to Siberia, the Ural region and the Altai *krai*. Considerable numbers of emigrants have come up against formidable difficulties in their new places of residence, and not a few have returned, especially to Kyrgyzstan, where there are still many Russians and living standards are still tolerable despite the economic crisis.

The Russian government has taken a passive stand with respect to these Russian migrants. Only those who have the status of 'refugees' or 'forced migrants'[18] receive help or support, although some local authorities, interested in attracting a labour force, give them credits and land to build settlements.

The most dynamic people of working age, young people with specialized training who find it hard to get jobs, and parents concerned about their children's education are in the forefront of those who leave Central Asia. As a result, the natural age balance of the Russian population is being upset, with the proportion of older people increasing and the birth rate decreasing. Moreover, the intellectual potential of those remaining is in decline. Those 'Europeans' with good prospects of settling outside Central Asia have already departed: in the ten years between the 1979 and 1989 censuses the net outflow amounted to 850,000.[19] The estimate for the 1990s is one million people, most of whom will move to Russia.[20] Much in this respect will depend on the policies of the Central Asian governments, which are interested, on the one hand, in retaining skilled personnel who are indispensable for the national economy, and, on the other, in providing jobs for today's unemployed and the tremendously increasing workforce, whose members belong basically to the indigenous population.

NOTES

1. In accordance with the rule explained in the Note on Orthography, Kyrgyzstan is used for the post-independence period and Kirgiziia, as it was then called, for the Soviet period.
2. Iu. V. Arutunian and Iu. V. Bromlei (eds.), *Sotsial'no-kul'turnyi oblik sovetskikh natsii. Po rezul'tatam etnosotsiologicheskogo issledovaniia* (Moscow: Nauka, 1986), pp. 34–5, Table 9.
3. L. Maksakova, *Migratsiia naseleniia Uzbekistana* (Tashkent, 1986), p. 53.
4. Iu. V. Arutiunian (ed.), *Russkie. Etno-sotsiologicheskie ocherki* (Moscow: Nauka, 1992), p. 52, Table 19.
5. Ibid., pp. 96–7, Table 3; pp. 122–4, Tables 12, 13.
6. R. N. Narzikulov, 'Respubliki Srednei Azii za 70 let', *Vostok* 5 (1991), p. 125.
7. *Russkie. Etno-sotsiologicheskie ocherki*, p. 113, Table 9.
8. Iu. V. Bromlei (ed.), *Sovremennye etnicheskie protsessy v SSSR*, 2nd ed. (Moscow: Nauka, 1977), pp. 493, 497, Table 4.
9. Arutiunian, *Russkie. Etno-sotsiologicheskie ocherki*, pp. 195, 196, Table 21.
10. O. I. Brusina, 'Vostochno-slavianskoe naselenie v sel'skikh raionakh Uzbekistana. Problemy adaptatsii i mezhetnicheskikh vzaimodeistvii', in A. N. Zhilina and S. V. Cheshko (eds.), *Sovremennoe razvitie etnicheskikh grupp Srednei Azii i Kazakhstana*, Part 2 (Moscow: IEA, RAN, 1992), p. 84.
11. A Soviet citizen, in addition to his 'Soviet patriotism', had, or was supposed to have, 'local patriotism', that is, an attachment to his 'little homeland' or region of origin.
12. See William Fierman, 'Independence and the Declining Priority of Language Law Implementation in Uzbekistan', in this volume.
13. *Sredniaia Aziia. Spravochnye materialy. Istoriia, politika, ekonomika* (Moscow, 1992), p. 18.

14. Sh. Kadyrov, 'Diktatura i massovye narusheniia prav cheloveka v Turkmenistane', paper presented at an international scientific and practical conference 'Rossiia i Vostok: problemy vzaimodeistviia', Moscow, Dec. 1992.
15. See interview with the deputy chairman of the community, 'Ia nikuda ne poedu', *Argumenty i fakty* 92 (1992).
16. *Sovremennaia obshchestvenno-politicheskaia situatsiia v Srednei Azii i Kazakhstane/Issledovaniia po prikladnoi i neotlozhnoi etnologii*, No. 50 (Moscow: IEA, Academy of Sciences, 1993).
17. Sh. Kadyrov, 'Diktatura i massovye narusheniia prav cheloveka v Turkmenistane'.
18. Basically, those who received refugee status were people compelled to leave areas where hostilities had broken out (e.g., Tajikistan). People forced to migrate to Russia and who accepted Russian citizenship qualified for 'forced migrant' status.
19. V. I. Perevedentsev, 'Raspad SSSR i problemy repatriatsii v Rossiiu', in S. G. Zdravomyshov (ed.), *Bezhentsy* (Moscow: The Russian-American 'Cultural Initiative' Foundation, 1993), p. 155.
20. Ibid.

Afterword

The chapters in this book, both those that focus on the Soviet period and those that specifically address themselves to aspects of post-independence, raise issues that are salient to understanding current and probable future trends and developments in the Muslim regions of the former Soviet Union.

In the realm of Islam it seems that secularization, which began in some areas before 1917, has indeed been a general phenomenon, especially among the intelligentsia and the urban population, as well as the official clergy that served in the Muslim spiritual directorates and the registered mosques. Yet, the last decade or two of Soviet rule saw an enhanced level of Islamic practice and consciousness that penetrated both the more secularized strata and the rural, and generally more religious, populations. This has made Islam a major social force in most of the Muslim areas as they have begun high-lighting their nationalist orientations. In some areas political implications are already manifest. Islam is likely to become an increasingly significant political force as socio-economic conditions deteriorate (which is widely expected to happen – Ro'i, Malashenko). At the same time, Muslim identity and belief in, and practice of, Islam are perhaps not so widespread as is often held, except in a few areas, such as the Fergana Valley. The adherence to Islam seems often to be cultural and traditional rather than religious (Lubin).

The exigencies of the last year or two of Soviet rule, and even more so of the first two years of independence, have obliterated or, at least, blurred the division that was created by the Soviet regime between official and unofficial Islam. The former has been able to use the new resources and authority that the religious establishment has received from the secular powers-that-be to extend its influence over the latter. Unofficial Islam has, for its part, been largely willing to benefit from material and other assistance, but without necessarily accepting the restraints that the governments have hoped to impose. Not a few religious figures and groups seem to be striving persistently to take political advantage of the general religious revival and the enhanced role of Islam in the national consciousness. They would politicize Islam as a counter-force to the prevalent, basically secular tendency of the rulers of the Muslim states. This trend is patently liable to gain momentum in the near future as these rulers fail to achieve the principal goals they have set themselves (Olcott).

It is not only in the independent Muslim states that there is a growth of Islamic awareness. In the Muslim areas of Russia, especially in the Middle Volga and the Northern Caucasus, Islam and politics are interweaving. Here, too, as in Central Asia, the Soviet religious establishment is disintegrating. New spiritual administrations have come into being on the basis of each national autonomous unit. In some of these, young clergy, who accuse their elders of collaborating with the Soviet and post-Soviet secular regimes, have taken over. Muslim political organizations have come into being and are causing a radicalization of Islam and, to an extent, also of politics. While less potent than in Central Asia, this fundamentalism, (which overlaps to some degree with Russian Orthodox fundamentalism), and the return to Islamic values and behaviour codes, seem to constitute a force that will have to be reckoned with (Malashenko).

If sociological surveys suggest that religious identity is less strong than is often believed, the same can basically be said for national or ethnic identity. Most people, especially in Central Asia, feel their primary attachment to be to the extended family or the *mahalla*, or wider-based locality, rather than to their nationality as defined by the Soviet authorities (Lubin, Carlisle). Yet, the general trend of indigenization has created a national intolerance among the local peoples. Interestingly, this phenomenon is not only or chiefly between them and the Russians who live in their midst (whom they distinguish from the authorities in Moscow). It is also manifest in the attitudes of the Muslim peoples to each other – of Uzbeks to Kazakhs, Kyrgyz and Uighurs; of Azerbaijanis to Lezgins and Talysh; of Ingush to Ossets – and to 'Russian-speakers' such as Armenians, Jews and Koreans (Lubin, Gammer, Wasserman). Conflicts between North Caucasian peoples, both within the administrative units created by the Soviet authorities and with peoples inhabiting neighbouring autonomous republics or regions, seem particularly bitter. They are partly historical and were partly engendered by Soviet policies. Some of them have, since the break-up of the USSR, erupted into military hostilities (Gammer).

Certainly in Uzbekistan and Tajikistan political life seems, even in conditions of post-independence, to be subordinate to the political infighting among regional élites. These constituted the traditional power-base of the republican leaderships under Soviet rule and determined the parameters of the power game throughout the Soviet period. In consequence, national interests can hardly be expected to surface, let alone play a predominant role in the country's political development, since the requisite administrative infrastructure has not been created, or priorities established. The semi-feudal political structures that reigned under Moscow's distinctly colonialist and distant, yet generally rigorous, control, have done little to prepare the Central Asian republics for independence (Carlisle, Vaisman, Kosach; while there are no separate studies in this volume on the political life of Kyrgyzstan and Turkmenistan, there can be little doubt that the situation there is not fundamentally different).

Indeed, in those states where political parties have developed, the differences between them do not seem to emanate from divergences of political goals, methods and values. In Tajikistan, for example, the various parties and movements, despite their apparently contradictory platforms and leitmotifs – officially communist, or 'social-democratic', secular-democratic and Islamic – are extremely similar in their social composition, political behaviour and attachments (Kosach). This hardly bodes well for the independent, democratic prospects of the Central Asian states, or even the likelihood of their peaceful development within borders that were determined by the Soviets in the 1920s and 1930s on the basis of the political needs and considerations of the RCP(b).

This conclusion is borne out by developments in the one Muslim state in which one of the new national parties in fact came to power, Azerbaijan. The Popular Front of Azerbaijan (PFA) ruled for just over a year, from early summer 1992 until autumn 1993, but proved itself singularly unable to meet the challenges of government. Perhaps, precisely because it was composed of inexperienced people who were not part of the traditional ruling élite or *nomenklatura*, the situation in the country worsened notably in this period, even in fields unrelated to the ongoing war with Armenia. One such example was the relations with the country's indigenous Muslim ethnic minorities, despite the ideological openness and liberalism of the PFA on this issue (Wasserman).

While the viability of a state and a political system is not normally determined by cultural standards, the position and prospects of the Muslim states and other administrative units in the CIS can, to an extent, be gauged by the situation in the field of culture – in particular, language. Since in Soviet nationality policy an ethnic group's claim to national existence derived largely from its linguistic distinctiveness, and its national rights were given expression primarily in the realm of language, the national renaissance of the late Soviet period placed major emphasis on language. The result has been to seek to purify the national language of 'Russianisms' and Russian influences and to consolidate it in everyday private and public life: in education, legislation, administration, as well as in cultural expression. There is also a trend towards returning to national 'roots' and the pre-Soviet literary heritage, which was made inaccessible to the Muslim peoples by the change of alphabet. Yet, so far, no Muslim nation has seriously thought of returning to the Arabic alphabet, although Uzbekistan's Law on State Language provides for the study of the Arabic-based script in all Uzbek-language groups in primary and secondary schools. Some schools in Tajikistan and Uzbekistan have in fact included its study in their curriculum, and its restoration as the national alphabet was part of the political program of the Islamic Renaissance Party of Tajikistan. Indeed, there seems to be a trend toward Latinization, as has been decreed by the Supreme Soviets of both Azerbaijan and Uzbekistan. Both Kreindler and Fierman try, by discussing the history of the language situation and language legislation, to evaluate the cultural equipment with which the new Muslim states have taken the road of national independence. Interestingly enough, despite the enthusiasm evoked by the language issue prior to independence, the social, political and economic implications of language legislation have led to a marked hesitancy and conspicuous tardiness in implementing its most meaningful aspects (see below).

Certainly, too, socio-economic data are crucial to any appraisal of the present viability and the future prospects of the states and regions under discussion. In the first place, it is evident that the demographic situation in Central Asia, which caused so much concern to Soviet policy makers in the 1970s and early 1980s, was beginning to change by the end of the 1980s. In Azerbaijan and Kazakhstan there had already been clear indications of demographic modernization by the 1979 census. By the time of the last population census of the Soviet period in 1989, all the Muslim union republics, even Tajikistan, were showing signs of modernizing demographic behaviour. True, no significant decrease in the crude birth rate had taken place by that date – among the Tajiks and Turkmen it had actually risen from 1979 – reflecting the higher number of women of child-bearing age. None-theless, all data indicate that this must be the expected trend for the 1990s. One might even presume that given the deteriorating economic and domestic security situation, and the very poor welfare services in the entire CIS, and in the Muslim states in particular, this trend will actually accelerate, although there is just a chance that a rise in islamicization and radical nationalism will operate in the opposite direction (Tolts).

If demographic trends give room for limited optimism, a survey of the Soviet legacy in the strictly economic field shows a wide range of forbidding obstacles. It is unrealistic to believe that the Central Asian states will be able to find the skills, enterprise, momentum and capital to overcome them. These are very basic problems, some of them characteristic of ex-socialist economies in general; others are more specific to the peculiar conditions of the region with its manifest economic and technological backwardness. The new states are going to experience formidable difficulties in overcoming both the distortions that resulted from the former category, and the additional disadvantages entailed in the latter, which emanated from Russian and Soviet colonialism *vis-à-vis* Central Asia. These include the cotton monoculture and its multifarious concomitants on the one hand; and, on the other, the unbalanced expectations and perceptions created by Marxist-Leninist norms, and even by the considerable investment involved in the provision of welfare services on an All-Union level, which was disproportionate to Central Asian productivity (McAuley). The obstacles are going to be all the more difficult to overcome given the ethnic and perhaps also the gender tensions created by employment patterns. These seem, to a large extent, to have been determined by the takeoff point and by the traditional attitudes and customs of the Central Asian republics, particularly in Tajikistan and Turkmenistan. In addition, younger cohorts have recently been discriminated against by employment trends, and this seems already to have led to signs of unrest (Sacks, Tishkov).

The chapters in this book have largely stayed clear of the foreign policy connections and orientations of the new Muslim states of the CIS. Discussion of this topic belongs basically to a second volume of papers that were presented at the same conference at Tel Aviv University on the Muslim states and the Middle East. Yet a few points worthy of mention have become apparent from the chapters in this book, for foreign policy is in many respects an outcome of domestic needs, constraints and aspirations.

In the first place, the newly independent Central Asian states have maintained their links with Russia; in fact, for the foreseeable future, Russia will remain *a*, if not *the*, main foreign power in the Muslim states' political considerations. The main reasons for this are the following. First is their economic dependence on Russia, which has been systematically and consistently moulded since the Tsars conquered the Muslim areas. Second, many states have significant, and in some cases very large, Russian populations, whose well-being and sometimes physical existence seem to be in jeopardy as a result of the new radical sentiments of the indigenous populations. Moscow prefers to assume its responsibility for these Russians in their countries of residence than to provide them with actual refuge, although many Russians would like to migrate to Russia (Lubin, Tishkov). Third is the complex military situation, which in some cases (Tajikistan, Azerbaijan, North Ossetiia, Abkhaziia) has brought about direct Russian intervention in order to restore stability, with the consent of at least some of the local actors; this intervention has evoked the phoenix of Russian imperialism (Carlisle, Gammer, Wasserman).

The attitude of the local Muslim populations to Russia and Russians may well be reflected in their reluctance to proceed with implementation of some of the more substantial aspects of their respective laws on state language, which all the union republics enacted before independence and which some of Russia's Muslim autonomous republics have meanwhile also adopted. Almost certainly, the implications of full-scale implementation for their Russian populations and even for some of their own intelligentsia who were educated in Russian schools and whose culture is in fact Russian, not to mention other Russian-speaking minorities in their midst, have been a serious factor in the failure to put this legislation into effect (Fierman). Perhaps because of an inherent inferiority complex in the face of the 'superior qualities' of Russian culture, perhaps because they are loathe to lose the experience and know-how of a largely Russian administrative and economic personnel who are most unlikely to master the local tongue, perhaps as a result of their expectations of a negative reaction in Russia to what must be perceived there as anti-Russian discrimination, the Muslim states are largely dragging their feet over the language issue, although, admittedly, there are also a number of grave technical impediments (Fierman). The one state where this does not hold is Azerbaijan, where the native language has been the official state language since 1978.

The perspective of the local Russian population is somewhat different. It largely believes that language law implementation is proceeding too quickly. The local Russians see in this law a threat to their traditional social status and professional predominance, indeed to their continued habitation in the Muslim areas. Some of them believe they must master the local tongues and finally integrate in a society from which they remained fundamentally and consciously estranged, although their roots in the region may go back for generations. The overall sense, however, seems to be that, given the ineffectiveness of Russia's support for their predicament, their inability to opt for dual citizenship, the prevalent, or potential, atmosphere of ethnic conflict, large numbers of Russians will, in the final event, leave the Muslim states and return to Russia. This already began to happen in the 1980s, and although the trend has progressed unevenly because of the difficulties inherent in emigration as a whole, especially for older people and the less professionally qualified, and because of Russia's generally unwelcoming attitude, it appears that it will gather momentum in the 1990s (Tishkov).

Russia is undoubtedly, then, the country with which the new Muslim states (not to mention the Muslim areas of Russia itself, which are officially still a part of Russia) have close and complex ties in a variety of fields. Other foreign countries to which the Muslim states feel an affinity and whose role may grow in the not-too-distant future are the Muslim countries of the Middle East, especially Turkey. (These connections sometimes seem to comprise an attempt on the part of the new states to counteract Russian influence; sometimes they may represent an endeavour on the part of Middle Eastern powers to expand their own spheres of influence: political, geo-strategic, cultural or economic.) There seems to be considerable apprehension in Central Asia regarding the encouragement of close ties with Pakistan and Iran, and most particularly Afghanistan (as well as with China and Israel). Central Asia seems not to be too enthusiastic about receiving foreign aid, but insofar as its population believes this to be advisable, the largest cohort favours approaching the US, Western Europe and Japan (Lubin). The role of Saudi Arabia in the religious revival – reconstructing mosques, creating educational facilities, helping finance the *hajj* – is also evident (Olcott).

All in all, however, it appears that the future of the Muslim states, and to an extent also that of the Muslim areas of Russia, lies first and foremost with internal developments and trends. Despite the great interest shown in them by Western governments and business corporations and of the Muslim world as a whole, it will be their own viability as independent or autonomous political and economic entities, their ability to modernize and to shake off some of the very serious constraints imposed upon them by the Soviet legacy, and the way they meet the challenges of a growing religiosity, radical nationalism and conflicting or competing loyalties that will be decisive in shaping their fates. Moreover, given the major differences between their various circumstances, despite certain commonly inherited features, it is possible that their future paths may deviate quite sharply one from another.

Notes on Contributors

DONALD S. CARLISLE is Professor of Political Science at Boston College and a Fellow at Harvard University's Russian Research Center. As an expert on Central Asia, he also serves as a consultant to the United Nations. His book *Uzbekistan under Soviet Rule* is to be published shortly.

WILLIAM FIERMAN is Professor in the Department of Uralic and Altaic Studies at Indiana University. He is the author of *Language Planning and National Development* (1991) and editor of *Soviet Central Asia: The Failed Transformation* (1991), and has written numerous book chapters and articles on the politics of language and culture and on youth problems in Central Asia.

MOSHE GAMMER is a Lecturer in the Department of Middle Eastern and African History, Tel Aviv University. His research interests include the modern history of Muslims of the Northern Caucasus, on which he has published a number of articles. He is also author of the book *Muslim Resistance to the Tsar: Shamil and the Conquest of Chechnia and Daghestan* (1994).

GRIGORII G. KOSACH is a Professor at the Political Science Centre of the Russian Academy of Management and in the Department of Near and Middle East History at Moscow State University's Institute of Asian and African Studies. His major publications are devoted to problems of the formation of political parties and movements in the Arab world and Central Asia and international relations in the Middle East.

ISABELLE T. KREINDLER is a Research Associate at Haifa University's Department of English. She has published extensively on the nationality problem in Tsarist Russia and the Soviet Union, with emphasis on the language question, and is the editor of *The Changing Status of Russian in the Soviet Union* (1982) and *Sociolinguistic Perspectives on Soviet National Languages: Their Past, Present and Future* (1985).

NANCY LUBIN is a Senior Associate at the Center for Post Soviet Studies and an Adjunct Professor at Georgetown University, as well as a member of the Council on Foreign Relations and of the Board of the Institute for US-Soviet Affairs. She is the author of *Labour and Nationality in Soviet Central Asia* (1984) and numerous articles, Congressional reports and Congressional testimony on the former USSR and Central Asia.

ALEXEI V. MALASHENKO is Head of the Islamic Studies Department of the Institute of Oriental Studies at the Russian Academy of Sciences. Recently, he has been studying the problems of Islam in the Muslim regions of the former USSR. He has published four books and over 100 articles in Russian.

ALASTAIR McAULEY is a Reader in Economics at the University of Essex. He is a specialist on the former Soviet economy and has recently acted as a consultant to the World Bank in both Russia and Uzbekistan. His work focuses on income inequality and the labour market under central planning and during the transition, and regional policy and development under socialism. He has written extensively on these topics, including *Economic Welfare in the Soviet Union* (1979).

MARTHA BRILL OLCOTT is Professor of Political Science at Colgate University. She is the author of *The Kazakhs* (1987) and editor of *The Soviet Multinational State* (1990), and has published numerous other articles on Soviet nationality problems.

YAACOV RO'I is Professor of History at Tel Aviv University and a Research Fellow at the Cummings Center for Russian and East European Studies there. He has published widely on Soviet policy toward the Middle East, Soviet Jewish policy, Islam in the Soviet period and Soviet Central Asia. His major publications include *From Encroachment to Involvement. A Documentary Study of Soviet Policy in the Middle East, 1945–1973; Soviet Decision Making in Practice: The USSR and Israel, 1947–1954;* and *The Struggle for Soviet Jewish Emigration 1948–1967.* He also edited *The USSR and the Muslim World* (1984).

MICHAEL PAUL SACKS is Professor of Sociology at Trinity College, Hartford, Connecticut. He is the author of *Women's Work in Soviet Russia: Continuity in the Midst of Change* (1976) and *Work and Equality: The Division of Labor by Age, Gender and Nationality* (1982) and coeditor of *Understanding Soviet Society* (1988). His current research focuses on ethnic and gender differences in the work force of Russia and problems facing the Russian minority elsewhere in the Soviet successor states.

VALERY I. TISHKOV is Director of the Institute of Ethnology and Anthropology at the Russian Academy of Sciences. He has also served as Chairman of the State Committee of the Russian Federation on National Policy and Minister of the Russian Federation, as well as Plenipotentiary charged with settling problems concerning the situation in Ossetia. He is the author of numerous books and articles on international and inter-ethnic relations.

MARK TOLTS is a Research Associate at the Institute of Contemporary Jewry at the Hebrew University of Jerusalem. Before his emigration to Israel in 1991, he was a staff member at the Institute for Socio-Economic Population Studies of the USSR Academy of Sciences. He has written widely on the demography of the USSR, in general, and of ex-Soviet Jewry in particular.

DEMIAN VAISMAN is a Research Fellow at the Cummings Center for Russian and East European Studies at Tel Aviv University. Before immigrating to Israel in 1990, he lectured in history at the University of Tashkent, Uzbekistan. His current research focuses on the political problems of the Muslim states of the former Soviet Union.

ARYEH WASSERMAN is a Research Fellow at the Cummings Center for Russian and East European Studies at Tel Aviv University. Before immigrating to Israel in 1990, he held senior positions in a number of institutes associated with the Academy of Sciences of Azerbaijan and published extensively in Russian. His special fields of interest are Soviet policy towards Turkey and Iran, and socio-political processes in modern Azerbaijan. His current research focuses on the Nagornyi-Karabakh conflict.

Glossary

CPSU	–	Communist Party of the Soviet Union
fetwa	–	formal Islamic legal opinion
gorispolkom	–	municipal executive committee or town council
hadith	–	narrative relating deeds and utterances of the Prophet and his Companions
hajj	–	the pilgrimage to the holy places of Mecca and Medina; one of the five pillars of Islam
ishan	–	a spiritual and religious mentor in Sufi *tariqat*
jadidism	–	from Arabic *jadid* – new; a movement or ideology that developed in the second half of the 19th century, propagating reformism and modernism within Islam
khoja	–	those who claim to be descendants of the first Arabs who came to Central Asia
krai	–	territorial unit within the RSFSR, usually containing one or more small national units (autonomous regions or national districts)
madrasa	–	religious school associated with a mosque
mahalla	–	city neighbourhood
maktab	–	elementary religious school
oblast	–	administrative unit within a union republic
qazi	–	religious judiciary authority
Qurban-Bairam	–	Feast of the Sacrifice, a major Muslim festival that lasts 3–4 days; Arabic – *'id al-adha*
raion	–	district; administrative unit; subdivision of an *oblast*
SADUM	–	Central Asian Spiritual Directorate of Muslims; full name, the Spiritual Directorate of Muslims of Central Asia and Kazakhstan
Sufism	–	a mystical discipline that guides the adept in his search for divine truth
tariqa (pl. *tariqat*)	–	lit., the way; school within Sufism
waqf	–	unalienable religious endowment, chiefly landed property

321

Index

INDEX

107–8, 125, 129, 137, 188; jadidism in, 74–7, 92n, 133, 191

Bukhara Oblast, 69, 76, 107, 109, 117

Bukhara, Soviet Peoples' Republic of, 74–5, 92n

Burhanov, M., 121n

Caucasus (*see also* Abkhaziia; Adygeia; Armenia; Azerbaijan; Chechnia; Dagestan; Georgia; Kabardino-Balkariia; Karachai-Cherkes Republic; North Ossetiia; South Ossetiia), 3, 8, 13, 85, 163, 172; Russians in, 163, 165, 172; Northern (*see* Northern Caucasus)

Central Asia (*see also* Kazakhstan; Kyrgyzstan; Tajikistan; Turkmenistan; Uzbekistan), 17n; demography of, 4, 277, 292, 314; economies of, 4, 89, 256–68, 315; élites in (*see also* awlads; khojas; seyyids), 22–5, 79, 91; ethnic and national identity in, 21, 62–70 *passim*, 83, 105, 301, 312; ethnic minorities in (*see* Armenians; Jews; Kazakhs; Koreans; Kyrgyz; Tajiks; Uighurs; Ukrainians); foreign relations of, 317; Islam in (*see also* SADUM), 21, 22–6, 32–3, 34, 37, 56–62 *passim*, 70, 92n, 296; modernization in, 4; 231–47; relations with Russian Federation, 315; Russians in, 4, 59, 63–7, 87–8, 289–310, 316

Central Asians, 56–70; attitudes towards Russia and Russians, 71, 301–2, 312

Central Asian Spiritual Directorate of Muslims (*see* SADUM)

Chagatay, 92n, 188

Checheno-Ingush ASSR, 13, 163, 170, 176n

Chechens (*see also* Shaykh Mansur), 164, 166, 169–74, 178n, 197, 199; in Dagestan (*see also* Aki district), 166–8; deportation of, 167, 176n

Chechnia/Chechen Republic (*see also* CMPC; OKChN), 42, 46–7, 164–5, 167, 169, 172–3, 177nn; conflicts in (*see also* Groznyi; Prigorodnyi district; Šunja district), 172–3, 175; Islam in, 46, 51n; Mehk Khel (Council of Elders), 46–7; nationalities in (*see* Cherkes; Cossacks)

Cherkes (*see also* Adyge; CMPC; Kabardinians; Kabardino-Balkariia; Karachai-Cherkes Republic), 164, 166, 171

Circassians (*see* Cherkes)

CIS (*see also* Azerbaijan; Belarus; Belovezhskaia Pushcha agreements; Kazakhstan; Kyrgyzstan; Russian Federation; Tajikistan; Turkmenistan; Ukraine), 41, 45, 66, 87, 90, 154, 160n, 305

clans (*see* tribalism)

CMPC (Confederation of the Mountain Peoples of the Caucasus), 173–4, 177n, 183–6; Mountain Republic (1918), 164, 173

Commissariat for Nationality Affairs (*see* Narkomnats)

Commonwealth of Independent States (*see* CIS)

communism, 2, 47–8, 195–6

Communist Party of the Soviet Union (*see* CPSU)

Confederation of the Mountain Peoples of the Caucasus (*see* CMPC)

Cossacks (*see also* Landsmannschaft of Kyrgyzstan Cossacks; Slav Foundation; Ural Cossack Host), 169, 174

Council for the Affairs of Religious Cults (CARC), 11–13, 19nn

CPSU (Communist Party of the Soviet Union; formerly, RCP(b) — Russian Communist Party (of Bolsheviks)), 2, 16, 22, 34, 105, 110–17, 134, 171, 176n, 190; CP of Azerbaijan, 151, 157n; CP of Tajikistan (*see* Socialist Party of Tajikistan); CP of Uzbekistan, 76, 78–80, 107, 110–12, 114, 116–18, 121n, 124, 141nn, 211, 213

Dagestan/Dagestan ASSR (*see also* Makhachkala), 17n, 29, 41, 43, 149, 164, 171, 191, 197; conflicts in (*see also* Aki district; Khasavyurt), 167–8; ethnic groups in (*see also* Avars; Chechens; Cossacks; Kumyks; Jews — Mountain Jews; Laks; Lezgins; Nogai; Russians; Rutuls; Tats; Tsakhurs), 163, 168, 195; Islam in, 18n, 47; parties in (*see* Islamic Democratic Party; Jama'ati Muslimi)

DDK (Demokraticheskoe dvizhenie Kyrgyzstana), 28

demography (*see* Azerbaijan, Central Asia, Kazakhstan, Kyrgyzstan, Tajikistan, Turkmenistan, Uzbekistan — demography of)

Den', 48–9

deported peoples (*see* Chechens; Ingush; Meskketians; Ossets)

dervishes (*see* Sufism)

diaspora (of Azerbaijanis), 156, 161nn

DPT (Democratic Party of Tajikistan) (*see also* Yusuf, Shodmon), 31, 86, 124–40, 141n

Dudko, Dmitrii, 49–50

DUMES (Spiritual Directorate of the Muslims of the European Part of Russia/the CIS and Siberia) (*see also*

INDEX

Iran (*see also* Khomeini, Ayatolla), 35, 38n, 46, 65–7, 70, 150, 156, 159n; Islamic Revolution in, 33

IRP (Islamic Renaissance Party) (*see also* Akhtaev, Ahmedqadi; Andijan; Biji-Ulu (Bijiev), Muhammed; Dunaev, Sergei; Fergana Valley; Heidar, Jemal; Namangan; Sadur, Vali Ahmed; Tawhid; Usman, Dawlat) , 29, 43–4, 47; in Tajikistan (*see also* Turajonzade, Qazi Akbar; Usman, Dawlat), 30–1, 33, 37, 43, 45, 51n, 124–140 *passim*, 141n; in Uzbekistan (*see also* Qari, Abdulwali; Qari, Hakim; Rahmatulla Alloma; Uta, Abdulla), 29, 37, 45, 61, 195; *al-Vahdat* (Edinenie), 44

ishan (*see* Naqshbandi movement)

Ishanbaev, Aqilbek, 29

Iskandarov, Akbarshoh, 28, 31

Iskender, Fazil, 198

Iskenderov, Mamed, 146

Islam (*see also* Central Asia; DUMES; *gortsy*; *hadith*; imam; Kazakhstan; Kyrgyzstan; *madrasas*; *maktabs*; mosques; Muslim clergy; Qur'an; Russian Federation; SADUM; secularization; Spiritual Directorate of the Muslims of the Northern Caucasus; Sufism; *tafsir*; Tajikistan; Turkmenistan; USSR; Uzbekistan), 7, 164, 199, 311; fundamentalism (*see also* ahl-i qur'an; gazavat; IRP; Jama'ati Muslimi; Qari, Abdulwali; Rahmatulla Alloma; Qari, Hakim; Qutb, Muhammed; Qutb, Sayyid; *umma*), 2, 5, 26, 32–3, 37, 41–2, 48–9, 81, 89, 131; Muslim intelligentsia and, 12, 15, 20nn, 50; and nationalism, 21; pan-Islam, 2, 5, 89, 150; politicization of, 20n, 37, 47–8, 56; practices (*see hajj*; *namaz*; Nawruz; Qurban-Bairam; Ramadan; *uraza*; *waqf*; *zakat*); secularization of, 6, 14–16, 188; Shariat law, 17n, 23, 30, 32, 46; Shi'a, 8, 175n; unofficial, 9, 12–13, 19nn, 21, 24–5, 31, 311

Islamic Democratic Party, 45

Islamic Renaissance Party (*see* IRP)

Ittifaq (Tatarstan), 45

Ivanov, Nikolai, 92n, 116

Jabbarov, Ismail, 118

jadidism (*see also* Behbudi, Mahmud; Bukhara; Fitrat, Abdurrauf; Qari, Munawwar), 8, 9, 17n, 34

Jama'ati Muslimi, 45

Jews, 63–4, 105, 134, 136, 147, 155
Mountain Jews, 161n

jihad (*see gazavat*)

Jordan, 30, 46

Judaism, 7–8

Kabardinians (*see also* CMPC), 166, 176n

Kabardino-Balkariia/Kabardino-Balkar ASSR, 13, 163, 171

Kalinin, Mikhail, 76

Kamalov, Kalibek, 112

Kamalov, Sabir, 111

Kamalov, Sadyqjan, 28, 31

Karachai (*see also* Biji-Ulu (Bijiev), Muhammed; Karachai-Balkars), 43, 47, 173, 197, 199

Karachai-Balkars (*see also* Karachai; Balkars), 166, 171, 192

Karachai-Cherkes Republic/Karachai-Cherkes Autonomous Oblast, 163, 171

Karakalpak (language), 54

Karakalpakistan/Karakalpak ASSR, 107, 112

Karakalpaks, 191–2, 199, 207

Karategin, 86

Karaganda Oblast, 19n

Karimov, Islam, 55, 59, 61, 62, 67, 79–91 *passim* 93n, 119, 218–19, 304–5; language policy of, 198, 205–6, 221; and Islam, 22, 28, 29–30, 37, 56, 224–25

Karshi, 80, 108

Kashka-Darya Oblast, 80, 108

Kazakh (language), 54, 188, 191, 197

Kazakhs, 27, 63–4, 72, 76, 191–2; attitudes toward local Russians, 63–4; ethnic and national identity among, 63–4, 87; Islam among, 8; in Kazakhstan, 51n; in Uzbekistan, 207

Kazakhstan (*see also* Almaty), 22, 54–5, 90, 167, 226; demography of, 226, 232–53 *passim*, 285n; ethnic and national identity in, 62–5, 70; Islam in (*see also* Alash; Nysanbai, Qazi Ratbek; SADUM), 21, 29, 45, 56–62; languages in, 197; Northern (*see also* Orenburg Governorate), 4, 88; political leadership in (*see* Kunaev, Dinmuhammed; Nazarbaev, Nursultan); regionalism in (*see also* Karaganda Oblast), 25, 88; Russians in (*see also* Edinstvo; Social Democratic Party), 63–7, 289–310 *passim*; Sufism in, 20n

Kazan (*see also* Tatars; Tatarstan), 19n, 51n

Khasavyurt, 168, 177n

Khasbulatov, Ruslan, 44

khatib (*see* Muslim clergy)

Khiva, 8, 73–6, 79, 105–8

Khojaev, Faizulla, 74–8, 92n, 109

325

INDEX

INDEX

INDEX

INDEX

INDEX

Turkey, 35, 46, 65–6, 70, 87, 150, 155, 165, 171, 193
Turkic (language), 71, 83, 90, 150–1, 153, 157, 176n, 187–92, 199–200
turkicization, 75, 83, 151–2
turkkomissia ('Turkestan Commission'), 92n
Turkmenistan/Turkmeniia (Turkmen SSR) (*see also* Ashgebat), 8n, 25, 74–5, 87, 89–90, 227, 255; demography of, 232–53 *passim*, 269; Islam in (*see also elat*), 22, 24, 33; political leadership in (*see* Niiazov, Sapurmurad); Russians in, 274–5, 290, 292–3
Turkmen (language), 188, 191–2

Ubykhs, 165, 176n
Uighurs, 63–4
Ukraine, 16, 64, 156
Ukrainians, 136, 272, 285n, 298
Umarov, Hamdan, 118
umma, 8, 50
United Nations, 87–8, 91, 156
unemployment, 219, 275, 301
Unity Movement (*see* Edinstvo)
Ural Cossack Host (Kazakhstan), 307
Urals, 43
uraza (ruza), 18n
urbanization, 245–6, 274–5
Urgench, 107
Usman, Dawlat, 31
Usmankhojaev, Inamjon, 116–17
USSR, 56, 62, 72, 78, 87, 111, 116, 119; August coup (1991), 50, 81–2; atheistic propaganda in, 9, 10, 19n; centralization policy of, 257–8, 267n; economy and economic policy of, 259–66; education policy of, 3, 145, 265, 266; industrialization policy of, 291; language policy of, 3, 176n, 189–200; nationalities policy of (*see also* deported peoples; inter-ethnic relations; Narkomnats; 'nation building'; 'national delimitation'; Sultan Galiev, Mir Said), 1–2, 76, 87, 116, 123, 145; policy toward Islam (*see also* DUMES; *hujum*; *maktabs*; *madrasas*; mosques; SADUM; Shariat law), 5, 6, 9, 14, 18n, 165–7; policy toward religion, 5–6; social policy of, 264–5
Uta, Abdulla, 29
Uzbek (language) (*see also* Uzbekistan — language law of, education in), 32, 34, 54, 188, 197–8, 207, 227
Uzbekistan, 1, 24, 72–3, 76–8, 84–7, 89–91, 154, 255; Academy of Sciences of, 112, 119; demography of, 207, 222–3, 228n, 232–53 *passim*, 269; economy of, 36,

107–8, 119, 218–19, 256–66 *passim*; education in, 64, 209, 212–13, 216, 220–1, 227, 228n, 229n; ethnic and national identity in, 62–5, 87; Islam in (*see also ahl-i qur'an*; SADUM), 224–5; language law of (adopted October 1989), 3, 205–30, 299, 314; parties in (*see also* Birlik; CPSU — Uzbekistan; Erk; IRP), 61; political élite in (*see also* Karimov, Islam; Mutalov, Abdulhashim; Nishanov, Rafiq; Rashidov, Sharaf; Usmankhojaev, Inamjon), 61, 77–83, 93n, 107–119, 220; regionalism in (*see also* Andijan Oblast; Bukhara Oblast; Fergana Valley; Fergana Oblast; Karakalpak; Karshi; Kashka-Darya Oblast; Namangan Oblast; Samarkand Oblast; Shakhrisabz; Surkhan-Darya Oblast; Syr-Darya Oblast; Tashkent Oblast; Termez), 77–83, 87, 93n, 107–119, 312; relations with Russian Federation, 86–7, 219–20, 226; Russians in, 56, 59, 63–7, 88, 207, 208, 219, 222–3, 228n, 272–5, 290, 298–309 *passim*
Uzbeks, 27, 72, 87, 92n, 105, 191–2, 199; in Kazakhstan, 64; in Kyrgyzstan (*see also* Osh Oblast), 88; in Tajikistan, 75, 83–4, 134, 136, 273; in Turkmenistan, 274; in Uzbekistan (*see also* Uzbekistan — demography of), 63–4, 72–3

Vakhsh Valley, 137
Validov, Zeki, 191
Vatan; Tajik, 86; Azerbaijani, 161n
Vestnik vospitaniia, 188
Vozrozhdenie movement (Kazakhstan), 307

'Wahhabis', 141n
waqf, 9
women (*see also* Azerbaijan, Kazakhstan, Kyrgyzstan, Tajikistan, Turkmenistan, Uzbekistan — demography in), 14, 35, 45, 59, 113, 265; in labour force, 4, 273, 275–85 *passim*, 286n
workforce (*see* labour force)
World War II, 9, 12, 20n, 110

Yagnob, 86
Yemen, 35
youth, 57, 66, 130, 132, 198
Yurddash (*see also* Safarli, Mais), 121, 161n
Yusuf, Shodmon, 31, 129, 139
Yusupov, Usman, 77, 110

zakat, 10, 18n
Zarafshan Valley (*see also* Yagnob), 86
Zargishiev, Murad, 44, 51n